Applied Mathematics and Machine Learning

Applied Mathematics and Machine Learning

Editors

Qun Li
Aihua Wood

Basel • Beijing • Wuhan • Barcelona • Belgrade • Novi Sad • Cluj • Manchester

Editors
Qun Li
Wright State University
Dayton, OH
USA

Aihua Wood
Air Force Institute of Technology
Wright-Patterson AFB, OH
USA

Editorial Office
MDPI
St. Alban-Anlage 66
4052 Basel, Switzerland

This is a reprint of articles from the Special Issue published online in the open access journal *Mathematics* (ISSN 2227-7390) (available at: https://www.mdpi.com/journal/mathematics/special_issues/Appl_Math_Mach_Learn).

For citation purposes, cite each article independently as indicated on the article page online and as indicated below:

Lastname, A.A.; Lastname, B.B. Article Title. *Journal Name* **Year**, *Volume Number*, Page Range.

ISBN 978-3-7258-1281-3 (Hbk)
ISBN 978-3-7258-1282-0 (PDF)
doi.org/10.3390/books978-3-7258-1282-0

© 2024 by the authors. Articles in this book are Open Access and distributed under the Creative Commons Attribution (CC BY) license. The book as a whole is distributed by MDPI under the terms and conditions of the Creative Commons Attribution-NonCommercial-NoDerivs (CC BY-NC-ND) license.

Contents

Nhat-Duc Hoang
Machine Learning-Based Estimation of the Compressive Strength of Self-Compacting Concrete: A Multi-Dataset Study
Reprinted from: *Mathematics* **2022**, *10*, 3771, doi:10.3390/math10203771 1

Hui Zhou, Yehui Huang and Yuqin Yao
Dbar-Dressing Method and N-Soliton Solutions of the Derivative NLS Equation with Non-Zero Boundary Conditions
Reprinted from: *Mathematics* **2022**, *10*, 4424, doi:10.3390/math10234424 21

Weng Hoe Lam, Weng Siew Lam, Kah Fai Liew and Pei Fun Lee
Decision Analysis on the Financial Performance of Companies Using Integrated Entropy-Fuzzy TOPSIS Model
Reprinted from: *Mathematics* **2023**, *11*, 397, doi:10.3390/math11020397 35

Pei Fun Lee, Weng Siew Lam and Weng Hoe Lam
Performance Evaluation of the Efficiency of Logistics Companies with Data Envelopment Analysis Model
Reprinted from: *Mathematics* **2023**, *11*, 718, doi:10.3390/math11030718 53

Kristina O. F. Williams and Benjamin F. Akers
Numerical Simulation of the Korteweg–de Vries Equation with Machine Learning
Reprinted from: *Mathematics* **2023**, *11*, 2791, doi:10.3390/math11132791 68

Weng Siew Lam, Weng Hoe Lam and Pei Fun Lee
A Bibliometric Analysis of Digital Twin in the Supply Chain
Reprinted from: *Mathematics* **2023**, *11*, 3350, doi:10.3390/math11153350 82

Na Ye, Dingguo Yu, Yijie Zhou, Ke-ke Shang and Suiyu Zhang
Graph Convolutional-Based Deep Residual Modeling for Rumor Detection on Social Media
Reprinted from: *Mathematics* **2023**, *11*, 3393, doi:10.3390/math11153393 106

Timothy Roche, Aihua Wood, Philip Cho and Chancellor Johnstone
Anomaly Detection in the Molecular Structure of Gallium Arsenide Using Convolutional Neural Networks
Reprinted from: *Mathematics* **2023**, *11*, 3428, doi:10.3390/math11153428 117

Annisa Nur Falah, Budi Nurani Ruchjana, Atje Setiawan Abdullah and Juli Rejito
The Hybrid Modeling of Spatial Autoregressive Exogenous Using Casetti's Model Approach for the Prediction of Rainfall
Reprinted from: *Mathematics* **2023**, *11*, 3783, doi:10.3390/math11173783 127

Imran Nasim and Michael E. Henderson
Dynamically Meaningful Latent Representations of Dynamical Systems
Reprinted from: *Mathematics* **2024**, *12*, 476, doi:10.3390/math12030476 148

Article

Machine Learning-Based Estimation of the Compressive Strength of Self-Compacting Concrete: A Multi-Dataset Study

Nhat-Duc Hoang [1,2]

[1] Institute of Research and Development, Duy Tan University, Da Nang 550000, Vietnam; hoangnhatduc@duytan.edu.vn; Tel.: +84-2036-382-7111 (ext. 809)
[2] Faculty of Civil Engineering, Duy Tan University, Da Nang 550000, Vietnam

Abstract: This paper aims at performing a comparative study to investigate the predictive capability of machine learning (ML) models used for estimating the compressive strength of self-compacting concrete (SCC). Seven prominent ML models, including deep neural network regression (DNNR), extreme gradient boosting machine (XGBoost), gradient boosting machine (GBM), adaptive boosting machine (AdaBoost), support vector regression (SVR), Levenberg–Marquardt artificial neural network (LM-ANN), and genetic programming (GP), are employed. Four experimental datasets, compiled in previous studies, are used to construct the ML-based methods. The models' generalization capabilities are reliably evaluated by 20 independent runs. Experimental results point out the superiority of the DNNR, which has excelled other models in three out of four datasets. The XGBoost is the second-best model, which has gained the first rank in one dataset. The outcomes point out the great potential of the utilized ML approaches in modeling the compressive strength of SCC. In more details, the coefficient of determination (R^2) surpasses 0.8 and the mean absolute percentage error (MAPE) is always below 15% for all datasets. The best results of R^2 and MAPE are 0.93 and 7.2%, respectively.

Keywords: self-compacting concrete; compressive strength; deep neural network; gradient boosting machine; machine learning

MSC: 65K05; 90C15

1. Introduction

SCC is typically characterized by its enhanced workability and good resistance to segregation. This type of concrete is able to settle by its own weight without the requirement of internal or external vibration during the placing phase [1–3]. Therefore, SCC is highly applicable in areas featuring congested reinforcements (e.g., high-rise shear walls) and at other narrow cross-sections [4]). Due to its excellent workability, SCC is often employed in elements that are unconventionally shaped or hardly reachable [5].

The compressive strength (CS) of SCC is a crucial mechanical parameter for both design and application purposes on construction sites as well as in ready-mixed concrete plants [6]. Other properties of SCC such as modulus of elasticity and tensile strength can be inferred from the CS [7]. The CS of a SCC mix is usually obtained via time-consuming and costly experiments [8]. Due to its importance, various research works have been conducted to measure the CS of SCC mixes corresponding to different proportions of their constituents. Therefore, it is highly beneficial to analyze the existing experimental records and construct intelligent models that can estimate the CS of SCC mixes. These data-driven models can be effective decision-support tools to assist in the design of SCC mixes. It is because designing a proper mixture of SCC is still a challenging task in civil engineering [9,10].

In recent years, the research community has observed a burgeoning trend of applying machine learning (ML) in modeling the CS of various types of concrete [11–13], including SCC. ML has demonstrated unquestionable advantages in terms of prediction accuracy and flexibility over conventional empirical models for concrete mechanical strength. Nevertheless, deriving accurate models for estimating the CS of SCC is by no means an easy task. The reason is that the mapping function between the CS and the concrete constituent is typically nonlinear and multivariate.

Moreover, various supplementary materials, cement replacement components, and environmentally friendly mineral additives (e.g., fly ash, silica fume, ground granulated blast furnace slag, rice husk ash, etc.) are often added to the mix [9,14,15]. This fact significantly complicates the function approximation process. For instance, Sukumar et al. [16] shows a significant effect of fly ash content to the development of strength at early ages of curing. Dinakar et al. [3] demonstrates that variations in cement, mineral additives, and aggregate type can bring about large changes in the properties of SCC.

Accordingly, various advanced ML methods have been proposed and applied to model the CS of SCC. Neural networks were used in [6] to predict the 28-day CS of normal and high-strength SCC mixes containing fly ash. Uysal and Tanyildizi [17] put forward an artificial neural network (ANN) model for estimating the CS of mixes that contain mineral additives and polypropylene (PP) fiber exposed to elevated temperature. In addition, Portland cement (PC) was substituted by mineral additives such as fly ash, granulated blast furnace slag, limestone powder, basalt powder, and marble powder in different proportions. The ANN model is then trained by a dataset consisting of 85 data samples.

Vakhshouri and Nejadi [18] relied on an adaptive neuro fuzzy inference model (ANFIS) to perform the task of interest. Although ANFIS is a capable tool for nonlinear regression analysis, its learning phase requires a significant effort in model configuration, which involves the setting of fuzzy membership functions. In addition, this study only employed a limited dataset, including only 55 data samples. To establish reliable and robust ML models, larger datasets should be used. Asteris and Kolovos [4] also employed ANN in estimating the 28-day CS of SCC; the authors relied on a fairly large dataset, consisting of 205 records and 11 predictor variables.

ML based on ANN and genetic programming (GP) was used in [19] to predict the strength properties of geopolymer blended SCC. The results show that both ANN and GP are capable of delivering good predictions with respect to the experimental data. Farooq et al. [20] investigated the performance of ANN, support vector regression (SVR), and gene expression programming (GEP) in modeling a dataset consisting of 300 samples. The cement, water–binder ratio, coarse aggregate, fine aggregate, fly ash, and superplasticizer are considered the influencing factors of the CS. The authors demonstrated that the GEP could obtain an accurate prediction outcome, but they also pointed out that this method might not deliver satisfactory results if it is trapped in a local optimal solution.

Levenberg-Marquardt ANN (LM-ANN) models were used in [8,21]. These models rely on the Levenberg-Marquardt (LM) algorithm, which is derived from Newton's method and highly suitable for minimizing functions that are sums of squares of nonlinear functions. This study reported a good correlation between the observed and predicted CS of SCC. However, the LM algorithm requires the calculation and storage of the Jacobian matrix [22], which might be computationally expensive for large-scale datasets and deep ANN.

As can be seen from the literature, the existing works have extensively relied on conventional ANN, GP, and SVR for estimating the SC of SCC. Apparently, there is a lack of comprehensive comparative study that analyzes the capability of state-of-the-art ML models that are feasible for the task of interest. Notably, the gradient boosting machine (GBM) and the extreme gradient boosting machine (XGBoost) have shown remarkable prediction performances in predicting the SC of high-performance concrete [23]. Deep learning is also a burgeoning research direction with high potential in modeling complex engineering processes [24]. However, gradient boosting machines and deep learning have not yet been used for estimating the CS of SCC.

To fill this gap in the literature, this paper conducts a comparative study that considers prominent ML-based regression analysis methods, including the GBM, XGBoost, and deep neural network regression (DNNR). In addition, an adaptive boosting machine (AdaBoost),

SVR, LM-ANN, and GP are also taken into account due to their good performances in previous studies [8,25,26]. The predictive capability of the employed ML models is evaluated reliably via four datasets and 20 independent runs.

Conceptually, the GBM, AdaBoost, and XGBoost rely on the idea of gradient boosting [27] which views a model's training process as an optimization of a cost function. Gradient boosting machines sequentially select a weak learner (e.g., a regression tree) that helps to drive the optimization process to the negative gradient direction. The AdaBoost improves the data fitting process by assigning weights to data points adaptively during the training phase. By doing so, this ML method is able to focus on the training samples that are not well fitted. The XGBoost model further improves the conventional boosting machine with the concept of Similarity Score and Gain index; these two metrics are used to determine the best node splits during the training phase of regression trees [28].

In addition, the SVR employs the concept of the margin of tolerance and kernel mapping to construct a robust model. The margin of tolerance is used to alleviate the effect of noisy data points. The kernel mapping function helps the SVR effectively cope with nonlinear functions. The LM-ANN relies on the LM algorithm to train the regression model; the LM algorithm can be viewed as a variant of the Newton algorithm for optimizing a nonlinear function. The GP is a technique for evolving a set of mathematical equations used for modeling a response variable; this algorithm employs operations that are similar to natural genetic processes. Meanwhile, the DNNR relies on the hierarchical organization of various hidden layers to model complex patterns. Each layer in a DNNR model serves as a feature engineering operator that sequentially constructs high-level representations of the input dataset [29]. This characteristic helps this deep learning method effectively capture and simulate complex functional mappings.

The novelty of the current work can be summarized as follows:

(1) The performance of prominent ML methods in a comparative manner to predict the CS of SCC is investigated. It is apparent that existing works lack a comprehensive comparison of the prominent ML models' performance applied to the problem of interest. Chou et al. [30] covered a wide range of ML approaches such as SVR and ANN; however, deep learning solutions and novel gradient boosting machines were unexplored. The ANN models have been utilized in [4]; however, this work did not take into account the potential of state-of-the-art gradient boosting machines. Nguyen et al. [23] has recently covered a wide variety of models and proven the superiority of the XGBoost; nevertheless, the performance of the DNNR were not included.

(2) The current work utilizes multiple datasets, instead of a single dataset, to train and test the ML models. Since each dataset has distinctive characteristics due to the materials used and the mixed design, employing multiple datasets provides a comprehensive view of the predictive capability of the ML approaches.

The rest of the paper is organized as follows: The next section reviews the employed ML models. Descriptions of the datasets are provided in the third section. Experimental results are reported in the next section, followed by the final section that summarizes the research findings.

2. The Machine Learning Methods for Estimating the CS of SCC

2.1. Deep Neural Network Regression (DNNR)

Deep learning (DL) is a powerful approach for pattern recognition and modeling complex mapping functions [29]. The advantage of DL stems from its hierarchical organization of hidden layers of individual processing units, called neurons. These stacked layers of neurons allow a DL-based model to capture, simulate, and represent complex patterns hidden in the data. A typical structure of a DNNR model, employed for estimating the CS of SCC, includes an input layer, a set of hidden layers, and an output layer. The first layer receives input signals in the form of the SCC constituent and curing age. The hidden layers contain individual information processing units organized into different layers.

Each hidden layer serves as a feature engineering operator that gradually distills increasingly high-level representations of the original dataset [29]. The stacked hidden layers equip a DNNR with the capability of learning multivariate and complex functional mapping between the CS and its influencing factors [31]. Notably, to cope with complex mapping relationships, nonlinear activation functions (f_A) are often employed in the neurons of the hidden layers. The commonly utilized f_A includes logistic sigmoid (Sigmoid), hyperbolic tangent sigmoid (Tanh), and rectified linear unit activation (ReLU). In addition, the output layer uses the linear function to derive the estimated value of the CS. The training phase of a DNNR involves the adaptation of the weight matrices, which represent the entire model structure [32]. This study employs the state-of-the-art adaptive moment estimation (Adam) to train the DNNR.

2.2. Extreme Gradient Boosting Machine (XGBoost)

The XGBoost, proposed in [28], is enhanced according to the original gradient boosting algorithm [33]. This ML approach can also be viewed as an ensemble of boosting decision trees. Notably, the model construction phase of the XGBoost can be executed very fast because it can be performed in parallel [34]. Similar to the GBM, the XGBoost for regression analysis also utilizes the mean squared error loss function. During the training phase, individual regression trees are fitted using the residuals of their predecessors.

To construct regression trees, an XGBoost model relies on the Similarity Score and Gain index to determine the best node splits [28]. The Similarity Score is a function of the model residuals. The Gain of a node is computed from the Similarity Score of the right leaf, left leaf, and root. Accordingly, the note split having the highest Gain index is selected to build the regression tree [35]. The progress of the construction phase is governed by the learning rate parameter. The complexity of each regression tree can be controlled by the tree depth parameter. In addition, a regularization parameter (λ), which is included in the calculation of the Similarity Score, can be used to alleviate the over-fitting issue during the model training phase.

2.3. Gradient Boosting Machine (GBM)

The GBM is a ML that sequentially combines a set of weak learners (e.g., regression trees) to establish a robust model [27]. The GBM can be considered as a numerical optimization method, used to formulate an additive model that minimizes a loss function. For the task of nonlinear function approximation, the mean squared error is commonly used as the loss function. During the training phase, the GBM sequentially adds a new decision tree to the current ensemble to minimize the mean squared error loss. By fitting decision trees to the residuals, the overall model is able to focus on the samples of the dataset which have not been well fitted.

2.4. Adaptive Gradient Boosting Machine (AdaBoost)

The AdaBoost [36] also relies on the principle of boosting algorithms to rectify the residual committed by a ML model, e.g., a decision tree. This method first builds a model on the training dataset. Initially, AdaBoost assigns equal weights to all of the data instances. Subsequent models are then built to rectify the existing error committed by their predecessors. This process is repeated until the error is lower than a specified threshold. It is noted that during the model fitting process, the AdaBoost gradually adjusts the weights of data points. In more detail, it increases the weights assigned to data points associated with high residuals. This ML method is adaptive in the sense that subsequent weak learners (e.g., regression trees) are trained with the inclination of fitting the data samples associated with high residuals. Hence, although an individual regression tree may not fit the entire dataset well, the aggregated model can converge to an accurate predictor [37].

2.5. Support Vector Regression (SVR)

The SVR [38,39] relies on a margin of tolerance (ε) and the concept of kernel functions for constructing a nonlinear and multivariate mapping relation. The goal of the SVR is to construct $f(x)$ that has at most ε deviation from the desired variable. To deal with nonlinear mapping functions, the SVR utilizes kernel functions that map the input data from the original space to a high-dimensional space where a linear hyper-plane can be used to fit the collected data. For nonlinear regression problems, the radial basis function (RBF) is often employed as the kernel function [23]. The training phase of a SVR model is formulated as a quadratic programming problem. Therefore, the SVR is suitable for modeling small- and medium-sized datasets because it demands substantial computational cost for dealing with large-scale datasets. In addition, the implementation of the SVR requires a proper setting of the RBF and the regularization parameters. These parameters can be determined via a grid search [40].

2.6. Levenberg–Marquardt Artificial Neural Network (LM-ANN)

An ANN model typically consists of an input layer, a hidden layer, and an output layer. This ML is designed as an attempt to mimic the information processing and knowledge generalization in the human brain [41]. Each neuron employs a nonlinear activation function (e.g., Sigmoid) to process the signals received from the input layer. An ANN model can be completely characterized by the weight matrix of the hidden layer (W_1), the weight matrix of the output layer (W_2), the bias vector of the hidden layer (b_1), and the bias vector of the output layer (b_2). The number of the neurons in the hidden layer strongly influences the learning capability of the LM-ANN and this parameter should be tuned to attain a robust prediction model [42].

Accordingly, an ANN model used for nonlinear function estimation can be generally stated as:

$$f(x) = b_2 + W_2 \times \sigma(b_1 + W_1 \times x) \tag{1}$$

where x denotes the matrix of input variables; σ represents the activation function.

The weight matrices and the biases of an ANN model can be adapted by the Levenberg–Marquardt (LM) algorithm [43]. Thus, the ANN model trained by the LM algorithm can be denoted as the LM-ANN. The LM algorithm can be viewed as a modification of the Newton algorithm for optimizing a nonlinear function, e.g., the Mean Square Error function. The LM–ANN is an effective method for modeling moderate-sized datasets as demonstrated in [4].

2.7. Genetic Programming (GP)

The GP [44] is a ML technique used for evolving programs. These programs can be used as functions to model complex and multivariate processes, such as the CS of SCC. The GP commences with a population of random programs consisting of a predefined set of mathematical operations (e.g., addition, subtraction, multiplication, etc.). The algorithm then evolves this population with operations that are analogous to the natural genetic processes. The employed operations are selection, crossover, and mutation, which imitate the concepts in the Genetic Algorithm [45]. The first operator aims at preserving the most desired programs and casting out inferior ones. The second operation involves swapping random genes of the selected parents to generate a new offspring that possesses the advantageous features of the parents. The third operation introduces some random changes in a program so that an offspring can have features that don't exist in the parents.

The GP can be used to construct mathematical equations automatically from the data (Searson 2015). However, since this ML method involves a stochastic search for the best program, it generally demands a considerable computational cost for evaluating the fitness of the programs and performing genetic operations (e.g., selection, crossover, and mutation). One significant advantage of the GP is that the constructed model can be explicitly presented as a mathematical equation used for predicting the CS from the mix's constituents. However, for decently describing complex mapping relationships, the resulting mathematical equations can be quite complicated [46]. This fact hinders the process of interpreting these GP-based mathematical equations by civil engineers. Moreover, the quality of a GP-based model in terms of prediction accuracy does not always outperform that of the prominent nonlinear regression methods such as the ANN [47].

3. The Collected Datasets

In this study, four datasets, compiled by the previous studies, are used to evaluate the employed ML approaches. It is noted that the dataset investigates different sets of predictor variables that influence the CS of SCC. Therefore, each dataset has distinctive features because of the materials employed and mix design. This paper relies on the four datasets to provide a comprehensive assessment of the modeling capabilities of the prominent ML approaches. General information about the collected datasets is provided in Table 1. The statistical descriptions of the variables in the datasets are reported in Tables 2–5. The minimum number of testing records in the datasets is 205. The number of predictor variables used as the CS's influencing factors ranges from 6 to 11. The 28-day CS of SCC specimens is used as a modeled variable in the first two datasets. Meanwhile, the concrete age, measured in days, is used as an influencing factor in Dataset 3 and 4. The desired characteristics of SCC are obtained via the use of supplementary cementitious materials such as fly ash, silica fume, and chemical additives (e.g., superplasticizers) [48].

Dataset 1 [4] contains 205 mixes of SCC. The predictor variables in this dataset are the cement, the coarse aggregate, the fine aggregate, the water, the limestone powder, the fly ash, the ground granulated blast furnace slag, the silica fume, the rice husk ash, superplasticizers, and the viscosity modifying admixtures. The mixes include the use of limestone powder and rice husk ash as supplementary cementing materials (SCMs). Blending SCMs with Portland cement has been shown to bring about significant environmental benefits (e.g., reducing CO_2 emission) and enhancement of the physical properties of the concrete mixes [49].

Table 1. The collected datasets of SCC.

Dataset	Number of Predictor Variables	Number of Data Points	General Description	Reference
1	11	205	28-days CS of SCC specimens	[4]
2	6	300	28-days CS of SCC specimens containing fly ash	[20]
3	7	327	Predicting the CS of SCC containing Class F fly ash at different curing ages	[8]
4	7	366	Predicting the CS of SCC containing with silica fume at different curing ages	[21]

Table 2. The variables used in the Dataset 1.

Variables	Notation	Unit	Min	Mean	Std.	Max
Cement	X_1	kg/m^3	110.00	349.22	93.43	600.00
Limestone powder	X_2	kg/m^3	0.00	25.67	60.78	272.00
Fly ash	X_3	kg/m^3	0.00	106.36	94.01	440.00
Ground granulated blast furnace slag	X_4	kg/m^3	0.00	17.39	52.01	330.00
Silica fume	X_5	kg/m^3	0.00	14.91	33.45	250.00
Rice husk ash	X_6	kg/m^3	0.00	6.55	24.29	200.00
Coarse aggregate	X_7	kg/m^3	500.00	772.35	175.36	1600.00
Fine aggregate	X_8	kg/m^3	336.00	827.93	144.33	1135.00
Water	X_9	kg/m^3	94.50	179.27	27.65	250.00
Superplasticizer	X_{10}	kg/m^3	0.00	5.96	4.35	22.50
Viscosity-modifying admixtures	X_{11}	kg/m^3	0.00	0.14	0.31	1.23
Compressive strength	Y	MPa	10.20	58.08	21.61	122.00

Table 3. The variables used in the Dataset 2.

Variables	Notations	Unit	Min	Mean	Std.	Max
Cement	X_1	kg/m^3	83.00	292.79	93.73	540.00
Fly ash	X_2	kg/m^3	0.00	115.34	87.26	525.00
Water-powder ratio	X_3	-	0.22	0.48	0.13	0.90
Sand	X_4	kg/m^3	478.00	805.74	98.47	1180.00
Coarse aggregate	X_5	kg/m^3	578.00	912.48	119.43	1125.00
Superplasticizer	X_6	%	0.00	0.17	0.26	1.36
Compressive strength	Y	MPa	8.54	36.60	15.80	79.19

Table 4. The variables used in the Dataset 3.

Variables	Notations	Unit	Min	Mean	Std.	Max
Cement	X_1	kg/m^3	61.00	293.08	89.78	503.00
Water	X_2	kg/m^3	132.00	197.00	37.62	390.39
Class F fly ash	X_3	kg/m^3	20.00	170.23	69.68	373.00
Coarse aggregate	X_4	kg/m^3	590.00	828.34	137.30	1190.00
Fine aggregate	X_5	kg/m^3	434.00	807.47	135.80	1109.00
Superplasticizer	X_6	%	0.00	0.98	1.11	4.60
Age of concrete	X_7	Days	1.00	44.31	63.76	365.00
Compressive strength	Y	MPa	4.44	36.45	19.07	90.60

Table 5. The variables used in the Dataset 4.

Variables	Notations	Unit	Min	Mean	Std.	Max
Water to binder ratio	X_1	kg/m^3	0.22	0.38	0.04	0.51
Binder	X_2	kg/m^3	359.00	493.09	53.00	600.00
Silica fume	X_3	kg/m^3	0.00	45.68	36.84	250.00
Fine aggregate	X_4	kg/m^3	680.00	902.90	101.22	1166.00
Coarse aggregate	X_5	kg/m^3	595.00	817.03	112.70	1000.00
Superplasticizer	X_6	kg/m^3	1.30	7.21	2.53	15.00
Age of specimen	X_7	Days	1.00	32.37	42.92	270.00
Compressive strength	Y	MPa	21.10	54.01	18.79	106.60

Dataset 2 [20] consists of 300 samples and 6 influencing factors: cement, water–binder ratio, coarse aggregate, fine aggregate, fly ash, and superplasticizer. Dataset 3 [8] focuses on the inclusion of class F fly ash as a partial cement replacement in concrete mixes. The use of class F fly ash is able to provide various desired features, including enhancements of the mechanical properties [50,51] and reductions in the construction costs [8]. This dataset contains 327 samples and 7 predictor variables (the cement, water, class F fly ash, coarse aggregate, fine aggregate, superplasticizer, and concrete age). Dataset 4 [21] aims at investigating the CS of SCC containing silica fume at different curing ages. It considers 366 samples and 7 predictor variables: the water to binder ratio, the binder, the silica fume, the fine aggregate, the coarse aggregate, the superplasticizer, and the age of concrete specimen. It is noted that fly ash is used in the first three datasets. Meanwhile, the silica fume is only used as a predictor variable in the Dataset 1 and Dataset 4.

The first dataset has the highest number of predictor variables, but it contains the smallest number of data points. The scatter plots showing the correlation between the predictor variable and the CS as the modeled variable of the 4 datasets are demonstrated in Figures 1–4. Generally, these figures show weak linear correlations between the predictor variables and the CS of CSS and point out the need for advanced nonlinear analysis methods to predict the CS effectively.

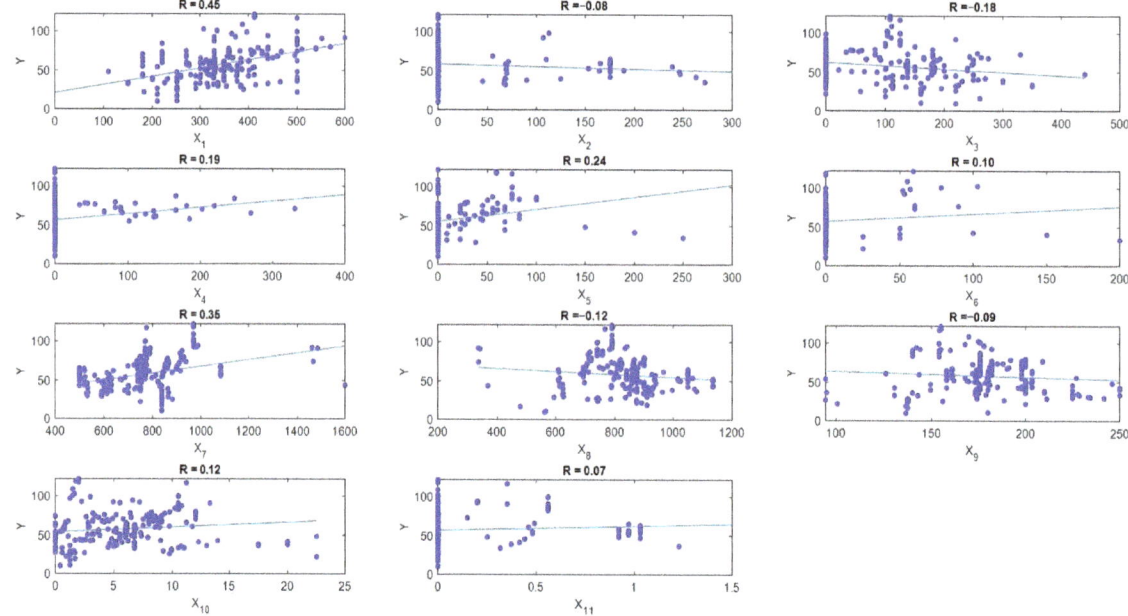

Figure 1. Scatter plots of variables in Dataset 1.

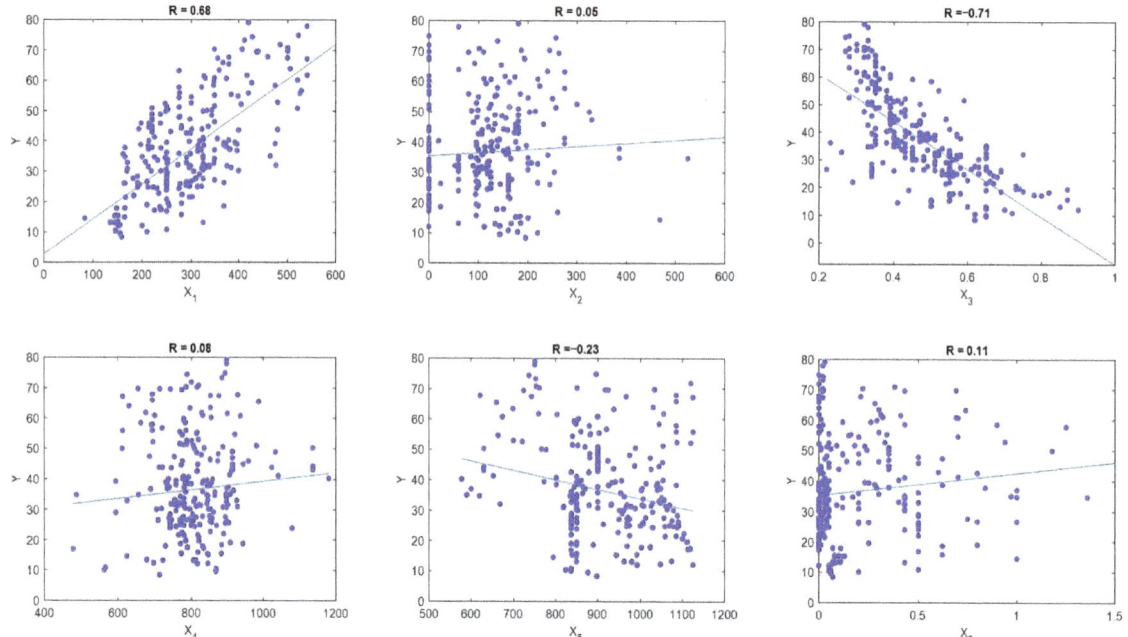

Figure 2. Scatter plots of variables in Dataset 2.

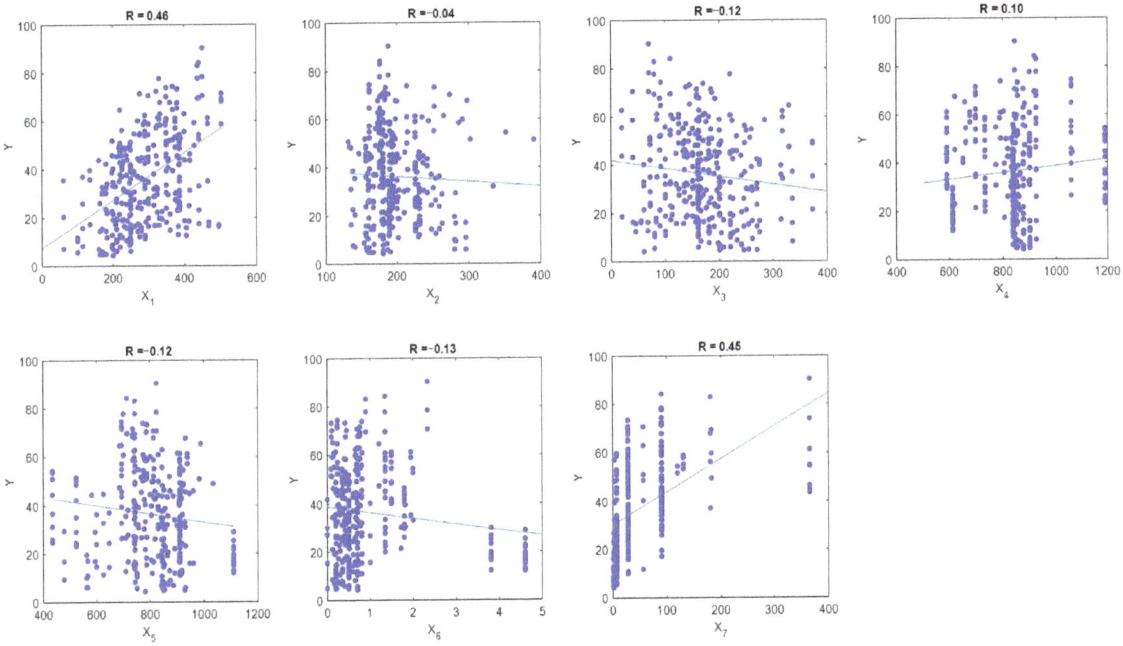

Figure 3. Scatter plots of variables in Dataset 3.

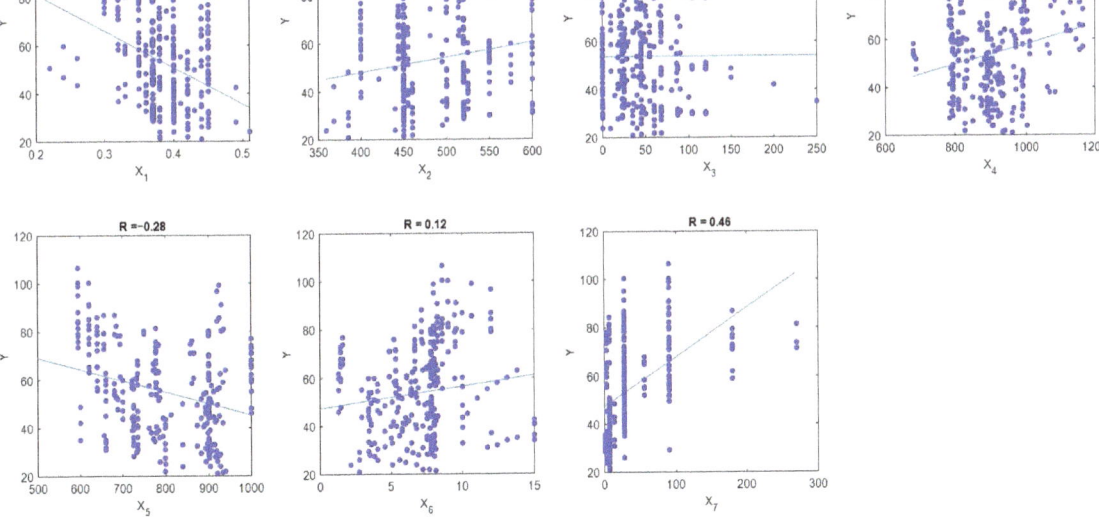

Figure 4. Scatter plots of variables in Dataset 4.

4. Experimental Results and Discussion

The aforementioned four datasets containing the CS of SCC specimens and their corresponding constituents are used to train and verify the ML approaches. Each dataset is randomly separated into two subsets: a training (85%) set and a testing (15%) set.

The former is used for model construction. The latter is reserved for evaluating the generalization capability of the trained ML models. To mitigate the effect of randomness due to the data sampling process, in this study, we conducted 20 independent experiments. The model performance is evaluated via the statistical indices, i.e., the mean and the standard deviation (std.), obtained from these independent experiments. It is noted that the experiments were performed on the Dell G15 (Core i7-11800H and 16 GB Ram). In addition, to standardize the range of the predictor variables (e.g., the concrete constituents and curing age) and target variable (i.e., the CS of SCC), this study relies on the Z-score normalization. This method transforms the original range of a variable into a standardized variable with a mean of 0 and a standard deviation of 1. The equation of the Z-score normalization is given by:

$$X_Z = \frac{X_O - \mu_X}{\sigma_X} \quad (2)$$

where X_Z and X_O are the standardized and the original variables, respectively. μ_X and σ_X denote the mean and standard deviation of the variable, respectively.

Furthermore, the root mean square error (RMSE), mean absolute percentage error (MAPE), and coefficient of determination (R^2) are the commonly employed metrics for evaluating the performance of a ML model. These metrics are computed as follows:

$$RMSE = \sqrt{\frac{1}{N} \sum_{i=1}^{N} (y_i - t_i)^2} \quad (3)$$

$$MAPE = \frac{100}{N} \times \sum_{i=1}^{N} \frac{|y_i - t_i|}{y_i} \quad (4)$$

$$R^2 = 1 - \frac{\sum_{i=1}^{N}(t_i - y_i)^2}{\sum_{i=1}^{N}(t_i - \bar{t})^2} \quad (5)$$

where t_i and y_i denote the actual and predicted CS of the SCC, respectively. N is the number of specimens. $\bar{t}$ denotes the mean of the observed CS values.

Notably, the RMSE indicates the deviations between the actual and predicted CS of SCC. This index is computed as the square root of the second sample moment of the residuals (or deviations) between the observed and predicted CS values. The RMSE aggregates the magnitudes of the deviations in predictions for all of the specimens into a unified measurement that demonstrates the predictive power of a ML model. Basically, the smaller the RMSE is, the better the prediction outcome is. The MAPE demonstrates the relative error of the prediction and is often expressed in terms of a percentage. Meanwhile, the R^2 denotes the proportion of the variation in target output that can be predicted by a model [52]. A perfect regression model is indicated by a $R^2 = 1$. The higher the index is, the better the prediction result is. The RMSE is a scale-dependent index; it is only valid for comparing different models in modeling the same dataset. On the contrary, the MAPE and R^2 are scale-independent; therefore, they can be used to assess the performance of a ML model in predicting the CS of different datasets.

This study employs 7 ML models: the DNNR, XGBoost, GBM, AdaBoost, SVR, LM-ANN, and GP. The DNNR model is coded in MATLAB by the author. The XGBoost is built with the assistance of the Python library provided in [53]. The GBM and SVR models are constructed with the help of built-in functions provided in the Scikit-Learn library [54]. The LM-ANN is implemented with the MATLAB's Statistics and Machine Learning Toolbox [55]. The library developed by [56] is used to construct the GP model.

The DNNR requires a proper setting of the number of hidden layers, the number of neurons, the learning rate, the activation function type, and the regularization coefficient. The regularization coefficient is used to penalize large values of the network's weight;

therefore, the issue of over-fitting can be alleviated [32]. In this study, the number of hidden layers ranging from 2 to 5 is investigated. The number of neurons in each hidden layer varies in the range of $[0.5D, 2D]$ where D is the number of the CS's influencing factors. The Sigmoid, Tanh, and ReLU activation functions are used. Various learning rates ranging from 0.001 to 0.1 are employed. The regularization parameters are selected from a set of $\{0.00001, 0.0001, 0.001, 0.01\}$.

The essential hyper-parameters of the XGBoost model are the learning rate, the maximum tree depth, and the regularization coefficient. The learning rate, the number of estimators, and the maximum tree depth are the hyper-parameters that govern the learning phase of a GBM model and an AdaBoost model. The SVR requires the specification of the penalty coefficient, the kernel function's parameter, and the margin of tolerance (ε). In this study, the LM-ANN is adapted during 300 epochs; its hyper-parameters include the number of neurons and the learning rate. The GP has a population size of 100, a maximum number of genes of 8, and a maximum number of evolutionary generations of 3000. In this study, the hyper-parameters of the ML models for each dataset were properly set with the use of the five-fold cross validation processes [57]. For the ANN models, the number of neurons in the hidden layer is allowed to range from $0.5D$ to $3D$, where D denotes the number of predictor variables.

The average performance of the ML models with respect to different datasets is reported in Table 6. It can be seen from the experimental results that the DNNR achieves outstanding results; it has outperformed other models in Dataset 1 (with RMSE = 7.73, MAPE = 11.21%, and R^2 = 0.81), 2 (with RMSE = 4.68, MAPE = 10.29%, and R^2 = 0.90), and 4 (with RMSE = 4.84, MAPE = 7.16%, and R^2 = 0.93). Additionally, the XGBoost achieved the best outcome in Dataset 3 (with RMSE = 5.49, MAPE = 14.36%, and R^2 = 0.91). The setting of the XGBoost model found by the cross-validation process is as follows: the learning rate = 0.5, the maximum tree depth = 3, and the regularization parameter = 1. The GBM is slightly inferior to the XGBoost with RMSE = 5.61, MAPE = 14.89%, and R^2 = 0.91. The DNNR achieved the third rank with RMSE = 6.68, MAPE = 17.40%, and R^2 = 0.87.

Table 6. Average performance of the ML models.

Dataset	Metrics	The ML Models						
		DNNR	XGBoost	GBM	AdaBoost	SVR	LM-ANN	GP
1	RMSE	**7.73**	8.91	9.59	9.14	8.32	10.96	9.82
	MAPE (%)	**11.21**	14.15	13.69	14.74	12.26	15.01	15.27
	R^2	**0.81**	0.82	0.77	0.79	0.80	0.73	0.73
2	RMSE	**4.68**	5.26	5.57	6.04	4.80	5.19	5.20
	MAPE (%)	**10.29**	11.52	11.39	13.26	11.36	12.33	12.24
	R^2	**0.90**	0.88	0.87	0.84	0.90	0.88	0.88
3	RMSE	6.68	**5.49**	5.61	7.60	7.28	8.67	8.15
	MAPE (%)	17.40	**14.36**	14.89	23.07	20.57	25.02	24.02
	R^2	0.87	**0.91**	0.91	0.84	0.84	0.77	0.79
4	RMSE	**4.84**	4.90	4.98	6.24	5.65	7.16	7.03
	MAPE (%)	**7.16**	6.69	6.41	10.50	7.60	10.61	10.15
	R^2	**0.93**	0.93	0.92	0.88	0.91	0.84	0.85

Note: Bold text indicate the best performance.

The values of R^2 obtained from the ML are at least 0.81, which indicates a good degree of data fitting results. For Dataset 1, the DNNR is able to explain 81% of the variation in the CS of SCC. For other datasets, the R^2 is always larger than 0.9; this outcome demonstrates that the fluctuations of the CS values are well captured and generalized by the ML models. In addition, the MAPE values within the range of 7% and 15% show an acceptable deviation between the predicted and observed variables [58]. More details of the prediction results obtained from the ML models are provided in Appendices A and B.

Based on the experimental results, it is found that those parameters of the DNNR are highly data dependent. The configurations of the DNNR models that help to achieve the most accurate predictions are reported in Table 7. It can be seen that the Tanh activation function is favored in Dataset 1, 2, and 4. Meanwhile, for Dataset 3, in which the DNNR is the second-best approach, the ReLU activation function is favored. The DNNR models in all datasets require two hidden layers. This means that a two-layer structure is considered to be deep enough for modeling the CS of SCC. However, the suitable number of neurons varies with respect to different datasets. The number of neurons can be as low as 6 in the case of Dataset 2 and as high as 16 in the case of Dataset 4. This can be explained by the fact that Dataset 4 includes a comparatively larger number of instances. Therefore, more neurons are required to model the mapping functions stored in those datasets.

In addition, the average computational time of each model is provided in Table 8. Generally, the training time of the ML models used for predicting the CS of SCC is minor. It is because the sizes of the currently collected datasets are moderate with the largest number of instances = 366. As shown in this table, the computational cost of the XGBoost is lower than that of the DNNR. It is because the training algorithm of the XGBoost can be executed in parallel. It is also observable that the GP consumes the largest amount of computational expense due to its genetic operators.

The detailed ranking of the ML models with respect to different datasets is reported in Table 9 and Figure 5. Herein, the model performance is ranked according to the average RMSE in the testing phase. As mentioned previously, the DNNR has gained the best outcomes in three out of four datasets. This model gains the third rank in Dataset 3. The XGBoost has gained the best performance once with dataset 3; it achieved the second, third, and fifth rank in Dataset 4, 1, and 2, respectively. The best outcomes of the GBM and the SVR are the second rank in Dataset 3 and 2, respectively. The LM-ANN achieved the third rank in Dataset 2 and obtained the worst performance in the other three datasets.

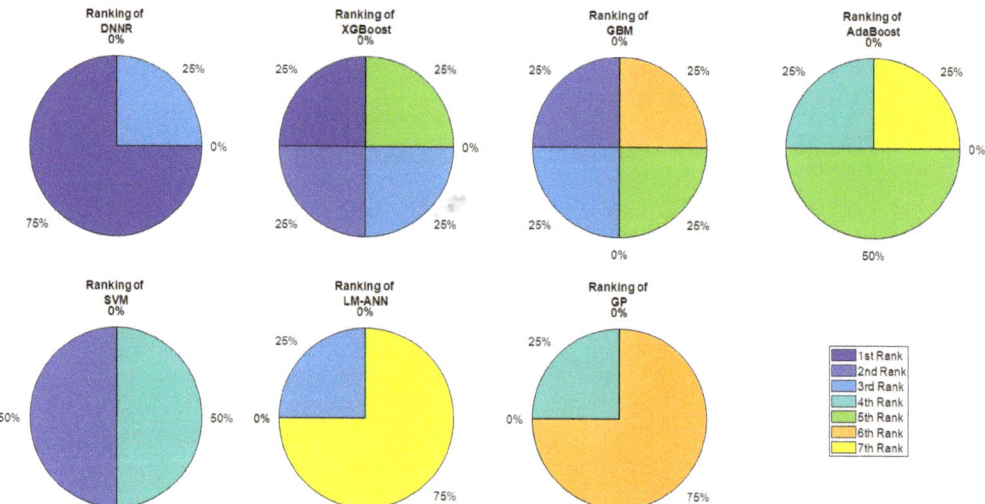

Figure 5. Summary of the models' rankings.

The GP only outperformed the LM-ANN in Dataset 2 and was worse than the ANN model in the other three datasets. Hence, the results of this paper are, to some degree, comply with that reported in the previous works of [23,59] which demonstrated the advantage of the XGBoost. In addition, the current paper also points out the great potential of the DNNR since it was able to outperform the XGBoost in three datasets. The GBM was able to excel the DNNR once (in Dataset 3) but it never outperformed the XGBoost. The deep neural network is always better than the shallow network of the LM-ANN. This fact clearly shows the superiority of deep learning over conventional ANN in the task of predicting the CS of SCC. The AdaBoost and GP generally show mediocre performances in comparison with the DNNR and the XGBoost.

Figure 6 illustrates the correlation between the actual and predicted CS with respect to different datasets. The line of best fit, ±10% bounds, and ±20% bounds are provided to assist the inspection of the prediction errors. The red straight line denotes a perfect fit where the CS of a specimen is correctly estimated. The nearer the data samples (shown as black circles) to the line of best fit, the better they are estimated by the ML approaches. In addition, the distribution of the residual (or error) committed by the ML models is presented by four histograms in Figure 7. Generally, the mean of the residuals is close to 0 and the values of the std. are less than 8 for all of the cases.

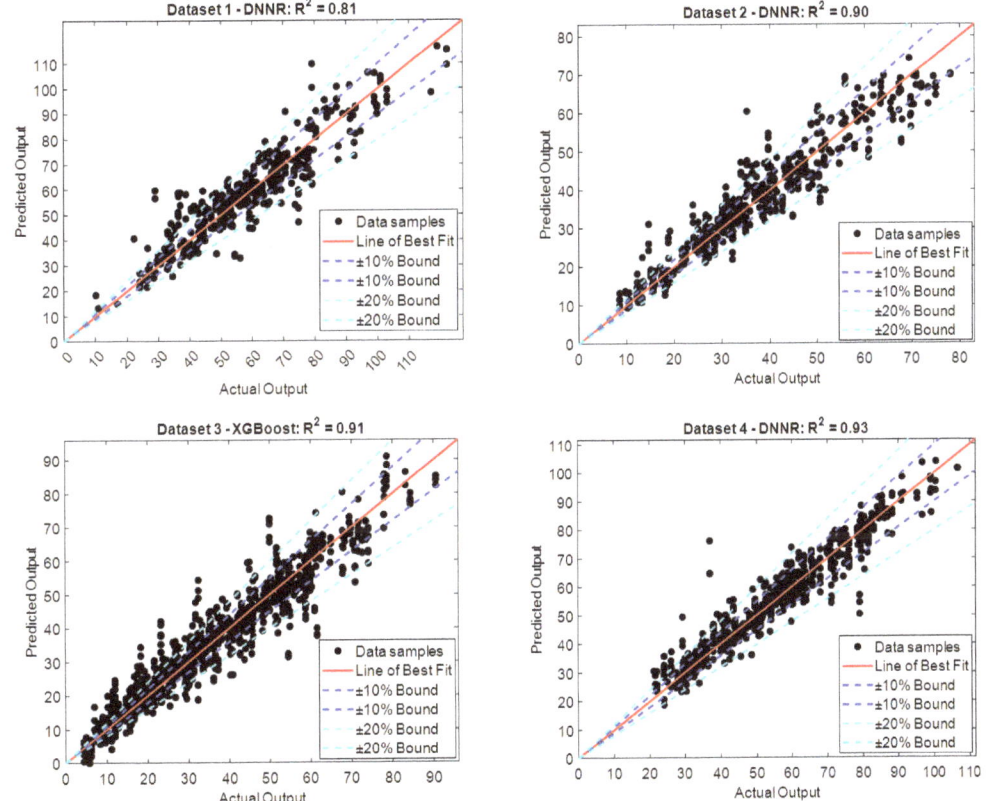

Figure 6. The correlation between the actual and predicted CS.

Table 7. Model configuration of the DNNR models that helps to attain the best performance.

Dataset	Parameters				
	Number of Hidden Layers	Number of Neurons	Learning Rate	Regularization Coefficient	Activation Function
1	2	10	0.03	0.001	Tanh
2	2	6	0.03	0.001	Tanh
4	2	16	0.01	0.001	Tanh

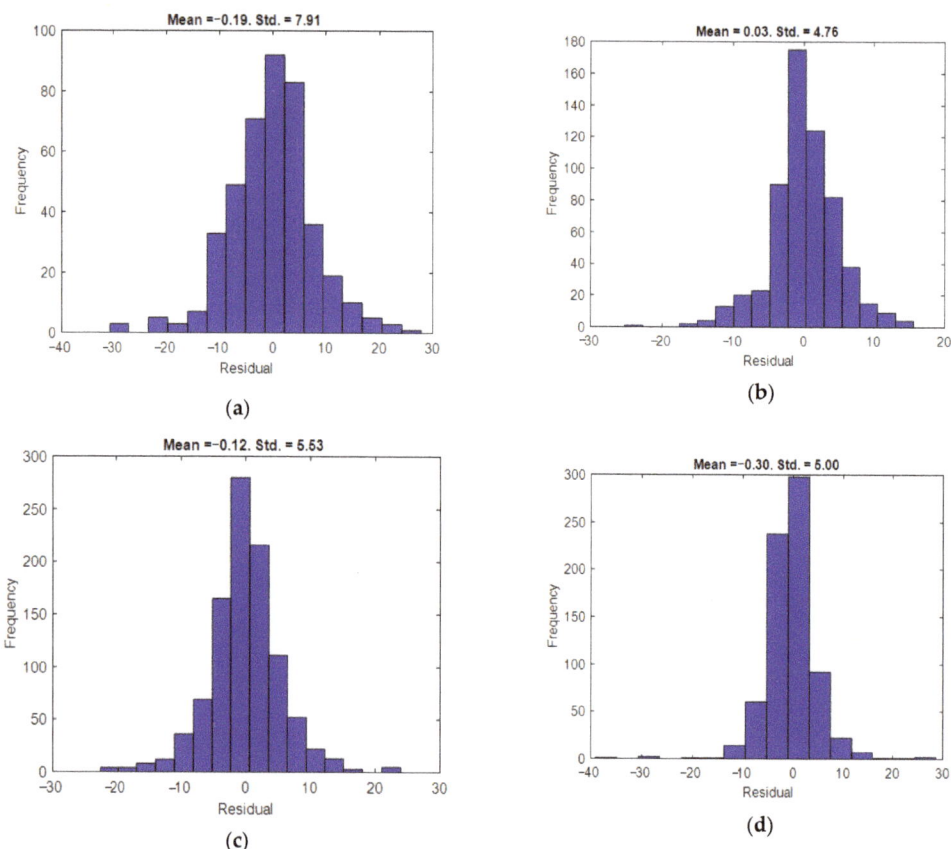

Figure 7. Histograms of residuals of the ML models used for predicting the CS: (**a**) Dataset 1, (**b**) Dataset 2, (**c**) Dataset 3, and (**d**) Dataset 4.

Table 8. Average computational time (s).

Dataset	The ML Models						
	DNNR	XGBoost	GBM	AdaBoost	SVR	LM-ANN	GP
1	3.82	0.11	0.05	0.17	0.06	0.62	297.20
2	5.43	0.05	0.14	0.13	0.07	0.96	289.25
3	6.44	0.08	0.14	0.38	0.04	0.55	736.70
4	7.64	0.13	0.14	0.38	0.04	0.55	795.50

Table 9. Detailed model ranking.

Dataset	The Employed ML Models						
	DNNR	XGBoost	GBM	AdaBoost	SVR	LM-ANN	GP
1	1	3	5	4	2	7	6
2	1	5	6	7	2	3	4
3	3	1	2	5	4	7	6
4	1	2	3	5	4	7	6

By inspecting the range of the residuals (refer to Figure 8), it can be seen that the data samples in all of the datasets lie within the ±20% bound. The best outcome in Dataset 3, predicted by the XGBoost, has 22% of the cases that stay beyond the ±20% bound. The results predicted by the DNNR has at most 14% of the samples that go beyond the ±20% bound. Particularly, prediction accuracy of the instances in Dataset 4 is remarkably high because only 6% of the samples have the residuals lying beyond the ±20% bound.

One possible explanation for this finding is that the number of data instances in Dataset 4 is decently high so that the DNNR can be effectively trained. Thus, this model can generalize the function that provides a mapping between the CS of SCC and its constituents. The proportion of the residual ≤ 5% for the case of interest is also notably high (52%). In the case of Dataset 3, the relatively high proportion of the residuals lying beyond the ±20% bound shows the high complexity of the functional mapping between the CS and the SCC mix containing class F fly ash. It is possible that the CS of SCC samples containing class F fly ash are governed by other explanatory variables that have not yet investigated.

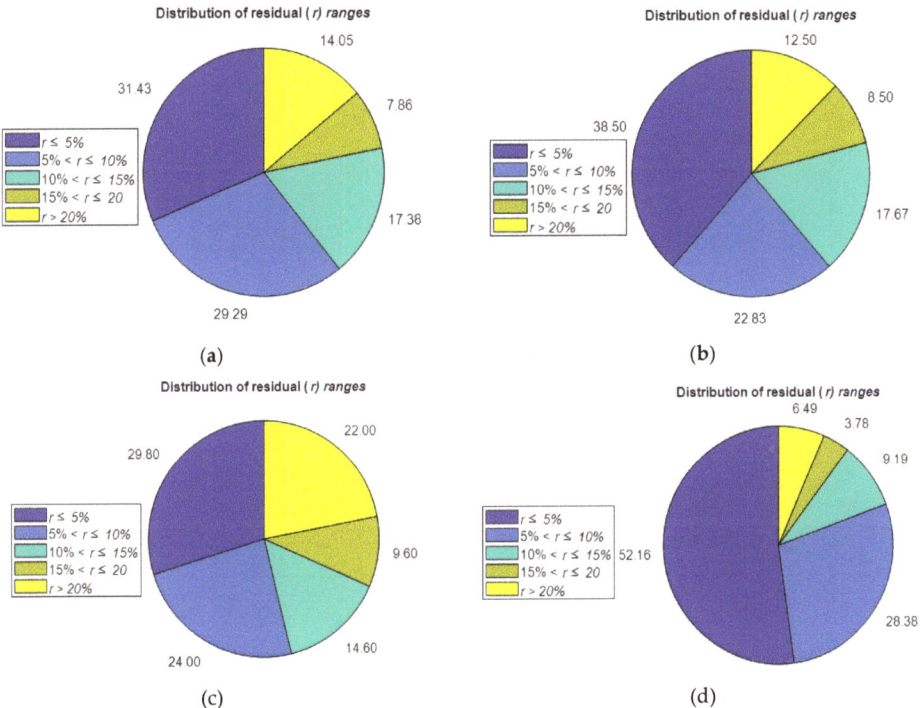

Figure 8. Distribution of the residual range: (**a**) the DNNR used for modeling Dataset 1, (**b**) the DNNR used for modeling Dataset 2, (**c**) the XGBoost used for modeling Dataset 3, and (**d**) the DNNR used for modeling Dataset 4.

5. Conclusions

The CS is a crucial mechanical property of SCC that must be considered during the phase of mix design and quality monitoring. An accurate and reliable estimation of the CS considerably facilitates the process of concrete mixture design. Data-driven models, which take into account past experimental tests of SCC, can effectively analyze the input information and quickly deliver estimations of the CS of SCC. These models are useful for reducing the cost and time required for performing laboratory tests. In addition, a good estimate of the CS with respect to different concrete ages is also desirable for scheduling the installation and removal of formwork or scaffolding on construction sites. It is because these activities highly depend on the development of the CS.

In this paper, we conduct a comparative work that takes into account the capability of prominent ML models used for predicting the CS of SCC. The employed models are

DNNR, XGBoost, GBM, AdaBoost, SVR, LM-ANN, and GP. Four historical datasets are used to train and verify the predictive ability of these ML models. The RMSE, MAPE, and R^2 are the metrics used for quantifying the modeling performance. This paper also performs a repetitive data sampling process, including 20 independent runs, to reliably evaluating the prediction results. Experimental results demonstrate the superiority of the DNNR which excels other models in three out of four datasets. The developed DNNR is about 7.0% and 2.5% better than the SVR for the cases of Dataset 1 and 2, respectively. In Dataset 4, the deep learning method outperformed the XGBoost by a minor margin of 1.3%. The XGBoost is the second-best method that achieves the first rank in one dataset. The R^2 values in all cases are greater than 0.8. The R^2 surpasses 0.9 in three datasets. These facts show a sufficient degree of variance explanation obtained by the selected ML models. The DNNR clearly outperformed the shallow ML approach of the LM-ANN. The improvement of the deep learning in comparison with the shallow neural network is at least 9.87% in Dataset 2 and can be as high as 36.6% in Dataset 3.

Future extensions of the current work may include the following directions: (1) the investigation of other advanced ML ensembles and boosting machines in the task of predicting the CS of SCC to reduce the prediction errors; (2) the use of sophisticated feature selection or transformation techniques for enhancing the model performance; and (3) the employment of metaheuristic approaches for tuning the hyper-parameters of the neural network models [60,61]; (4) investigation of other crucial mechanical properties of SCC [62,63] such as elastic modulus, peak strain, ultimate strain, and residual strain; and (5) analyzing the effect of the material properties on the CS of SCC [64,65].

Funding: This research received no external funding.

Data Availability Statement: The data presented in this study are openly available at in https://github.com/NHDDTUEDU/CS_SCC_ML.

Conflicts of Interest: The author of the paper confirms that there are no conflict of interest regarding the publication of the paper.

Appendix A

Table A1. Detailed statistical performance of the ML models.

ML Models	Metrics	Dataset 1		Dataset 2		Dataset 3		Dataset 4	
		Mean	Std.	Mean	Std.	Mean	Std.	Mean	Std.
DNNR	RMSE	7.73	1.69	4.68	0.90	6.68	0.97	4.84	1.34
	MAPE (%)	11.21	2.49	10.29	1.94	17.40	3.28	7.16	1.42
	R^2	0.81	0.10	0.90	0.05	0.87	0.04	0.93	0.05
XGBoost	RMSE	8.91	1.42	5.26	0.74	5.49	0.65	4.90	1.20
	MAPE (%)	14.15	3.07	11.52	2.25	14.36	1.98	6.69	0.93
	R^2	0.82	0.08	0.88	0.03	0.91	0.02	0.93	0.04
GBM	RMSE	9.59	3.03	5.57	0.62	5.61	0.78	4.98	1.35
	MAPE (%)	13.69	4.04	11.39	1.73	14.89	2.70	6.41	1.21
	R^2	0.77	0.18	0.87	0.04	0.91	0.03	0.92	0.07
AdaBoost	RMSE	9.14	1.58	6.04	1.06	7.60	1.45	6.24	0.96
	MAPE (%)	14.74	3.49	13.26	2.35	23.07	3.90	10.50	1.36
	R^2	0.79	0.08	0.84	0.07	0.84	0.06	0.88	0.03
SVR	RMSE	8.32	1.74	4.80	0.96	7.28	0.66	5.65	1.21
	MAPE (%)	12.26	2.85	11.36	2.09	20.57	3.87	7.60	1.24
	R^2	0.80	0.11	0.90	0.05	0.84	0.03	0.91	0.04
LM-ANN	RMSE	10.96	3.42	5.19	0.78	8.67	1.53	7.16	1.82
	MAPE (%)	15.01	4.53	12.33	2.25	25.02	6.64	10.61	2.51
	R^2	0.73	0.18	0.88	0.04	0.77	0.09	0.84	0.09
GP	RMSE	9.82	2.21	5.20	1.09	8.15	1.72	7.65	0.40
	MAPE (%)	15.27	3.54	12.24	2.00	24.02	3.51	11.55	0.80
	R^2	0.73	0.19	0.88	0.07	0.79	0.10	0.85	0.01

Appendix B

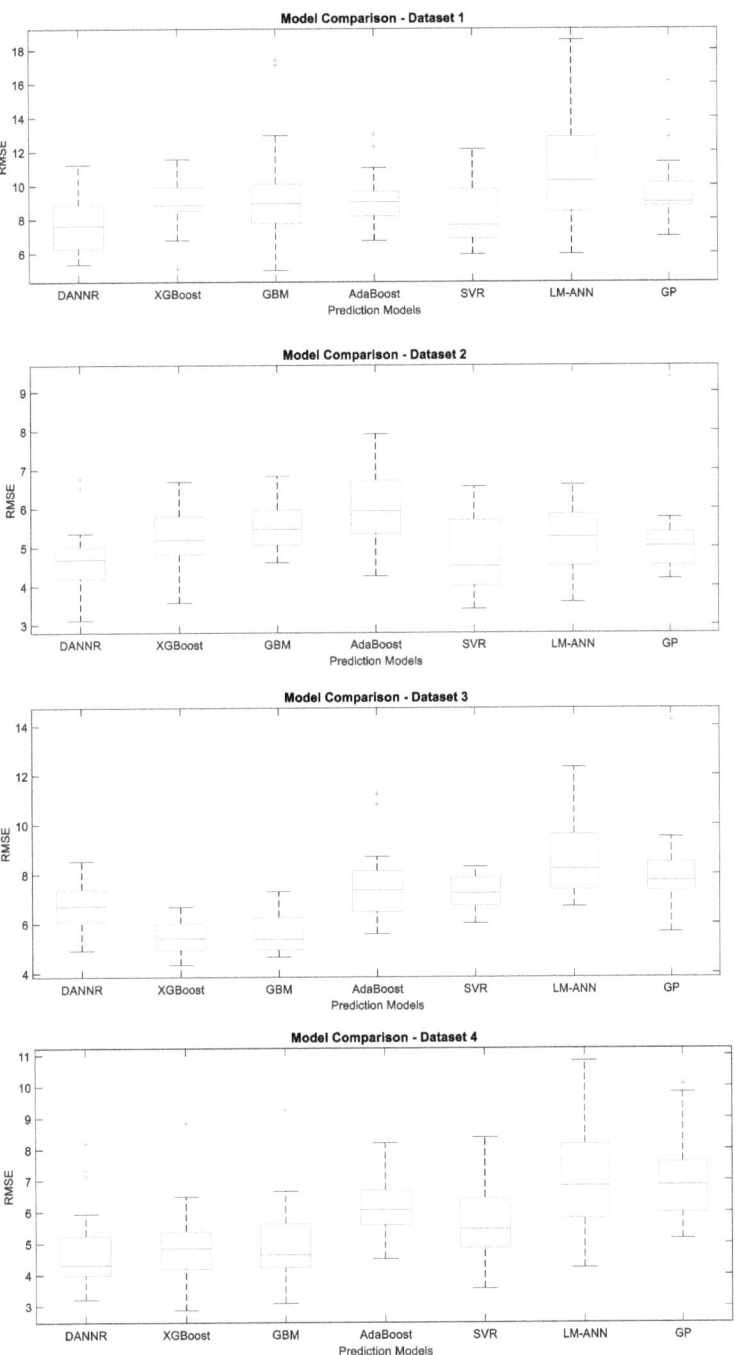

Figure A1. Boxplots of the model performance (The blue box denotes the 25th and 75th percentiles of RMSE. The red line represents the median value. The symbol "+" denotes an outlier.)

References

1. Alyamaç, K.E.; Ince, R. A preliminary concrete mix design for SCC with marble powders. *Constr. Build. Mater.* **2009**, *23*, 1201–1210. [CrossRef]
2. Chabane, A.; Belebchouche, C.; Bensebti, S.-E.; Czarnecki, S.; Amira, B. Comparison of the accuracy of regulation models for self-compacting concrete creep evaluation. *J. Build. Eng.* **2022**, *59*, 105069. [CrossRef]
3. Dinakar, P.; Sethy, K.P.; Sahoo, U.C. Design of self-compacting concrete with ground granulated blast furnace slag. *Mater. Des.* **2013**, *43*, 161–169. [CrossRef]
4. Asteris, P.G.; Kolovos, K. Self-compacting concrete strength prediction using surrogate models. *Neural Comput. Appl.* **2019**, *31*, 409–424. [CrossRef]
5. Li, H.; Yin, J.; Yan, P.; Sun, H.; Wan, Q. Experimental Investigation on the Mechanical Properties of Self-Compacting Concrete under Uniaxial and Triaxial Stress. *Materials* **2020**, *13*, 1830. [CrossRef]
6. Prasad, B.R.; Eskandari, H.; Reddy, B.V. Prediction of compressive strength of SCC and HPC with high volume fly ash using ANN. *Constr. Build. Mater.* **2009**, *23*, 117–128. [CrossRef]
7. Filho, F.M.A.; Barragán, B.E.; Casas, J.R.; El Debs, A.L.H.C. Hardened properties of self-compacting concrete—A statistical approach. *Constr. Build. Mater.* **2010**, *24*, 1608–1615. [CrossRef]
8. Pazouki, G.; Golafshani, E.M.; Behnood, A. Predicting the compressive strength of self-compacting concrete containing Class F fly ash using metaheuristic radial basis function neural network. *Struct. Concr.* **2021**, *23*, 1191–1213. [CrossRef]
9. Esfandiari, J.; Loghmani, P. Effect of perlite powder and silica fume on the compressive strength and microstructural characterization of self-compacting concrete with lime-cement binder. *Measurement* **2019**, *147*, 106846. [CrossRef]
10. Faraj, R.H.; Sherwani, A.F.H.; Daraei, A. Mechanical, fracture and durability properties of self-compacting high strength concrete containing recycled polypropylene plastic particles. *Build. Eng.* **2019**, *25*, 100808. [CrossRef]
11. Alidoust, P.; Goodarzi, S.; Amlashi, A.T.; Sadowski, Ł. Comparative analysis of soft computing techniques in predicting the compressive and tensile strength of seashell containing concrete. *Eur. J. Environ. Civ. Eng.* **2022**, 1–23. [CrossRef]
12. Ben Chaabene, W.; Flah, M.; Nehdi, M.L. Machine learning prediction of mechanical properties of concrete: Critical review. *Constr. Build. Mater.* **2020**, *260*, 119889. [CrossRef]
13. Golafshani, E.M.; Behnood, A.; Arashpour, M. Predicting the compressive strength of normal and High-Performance Concretes using ANN and ANFIS hybridized with Grey Wolf Optimizer. *Constr. Build. Mater.* **2020**, *232*, 117266. [CrossRef]
14. Boukendakdji, O.; Kadri, E.-H.; Kenai, S. Effects of granulated blast furnace slag and superplasticizer type on the fresh properties and compressive strength of self-compacting concrete. *Cem. Concr. Compos.* **2012**, *34*, 583–590. [CrossRef]
15. Güneyisi, E.; Gesoglu, M.; Azez, O.A.; Öz, H. Effect of nano silica on the workability of self-compacting concretes having untreated and surface treated lightweight aggregates. *Constr. Build. Mater.* **2016**, *115*, 371–380. [CrossRef]
16. Sukumar, B.; Nagamani, K.; Raghavan, R.S. Evaluation of strength at early ages of self-compacting concrete with high volume fly ash. *Constr. Build. Mater.* **2008**, *22*, 1394–1401. [CrossRef]
17. Uysal, M.; Tanyildizi, H. Estimation of compressive strength of self compacting concrete containing polypropylene fiber and mineral additives exposed to high temperature using artificial neural network. *Constr. Build. Mater.* **2012**, *27*, 404–414. [CrossRef]
18. Vakhshouri, B.; Nejadi, S. Prediction of compressive strength of self-compacting concrete by ANFIS models. *Neurocomputing* **2018**, *280*, 13–22. [CrossRef]
19. Awoyera, P.O.; Kirgiz, M.S.; Viloria, A.; Ovallos-Gazabon, D. Estimating strength properties of geopolymer self-compacting concrete using machine learning techniques. *J. Mater. Res. Technol.* **2020**, *9*, 9016–9028. [CrossRef]
20. Farooq, F.; Czarnecki, S.; Niewiadomski, P.; Aslam, F.; Alabduljabbar, H.; Ostrowski, K.A.; Śliwa-Wieczorek, K.; Nowobilski, T.; Malazdrewicz, S. A Comparative Study for the Prediction of the Compressive Strength of Self-Compacting Concrete Modified with Fly Ash. *Materials* **2021**, *14*, 4934. [CrossRef]
21. Serraye, M.; Kenai, S.; Boukhatem, B. Prediction of Compressive Strength of Self-Compacting Concrete (SCC) with Silica Fume Using Neural Networks Models. *Civ. Eng. J.* **2021**, *7*, 118–139. [CrossRef]
22. Lv, C.; Xing, Y.; Zhang, J.; Na, X.; Li, Y.; Liu, T.; Cao, D.; Wang, F.-Y. Levenberg–Marquardt Backpropagation Training of Multilayer Neural Networks for State Estimation of a Safety-Critical Cyber-Physical System. *IEEE Trans. Ind. Inform.* **2018**, *14*, 3436–3446. [CrossRef]
23. Nguyen, H.; Vu, T.; Vo, T.P.; Thai, H.-T. Efficient machine learning models for prediction of concrete strengths. *Constr. Build. Mater.* **2021**, *266*, 120950. [CrossRef]
24. Asghari, V.; Leung, Y.F.; Hsu, S.-C. Deep neural network based framework for complex correlations in engineering metrics. *Adv. Eng. Inform.* **2020**, *44*, 101058. [CrossRef]
25. Feng, D.-C.; Liu, Z.-T.; Wang, X.-D.; Chen, Y.; Chang, J.-Q.; Wei, D.-F.; Jiang, Z.-M. Machine learning-based compressive strength prediction for concrete: An adaptive boosting approach. *Constr. Build. Mater.* **2020**, *230*, 117000. [CrossRef]
26. Ling, H.; Qian, C.X.; Kang, W.C.; Liang, C.Y.; Chen, H.C. Combination of Support Vector Machine and K-Fold cross validation to predict compressive strength of concrete in marine environment. *Constr. Build. Mater.* **2019**, *206*, 355–363. [CrossRef]
27. Friedman, J.H. Greedy Function Approximation: A Gradient Boosting Machine. *Ann. Stat.* **2001**, *29*, 1189–1232. [CrossRef]
28. Chen, T.; Guestrin, C. XGBoost: A Scalable Tree Boosting System. In Proceedings of the 22nd ACM SIGKDD International Conference on Knowledge Discovery and Data Mining, San Francisco, CA, USA, 13–17 August 2016; pp. 785–794. [CrossRef]

29. Goodfellow, I.; Bengio, Y.; Courville, A. *Deep Learning (Adaptive Computation and Machine Learning Series)*; The MIT Press: Cambridge, MA, USA, 2016; ISBN 10 0262035618.
30. Chou, J.-S.; Tsai, C.-F.; Pham, A.-D.; Lu, Y.-H. Machine learning in concrete strength simulations: Multi-nation data analytics. *CConstr. Build. Mater.* **2014**, *73*, 771–780. [CrossRef]
31. Latif, S.D. Concrete compressive strength prediction modeling utilizing deep learning long short-term memory algorithm for a sustainable environment. *Environ. Sci. Pollut. Res.* **2021**, *28*, 30294–30302. [CrossRef]
32. Kim, P. *MatLab Deep Learning with Machine Learning, Neural Networks and Artificial Intelligence*; Apress: New York, NY, USA, 2017; ISBN 1484228448.
33. Friedman, J.H. Stochastic gradient boosting. *Comput. Stat. Data Anal.* **2002**, *38*, 367–378. [CrossRef]
34. Zhang, X.; Nguyen, H.; Bui, X.N.; Tran, Q.H.; Nguyen, D.A.; Bui, D.T.; Moayedi, H. Novel Soft Computing Model for Predicting Blast-Induced Ground Vibration in Open-Pit Mines Based on Particle Swarm Optimization and XGBoost. *Nat. Resour. Res.* **2019**, *29*, 711–721. [CrossRef]
35. Dobilas, S. XGBoost: Extreme Gradient Boosting—How to Improve on Regular Gradient Boosting? Towards Data Science. 2021. Available online: https://towardsdatascience.com/ (accessed on 17 September 2022).
36. Freund, Y.; Schapire, R.E. A Decision-Theoretic Generalization of On-Line Learning and an Application to Boosting. *J. Comput. Syst. Sci.* **1997**, *55*, 119–139. [CrossRef]
37. Wyner, A.J.; Olson, M.; Bleich, J.; Mease, D. Explaining the Success of AdaBoost and Random Forests as Interpolating Classifiers. *J. Mach. Learn. Res.* **2017**, *18*, 1–33.
38. Drucker, H.; Burges, C.J.C.; Kaufman, L.; Smola, A.; Vapnik, V. Support vector regression machines. In Proceedings of the 9th International Conference on Neural Information Processing Systems, Denver, CO, USA, 3–5 December 1996.
39. Vapnik, V.N. *Statistical Learning Theory*; John Wiley & Sons, Inc.: Hoboken, NJ, USA, 1998; ISBN 10 0471030031.
40. Tang, F.; Wu, Y.; Zhou, Y. Hybridizing Grid Search and Support Vector Regression to Predict the Compressive Strength of Fly Ash Concrete. *Adv. Civ. Eng.* **2022**, *2022*, 3601914. [CrossRef]
41. Haykin, S.O. Neural Networks and Learning Machines. Pearson: Hong Kong, China, 2008.
42. Skare, E.L.; Sheiati, S.; Cepuritis, R.; Mørtsell, E.; Smeplass, S.; Spangenberg, J.; Jacobsen, S. Rheology modelling of cement paste with manufactured sand and silica fume: Comparing suspension models with artificial neural network predictions. *Constr. Build. Mater.* **2022**, *317*, 126114. [CrossRef]
43. Hagan, M.T.; Menhaj, M.B. Training feedforward networks with the Marquardt algorithm. *IEEE Trans. Neural Netw.* **1994**, *5*, 989–993. [CrossRef]
44. Koza, J.R. Genetic programming as a means for programming computers by natural selection. *Stat. Comput.* **1994**, *4*, 87–112. [CrossRef]
45. Mitchell, M. *An Introduction to Genetic Algorithms*; MIT Press: Cambridge, MA, USA, 1996; ISBN 9780585030944.
46. Cheng, M.-Y.; Firdausi, P.M.; Prayogo, D. High-performance concrete compressive strength prediction using Genetic Weighted Pyramid Operation Tree (GWPOT). *Eng. Appl. Artif. Intell.* **2014**, *29*, 104–113. [CrossRef]
47. Tran, T.-H.; Hoang, N.-D. Predicting Colonization Growth of Algae on Mortar Surface with Artificial Neural Network. *J. Comput. Civ. Eng.* **2016**, *30*, 04016030. [CrossRef]
48. Verian, K.P.; Behnood, A. Effects of deicers on the performance of concrete pavements containing air-cooled blast furnace slag and supplementary cementitious materials. *Cem. Concr. Compos.* **2018**, *90*, 27–41. [CrossRef]
49. Amlashi, A.T.; Golafshani, E.M.; Ebrahimi, S.A.; Behnood, A. Estimation of the compressive strength of green concretes containing rice husk ash: A comparison of different machine learning approaches. *Eur. J. Environ. Civ. Eng.* **2022**, 1–23. [CrossRef]
50. Jalal, M.; Pouladkhan, A.; Harandi, O.F.; Jafari, D. RETRACTED: Comparative study on effects of Class F fly ash, nano silica and silica fume on properties of high performance self compacting concrete. *Constr. Build. Mater.* **2015**, *94*, 90–104. [CrossRef]
51. de Matos, P.R.; Foiato, M.; Prudêncio, L.R., Jr. Ecological, fresh state and long-term mechanical properties of high-volume fly ash high-performance self-compacting concrete. *Constr. Build. Mater.* **2019**, *203*, 282–293. [CrossRef]
52. Mendenhall, W.; Sincich, T.T. *A Second Course in Statistics: Regression Analysis*, 7th ed.; Pearson: London, UK, 2011; ISSN 978-0321691699.
53. XGBoost. XGBoost Documentation. 2021. Available online: https://xgboostreadthedocsio/en/stable/indexhtml (accessed on 30 December 2021).
54. Pedregosa, F.; Varoquaux, G.; Gramfort, A.; Michel, V.; Thirion, B.; Grisel, O.; Blondel, M.; Prettenhofer, P.; Weiss, R.; Dubourg, V.; et al. Scikit-learn: Machine Learning in Python. *J. Mach. Learn. Res.* **2011**, *12*, 2825–2830.
55. MathWorks. Statistics and Machine Learning Toolbox User's Guide. Matwork Inc. 2017. Available online: https://www.mathworks.com/help/pdf_doc/stats/stats.pdf (accessed on 28 April 2018).
56. Searson, D.P. GPTIPS 2: An Open-Source Software Platform for Symbolic Data Mining. In *Handbook of Genetic Programming Applications*; Gandomi, A.H., Alavi, A.H., Ryan, C., Eds.; Springer International Publishing: Cham, Switzerland, 2015; pp. 551–573. [CrossRef]
57. Wong, T.-T.; Yeh, P.-Y. Reliable Accuracy Estimates from k-Fold Cross Validation. *IEEE Trans. Knowl. Data Eng.* **2020**, *32*, 1586–1594. [CrossRef]
58. Lewis, C.D. *Industrial and Business Forecasting Methods: A Practical Guide to Exponential Smoothing and Curve Fitting*; Butterworth-Heinemann: Oxford, UK, 1982; ISBN 0408005599.

59. Kang, M.-C.; Yoo, D.-Y.; Gupta, R. Machine learning-based prediction for compressive and flexural strengths of steel fiber-reinforced concrete. *Constr. Build. Mater.* **2021**, *266*, 121117. [CrossRef]
60. Pham, T.A.; Tran, V.Q.; Vu, H.-L.T.; Ly, H.-B. Design deep neural network architecture using a genetic algorithm for estimation of pile bearing capacity. *PLoS ONE* **2020**, *15*, e0243030. [CrossRef]
61. Sheiati, S.; Ranjbar, N.; Frellsen, J.; Skare, E.L.; Cepuritis, R.; Jacobsen, S.; Spangenberg, J. Neural network predictions of the simulated rheological response of cement paste in the FlowCyl. *Neural Comput. Appl.* **2021**, *33*, 13027–13037. [CrossRef]
62. Revilla-Cuesta, V.; Ortega-López, V.; Skaf, M.; Manso, J.M. Effect of fine recycled concrete aggregate on the mechanical behavior of self-compacting concrete. *Constr. Build. Mater.* **2020**, *263*, 120671. [CrossRef]
63. Salari, Z.; Vakhshouri, B.; Nejadi, S. Analytical review of the mix design of fiber reinforced high strength self-compacting concrete. *J. Build. Eng.* **2018**, *20*, 264–276. [CrossRef]
64. Akbari, M.; Khalilpour, S.; Dehestani, M. Analysis of material size and shape effects for steel fiber reinforcement self-consolidating concrete. *Eng. Fract. Mech.* **2019**, *206*, 46–63. [CrossRef]
65. Wang, C.; Xiao, J.; Liu, W.; Ma, Z. Unloading and reloading stress-strain relationship of recycled aggregate concrete reinforced with steel/polypropylene fibers under uniaxial low-cycle loadings. *Cem. Concr. Compos.* **2022**, *131*, 104597. [CrossRef]

Article

Dbar-Dressing Method and N-Soliton Solutions of the Derivative NLS Equation with Non-Zero Boundary Conditions

Hui Zhou [1], Yehui Huang [2] and Yuqin Yao [1,*]

[1] College of Science, China Agricultural University, Beijing 100083, China
[2] School of Mathematics and Physics, North China Electric Power University, Beijing 102206, China
* Correspondence: yaoyq@cau.edu.cn

Abstract: The Dbar-dressing method is extended to investigate the derivative non-linear Schrödinger equation with non-zero boundary conditions (DNLSENBC). Based on a meromorphic complex function outside an annulus with center 0, a local Dbar-problem inside the annulus is constructed. By use of the asymptotic expansion at infinity and zero, the spatial and temporal spectral problems of DNLSENBC are worked out. Thus, the relation between the potential of DNLSENBC with the solution of the Dbar-problem is established. Further, symmetry conditions and a special spectral distribution matrix are presented to construct the explicit solutions of DNLSENBC. In addition, the explicit expressions of the soliton solution, the breather solution and the solution of the interaction between solitons and breathers are given.

Keywords: Dbar-dressing method; Cauchy matrix; Lax pair; soliton solutions

MSC: 35Q51

1. Introduction

As a result of a specific balance between non-linear effects and dispersion effects, the soliton plays a pivotal role in three-level atomic systems, microcavity wires, and other physical systems [1–3]. Non-linear integrable differential equations have soliton solutions and elastic collision properties during propagation. In some suitable conditions, we can use integrable equations to depict many important wave propagation phenomena. The non-linear Schrödinger (NLS) equation is a classical physical model. It has extensive applications in physical fields, such as the disturbance of water waves [4], the action of a particle's gravitational field on the quantum potential [5], and others [6–8]. The derivative non-linear Schrödinger (DNLS) equation

$$iq_t + q_{xx} - i(|q|^2 q)_x = 0, \qquad (1)$$

is an important non-linear physical model, which can describe the propagation of circular polarized non-linear Alfvén waves in plasmas [9–14]. The DNLS equation has been studied extensively in recent decades. For example, in [15–17], the involutive solutions of the DNLS equation and generalized DNLS equation were developed, respectively. The multi-soliton solutions were derived via Darboux transformation and Bäcklund transformation [18,19]. The high-order rational solution and rogue wave of the DNLS equation were determined in 2012 [20]. The N-double-pole solution was investigated by means of inverse scattering transformation in 2020 [21]. In addition, the existence of global solutions of the model (1) was fully discussed in [22]. In 2022, combining profile decomposition techniques with the integrability structure of the model (1), the global well-posedness of the DNLS equation was proved in [23].

The Dbar-dressing method, which can also be referred to as the $\bar{\partial}$-dressing method, is a powerful tool to explore integrable non-linear systems and to derive corresponding soliton solutions. This approach was first introduced by Zakharov and Shabat [24]. Thereafter, Beals, Coifman, Manakov, Ablowitz and Fokas developed it further [25–29]. By generalizing a Riemann–Hilbert problem, a corresponding $\bar{\partial}$-problem can be constructed. Then, based on the obtained $\bar{\partial}$-problem, the equation to be studied can be solved using the Dbar-dressing procedure. In contrast to the numerical solutions provided in [30,31], the Dbar-dressing method can be used to obtain the explicit solutions of soliton equations. At present, varieties of well-known non-linear integrable equations, such as the NLS equation, the sine-Gordon equation, the Gerdjikov–Ivanov equation and others, have been solved successfully by means of this approach [32–40]. In particular, a new calculating rule of the Lie bracket which contains the standard calculating rule was proposed in [41]. Based on this, a new generalized NLS hierarchy and its reduction equations were worked out using the $\bar{\partial}$-method. The $\bar{\partial}$-method is also a valuable method for researching high-dimensional systems; in [42], it was applied to the Sawada–Kotera equation and some interesting results were obtained.

Based on the dressing method proposed by Zakharov and Shabat, the inverse scattering transformation (IST) method is mainly used for the factorization of integral operators on a line into a product of two Volterra operators and the Riemann–Hilbert (RH) problem. In our work, the Dbar-dressing method is the most powerful version of the dressing method, which incorporates the $\bar{\partial}$-problem formalism. New spectral problems, hierarchy and soliton solutions can be readily discovered using the Dbar-dressing method. Compared with other classical methods, the advantage of the Dbar-dressing method is that it can deal with the RH problem with non-analytical jump matrices. From this perspective, this method is an improved and upgraded version of the IST method and the RH method [43]. Moreover, compared to the existing reports described above, such as [38], our aim is to construct N-soliton solutions of DNLSENBC using the Dbar-dressing method and to fully analyze the properties of the solution. In our investigation, we mainly seek to improve the analysis of solutions and to explore the relationship between the types of solutions and the discrete spectrum.

For the purpose of describing and investigating complex magnetic fields more accurately, the non-zero boundary conditions on the non-linear integrable equations are imposed. In this paper, we extend the $\bar{\partial}$-dressing method to construct the Lax pair and N-soliton of the DNLS equation with non-zero boundary conditions (DNLSENBC)

$$iq_t + q_{xx} - 2i(|q|^2 + q_0^2)q_x + q_0^2(-|q|^2 + q_0^2)q - iq^2\bar{q}_x = 0, \qquad (2)$$

and

$$q(x,t) \to \rho, \ |x| \to \infty, \qquad (3)$$

where ρ is a constant and $|\rho| = q_0 \neq 0$.

The structure of this paper is as follows: In Section 2, we obtain the symmetry condition of the eigenfunction as $z \to \infty$ and $z \to 0$ by considering a local 2×2 matrix $\bar{\partial}$-problem with special non-canonical normalization. In Section 3, the Lax pair of DNLSENBC is constructed. In Section 4, the symmetry conditions and particular spectral transformation matrix are introduced to construct the N-soliton solutions of DNLSENBC. Moreover, as applications of the N-soliton solutions, the explicit one- and two-soliton solutions, one- and two-breather solutions, and soliton-breather solution are presented. The conclusions are presented in the final section.

2. Dbar-Dressing Method and $\bar{\partial}$-Problem for DNLSENBC

We introduce the framework of the Dbar-dressing method, in general, in Section 2.1 and obtain the symmetric constraint of the eigenfunction based on the eigenvalue problem and the $\bar{\partial}$-problem in Section 2.2, which plays a key role in the asymptotic expansion and construction of the N-soliton solutions.

2.1. Dbar-Dressing Method

As necessary knowledge for the Dbar-dressing method, we introduce the $\bar{\partial}$-operator and the Cauchy integral formula. By introducing the complex variable $z = x + iy$, $\bar{z} = x - iy$ and directly calculating, we have

$$\frac{\partial}{\partial \bar{z}} = \frac{1}{2}(\partial_x + i\partial_y) \equiv \bar{\partial}, \quad \frac{\partial}{\partial z} = \frac{1}{2}(\partial_x - i\partial_y) \equiv \partial, \quad \partial_x = \partial + \bar{\partial}, \quad \partial_y = i(\partial - \bar{\partial}). \tag{4}$$

The partial derivative $\frac{\partial}{\partial \bar{z}}$ is called the $\bar{\partial}$-operator and $\bar{\partial}$ is the conjecture of ∂. Suppose that $g(z)$ is a given function in a simply connected domain D of the complex z plane, then the equation

$$\bar{\partial} f(z) = g(z), \ z \in D, \tag{5}$$

is called a $\bar{\partial}$-problem, where $f(z) = f(z, \bar{z})$ is a complex function; here, we represent it as $f(z)$ for simplicity. If $f(z)$ is analytical in a simply connected domain D, then, along its closed contour ∂D, we have the Cauchy integral theorem

$$\oint_{\partial D} f(z) dz = 0, \tag{6}$$

and the Cauchy integral formula

$$f(z) = \frac{1}{2\pi i} \oint_{\partial D} \frac{f(\xi)}{\xi - z} d\xi, \ z \in D. \tag{7}$$

In order to facilitate the calculation of Section 2.2, we provide the following propositions:

Proposition 1. *Suppose that D is a domain with closed curve ∂D, $f(z)$, $g(z)$ and their derivatives are continuous in D, then*

$$\oint_{\partial D} f(z) dz = -\int\int_D \bar{\partial} f(z) dz \wedge d\bar{z},$$
$$\oint_{\partial D} g(z) d\bar{z} = \int\int_D \partial g(z) dz \wedge d\bar{z}, \tag{8}$$

where $dz \wedge d\bar{z} = -2i dx \wedge dy = -2i dx dy$, $dx \wedge dy$ is a Lebesgue measure.

Proposition 2. *Suppose that ∂D is a closed curve with boundary D, $f(z)$ and its derivatives are continuous and bounded in D, then we have the Cauchy–Green formula*

$$f(z) = \frac{1}{2\pi i} \oint_{\partial D} \frac{f(\xi)}{\xi - z} d\xi + \frac{1}{2\pi i} \int\int_D \frac{\bar{\partial} f(\xi)}{\xi - z} d\xi \wedge d\bar{\xi}, \tag{9}$$

where $\xi = \zeta + i\eta$ and $d\xi \wedge d\bar{\xi} = (d\zeta + id\eta) \wedge (d\zeta - id\eta) = -2i d\zeta d\eta$.

Define the complex δ function

$$\int\int_D \psi(z) \delta(z - z_0) dz \wedge d\bar{z} = -2i\psi(z_0), \tag{10}$$

and suppose that $g(z) \in L^1(z) \cap L^\infty(z)$, then we can find that the $\bar{\partial}$-problem (5) admits a general solution

$$f(z) = a(z) + \frac{1}{2\pi i} \int\int_D \frac{g(\xi)}{\xi - z} d\xi \wedge d\bar{\xi}, \tag{11}$$

where $a(z)$ is an arbitrary analytical function. If $f(z)$ is Hölder continuous on ∂D and $g(z) \in L^1(z) \cap L^\infty(z)$, then, using the Cauchy integral formula, we get

$$f(z) = \frac{1}{2\pi i} \oint_{\partial D} \frac{f(\xi)}{\xi - z} d\xi + \frac{1}{2\pi i} \int \int_D \frac{g(\xi)}{\xi - z} d\xi \wedge d\bar{\xi}, \tag{12}$$

satisfying the $\bar{\partial}$-problem (5) on D.

2.2. $\bar{\partial}$-Problem for DNLSENBC

The DNLS equation has the following eigenvalue problem [44]

$$\Phi_x = U\Phi, \quad \Phi_t = V\Phi, \tag{13}$$

where

$$U = \begin{bmatrix} ik^2 & kq \\ -k\bar{q} & -ik^2 \end{bmatrix}, \quad V = \begin{bmatrix} -2ik^4 + i|q|^2 k^2 & -2k^3 q + |q|^2 qk + iq_x k \\ 2k^3 \bar{q} - |q|^2 \bar{q} k + i\bar{q}_x k & 2ik^4 - i|q|^2 k^2 \end{bmatrix}. \tag{14}$$

Here the bar represents the complex conjugate and the subscript x (or t) stands for the partial derivative of x (or t). As an arbitrary number, k is called the eigenvalue (or spectral parameter) and Φ is called the eigenfunction associated with k.

In the asymptotic behavior of $|x| \to \infty$, we note the variable z as $z = k + \lambda$ and solve the eigenvalues of U and V, and obtain

$$\lambda(z) = \tfrac{1}{2}(z + \tfrac{q_0^2}{z}), \quad k(z) = \tfrac{1}{2}(z - \tfrac{q_0^2}{z}), \\ \theta(x,t,z) = k(z)\lambda(z)(x - 2k(z)^2 t + q_0^2 t), \tag{15}$$

and the eigenfunction of (13)

$$(I + \frac{i}{z}\sigma_3 Q_0) e^{i\theta(x,t,z)\sigma_3},$$

where

$$Q_0 = \begin{bmatrix} 0 & \rho \\ -\bar{\rho} & 0 \end{bmatrix}, \quad \sigma_3 = \begin{bmatrix} 1 & 0 \\ 0 & -1 \end{bmatrix}. \tag{16}$$

Here, we consider a 2×2 matrix $\bar{\partial}$-problem

$$\bar{\partial}\Psi(x,t,z) = \Psi(x,t,z) r(z), \quad z \in \mathbb{C} \setminus \{0\}, \tag{17}$$

where $r(z)$ is a 2×2 matrix and is independent of x and t. Moreover, $\Psi(x,t,z)$ is a 2×2 matrix and has the non-canonical normalization conditions

$$\Psi(x,t,z) \sim e^{i\theta(x,t,z)\sigma_3}, \quad z \to \infty, \\ \Psi(x,t,z) \sim \tfrac{i}{z}\sigma_3 Q_0 e^{i\theta(x,t,z)\sigma_3}, \quad z \to 0. \tag{18}$$

For simplicity, we define

$$\hat{\Psi}(x,t,z) = \Psi(x,t,z) e^{-i\theta(x,t,z)\sigma_3}, \tag{19}$$

then $\hat{\Psi}$ has the following asymptotic behavior

$$\hat{\Psi}(x,t,z) \to I, \quad z \to \infty, \quad \hat{\Psi}(x,t,z) \to \frac{i}{z}\sigma_3 Q_0, \quad z \to 0. \tag{20}$$

Now, we consider a new $\bar{\partial}$-problem

$$\bar{\partial}\hat{\Psi}(x,t,z) = \hat{\Psi}(x,t,z) R(x,t,z), \quad R(x,t,z) = e^{i\theta(x,t,z)\sigma_3} r(z) e^{-i\theta(x,t,z)\sigma_3}, \quad z \in \mathbb{C} \setminus \{0\}. \tag{21}$$

Based on the generalized Cauchy integral formula, we have

$$\hat{\Psi}(z) = \lim_{\varepsilon \to 0, R \to \infty} \frac{1}{2\pi i} \oint_{\Gamma_R + \Gamma_\varepsilon} \frac{\hat{\Psi}(\xi)}{\xi - z} d\xi + \frac{1}{2\pi i} \int\int_{\varepsilon < |\xi| < R} \frac{\bar{\partial}\hat{\Psi}(\xi)}{\xi - z} d\xi \wedge d\bar{\xi}$$

$$= I + \frac{i}{z}\sigma_3 Q_0 + \frac{1}{2\pi i} \int\int_{\varepsilon < |\xi| < R} \frac{\bar{\partial}\hat{\Psi}(\xi)}{\xi - z} d\xi \wedge d\bar{\xi} = \mathcal{N}(\Psi) + J\hat{\Psi}(z), \quad (22)$$

where Γ_ε and Γ_R are oriented circles with centers at the origin of the z plane with radii R and ε.

We note the solution space $\mathcal{F}$ of the $\bar{\partial}$-problem (17) as

$$\mathcal{F} = \{\Psi(x,t,z) | \bar{\partial}\Psi(x,t,z) = \Psi(x,t,z)r(z), z \in \mathbb{C} \setminus \{0\}\}. \quad (23)$$

To investigate the DNLSENBC through the $\bar{\partial}$-problem (17), we first introduce the following constraint:

Proposition 3. *Let $\Phi \in \mathcal{F}$ and $\mathcal{N}(\Phi) = I + \frac{i}{z}\sigma_3 Q_0$, then it satisfies*

$$\Phi(x,t,z) = \frac{i}{z}\Phi(x,t,-\frac{q_0^2}{z})\sigma_3 Q_0. \quad (24)$$

Suppose that $\Phi(x,t,z)$ has the asymptotic expansion at $z \to \infty$ and $z \to 0$,

$$\begin{aligned}\Phi(x,t,z) &\sim (I + \sum_{l=1}^{\infty} a_l(x,t)z^{-l})e^{i\theta(x,t,z)\sigma_3}, \quad z \to \infty, \\ \Phi(x,t,z) &\sim (\sum_{l=-1}^{\infty} b_m(x,t)z^m)e^{i\theta(x,t,z)\sigma_3}, \quad z \to 0. \end{aligned} \quad (25)$$

By making use of the formula $\oint_{\partial D} f(z)dz = -\int\int_D \bar{\partial}f(z)dz \wedge d\bar{z}$, the coefficients a_l and b_m can be determined

$$a_l(x,t) = \delta_{l,1}i\sigma_3 Q_0 - \frac{1}{2\pi i}\int\int_{\mathbb{C}\setminus\{0\}} \Phi(\xi,x,t)r(\xi)e^{-i\theta(\xi)\sigma_3}\xi^{l-1}d\xi \wedge d\bar{\xi}, \quad l = 1,2,\cdots, \quad (26)$$

$$b_m(x,t) = \begin{cases} \delta_{m,0} + \frac{1}{2\pi i}\int\int_{\mathbb{C}\setminus\{0\}} \Phi(\xi,x,t)r(\xi)e^{-i\theta(\xi)\sigma_3}\xi^{-m-1}d\xi \wedge d\bar{\xi}, & m \geq 0, \\ i\sigma_3 Q_0, & m = -1. \end{cases} \quad (27)$$

Remark 1. *Based on the Proposition 3, we can find that the coefficients $a_l(x,t)$ and $b_m(x,t)$ are not independent and that satisfy*

$$b_{m-1}(x,t) = \frac{i}{(-1)^m q_0^{2m}} a_m(x,t)\sigma_3 Q_0, \quad m = 1,2,\cdots. \quad (28)$$

3. Lax Pair of the DNLSENBC

In this section, we deduce the Lax pair of the DNLSENBC. We first introduce the conclusion.

Proposition 4 ([37,38]). *Suppose $\Psi R \in L^1(\mathbb{C}\setminus\{0\}) \cap L^\infty(\mathbb{C}\setminus\{0\})$, then the homogeneous equation of (22) only has a zero solution for a small norm of the operator J, i.e., $\hat{\Psi}(I - J) = 0 \Rightarrow \hat{\Psi} = 0$.*

For $\Psi_1(x,t,z), \Psi_2(x,t,z) \in \mathcal{F}$, the following conclusion can be derived from Proposition 4:

$$\mathcal{N}(\hat{\Psi}_1(x,t,z)) = \mathcal{N}(\hat{\Psi}_2(x,t,z)) \Leftrightarrow \Psi_1(x,t,z) = \Psi_2(x,t,z), \quad (29)$$

which plays a crucial role in constructing the Lax pair of the DNLSENBC.

Theorem 1. *The DNLSENBC (2) has the following Lax pair*

$$\Phi_x = X\Phi, \quad \Phi_t = T\Phi, \tag{30}$$

with

$$X = i(k^2 + \tfrac{1}{2}q_0^2)\sigma_3 + kQ, \quad Q = \begin{bmatrix} 0 & q \\ -\bar{q} & 0 \end{bmatrix},$$
$$T = (-2ik^4 + iq_0^4)\sigma_3 - ik^2Q^2\sigma_3 - 2k^3Q - kQ^3 - ikQ_x\sigma_3 + kq_0^2Q. \tag{31}$$

which implies that DNLSENBC is Lax integrable.

Proof. If $\Phi \in \mathcal{F}$, then Φ_t and Φ_x belongs to the solution space $\mathcal{F}$. From (25), we have, at $z \to \infty$,

$$\Phi_x = \left[\sum_{l=1}^{\infty} a_{l,x} z^{-l} + (I + \sum_{l=1}^{\infty} a_l z^{-l}) i\theta_x \sigma_3 \right] e^{i\theta\sigma_3}$$

$$= \left[\sum_{l=1}^{\infty} a_{l,x} z^{-l} + \frac{i}{4}(z - \frac{q_0^2}{z})(z + \frac{q_0^2}{z})\sigma_3 + \frac{i}{4}\sum_{l=1}^{\infty} a_l(z - \frac{q_0^2}{z})(z + \frac{q_0^2}{z})\sigma_3 z^{-l}\right] e^{i\theta\sigma_3} \tag{32}$$

$$= \frac{i}{4}\left[z^2 \sigma_3 + a_1 \sigma_3 z + a_2 \sigma_3 + O(\frac{1}{z})\right] e^{i\theta\sigma_3}.$$

At $z \to 0$, we have

$$\Phi_x = (\sum_{m=-1}^{\infty} b_{m,x} z^m + i \sum_{m=-1}^{\infty} b_m z^m \theta_x \sigma_3) e^{i\theta\sigma_3}$$

$$= \left[b_{-1,x} z^{-1} + \sum_{m=0}^{\infty} b_{m,x} z^m + \frac{i}{4}\sum_{m=-1}^{\infty} b_m z^m (z - \frac{q_0^2}{z})(z + \frac{q_0^2}{z})\sigma_3\right] e^{i\theta\sigma_3} \tag{33}$$

$$= \left[b_{-1,x} z^{-1} - \frac{i}{4} q_0^4 b_{-1} z^{-3} \sigma_3 - \frac{i}{4} q_0^4 b_0 z^{-2} \sigma_3 - \frac{i}{4} q_0^4 b_1 z^{-1} \sigma_3 + O(1)\right] e^{i\theta\sigma_3}.$$

By direct calculation, we find

$$\left[i(k^2 + \tfrac{1}{2}q_0^2)\sigma_3 + \tfrac{i}{2}k(a_1\sigma_3 - \sigma_3 a_1)\right]\Phi = \frac{i}{4}\left[z^2\sigma_3 + a_1\sigma_3 z + a_2\sigma_3 + O(\frac{1}{z})\right]e^{i\theta\sigma_3}, \quad z \to \infty,$$

$$\left[i(k^2 + \tfrac{1}{2}q_0^2)\sigma_3 - \tfrac{i}{2}kq_0^2(b_0\sigma_3 + \sigma_3 b_0)b_{-1}^{-1}\right]\Phi = \left[(b_{-1,x} z^{-1} - \frac{i}{4}q_0^4 b_{-1} z^{-3}\sigma_3 - \frac{i}{4}q_0^4 b_0 z^{-2}\sigma_3\right. \tag{34}$$

$$\left. - \frac{i}{4}q_0^4 b_1 z^{-1}\sigma_3 + O(1)\right]e^{i\theta\sigma_3}, \quad z \to 0.$$

The relation of the coefficients a_l and b_m in (28) gives that $\tfrac{i}{2}k(a_1\sigma_3 - \sigma_3 a_1) = -\tfrac{i}{2}kq_0^2(b_0\sigma_3 + \sigma_3 b_0)b_{-1}^{-1}$. Thus, using (22), we obtain

$$\mathcal{N}(\widehat{\Phi_x}) = \mathcal{N}\left[(i(k^2 + \tfrac{1}{2}q_0^2)\sigma_3 + \tfrac{i}{2}k(a_1\sigma_3 - \sigma_3 a_1))\widehat{\Phi}\right], \tag{35}$$

which gives the spatial linear spectral problem based on (29)

$$\Phi_x = \left[i(k^2 + \tfrac{1}{2}q_0^2)\sigma_3 + kQ\right]\Phi, \quad Q = \frac{i}{2}[a_1, \sigma_3]. \tag{36}$$

Similarly, we can have

$$\Phi_t = -\frac{i}{8}\left[z^4 - 4q_0^2 z^2 + a_1 z^3 + a_2 z^2 + a_3 z + a_4 - 4q_0^2 a_1 z - 4q_0^2 a_2 + O(\frac{1}{z})\right], \quad z \to \infty,$$

$$\Phi_t = \frac{i}{8}q_0^6\left[q_0^2(b_{-1} z^{-5} + b_0 z^{-4} + b_1 z^{-3} + b_2 z^{-2} + b_3 z^{-1}) - 4(b_{-1} z^{-3} + b_0 z^{-2} + b_1 z^{-1}) + O(1)\right], \quad z \to 0. \tag{37}$$

And

$$T\Phi = -\frac{i}{8}\left[z^4 - 4q_0^2 z^2 + a_1 z^3 + a_2 z^2 + a_3 z + a_4 - 4q_0^2 a_1 z - 4q_0^2 a_2 + O\left(\frac{1}{z}\right)\right], \quad z \to \infty,$$
$$T\Phi = \frac{i}{8}q_0^6\left[q_0^2(b_{-1}z^{-5} + b_0 z^{-4} + b_1 z^{-3} + b_2 z^{-2} + b_3 z^{-1}) - 4(b_{-1}z^{-3} + b_0 z^{-2} + b_1 z^{-1}) + O(1)\right], \quad z \to 0.$$
(38)

Again using (22), (29), (37) and (38) gives the temporal linear spectral problem. □

Theorem 1 forms a connecting link between the preceding and the following: Starting from the asymptotic expression of $\Phi(x,t,z)$ in Section 2, we obtain the spatial and temporal linear spectral problem that $\Phi(x,t,z)$ satisfies in Theorem 1. Integrability is an extremely important property of non-linear equations and Theorem 1 proves that the DNLSENBC is Lax integrable. Moreover, Theorem 1 establishes the connection between the potential of the DNLSENBC and the solution of the Dbar-problem, which paves the way for construction of the N-soliton solutions of the DNLSENBC in the next section.

4. Solutions

In this section, we construct the N-soliton solutions of the DNLSENBC.

4.1. $\bar{\partial}$-Dressing Method and N-Soliton Solutions

We first introduce the symmetry condition on the off-diagonal matrix Q in (36)

$$\sigma_2 \overline{Q} \sigma_2 = Q, \quad \sigma_2 = \begin{bmatrix} 0 & -i \\ i & 0 \end{bmatrix}. \tag{39}$$

Based on (39), we can find that the matrix eigenfunction Φ and the distribution $r(z)$ satisfy the symmetry conditions

$$\Phi(x,t,z) = \sigma_2 \overline{\Phi(x,t,\bar{z})} \sigma_2, \quad r(z) = \sigma_2 \overline{r(\bar{z})} \sigma_2, \tag{40}$$

which plays a key role in the construction of solutions.

Theorem 2. *Suppose that η_j are $2N_1 + N_2$ discrete spectra in a complex plane $\mathbb{C}$. For the purpose of obtaining the soliton solutions of the DNLSENBC, we choose a spectral transformation matrix $r(z)$ as*

$$r(z) = \pi \sum_{j=1}^{2N_1+N_2} \begin{bmatrix} 0 & c_j(\delta(z-\eta_j) + \delta(z+\eta_j)) \\ -\bar{c}_j(\delta(z-\bar{\eta}_j) + \delta(z+\bar{\eta}_j)) & 0 \end{bmatrix}, \tag{41}$$

where $c_j \in \mathbb{C}$ are all constants and

$$\eta_j = z_j, \quad \eta_{N_1+j} = -\frac{q_0^2}{\bar{z}_j}, \quad \eta_{2N_1+n} = \zeta_n, \quad c_{N_1+j} = \frac{\rho q_0^2}{\rho \cdot \bar{\eta}_j^2} \bar{c}_j, \quad j = 1, 2, \cdots N_1, \quad n = 1, 2, \cdots N_2. \tag{42}$$

Then, the DNLS Equation (2) with a non-zero boundary condition (3) admits the solutions

$$q = \rho - 2i\frac{\det M^a}{\det M}, \quad M = I + A_{n,m}, \tag{43}$$

where M^a are $(2N_1 + N_2 + 1) \times (2N_1 + N_2 + 1)$ matrices defined as

$$M^a = \begin{bmatrix} 0 & Y \\ F & M \end{bmatrix}, \quad Y = (Y_1, Y_2, \cdots Y_{2N_1+N_2}), \quad Y_j = c_j e^{2i\theta(\eta_j)}, \quad D_j(z) = \frac{c_j}{z^2 - \eta_j^2} e^{2i\theta(\eta_j)},$$

$$F = (f_1, f_2, \cdots f_{2N_1+N_2}), \quad f_n = 1 - 2i\rho \sum_{n=1}^{2N_1+N_2} \overline{D_j(\bar{\eta}_n)}, \quad A_{n,m} = 4 \sum_{j=1}^{2N_1+N_2} \bar{\eta}_j^2 \overline{D_j(\bar{\eta}_n)} D_m(\bar{\eta}_j),$$

$$\theta(x,t,\eta_j) = \frac{1}{4}(\eta_j^2 - \frac{q_0^4}{\eta_j^2})\left[x - \frac{1}{2}(\eta_j^2 + \frac{q_0^4}{\eta_j^2})t + 2q_0^2 t\right].$$

Proof. From Equations (26) and (36), we have

$$Q = Q_0 + \frac{1}{4\pi}\left[\sigma_3, \int\int_{\mathbb{C}^0} \widehat{\Phi}(x,t,z)e^{i\theta(z)\sigma_3}r(z)e^{-i\theta(z)\sigma_3}dz \wedge d\bar{z}\right]. \tag{44}$$

Substituting (41) into (44), we have the solution of the DNLSENBC

$$q = \rho - 2i \sum_{j=1}^{2N_1+N_2} c_j e^{2i\theta(\eta_j)} \widehat{\Phi}_{11}(\eta_j). \tag{45}$$

In order to obtain the explicit expression of q, the key is to determine the functions $\widehat{\Phi}_{11}$. Making use of the properties of the δ function and the symmetry (24), from (22), we have

$$\widehat{\Phi}_{11}(z) = 1 - 2\sum_{j=1}^{2N_1+N_2} \bar{c}_j \frac{\bar{\eta}_j}{z^2 - \bar{\eta}_j^2} e^{-2i\theta(\bar{\eta}_j)} \widehat{\Phi}_{12}(\bar{\eta}_j), \tag{46}$$

$$\widehat{\Phi}_{12}(z) = \frac{i}{z}\rho + 2\sum_{m=1}^{2N_1+N_2} c_m \frac{z}{z^2 - \eta_m^2} e^{2i\theta(\eta_m)} \widehat{\Phi}_{11}(\eta_m). \tag{47}$$

Taking $z = \eta_n$ in (46) and $z = \bar{\eta}_j$ in (47), a system of linear equations is obtained

$$\widehat{\Phi}_{11}(\eta_n) + \sum_{m=1}^{2N_1+N_2} A_{n,m}\widehat{\Phi}_{11}(\eta_m) = f_n, \quad n = 1, 2, \cdots 2N_1 + N_2, \tag{48}$$

with

$$f_n = 1 - 2i\rho \sum_{n=1}^{2N_1+N_2} \overline{D}_j(\bar{\eta}_n), \quad A_{n,m} = 4\sum_{j=1}^{2N_1+N_2} \bar{\eta}_j^2 \overline{D}_j(\bar{\eta}_n) D_m(\bar{\eta}_j), \quad D_j(z) = \frac{c_j}{z^2 - \eta_j^2} e^{2i\theta(\eta_j)}.$$

For simplicity, we further note

$$M = I + A_{n,m}, \quad F = (f_1, f_2, \cdots f_{2N_1+N_2})^T, \quad \Phi = (\widehat{\Phi}_{11}(\eta_1), \widehat{\Phi}_{11}(\eta_2), \cdots \widehat{\Phi}_{11}(\eta_{2N_1+N_2}))^T.$$

Then (48) can be written in the matrix form

$$M\Phi_{11} = F. \tag{49}$$

Substituting the solution Φ_{11} of (49) into (45) gives the Formula (43). □

4.2. Application of N-Soliton Formula

As applications of the Formula (43), we present explicit soliton solutions of the DNLSENBC. For simplicity, we take $|\rho| = 1$ in the following.

Case 1. One-breather

In this case, we take $N_1 = 1$, $N_2 = 0$, $\eta_1 = re^{i\alpha}$, $c_1 = e^{\mu+iv}$, and $\rho = e^{i\phi}$. From (42), we can determine $\eta_2 = -\frac{1}{r}e^{i\alpha}$, $c_2 = \frac{1}{r^2}e^{\mu+i(2\phi+2\alpha-v)}$. Substituting the above parameters in (43), we have the one-breather solution (see Figure 1)

$$q(x,t) = 1 - 2i\frac{\det\begin{bmatrix} 0 & Y_1 & Y_2 \\ f_1 & 1+A_{1,1} & A_{1,2} \\ f_2 & A_{2,1} & 1+A_{2,2} \end{bmatrix}}{\det\begin{bmatrix} 1+A_{1,1} & A_{1,2} \\ A_{2,1} & 1+A_{2,2} \end{bmatrix}}, \tag{50}$$

where
$$\theta(x,t,\eta_j) = \frac{1}{4}(\eta_j^2 - \frac{1}{\eta_j^2})[x - \frac{1}{2}(\eta_j^2 + \frac{1}{\eta_j^2})t + 2t], \ j = 1,2,$$
$$D_j(z) = \frac{c_j}{z^2 - \eta_j^2}e^{2i\theta(x,t,\eta_j)}, \ Y_j = c_j e^{2i\theta(x,t,\eta_j)}, \ j = 1,2, \quad (51)$$
$$f_n = 1 - 2i\sum_{n=1}^{2} \overline{D}_j(\overline{\eta}_n), \ A_{n,m} = 4\sum_{j=1}^{2} \overline{\eta}_j^2 \overline{D}_j(\overline{\eta}_n)D_m(\overline{\eta}_j), \ m,n = 1,2.$$

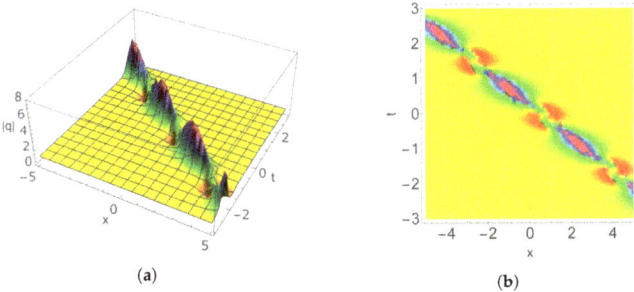

Figure 1. (**a**) One-breather of (50) with $r = 0.5, \alpha = 0.8, \mu = 0.5, \nu = 0.5, \phi = 2\pi, q_0 = 1$, (**b**) the corresponding density profile.

Case 2. One-soliton

Let $N_1 = 0$ and $N_2 = 1$. Based on (42), we take $\eta_1 = e^{i\beta}$, $c_1 = e^{\kappa + i\tau}$ and $\rho = e^{i\phi}$. The relation (43) gives rise to the one-soliton solution (see Figure 2)

$$q(x,t) = 1 - 2i\frac{-Y_1 f_1}{1 + A_{1,1}}, \quad (52)$$

where
$$\theta(x,t,\eta_1) = \frac{1}{4}(\eta_1^2 - \frac{1}{\eta_1^2})[x - \frac{1}{2}(\eta_1^2 + \frac{1}{\eta_1^2})t + 2t], \ D_1(\overline{\eta}_1) = \frac{\overline{c}_1}{\eta_1^2 - \overline{\eta}_1^2}e^{2i\theta(x,t,\overline{\eta}_1)},$$
$$Y_1 = c_1 e^{2i\theta(x,t,\eta_1)}, \ f_1 = 1 - 2i\overline{D}_1(\overline{\eta}_1), \ A_{1,1} = 4\overline{\eta}_1^2 \overline{D}_1(\overline{\eta}_1)D_1(\overline{\eta}_1). \quad (53)$$

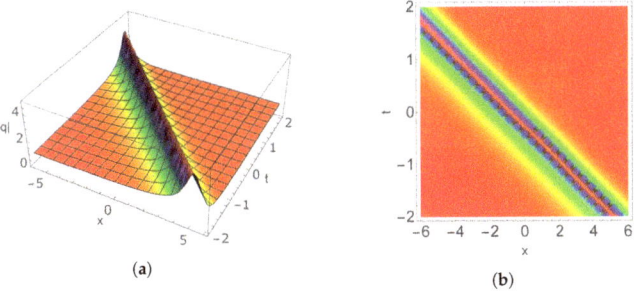

Figure 2. (**a**) One-soliton of (52) with $\beta = -1.46, \kappa = -1.35, \tau = -1.35, \phi = 2\pi, q_0 = 1$, (**b**) the corresponding density profile.

On the one hand, when $N_1 = 1, N_2 = 0$, the one breather occurs for the parameters $r = 0.5, \alpha = 0.8, \mu = 0.5, \nu = 0.5, \phi = 2\pi, q_0 = 1$. On the other hand, when selecting $N_1 = 0, N_2 = 1$, one soliton is displayed with $\beta = -1.46, \kappa = -1.35, \tau = -1.35, \phi = 2\pi, q_0 = 1$.

Thus, Figures 1 and 2 reveal that a single specific discrete spectrum leads to the appearance of a specific type of soliton.

Case 3. Soliton-breather solution

Let $N_1 = 1$ and $N_2 = 1$. Based on (42), we can take $\eta_1 = re^{i\alpha}$, $\eta_2 = -\frac{1}{r}e^{i\alpha}$, $\eta_3 = e^{i\beta}$, $\rho = 1$, $c_1 = e^{\mu+i\nu}$, $c_2 = \frac{1}{r^2}e^{\mu+i(2\alpha-\nu)}$, and $c_3 = e^{\kappa+i\tau}$. Substituting these data in (43) gives the soliton-breather solution (see Figure 3)

$$q(x,t) = 1 - 2i\frac{det\begin{bmatrix} 0 & Y \\ f & I+A \end{bmatrix}}{det[I+A]}, \qquad (54)$$

where

$$Y = (Y_1, Y_2, Y_3), \ f = (f_1, f_2, f_3)^T, \ A = (A_{i,j}), \ i,j = 1,2,3,$$

$$\theta(x,t,\eta_j) = \frac{1}{4}(\eta_j^2 - \frac{1}{\eta_j^2})[x - \frac{1}{2}(\eta_j^2 + \frac{1}{\eta_j^2})t + 2t], \ j = 1,2,3,$$

$$D_j(z) = \frac{c_j}{z^2 - \eta_j^2}e^{2i\theta(x,t,\eta_j)}, \ Y_j = c_j e^{2i\theta(x,t,\eta_j)}, \ j = 1,2,3, \qquad (55)$$

$$f_n = 1 - 2i\sum_{n=1}^{3} \overline{D}_j(\overline{\eta}_n), \ A_{n,m} = 4\sum_{j=1}^{3} \overline{\eta}_j^2 \overline{D}_j(\overline{\eta}_n) D_m(\overline{\eta}_j), \ m,n = 1,2,3.$$

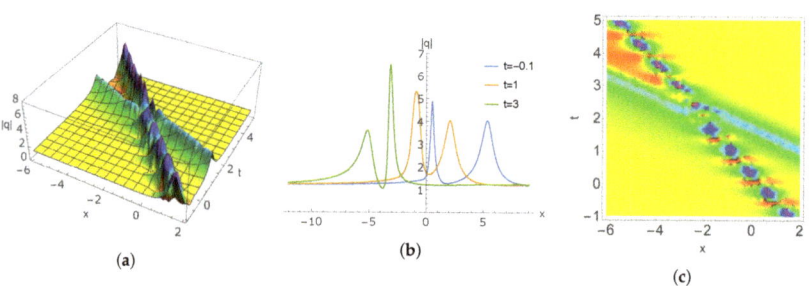

Figure 3. (**a**,**b**) Interaction of the soliton and breather with $r = 2.5$, $\alpha = -0.72$, $\beta = 1.45$, $\mu = -0.45$, $\nu = 1.5$, $\kappa = -0.5$, $\tau = 1.55$, $\rho = 1$, $q_0 = 1$, (**c**) the corresponding density profile.

Under the specific parameters $r = 2.5$, $\alpha = -0.72$, $\beta = 1.45$, $\mu = -0.45$, $\nu = 1.5$, $\kappa = -0.5$, $\tau = 1.55$, $\rho = 1$, $q_0 = 1$ of case 3, we can find that the soliton-breather solution propagates from right to left and the collision is elastic. Due to a mixed discrete spectrum, ($N_1 = 1$, $N_2 = 1$) is introduced in (43), and the interaction of the bright soliton and the bright breather emerges. This further reflects that the discrete spectrum N_1 and N_2 have different effects on the type of solitons.

Case 4. Two-breather

Let $N_1 = 2$ and $N_2 = 0$. From (42), we can choose $\eta_j = r_j e^{i\alpha_j}$, $\eta_{N_1+j} = -\frac{1}{r_j}e^{i\alpha_j}$ ($j = 1,2$), $\rho = 1$, $c_1 = e^{\mu+i\nu}$, $c_2 = e^{\kappa+i\tau}$, $c_{N_1+j} = \frac{1}{r_j^2}e^{\mu+i(2\alpha_j-\nu)}$. From (43), we obtain the two-breather solution (see Figure 4)

$$q(x,t) = 1 - 2i\frac{det\begin{bmatrix} 0 & Y \\ f & I+A \end{bmatrix}}{det[I+A]}, \qquad (56)$$

where

$$Y = (Y_1, Y_2, Y_3, Y_4), \ f = (f_1, f_2, f_3, f_4)^T, \ A = (A_{i,j}), \ i,j = 1,2,3,4,$$

$$\theta(x,t,\eta_j) = \frac{1}{4}(\eta_j^2 - \frac{1}{\eta_j^2})[x - \frac{1}{2}(\eta_j^2 + \frac{1}{\eta_j^2})t + 2t], \ j = 1,2,3,4,$$

$$D_j(z) = \frac{c_j}{z^2 - \eta_j^2} e^{2i\theta(x,t,\eta_j)}, \ Y_j = c_j e^{2i\theta(x,t,\eta_j)}, \ j = 1,2,3,4, \quad (57)$$

$$f_n = 1 - 2i \sum_{n=1}^{4} \overline{D}_j(\overline{\eta}_n), \ A_{n,m} = 4 \sum_{j=1}^{4} \overline{\eta}_j^2 \overline{D}_j(\overline{\eta}_n) D_m(\overline{\eta}_j), \ m,n = 1,2,3,4.$$

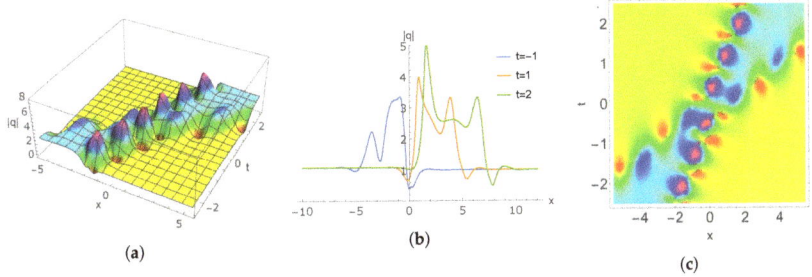

Figure 4. (**a**,**b**) Interaction of the two breathers with $r_1 = 0.42$, $r_2 = 0.42$, $\alpha_1 = 0.25$, $\alpha_2 = 0.5$, $\mu = 0.2$, $\nu = 0.2$, $\kappa = 0.5$, $\tau = 0.5$, $\rho = 1$, $q_0 = 1$, (**c**) the corresponding density profile.

Figure 4 corresponds to the case where only N_1 exists in the discrete spectrum and $N_1 = 2$, so the interaction of the two breathers naturally appears. As can be seen in Figure 4, for the parameters $r_1 = 0.42$, $r_2 = 0.42$, $\alpha_1 = 0.25$, $\alpha_2 = 0.5$, $\mu = 0.2$, $\nu = 0.2$, $\kappa = 0.5$, $\tau = 0.5$, $\rho = 1$, $q_0 = 1$, the two-breather solution propagates from left to right and the two breathers collide elastically.

Case 5. Two-soliton

Let $N_1 = 0$ and $N_2 = 2$. From (42), we can choose $\eta_j = e^{i\beta_j}$ ($j = 1,2$), $c_1 = e^{\mu + i\nu}$, $c_2 = e^{\kappa + i\tau}$. Based on (43), we gain the two-soliton solution (see Figure 5)

$$q(x,t) = 1 - 2i \frac{\det \begin{bmatrix} 0 & Y_1 & Y_2 \\ f_1 & 1+A_{1,1} & A_{1,2} \\ f_2 & A_{2,1} & 1+A_{2,2} \end{bmatrix}}{\det \begin{bmatrix} 1+A_{1,1} & A_{1,2} \\ A_{2,1} & 1+A_{2,2} \end{bmatrix}}, \quad (58)$$

where

$$\theta(x,t,\eta_j) = \frac{1}{4}(\eta_j^2 - \frac{1}{\eta_j^2})[x - \frac{1}{2}(\eta_j^2 + \frac{1}{\eta_j^2})t + 2t], \ j = 1,2,$$

$$D_j(z) = \frac{c_j}{z^2 - \eta_j^2} e^{2i\theta(x,t,\eta_j)}, \ Y_j = c_j e^{2i\theta(x,t,\eta_j)}, \ j = 1,2, \quad (59)$$

$$f_n = 1 - 2i \sum_{n=1}^{2} \overline{D}_j(\overline{\eta}_n), \ A_{n,m} = 4 \sum_{j=1}^{2} \overline{\eta}_j^2 \overline{D}_j(\overline{\eta}_n) D_m(\overline{\eta}_j), \ m,n = 1,2.$$

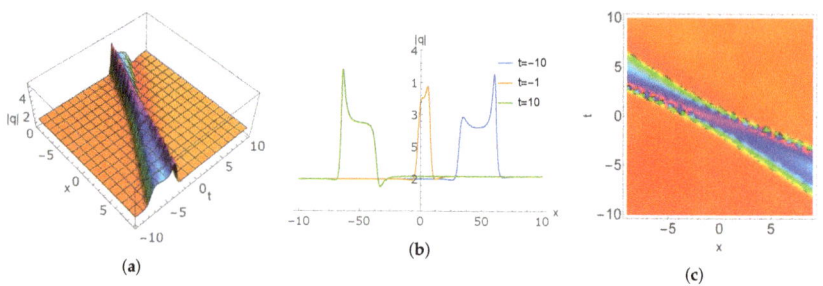

Figure 5. (**a**,**b**) Interaction of the two solitons with $\beta_1 = -0.5$, $\beta_2 = -1$, $\mu = 1.2$, $\nu = 0.3$, $\kappa = 1.2$, $\tau = 0.3$, $\rho = 1$, $q_0 = 1$, (**c**) the corresponding density profile.

Compared with case 4, case 5 has only N_2 in the discrete spectrum and $N_2 = 2$, so we obtain the two soliton solution in Figure 5 for the parameters $\beta_1 = -0.5$, $\beta_2 = -1$, $\mu = 1.2$, $\nu = 0.3$, $\kappa = 1.2$, $\tau = 0.3$, $\rho = 1$, $q_0 = 1$. At this time, the two-soliton solution propagates from right to left and collides elastically.

The above results can be briefly described in Table 1:

Table 1. The relation between the type of soliton and the discrete spectrum N_1 and N_2.

$N_1 = 1, N_2 = 0$	$N_1 = 0, N_2 = 1$	$N_1 = 1, N_2 = 1$	$N_1 = 2, N_2 = 0$	$N_1 = 0, N_2 = 2$
one-breather	one-soliton	soliton-breather	two-breather	two-soliton

It is straightforward to find that the discrete spectrum N_1 controls the generation of breathers, while the discrete spectrum N_2 leads to the appearance of solitons. When we take the mixed discrete spectrum (i.e., $N_1 = N_2 = 1$), the interaction of the bright soliton and the bright breather occurs. In the case of $N_1 = 2, N_2 = 0$, the solution of (56) displays the interaction of the bright breather and the bright breather, which is shown in Figure 4. When we take $N_1 = 0, N_2 = 2$, as shown in Figure 5, the solution of (58) exhibits the interaction of the bright soliton and the bright soliton. Case 3 to case 5 show that the collision is elastic, because the size and shape of the solitons remain unchanged before and after the collision.

5. Conclusions

In this paper, a special distribution and a symmetry matrix function were presented to construct the DNLSENBC and its linear spectral problem. Thus, the the relation between the potential of the DNLSENBC with the solution of the Dbar-problem was established. We extended the Dbar-dressing method to study the DNLSENBC based on the fact that the solution of the Dbar-problem was meromorphic outside an annulus with center 0 and satisfied a local Dbar-problem inside the annulus. Further, $2N_1 + N_2$ discrete eigenvalues were introduced in the distribution and the N-soliton solution was worked out. An innovative aspect of this investigation is the exploration of the relation between the type of soliton and the values of the discrete spectrum N_1 and N_2. The discrete spectrum N_1 is related to the appearance of breathers, while the discrete spectrum N_2 affects the generation of solitons. The interaction of the soliton and the breather occurs with the introduction of the mixed discrete spectrum. The dynamic behaviors of the soliton solution, the breather solution, and the solution of the interaction between the solitons and the breathers, are further elaborated in the figures and tables. Based on the results obtained in this study, we intend to investigate the long time asymptotic behavior of the DNLSENBC in another paper in the near future.

Author Contributions: The authors have made equal contributions to the paper. All authors have read and approved the final paper. All authors have read and agreed to the published version of the manuscript.

Funding: This work is supported by the National Natural Science Foundation of China (No.12171475) and the Fundamental Research Funds of the Central Universities (No.2020MS043).

Institutional Review Board Statement: Not applicable.

Informed Consent Statement: Not applicable.

Data Availability Statement: Not applicable.

Conflicts of Interest: The authors declare no conflict of interest.

References

1. Boutabbaa, N.; Eleucha, H.; Bouchriha, H. Thermal bath effect on soliton propagation in three-level atomic system. *Synth. Met.* **2009**, *159*, 1239–1243. [CrossRef]
2. Eleuch, H.; Elser, D.; Bennaceur, R. Soliton propagation in an absorbing three-level atomic system. *Laser Phys. Lett.* **2004**, *1*, 391–396. [CrossRef]
3. Al Khawaja, U.; Eleuchb, H.; Bahlouli, H. Analytical analysis of soliton propagation in microcavity wires. *Results Phys.* **2019**, *12*, 471–474. [CrossRef]
4. Johnson, R.S. On the modulation of water waves in the neighbourhood of $kh \approx 1.363$. *Proc. R. Soc. Lond. Ser. A Math. Phys. Eng. Sci.* **1977**, *357*, 131–141.
5. Rosales, J.L.; Sánchez-Gómez, J.L. Non-linear Schrödinger equation coming from the action of the particle's gravitational field on the quantum potential. *Phys. Lett. A* **1992**, *166*, 111–115. [CrossRef]
6. Eleuch, H.; Rotter, I. Width bifurcation and dynamical phase transitions in open quantum systems. *Phys. Rev. E* **2013**, *87*, 052136. [CrossRef]
7. Eleuch, H.; Rotter, I. Nearby states in non-Hermitian quantum systems I: Two states. *Eur. Phys. J. D* **2015**, *69*, 229. [CrossRef]
8. Karjanto, N. The nonlinear Schrödinger equation: A mathematical model with its wide-ranging applications. *arXiv* **2019**, arXiv:1912.10683v1.
9. Rogister, A. Parallel propagation of nonlinear low-frequency waves in high-β plasma. *Phys. Fluids* **1971**, *14*, 2733–2739. [CrossRef]
10. Mjølhus, E. On the modulational instability of hydromagnetic waves parallel to the magnetic field. *J. Plasma Phys.* **1976**, *16*, 321–334. [CrossRef]
11. Mio, K.; Ogino, T.; Minami, K.; Takeda, S. Modified nonlinear Schrödinger equation for Alfvén waves propagating along the magnetic field in cold plasmas. *J. Phys. Soc. Jpn.* **1976**, *41*, 265–271. [CrossRef]
12. Wadati, M.; Sanuki, H.; Konno, K.; Ichikawa, Y. Circular polarized nonlinear Alfvén waves-A new type of nonlinear evolution equation in plasma physics. *Rocky Mt. J. Math.* **1978**, *8*, 323–331. [CrossRef]
13. Ichikawa, Y.H.; Sanuki, H.; Konno, K.; Sanuki, H. Spiky soliton in circular polarized Alfvén wave. *J. Phys. Soc. Jpn.* **1980**, *48*, 279–286. [CrossRef]
14. Mjølhus, E. Nonlinear Alfvén waves and the DNLS equation: Oblique aspects. *Phys. Scr.* **1989**, *40*, 227–237. [CrossRef]
15. Bosanac, S. A method for calculation of Regge poles in atomic collisions. *J. Math. Phys.* **1978**, *19*, 789–797. [CrossRef]
16. Qiao, Z.J. A new completely integrable Liouville's system produced by the Kaup-Newell eigenvalue problem. *J. Math. Phys.* **1993**, *34*, 3110–3120. [CrossRef]
17. Qiao, Z.J. A hierarchy of nonlinear evolution equations and finite-dimensional involutive systems. *J. Math. Phys.* **1994**, *35*, 2971–2977. [CrossRef]
18. Steudel, H. The hierarchy of multi-soliton solutions of the derivative nonlinear Schrödinger equation. *J. Phys. A Math. Gen.* **2003**, *36*, 1931–1946. [CrossRef]
19. Xu, S.W.; He, J.S.; Wang, L.H. The Darboux transformation of the derivative nonlinear Schrödinger equation. *J. Phys. A Math. Theor.* **2001**, *44*, 6629–6630. [CrossRef]
20. Guo, B.; Ling, L.M.; Liu, Q.P. High-order solutions and generalized Darboux transformations of derivative nonlinear Schrödinger equations. *Stud. Appl. Math.* **2012**, *130*, 317–344. [CrossRef]
21. Zhang, G.Q.; Yan, Z.Y. The derivative nonlinear Schrödinger equation with zero/nonzero boundary conditions: inverse scattering transforms and N-double-pole solutions. *J. Nonlinear Sci.* **2020**, *30*, 3089–3127. [CrossRef]
22. Pelinovsky, D.E.; Shimabukuro, Y. Existence of global solutions to the derivative NLS equation with the inverse scattering transform method. *Int. Math. Res. Not.* **2016**, *2018*, 5663–5728. [CrossRef]
23. Bahouri, H.; Perelman, G. Global well-posedness for the derivative nonlinear Schrödinger equation. *Invent. Math.* **2022**, *229*, 639–688. [CrossRef]
24. Zakharov, V.E.; Shabat, A.B. A scheme for integrating the nonlinear equations of mathematical physics by the method of the inverse scattering problem. I. *J. Funct. Anal. Appl.* **1974**, *8*, 226–235. [CrossRef]
25. Beals, R.; Coifman, R.R. The D-bar approach to inverse scattering and nonlinear evolutions. *Physica D* **1986**, *18*, 242–249. [CrossRef]
26. Beals, R.; Coifman, R.R. Linear spectral problems, non-linear equations and the $\bar{\partial}$-method. *Inverse Problem* **1989**, *5*, 87–130. [CrossRef]
27. Bogdanov, L.V.; Manakov, S.V. The non-local $\bar{\partial}$-problem and (2+1)-dimensional soliton equations. *J. Phys. A Math. Gen.* **1988**, *21*, L537–L544. [CrossRef]

28. Doktorov, E.V.; Leble, S.B. *A Dressing Method in Mathematical Physics*; Springer: Berlin, Germany, 2007.
29. Fokas, A.S.; Zakharov, V.E. The dressing method and nonlocal Riemann-Hilbert problem. *J. Nonlinear Sci.* **1992**, *2*, 109–134. [CrossRef]
30. Parvizi, M.; Khodadadian, A.; Eslahchi, M.R. Analysis of Ciarlet-Raviart mixed finite element methods for solving damped Boussinesq equation. *J. Comput. Appl. Math.* **2020**, *379*, 112818. [CrossRef]
31. Khodadadian, A.; Parvizia, M.; Heitzinger, C. An adaptive multilevel Monte Carlo algorithm for the stochastic drift-diffusion-Poisson system. *Comput. Methods Appl. Mech. Eng.* **2020**, *368*, 113169. [CrossRef]
32. Jaulent, M.; Manna, M.; Alonso, L.M. $\bar{\partial}$ equations in the theory of integrable systems. *Inverse Probl.* **1988**, *4*, 123–150. [CrossRef]
33. Kuang, Y.H.; Zhu, J.Y. A three-wave interaction model with self-consistent sources: The $\bar{\partial}$-dressing method and solutions. *J. Math. Anal. Appl.* **2015**, *426*, 783–793. [CrossRef]
34. Mikhailov, A.V.; Papamikos, G.; Wang, J.P. Dressing method for the vector sine-Gordon equation and its soliton interactions. *Physica D* **2016**, *325*, 53–62. [CrossRef]
35. Ivanov, R.; Lyons, T.; Orr, N. A dressing method for soliton solutions of the Camass-Holm equation. *AIP Conf. Proc.* **2017**, *1895*, 040003.
36. Luo, J.H.; Fan, E.G. Dbar-dressing method for the coupled Gerdjikov-Ivanov equation. *Appl. Math. Lett.* **2020**, *110*, 106589. [CrossRef]
37. Luo, J.H.; Fan, E.G. Dbar-dressing method for the Gerdjikov-Ivanov equation with nonzero boundary conditions. *Appl. Math. Lett.* **2021**, *120*, 107297. [CrossRef]
38. Zhu, J.Y.; Jiang, X.L.; Wang, X.R. Dbar dressing method to nonlinear Schrödinger equation with nonzero boundary conditions. *arXiv* **2021**, arXiv:2011.09028v2.
39. Yao, Y.Q.; Huang, Y.H.; Fan, E.G. The $\bar{\partial}$-dressing method and Cauchy matrix for the defocuing matrix NLS system. *Appl. Math. Lett.* **2021**, *117*, 107143. [CrossRef]
40. Li, Z.Q.; Tian, S.F. A hierarchy of nonlocal nonlinear evolution equations and $\bar{\partial}$-dressing method. *Appl. Math. Lett.* **2021**, *120*, 107254. [CrossRef]
41. Zhao, S.Y.; Zhang, Y.F.; Zhang, X.Z. A New Application of the $\bar{\partial}$-Method. *J. Nonlinear Math. Phys.* **2021**, *28*, 492–506. [CrossRef]
42. Chai, X.D.; Zhang, Y.F.; Zhao, S.Y. Application of the $\bar{\partial}$-dressing method to a (2+1)-dimensional equation. *Theor. Math. Phys.* **2021**, *209*, 1717–1725. [CrossRef]
43. Peng, W.Q.; Chen, Y. Double and triple pole solutions for the Gerdjikov–Ivanov type of derivative nonlinear Schrödinger equation with zero/nonzero boundary conditions. *arXiv* **2021**, arXiv:2104.12073.
44. Kaup, D.J.; Newell, A.C. An exact solution for a derivative nonlinear Schrödinger equation. *J. Math. Phys.* **1978**, *19*, 798. [CrossRef]

Article

Decision Analysis on the Financial Performance of Companies Using Integrated Entropy-Fuzzy TOPSIS Model

Weng Hoe Lam, Weng Siew Lam *, Kah Fai Liew and Pei Fun Lee

Department of Physical and Mathematical Science, Faculty of Science, Universiti Tunku Abdul Rahman, Kampar Campus, Jalan Universiti, Bandar Barat, Kampar 31900, Perak, Malaysia; whlam@utar.edu.my (W.H.L.); liewkf@utar.edu.my (K.F.L.); pflee@utar.edu.my (P.F.L.)
* Correspondence: lamws@utar.edu.my

Citation: Lam, W.H.; Lam, W.S.; Liew, K.F.; Lee, P.F. Decision Analysis on the Financial Performance of Companies Using Integrated Entropy-Fuzzy TOPSIS Model. *Mathematics* 2023, *11*, 397. https://doi.org/10.3390/math11020397

Academic Editors: Qun Li and Aihua Wood

Received: 21 December 2022
Revised: 8 January 2023
Accepted: 9 January 2023
Published: 12 January 2023

Copyright: © 2023 by the authors. Licensee MDPI, Basel, Switzerland. This article is an open access article distributed under the terms and conditions of the Creative Commons Attribution (CC BY) license (https:// creativecommons.org/licenses/by/ 4.0/).

Abstract: Sustainable economic development plans have been shattered by the devastating COVID-19 crisis, which brought about an economic recession. The companies are suffering from financial losses, leading to financial distress and disengagement from sustainable economic goals. Many companies fail to achieve considerable financial performances, which may lead to unachieved organizational goal and a loss of direction in decision-making and investment. According to the past studies, there has been no comprehensive study done on the financial performance of the companies based on liquidity, solvency, efficiency, and profitability ratios by integrating the entropy method and fuzzy technique for order reference based on similarity to the ideal solution (TOPSIS) model in portfolio investment. Therefore, this paper aims to propose a multi-criteria decision-making (MCDM) model, namely the entropy-fuzzy TOPSIS model, to evaluate the financial performances of companies based on these important financial ratios for portfolio investment. The fuzzy concept helps reduce vagueness and strengthen the meaningful information extracted from the financial ratios. The proposed model is illustrated using the financial ratios of companies in the Dow Jones Industrial Average (DJIA). The results show that return on equity and debt-to-equity ratios are the most influential financial ratios for the performance evaluation of the companies. The companies with good financial performance, such as the best HD company, have been determined based on the proposed model for portfolio selection. A mean-variance (MV) model is used to validate the proposed model in the portfolio investment. At a minimum level of risk, the proposed model is able to generate a higher mean return than the benchmark DJIA index. This paper is significant as it helps to evaluate the financial performance of the companies and select the well-performing companies with the proposed model for portfolio investment.

Keywords: entropy; fuzzy; TOPSIS; multi-criteria decision making; financial ratio; ranking

MSC: 90B50

1. Introduction

The present needs must be attained without adversely affecting our future or the Earth, our home. This notion has moved into the center of discussion since the late 1980s and has since been put into writing as the Sustainable Development Goals (SDGs) in 2015 to be achieved in the next 15 years [1]. The call for the understanding, implementation, and management of SDGs is urgent, with the ultimate goal of generating long-term values for businesses, societies, and the environment. Several insightful companies have taken this initiative to apply various indicators under the SDGs to scan for business opportunities and global risks to enhance their financial performances through sustainable economic developments [2]. The companies pay notable attention to their financial performances because financial results reflect the quantifiable aspects of organizational goal achievements and, hence, allow companies to gauge their successes on a timely basis. In addition, based on recent financial performances, the management team is able to make prudent budgets and decisions to position the company strategically in the local and international markets. Investors also look at financial performances to establish their intentions for initial or continuous support of a company after weighing the risks and returns.

However, COVID-19 has impeded some progress toward sustainable economic developments in many parts of the world, which has then affected their financial performances. Safitri et al. [3] studied the impacts of COVID-19 on these efforts in Indonesia and found that social and economic sectors had been hit hard since 2020. Many industrial activities were also disrupted due to strict protocols to control this infectious disease. A study by Suriyankietkaew and Nimsai [4] also proved that economic activities have been stagnant as COVID-19 cases soared. In addition, the International Monetary Fund (IMF) pointed out that fiscal stimulus during this time could help improve resiliency and reduce the divergence from sustainable economic development goal attainment. As a result, countries in America, Asia, and Europe are standing together in solidarity and have responded by providing assistance to individuals and businesses [5]. However, despite governmental aid, high financial impacts are still felt by businesses, with many facing closure due to financial instability [6].

Over the years, sustainable economic development has helped countries develop economies and assisted companies in strengthening their financial statuses. However, as a result of the outbreak, commercial activities face labor, occupational health and safety, sales, and cash flow challenges that blur the future of businesses. In addition, individuals, families, and corporations tend to be conservative and save their capital, which then results in slower economic growth [7]. Furthermore, amid Omicron-variant concerns in the United States, with many flights halted for the 2021 year-end holidays, the Dow Jones Industrial Average (DJIA) plummeted more than 400 points, leading to growing anxieties among the listed companies [8]. This has reversed many companies' plans to perform expansions deemed risky, as there is a clear sign of a sluggish recovery from the recession and businesses could continue to suffer from weak balance sheets [9]. As much as they focus on strengthening their bottom lines, companies also realize the necessity of improving liquidity and leverage levels in a financial crisis [10]. In fact, financial strategies should be in place to be activated instantly during a crisis to reduce its daunting consequences [11].

Achim et al. [12] found that the large listed companies in Romania still faced a notable drop in quick ratio (QR), return on equity (ROE), and return on assets (ROA) in 2020. The results from Karim et al. [13] also indicated drops in liquidity, solvency, and operating efficiency of companies in Bangladesh during this health crisis. As a large economic zone, companies in the European Union began suffering from revenue shocks and deteriorating solvency levels since the start of the pandemic, with no definite timetable for recovery, as proven in research by Mirza et al. [14]. In China, listed companies also saw reductions in ROE and asset turnover (AT) [15]. Vito and Gómez [16] explained that companies tend to experience lower sales, which led to a cash crunch, causing the companies to resort to borrowing to reduce short-term liquidity concerns. Rababah et al. [17] revealed that some industries had worrying declines in financial performances as they were worst hit by the outbreak. In addition, financial distress could lead to operational issues such as debts, lower employee morale, and reduced productivity [18]. Given that the financial positions of a large number of companies are highly volatile, there is a pressing need for companies to continuously assess their financial health.

The financial performance of a company can be assessed using a multi-criteria decision-making (MCDM) model. The MCDM is popular due to its success in allowing simultaneous assessment of both optimistic and pessimistic decision criteria, where some criteria generate values while others incur expenses for a decision alternative [19]. Generally, the MCDM model involves the ranking of decision alternatives with regards to various criteria in order to obtain the best solution. Shaverdi et al. [20] studied the financial performance of petrochemical companies in Iran using a combination of the fuzzy analytic hierarchy process (AHP) and the fuzzy Technique for Order Performance by Similarity to an Ideal Solution (TOPSIS). In this study, the decision criteria were made up of liquidity, leverage, activity, and profitability ratios such as the current ratio (CR), the quick ratio (QR), the debt-to-equity ratio (DER), the debt-to-assets ratio (DAR), the AT, the ROA, and the ROE. Shaverdi et al. [20] also noted that uncertainties in real-life situations could be mitigated using fuzzy logic to overcome the limitations of the traditional MCDM model. A fuzzy AHP with CR, QR, DER, DAR, ROA, and ROE was also used in a separate study in Iran [21]. Further, researchers in India also categorized financial ratios into liquidity, leverage, and profitability ratios and adopted CR, QR, DAR, and ROE to evaluate the performances of companies in India with AHP [22]. In Turkey, commercial banks were investigated based on their financial performances with various financial indicators using AHP [23]. The financial aspects of the service and banking industries were examined with financial indicators using fuzzy AHP in Taiwan [24]. CR, QR, DER, DAR, AT, ROA, and ROE were also applied to assess technology companies in Turkey using TOPSIS to increase the power of assessment [25]. In measuring the efficiency of ports in India, Gayathri et al. [26] found that debt ratios had the greatest significance and that integrated MCDM models offered better evaluation.

According to Shannon [27], in decision-making analysis, the quantity and quality of data greatly influence the precision and reliability of the results. Shannon's entropy reflects the amount of useful information within a set of data to determine criteria weights in MCDM models such as TOPSIS. In addition, Shannon theorized that as an entropy value gets smaller, the criterion weight shall be greater with additional information carried by the criterion and greater effects on the research objective [28]. Shannon's entropy's application to determining the objective weights of decision criteria before the alternatives are ranked using the TOPSIS model can be found in a study on the selection of industrial robots in India, and the results of entropy TOPSIS were found to be useful [29]. Furthermore, Shannon's entropy was proven to be prominent when this method was integrated with TOPSIS to assess the risks present in heritage sites in China, which then assisted the local government in risk mitigation in culturally preserved areas [30]. Moreover, flood vulnerability assessments and rail system performance research were also done with Shannon's entropy and TOPSIS [31,32].

The introduction of fuzzy set theory by Zadeh [33] has had extensive use for the quantification of linguistic aspects of data. The fuzzy set theory offers higher flexibility in decision boundaries and can therefore, reflect particularities more precisely [34]. In addition, when crisp data is less suitable to model an event due to vagueness, interval judgment with linguistic terms can be used for initial evaluation. All linguistic terms can be transformed into triangular fuzzy numbers (TFNs) for quantitative computations [35]. The TOPSIS model is applicable to rank decision alternatives by calculating Euclidean intervals. This means obtaining distances from positive (PIS) and negative ideal solutions (NIS). The most feasible alternative shall have the shortest Euclidean interval from PIS and the furthest interval from NIS simultaneously. After identifying the decision criteria and alternatives in TOPSIS, the next step is to assign significance levels to the decision criteria by assigning weights to each criterion. The literature does not provide a definite computational method to find criteria weights [36]. Therefore, in this research, entropy is proposed to quantify the weights of the criteria before fuzzy TOPSIS is applied. The fuzzy integration with TOPSIS has been applied for project selection [37,38], dry bulk carrier selection [39], and website evaluation [40].

According to the past studies, there has been no comprehensive study done on the financial performance of the companies based on liquidity, solvency, efficiency, and profitability ratios by integrating the entropy method and fuzzy TOPSIS model in portfolio investment. The novelty of this research lies in the integrated entropy-fuzzy TOPSIS model used to evaluate the financial performance of companies and determine the best performing companies for portfolio investment. Secondly, this paper employs TFNs to reduce the vagueness of data obtained from financial ratios. Therefore, this research adopts a comprehensive set of financial ratios that involve liquidity, solvency, efficiency, and profitability ratios for their financial performance evaluation of companies based on the financial statements. This paper intends to contribute by identifying the influential financial ratios that contribute to the financial performance of the companies so that the companies can work on enhancing critical ratios to increase the companies' values. This study can also serve as a reference for investors making portfolio investments. The investors can determine an optimal portfolio from the well-performing companies in terms of financial performance for portfolio investment based on the proposed model. Section 2 demonstrates the methodology of the proposed entropy-fuzzy TOPSIS model. Section 3 presents the empirical results of this study. Section 4 summarizes the findings of this research and its conclusion.

2. Materials and Methods

This research aims to propose an MCDM model, namely the entropy-fuzzy TOPSIS model, to assess and compare the financial performance of all components of the DJIA with a total of 30 companies from 2015 to 2021 for portfolio investment. Throughout the years, TOPSIS has emerged as one of the most powerful and reliable methods to provide resolutions to managerial policy implementations and complications [41]. In real life, financial information incorporated into the coefficients of objective functions and constraints contains vagueness, which could be eliminated with fuzzy set theory.

In fact, there has been no proper judgment on the exact value of a financial ratio that reflects the best performance of a company. Moreover, a considerably fair ratio value in an industry in a region may not reflect the same information in other sectors and nations due to the adoption of different strategies and external factors such as legalities and level of competition. However, a rise or decline in a ratio value over consecutive years may not necessarily signal a success or hazard in a company's business structure and operation [42]. Therefore, due to subjectivity, the entropy-fuzzy TOPSIS model is proposed in this research. Figure 1 shows the flowchart for this research.

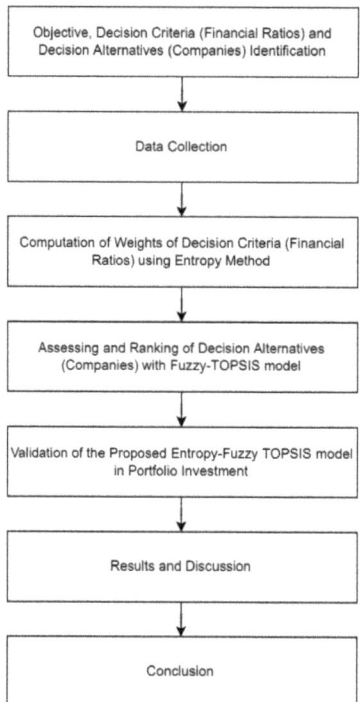

Figure 1. Process flowchart.

The proposed model consists of two stages, as shown below:

Stage-1: Compute the weights of decision criteria (financial ratios) using Shannon's entropy method.

Stage-2: Assess and rank the decision alternatives (companies) with a fuzzy TOPSIS model.

Table 1 presents the research framework proposal to assess the financial performances of 30 companies under the DJIA using the entropy-fuzzy TOPSIS model.

Table 1. Research framework proposal.

Hierarchy	Description			
Objective	Assessment and Ranking of the Financial Performances of Companies under DJIA			
Decision Criteria	Current Ratio (CR) Quick Ratio (QR) Debt-to-Equity Ratio (DER) Debt-to-Assets Ratio (DAR) Asset Turnover (AT) Return on Asset (ROA) Return on Equity (ROE)			
Decision Alternatives	AXP AMGN AAPL BA CAT CSCO CVX GS HD HON	IBM INTC JNJ KO JPM MCD MMM MRK MSFT NKE	PG TRV UNH CRM VZ V WBA WMT DIS DOW	

Table 1 highlights the framework proposal of this research, including the objective, decision criteria, and decision alternatives to assess and rank the financial performance of companies under the DJIA. The DJIA is a prominent US equity index, which consists of the 30 listed companies in the United States [43,44]. In addition, the DJIA measures the entire direction of the stock market. As the index goes up, the market is usually doing well. If the index falls, the stocks are underperforming [45,46]. Seven sets of prominent financial ratios, including CR, QR, DER, DAR, AT, ROA, and ROE, are fixed as the decision criteria. According to González et al. [47], financial ratios are categorized into four types: liquidity, solvency, efficiency, and profitability. The liquidity-type ratios reflect information on the ability to meet short-term obligations. However, solvency ratios consider the potential to meet long-term debts and are most likely linked to the financial health of a company. The efficiency ratios are highly operational measures that analyze the effective deployment of resources for sales generation and are commonly related to cash flows. In fact, investors and shareholders postulate on profitability ratios, which indicate the value creation of a company [48,49]. Furthermore, these four categories of financial ratios have also been supported in a study by Horta [50] and reported by S&P, a giant credit rating company [51]. As a result, this research incorporates all four categories of financial ratios, in which CR and QR are used to study liquidity, DER and DAR for solvency, AT for efficiency, and ROA and ROE are adopted to observe the profitability of a company [52–54]. The 30 companies under DJIA then serve as the decision alternatives in this research. The proposed model is presented in Section 2.1.

2.1. Proposed Entropy-Fuzzy TOPSIS Model

Upon the collection of financial ratio data from the financial statements of the 30 companies, Shannon's entropy method is applied in Stage-1 to compute the objective weights of the decision criteria due to the vagueness and ambiguity of the financial ratios [55,56]. The implicit information existing among various criteria can be captured to obtain the value dispersion for analysis, which is the strength of Shannon's entropy method [57]. However, as the entropy value gets larger, the entropy weight will become smaller, reflecting less information and the lesser importance of the criteria in a research study, and vice versa. In addition, Shannon's entropy has also received great interest in TOPSIS studies [58]. The details of Shannon's entropy method in Stage-1 are presented in the following steps:

Step-1: Determine the weights of the decision criteria with Shannon's entropy method [59]. When there are h alternatives and k criteria, the initial decision matrix, D, is:

$$D = (x_{ij})_{h \times k} \qquad (1)$$

x_{ij} shows the value of jth criterion from the ith alternative.

Step-2: Normalize the initial decision matrix, D.

$$p_{ij} = \frac{x_{ij}}{\sum_{i=1}^{h} x_{ij}}, \; i = 1,2,3,\ldots,h; \; j = 1,2,3,\ldots,k \qquad (2)$$

Step-3: Obtain the information entropy, e_j, of criterion k.

$$e_j = -\frac{1}{\ln m} \sum_{i=1}^{h} p_{ij} \ln p_{ij}, \; j = 1,2,3,\ldots,k \qquad (3)$$

Step-4: Compute the entropy weight, w_j of criterion k.

$$w_j = \frac{1 - e_j}{\sum_{j=1}^{k} (1 - e_j)}, \; j = 1,2,3,\ldots,k \qquad (4)$$

where $0 \leq w_j \leq 1$ and $\sum_{j=1}^{k} w_j = 1$.

Stage-2 of this research incorporates a fuzzy TOPSIS model to assess and rank the decision alternatives. Due to the limitation of providing unconcise information in TOPSIS, a fuzzy TOPSIS was then proposed by Chen [60]. The fuzzy TOPSIS is based from cardinal data on the criteria. The most critical concept of fuzzy TOPSIS is the interval or extent between fuzzy positive ideal solutions (PIS) and fuzzy negative ideal solutions (NIS) for the alternatives, respectively. In order to improve the suitability and reputability of this research, the assessment and ranking of the alternatives engage the use of linguistic variables with triangular fuzzy numbers (TFNs), which could exist in vector forms $\tilde{x} = (p, q, r)$. The membership of a TFN can be found below:

$$x(g) = \begin{cases} 0 & \text{if } g < p \\ \frac{g-p}{q-p} & \text{if } p \leq g < q \\ \frac{r-t}{r-q} & \text{if } q \leq g < r \\ 0 & \text{if } g > r \end{cases} \qquad (5)$$

where $p \leq q \leq r$.

Due to this, the chances of capturing imprecise data will be reduced with the adoption of mathematical means [61]. The steps for the entropy-fuzzy TOPSIS model are explained below.

Step-5: Construct a fuzzy decision matrix, $\tilde{D}$ from the ratings of h alternatives and k criteria [58]. Rating is given to each alternative using linguistic variables of TFNs as shown in Table 2 [61–64].

$$\tilde{D} = \begin{bmatrix} \tilde{x}_{11} & \tilde{x}_{12} & \cdots & \tilde{x}_{1j} \\ \tilde{x}_{21} & \tilde{x}_{22} & \cdots & \tilde{x}_{2j} \\ \vdots & \vdots & \vdots & \vdots \\ \tilde{x}_{i1} & \tilde{x}_{i2} & \cdots & \tilde{x}_{ij} \end{bmatrix}, \; i = 1,2,3,\ldots,h; j = 1,2,3,\ldots k \qquad (6)$$

where $\tilde{x}_{ij} = (a_{ij}, b_{ij}, c_{ij})$ where a_{ij} is the lower bound, b_{ij} is the median, and c_{ij} is the upper bound, with $i = 1, 2, 3, \ldots, h; j = 1, 2, 3, \ldots, k$.

Table 2. Linguistic variables corresponding to TFNs.

Linguistic Terms	TFNs
Very low	1, 1, 3
Low	1, 3, 5
Medium	3, 5, 7
High	5, 7, 9
Very high	7, 9, 9

According to Table 2, the rating from the fuzzy decision matrix is converted into TFNs. This conversion is based on where the rating will fall between the intervals of minimum value and maximum value for each financial ratio. For instance, the ratings with lower values will be rated as having very low linguistic terms. On the other hand, the ratings with higher values will be classified as very high linguistic terms. The ratings with intermediate values will be categorized as low, medium, or high in linguistic terms based on the interval between the minimum value and maximum value of the financial ratios.

Step-6: Compute the normalized fuzzy decision matrix, $\tilde{p}_{ij}$.

In this step, the optimistic and pessimistic criteria are classified. In this research, CR, QR, AT, ROA, and ROE are the optimistic criteria expecting maximum values, whereas DER and DAR are the pessimistic criteria with a minimum value to be obtained [59,62].

For the optimistic criteria, normalization can be computed as follows.

$$\tilde{p}_{ij} = \left(\frac{a_{ij}}{c_j^+}, \frac{b_{ij}}{c_j^+}, \frac{c_{ij}}{c_j^+} \right), j \in G, c_j^+ = max_i\{c_{ij} : i = 1, 2, 3, \ldots, h\} \quad (7)$$

For the pessimistic criterion, normalization can be performed as follows.

$$\tilde{p}_{ij} = \left(\frac{a_j^-}{a_{ij}}, \frac{a_j^-}{b_{ij}}, \frac{a_j^-}{c_{ij}} \right), j \in H, a_j^- = min_i\{a_{ij} : i = 1, 2, 3, \ldots, h\} \quad (8)$$

where G = optimistic criterion and H = pessimistic criterion.

Step-7: Calculate the weighted normalized fuzzy decision matrix, $\tilde{v}_{ij}$ by multiplying the normalized fuzzy decision matrix, $\tilde{p}_{ij}$, with the entropy weight of criteria, w_j.

$$\tilde{v}_{ij} = \tilde{p}_{ij} \times w_j \quad (9)$$

Step-8: Determine the fuzzy PIS, A^+ and fuzzy NIS, A^-.

$$A^+ = \left(\tilde{v}_1^+, \tilde{v}_2^+, \tilde{v}_3^+, \ldots, \tilde{v}_k^+ \right), \text{ where } \tilde{v}_j^+ = max_i(\tilde{v}_{ij}) \quad (10)$$

$$A^- = \left(\tilde{v}_1^-, \tilde{v}_2^-, \tilde{v}_3^-, \ldots, \tilde{v}_k^- \right), \text{ where } \tilde{v}_j^- = min_i(\tilde{v}_{ij}) \quad (11)$$

Step-9: Calculate the extent of every alternative with A^+ and A^-.

Extent of alternative to A^+:

$$d\left(\tilde{v}_{ij}, \tilde{v}_j^+\right) = \sqrt{\frac{1}{3}[(a_{ij} - a_j^+)^2 + (b_{ij} - b_j^+)^2 + (c_{ij} - c_j^+)^2]} \quad (12)$$

Extent of alternative to A^-:

$$d\left(\tilde{v}_{ij}, \tilde{v}_j^-\right) = \sqrt{\frac{1}{3}[(a_{ij} - a_j^-)^2 + (b_{ij} - b_j^-)^2 + (c_{ij} - c_j^-)^2]} \quad (13)$$

Step-10: Determine the overall extent of an alternative to A^+, Y_i^+, and A^-, Y_i^-.

$$Y_i^+ = \sum_{j=1}^{k} d\left(\tilde{v}_{ij}, \tilde{v}_j^+\right), \, i = 1,2,3,\ldots,h; j = 1,2,3,\ldots,k \tag{14}$$

$$Y_i^- = \sum_{j=1}^{k} d\left(\tilde{v}_{ij}, \tilde{v}_j^-\right), \, i = 1,2,3,\ldots,h; j = 1,2,3,\ldots,k \tag{15}$$

Step-11: Calculate the closeness coefficient (CC_i) for every alternative [63].

$$CC_i = \frac{Y_i^-}{Y_i^- + Y_i^+} \tag{16}$$

The alternative with the greatest CC_i value is the best alternative, while the remaining alternatives can be ranked based on the descending order of CC_i values [64].

2.2. Validation of the Proposed Model in Portfolio Investment

In this paper, the proposed model is validated in portfolio investment with a real-life case study on the DJIA. The portfolio optimization is determined by the mean-variance (MV) model. The MV model is developed by Markowitz [65] to construct an optimal portfolio to achieve the expected return at a minimum level of risk [66–70]. Furthermore, the investor is assumed to be rational in maximizing returns and minimizing risks. In this study, the top 15 companies, which are determined by the ranking of the proposed model, are selected for portfolio investment. Further, the MV portfolio optimization model is adopted to determine an optimal portfolio [71]. According to the previous studies, the researchers used the MV model to construct the optimal portfolio [72–78].

The MV portfolio optimization model's formulation is demonstrated as follows:

$$\text{Minimize} \sum_{i=1}^{n} \sum_{j=1}^{n} \sigma_{ij} x_i x_j \tag{17}$$

Subject to

$$\sum_{j=1}^{n} x_j = 1 \tag{18}$$

$$\sum_{j=1}^{n} r_j x_j \geq \rho \tag{19}$$

$$x_j \geq 0, \, j = 1,2,3,\ldots,n \tag{20}$$

where

ρ denotes a parameter representing the target rate of return required by an investor,
x_j denotes the weight invested in asset j,
σ_{ij} denotes covariance between assets i and j,
r_j denotes the expected return of asset j per period,
n denotes the number of assets,
x_i denotes weight invested in asset i.

The objective function of the MV portfolio optimization model is to minimize portfolio risk, which is indicated in Equation (17). The purpose of Equation (18) is to make sure that the total of all the weights of assets is equal to one. In addition, Equation (19) is utilized to get the returns at the desired level of return. Moreover, the weights of the assets must be positive. This constraint is presented in Equation (20). The Equation (20) shows that short sales are also not allowed for the MV portfolio optimization model since they require positive weights for assets. Therefore, it is a limitation of the proposed entropy-fuzzy TOPSIS model integrated into a portfolio optimization model for portfolio investment. Equation (21) shows the portfolio mean return [79].

$$r_p = \sum_{j=1}^{n} r_j x_j \qquad (21)$$

where

r_j denotes the expected return of asset j per period,
x_j denotes the weight invested in asset j,
r_p denotes the portfolio's mean return.

The portfolio performance ratio is determined based on the equation below [75].

$$\text{Portfolio performance ratio} = \frac{\text{Portfolio mean return}}{\text{Portfolio risk}} \qquad (22)$$

The performance of the optimal portfolio is compared with the benchmark DJIA in terms of mean return.

3. Empirical Results

The results of this study consist of three sections. Section 3.1 presents the priorities of financial ratios using the entropy weight method as described in Stage 1 of the proposed model. In addition, Section 3.2 presents the financial performance evaluation and ranking of the companies using fuzzy TOPSIS as presented in Stage 2 of the proposed model. Finally, Section 3.3 presents the validation of the proposed entropy-fuzzy TOPSIS model in portfolio investment.

3.1. Priorities of Financial Ratios with Entropy Weight Method

The weights of the financial ratios are determined using the entropy weight method. Table 3 displays the initial decision matrix for the companies with respect to all financial ratios.

Table 3. The initial decision matrix for the companies with respect to all financial ratios.

Companies	CR	QR	DER	DAR	AT	ROA	ROE
MMM	1.7400	1.2100	134.4386	38.3543	0.8386	13.8314	46.3529
AXP	1.1347	1.1347	257.5771	30.3486	0.1673	3.2200	26.5114
AMGN	3.0971	2.8086	256.5757	48.6843	0.3471	10.8200	49.4629
AAPL	1.2629	1.2271	115.2043	30.5629	0.8043	18.1143	63.9543
BA	1.2271	0.3586	1329.2100	21.0657	0.7671	2.1971	459.5800
CAT	1.3829	0.9800	253.5143	47.2471	0.6043	4.8886	26.2443
CVX	1.1529	0.9314	25.5686	14.8700	0.5257	2.2371	3.8286
CSCO	2.3329	2.2757	48.2171	21.1129	0.4557	9.7943	22.5071
KO	1.1343	1.0000	203.8743	50.3757	0.4314	8.4271	35.9286
DOW	1.8500	1.3250	97.3975	25.7400	0.7033	3.3433	14.1867
GS	1.1002	1.1002	435.3043	39.2800	0.0474	1.0057	11.8657
HD	1.2171	0.3671	810.5420	55.6857	2.2414	20.1857	2932.2020
HON	1.3257	1.0786	93.5800	29.1529	0.6686	9.3443	29.0271
IBM	1.1357	1.0929	272.6314	38.0429	0.5557	7.3100	54.6171
INTC	1.8657	1.5014	38.5686	22.0929	0.5400	13.3329	23.1929
JNJ	1.6200	1.3543	45.9986	18.8486	0.5200	10.2650	25.0067
JPM	1.1050	1.1050	195.3814	18.5686	0.0396	1.1443	12.7429
MCD	1.6629	1.6443	340.3300	76.9371	0.5857	14.4514	118.6800
MRK	1.3371	1.0800	85.3800	29.6357	0.4529	6.5629	18.8200
MSFT	2.5386	2.5000	72.3214	26.8100	0.4843	12.9114	34.0871
NKE	2.5714	1.7586	48.5114	17.7286	1.5000	16.1900	36.4957
PG	0.8729	0.7043	60.3671	25.9871	0.5614	8.1900	18.8129
CRM	0.9786	0.9792	27.0286	11.7143	0.4929	1.8514	3.1914
TRV	1.3065	1.3065	26.2729	6.1457	0.2838	2.6986	11.3929
UNH	1.5156	1.5156	72.0386	24.2114	1.5049	7.6743	22.6257
VZ	0.9100	0.8650	271.4600	42.2200	0.4786	6.3843	50.7843
V	1.7543	1.7551	46.2486	21.9929	0.3029	14.1786	30.5643
WBA	0.9600	0.5214	61.7471	22.5371	1.7414	5.0429	12.5686
WMT	0.8686	0.2686	59.2043	22.7214	2.3871	6.2714	16.4629
DIS	1.0129	0.9414	49.9386	24.2100	0.5100	7.1771	14.2443

Next, the initial decision matrix is normalized to form the normalized decision matrix as presented in Table 4.

Table 4. The normalized decision matrix for the companies with respect to all financial ratios.

Companies	CR	QR	DER	DAR	AT	ROA	ROE
MMM	0.0396	0.0330	0.0230	0.0425	0.0389	0.0555	0.0110
AXP	0.0258	0.0309	0.0441	0.0336	0.0078	0.0129	0.0063
AMGN	0.0704	0.0765	0.0440	0.0539	0.0161	0.0434	0.0117
AAPL	0.0287	0.0334	0.0197	0.0339	0.0373	0.0727	0.0151
BA	0.0279	0.0098	0.2278	0.0233	0.0356	0.0088	0.1088
CAT	0.0314	0.0267	0.0435	0.0523	0.0280	0.0196	0.0062
CVX	0.0262	0.0254	0.0044	0.0165	0.0244	0.0090	0.0009
CSCO	0.0531	0.0620	0.0083	0.0234	0.0212	0.0393	0.0053
KO	0.0258	0.0273	0.0349	0.0558	0.0200	0.0338	0.0085
DOW	0.0421	0.0361	0.0167	0.0285	0.0326	0.0134	0.0034
GS	0.0250	0.0300	0.0746	0.0435	0.0022	0.0040	0.0028
HD	0.0277	0.0100	0.1389	0.0617	0.1040	0.0811	0.6939
HON	0.0301	0.0294	0.0160	0.0323	0.0310	0.0375	0.0069
IBM	0.0258	0.0298	0.0467	0.0421	0.0258	0.0294	0.0129
INTC	0.0424	0.0409	0.0066	0.0245	0.0251	0.0535	0.0055
JNJ	0.0368	0.0369	0.0079	0.0209	0.0241	0.0412	0.0059
JPM	0.0251	0.0301	0.0335	0.0206	0.0018	0.0046	0.0030
MCD	0.0378	0.0448	0.0583	0.0852	0.0272	0.0580	0.0281
MRK	0.0304	0.0294	0.0146	0.0328	0.0210	0.0264	0.0045
MSFT	0.0577	0.0681	0.0124	0.0297	0.0225	0.0518	0.0081
NKE	0.0585	0.0479	0.0083	0.0196	0.0696	0.0650	0.0086
PG	0.0198	0.0192	0.0103	0.0288	0.0261	0.0329	0.0045
CRM	0.0223	0.0267	0.0046	0.0130	0.0229	0.0074	0.0008
TRV	0.0297	0.0356	0.0045	0.0068	0.0132	0.0108	0.0027
UNH	0.0345	0.0413	0.0123	0.0268	0.0699	0.0308	0.0054
VZ	0.0207	0.0236	0.0465	0.0468	0.0222	0.0256	0.0120
V	0.0399	0.0478	0.0079	0.0244	0.0141	0.0569	0.0072
WBA	0.0218	0.0142	0.0106	0.0250	0.0808	0.0202	0.0030
WMT	0.0198	0.0073	0.0101	0.0252	0.1108	0.0252	0.0039
DIS	0.0230	0.0257	0.0086	0.0268	0.0237	0.0288	0.0034

After that, the information entropy (e_j) and the entropy weight (w_j) of the financial ratios are determined as shown in Table 5.

Table 5. The information entropy (e_j) and the entropy weight (w_j) of the financial ratios.

Financial Ratio	CR	QR	DER	DAR	AT	ROA	ROE
e_j	0.9816	0.9681	0.8271	0.9681	0.9215	0.9403	0.4190
w_j	0.0188	0.0328	0.1774	0.0327	0.0806	0.0613	0.5964

Based on Table 5, the information entropy (e_j) for CR, QR, DER, DAR, AT, ROA, and ROE are 0.9816, 0.9681, 0.8271, 0.9681, 0.9215, 0.9403, and 0.4190, respectively. Next, the entropy weight (w_j) of the financial ratios can be determined. Figure 2 displays the entropy weights of the financial ratios.

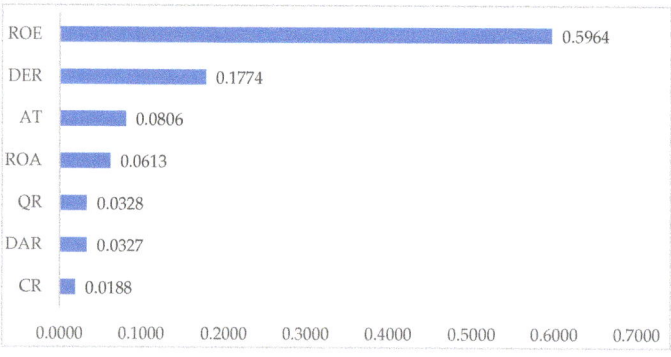

Figure 2. Entropy weights of financial ratios.

According to Figure 2, the weights of financial ratios are determined using the entropy weight method. Based on the results, ROE is identified as the most influential financial ratio in determining the companies' financial performance. The ROE has the highest weight of 0.5964. In addition, the DER achieves the second highest weight of 0.1774. The AT obtained a weight of 0.0806, followed by ROA (0.0613), QR (0.0328), DAR (0.0327), and finally CR (0.0188).

3.2. Financial Performance Evaluation and Ranking of Companies with the Proposed Entropy-Fuzzy TOPSIS Model

The financial performance of the companies is assessed by the proposed entropy-fuzzy TOPSIS model. The initial decision matrix from Table 3 is used to assess the financial performance and determine the ranking of the companies. Initially, the ratings from Table 3 are converted into TFNs, and then the fuzzy decision matrix is formed. This conversion is based on where the rating will fall between the intervals of minimum value and maximum value for each financial ratio. The fuzzy decision matrix for the companies with respect to all financial ratios is shown in Table 6.

Table 6. The fuzzy decision matrix for the companies with respect to all financial ratios.

Companies	CR	QR	DER	DAR	AT	ROA	ROE
MMM	(1, 3, 5)	(1, 3, 5)	(1, 1, 3)	(3, 5, 7)	(1, 3, 5)	(5, 7, 9)	(1, 1, 3)
AXP	(1, 1, 3)	(1, 3, 5)	(1, 1, 3)	(1, 3, 5)	(1, 1, 3)	(1, 1, 3)	(1, 1, 3)
AMGN	(7, 9, 9)	(7, 9, 9)	(1, 1, 3)	(5, 7, 9)	(1, 1, 3)	(3, 5, 7)	(1, 1, 3)
AAPL	(1, 1, 3)	(1, 3, 5)	(1, 1, 3)	(1, 3, 5)	(1, 3, 5)	(7, 9, 9)	(1, 1, 3)
BA	(1, 1, 3)	(1, 1, 3)	(7, 9, 9)	(1, 3, 5)	(1, 3, 5)	(1, 1, 3)	(1, 1, 3)
CAT	(1, 3, 5)	(1, 3, 5)	(1, 1, 3)	(3, 5, 7)	(1, 3, 5)	(1, 3, 5)	(1, 1, 3)
CVX	(1, 1, 3)	(1, 3, 5)	(1, 1, 3)	(1, 1, 3)	(1, 3, 5)	(1, 1, 3)	(1, 1, 3)
CSCO	(5, 7, 9)	(5, 7, 9)	(1, 1, 3)	(1, 3, 5)	(1, 1, 3)	(3, 5, 7)	(1, 1, 3)
KO	(1, 1, 3)	(1, 3, 5)	(1, 1, 3)	(5, 7, 9)	(1, 1, 3)	(1, 3, 5)	(1, 1, 3)
DOW	(3, 5, 7)	(3, 5, 7)	(1, 1, 3)	(1, 3, 5)	(1, 3, 5)	(1, 1, 3)	(1, 1, 3)
GS	(1, 1, 3)	(1, 3, 5)	(1, 3, 5)	(3, 5, 7)	(1, 1, 3)	(1, 1, 3)	(1, 1, 3)
HD	(1, 1, 3)	(1, 1, 3)	(5, 7, 9)	(5, 7, 9)	(7, 9, 9)	(7, 9, 9)	(7, 9, 9)
HON	(1, 3, 5)	(1, 3, 5)	(1, 1, 3)	(1, 3, 5)	(1, 3, 5)	(3, 5, 7)	(1, 1, 3)
IBM	(1, 1, 3)	(1, 3, 5)	(1, 1, 3)	(3, 5, 7)	(1, 1, 3)	(1, 3, 5)	(1, 1, 3)
INTC	(3, 5, 7)	(3, 5, 7)	(1, 1, 3)	(1, 3, 5)	(1, 3, 5)	(5, 7, 9)	(1, 1, 3)
JNJ	(1, 3, 5)	(3, 5, 7)	(1, 1, 3)	(1, 1, 3)	(1, 3, 5)	(3, 5, 7)	(1, 1, 3)
JPM	(1, 1, 3)	(1, 3, 5)	(1, 1, 3)	(1, 1, 3)	(1, 1, 3)	(1, 1, 3)	(1, 1, 3)
MCD	(1, 3, 5)	(3, 5, 7)	(1, 3, 5)	(7, 9, 9)	(1, 3, 5)	(5, 7, 9)	(1, 1, 3)
MRK	(1, 3, 5)	(1, 3, 5)	(1, 1, 3)	(1, 3, 5)	(1, 1, 3)	(1, 3, 5)	(1, 1, 3)
MSFT	(5, 7, 9)	(7, 9, 9)	(1, 1, 3)	(1, 3, 5)	(1, 1, 3)	(5, 7, 9)	(1, 1, 3)
NKE	(5, 7, 9)	(3, 5, 7)	(1, 1, 3)	(1, 1, 3)	(5, 7, 9)	(5, 7, 9)	(1, 1, 3)
PG	(1, 1, 3)	(1, 1, 3)	(1, 1, 3)	(1, 3, 5)	(1, 3, 5)	(1, 3, 5)	(1, 1, 3)
CRM	(1, 1, 3)	(1, 3, 5)	(1, 1, 3)	(1, 1, 3)	(1, 1, 3)	(1, 1, 3)	(1, 1, 3)
TRV	(1, 1, 3)	(3, 5, 7)	(1, 1, 3)	(1, 1, 3)	(1, 1, 3)	(1, 1, 3)	(1, 1, 3)
UNH	(1, 3, 5)	(3, 5, 7)	(1, 1, 3)	(1, 3, 5)	(5, 7, 9)	(1, 3, 5)	(1, 1, 3)
VZ	(1, 1, 3)	(1, 3, 5)	(1, 1, 3)	(3, 5, 7)	(1, 1, 3)	(1, 3, 5)	(1, 1, 3)
V	(1, 3, 5)	(3, 5, 7)	(1, 1, 3)	(1, 3, 5)	(1, 1, 3)	(5, 7, 9)	(1, 1, 3)
WBA	(1, 1, 3)	(1, 1, 3)	(1, 1, 3)	(1, 3, 5)	(5, 7, 9)	(1, 3, 5)	(1, 1, 3)
WMT	(1, 1, 3)	(1, 1, 3)	(1, 1, 3)	(1, 3, 5)	(7, 9, 9)	(1, 3, 5)	(1, 1, 3)
DIS	(1, 1, 3)	(1, 3, 5)	(1, 1, 3)	(1, 3, 5)	(1, 3, 5)	(1, 3, 5)	(1, 1, 3)

For the fuzzy decision matrix, all the financial ratios for each company are translated into TFNs due to the presence of uncertainty and ambiguity in the data. Next, the normalized fuzzy decision matrix is created by normalizing the fuzzy decision matrix. The weighted normalized fuzzy decision matrix is formed by multiplying the normalized fuzzy decision matrix with the entropy weights of the financial ratios. The weighted normalized fuzzy decision matrix for the companies with respect to their financial ratios is presented in Table 7.

Table 7. The weighted normalized fuzzy decision matrix for the companies with respect to all financial ratios.

Companies	CR	QR	DER	DAR	AT	ROA	ROE
MMM	(0.002, 0.006, 0.010)	(0.004, 0.011, 0.018)	(0.059, 0.177, 0.177)	(0.005, 0.007, 0.011)	(0.009, 0.027, 0.045)	(0.034, 0.048, 0.061)	(0.066, 0.066, 0.199)
AXP	(0.002, 0.002, 0.006)	(0.004, 0.011, 0.018)	(0.059, 0.177, 0.177)	(0.007, 0.011, 0.033)	(0.009, 0.009, 0.027)	(0.007, 0.007, 0.020)	(0.066, 0.066, 0.199)
AMGN	(0.015, 0.019, 0.019)	(0.025, 0.033, 0.033)	(0.059, 0.177, 0.177)	(0.004, 0.005, 0.007)	(0.009, 0.009, 0.027)	(0.020, 0.034, 0.048)	(0.066, 0.066, 0.199)
AAPL	(0.002, 0.002, 0.006)	(0.004, 0.011, 0.018)	(0.059, 0.177, 0.177)	(0.007, 0.011, 0.033)	(0.009, 0.027, 0.045)	(0.048, 0.061, 0.061)	(0.066, 0.066, 0.199)
BA	(0.002, 0.002, 0.006)	(0.004, 0.004, 0.011)	(0.020, 0.020, 0.025)	(0.007, 0.011, 0.033)	(0.009, 0.027, 0.045)	(0.007, 0.007, 0.020)	(0.066, 0.066, 0.199)
CAT	(0.002, 0.006, 0.010)	(0.004, 0.011, 0.018)	(0.059, 0.177, 0.177)	(0.005, 0.007, 0.011)	(0.009, 0.027, 0.045)	(0.007, 0.020, 0.034)	(0.066, 0.066, 0.199)
CVX	(0.002, 0.002, 0.006)	(0.004, 0.011, 0.018)	(0.059, 0.177, 0.177)	(0.011, 0.033, 0.033)	(0.009, 0.027, 0.045)	(0.007, 0.007, 0.020)	(0.066, 0.066, 0.199)
CSCO	(0.010, 0.015, 0.019)	(0.018, 0.025, 0.033)	(0.059, 0.177, 0.177)	(0.007, 0.011, 0.033)	(0.009, 0.009, 0.027)	(0.020, 0.034, 0.048)	(0.066, 0.066, 0.199)
KO	(0.002, 0.002, 0.006)	(0.004, 0.011, 0.018)	(0.059, 0.177, 0.177)	(0.004, 0.005, 0.007)	(0.009, 0.009, 0.027)	(0.007, 0.020, 0.034)	(0.066, 0.066, 0.199)
DOW	(0.006, 0.010, 0.015)	(0.011, 0.018, 0.025)	(0.059, 0.177, 0.177)	(0.007, 0.011, 0.033)	(0.009, 0.027, 0.045)	(0.007, 0.007, 0.020)	(0.066, 0.066, 0.199)
GS	(0.002, 0.002, 0.006)	(0.004, 0.011, 0.018)	(0.035, 0.059, 0.177)	(0.005, 0.007, 0.011)	(0.009, 0.009, 0.027)	(0.007, 0.007, 0.020)	(0.066, 0.066, 0.199)
HD	(0.002, 0.002, 0.006)	(0.004, 0.004, 0.011)	(0.020, 0.025, 0.035)	(0.004, 0.005, 0.007)	(0.063, 0.081, 0.081)	(0.048, 0.061, 0.061)	(0.464, 0.596, 0.596)
HON	(0.002, 0.006, 0.010)	(0.004, 0.011, 0.018)	(0.059, 0.177, 0.177)	(0.007, 0.011, 0.033)	(0.009, 0.027, 0.045)	(0.020, 0.034, 0.048)	(0.066, 0.066, 0.199)
IBM	(0.002, 0.002, 0.006)	(0.004, 0.011, 0.018)	(0.059, 0.177, 0.177)	(0.005, 0.007, 0.011)	(0.009, 0.027, 0.045)	(0.007, 0.020, 0.034)	(0.066, 0.066, 0.199)
INTC	(0.006, 0.010, 0.015)	(0.011, 0.018, 0.025)	(0.059, 0.177, 0.177)	(0.007, 0.011, 0.033)	(0.009, 0.027, 0.045)	(0.034, 0.048, 0.061)	(0.066, 0.066, 0.199)
JNJ	(0.002, 0.006, 0.010)	(0.011, 0.018, 0.025)	(0.059, 0.177, 0.177)	(0.011, 0.033, 0.033)	(0.009, 0.027, 0.045)	(0.020, 0.034, 0.048)	(0.066, 0.066, 0.199)
JPM	(0.002, 0.002, 0.006)	(0.004, 0.011, 0.018)	(0.059, 0.177, 0.177)	(0.011, 0.033, 0.033)	(0.009, 0.009, 0.027)	(0.007, 0.007, 0.020)	(0.066, 0.066, 0.199)
MCD	(0.002, 0.006, 0.010)	(0.011, 0.018, 0.025)	(0.035, 0.059, 0.177)	(0.004, 0.004, 0.005)	(0.009, 0.027, 0.045)	(0.034, 0.048, 0.061)	(0.066, 0.066, 0.199)
MRK	(0.002, 0.006, 0.010)	(0.004, 0.011, 0.018)	(0.059, 0.177, 0.177)	(0.007, 0.011, 0.033)	(0.009, 0.009, 0.027)	(0.007, 0.020, 0.034)	(0.066, 0.066, 0.199)
MSFT	(0.010, 0.015, 0.019)	(0.025, 0.033, 0.033)	(0.059, 0.177, 0.177)	(0.007, 0.011, 0.033)	(0.009, 0.009, 0.027)	(0.034, 0.048, 0.061)	(0.066, 0.066, 0.199)
NKE	(0.010, 0.015, 0.019)	(0.011, 0.018, 0.025)	(0.059, 0.177, 0.177)	(0.011, 0.033, 0.033)	(0.045, 0.063, 0.081)	(0.034, 0.048, 0.061)	(0.066, 0.066, 0.199)
PG	(0.002, 0.002, 0.006)	(0.004, 0.004, 0.011)	(0.059, 0.177, 0.177)	(0.007, 0.011, 0.033)	(0.009, 0.027, 0.045)	(0.007, 0.020, 0.034)	(0.066, 0.066, 0.199)
CRM	(0.002, 0.002, 0.006)	(0.004, 0.011, 0.018)	(0.059, 0.177, 0.177)	(0.011, 0.033, 0.033)	(0.009, 0.009, 0.027)	(0.007, 0.007, 0.020)	(0.066, 0.066, 0.199)
TRV	(0.002, 0.002, 0.006)	(0.011, 0.018, 0.025)	(0.059, 0.177, 0.177)	(0.011, 0.033, 0.033)	(0.009, 0.009, 0.027)	(0.007, 0.007, 0.020)	(0.066, 0.066, 0.199)
UNH	(0.002, 0.006, 0.010)	(0.011, 0.018, 0.025)	(0.059, 0.177, 0.177)	(0.007, 0.011, 0.033)	(0.045, 0.063, 0.081)	(0.007, 0.020, 0.034)	(0.066, 0.066, 0.199)
VZ	(0.002, 0.002, 0.006)	(0.004, 0.011, 0.018)	(0.059, 0.177, 0.177)	(0.005, 0.007, 0.011)	(0.009, 0.009, 0.027)	(0.007, 0.020, 0.034)	(0.066, 0.066, 0.199)
V	(0.002, 0.006, 0.010)	(0.011, 0.018, 0.025)	(0.059, 0.177, 0.177)	(0.007, 0.011, 0.033)	(0.009, 0.009, 0.027)	(0.034, 0.048, 0.061)	(0.066, 0.066, 0.199)
WBA	(0.002, 0.002, 0.006)	(0.004, 0.004, 0.011)	(0.059, 0.177, 0.177)	(0.007, 0.011, 0.033)	(0.045, 0.063, 0.081)	(0.007, 0.020, 0.034)	(0.066, 0.066, 0.199)
WMT	(0.002, 0.002, 0.006)	(0.004, 0.004, 0.011)	(0.059, 0.177, 0.177)	(0.007, 0.011, 0.033)	(0.063, 0.081, 0.081)	(0.007, 0.020, 0.034)	(0.066, 0.066, 0.199)
DIS	(0.002, 0.002, 0.006)	(0.004, 0.011, 0.018)	(0.059, 0.177, 0.177)	(0.007, 0.011, 0.033)	(0.009, 0.027, 0.045)	(0.007, 0.020, 0.034)	(0.066, 0.066, 0.199)

The fuzzy PIS (A^+) and the fuzzy NIS (A^-) for each financial ratio are determined and shown in Table 8.

Table 8. The fuzzy PIS (A^+) and the fuzzy NIS (A^-).

Financial Ratio	CR	QR	DER	DAR	AT	ROA	ROE
A^+	(0.015, 0.019, 0.019)	(0.025, 0.033, 0.033)	(0.059, 0.177, 0.177)	(0.011, 0.033, 0.033)	(0.063, 0.081, 0.081)	(0.048, 0.061, 0.061)	(0.464, 0.596, 0.596)
A^-	(0.002, 0.002, 0.006)	(0.004, 0.004, 0.011)	(0.020, 0.020, 0.025)	(0.004, 0.004, 0.005)	(0.009, 0.009, 0.027)	(0.007, 0.007, 0.020)	(0.066, 0.066, 0.199)

The fuzzy PIS (A^+) and the fuzzy NIS (A^-) for each financial ratio in the weighted normalized fuzzy decision matrix are established. In this study, the fuzzy PIS (A^+) for CR, QR, DER, DAR, AT, ROA, and ROE are (0.015, 0.019, 0.019), (0.025, 0.033, 0.033), (0.059, 0.177, 0.177), (0.011, 0.033, 0.033), (0.063, 0.081, 0.081), (0.048, 0.061, 0.061), and (0.464, 0.596, 0.596) respectively. On the other hand, the fuzzy NIS (A^-) for CR, QR, DER, DAR, AT, ROA, and ROE are (0.002, 0.002, 0.006), (0.004, 0.004, 0.011), (0.020, 0.020, 0.025), (0.004, 0.004, 0.005), (0.009, 0.009, 0.027), (0.007, 0.007, 0.020), and (0.066, 0.066, 0.199), respectively.

For the next step, the extent of each company from the fuzzy PIS and the fuzzy NIS is computed and presented in Table 9.

Table 9. Extent of all companies with fuzzy PIS and fuzzy NIS.

Companies	Extent with Fuzzy PIS	Extent with Fuzzy NIS
MMM	0.557	0.193
AXP	0.599	0.151
AMGN	0.553	0.192
AAPL	0.541	0.212
BA	0.720	0.031
CAT	0.583	0.168
CVX	0.574	0.173
CSCO	0.552	0.200
KO	0.600	0.147
DOW	0.573	0.180
GS	0.676	0.101
HD	0.183	0.560
HON	0.562	0.193
IBM	0.585	0.164
INTC	0.538	0.217
JNJ	0.542	0.206
JPM	0.586	0.158
MCD	0.623	0.159
MRK	0.587	0.166
MSFT	0.534	0.218
NKE	0.488	0.262
PG	0.583	0.171
CRM	0.586	0.158
TRV	0.579	0.165
UNH	0.534	0.221
VZ	0.597	0.150
V	0.554	0.198
WBA	0.549	0.205
WMT	0.534	0.217
DIS	0.578	0.177

After that, the closeness coefficients of the companies are determined. The companies' rankings are determined based on the closeness coefficients achieved. Table 10 presents the entropy-fuzzy TOPSIS closeness coefficients as well as the ranking of companies.

Table 10. The entropy-fuzzy TOPSIS closeness coefficients and ranking of companies.

Companies	Entropy-Fuzzy TOPSIS Closeness Coefficients	Ranking
MMM	0.2578	13
AXP	0.2017	26
AMGN	0.2578	12
AAPL	0.2812	7
BA	0.0418	30
CAT	0.2235	19
CVX	0.2313	17
CSCO	0.2659	10
KO	0.1967	28
DOW	0.2388	15
GS	0.1302	29
HD	0.7534	1
HON	0.2555	14
IBM	0.2191	22
INTC	0.2870	6
JNJ	0.2758	8
JPM	0.2125	23
MCD	0.2030	25
MRK	0.2202	21
MSFT	0.2900	4
NKE	0.3490	2
PG	0.2269	18
CRM	0.2125	23
TRV	0.2216	20
UNH	0.2925	3
VZ	0.2004	27
V	0.2634	11
WBA	0.2718	9
WMT	0.2885	5
DIS	0.2344	16

3.3. Validation of the Proposed Entropy-Fuzzy TOPSIS Model in Portfolio Investment

Finally, the validation of the proposed entropy-fuzzy TOPSIS model in portfolio investment is performed with a real-world case study on DJIA. Based on the proposed model, the optimal MV portfolio is determined by the selected companies with good financial performance. Table 11 presents the summary statistics and performance of the optimal MV portfolio.

Table 11. Summary statistics and performance of the optimal MV portfolio.

Optimal Portfolio	Value
Portfolio mean return	0.0225
Portfolio risk	0.0445
Portfolio performance ratio	0.5056
DJIA index return (Benchmark)	0.0095

According to Table 10, the values of the closeness coefficients are determined based on the proposed entropy-fuzzy TOPSIS model. A larger value of the closeness coefficients implies the most performing companies. Based on the results, the closeness coefficients of the companies range from 0.0418 to 0.7534. Among the companies, HD is identified as the best company in terms of financial performance, with the largest closeness coefficient of 0.7534. This implies that HD has the closest proximity to the ideal solution, considering the presence of uncertainty and fuzziness in the data. As a result, HD outperforms other companies and thus achieves the first ranking based on the proposed entropy-fuzzy TOPSIS model. The second ranking is obtained by NKE, followed by UNH, MSFT, WMT, INTC,

AAPL, JNJ, WBA, CSCO, V, AMGN, MMM, HON, DOW, DIS, CVX, PG, CAT, TRV, MRK, IBM, JPM, CRM, MCD, AXP, VZ, KO, GS, and finally BA. In this study, BA scored the lowest value of 0.0418. Additionally, this study has indicated that there are ample opportunities for the companies with low performances to make continuous improvements by considering the good companies for future benchmarking.

The entropy-fuzzy TOPSIS model is proposed in this paper because the fuzzy analysis takes the vagueness and uncertainty of the data into account. The results of this study are converted into TFNs, and then the fuzzy decision matrix is formed. The fuzzy method is taken into consideration in this study since uncertainty and vagueness of data are involved. In this paper, the companies' financial performances are assessed by seven important financial ratios, which are CR, QR, DER, DAR, AT, ROA, and ROE. After analyzing the financial ratios with the entropy weight method, the weights and priorities of the financial ratios are determined. The financial ratio with the highest weight is ROE, followed by DER, AT, ROA, QR, DAR, and CR. In this research, an entropy-fuzzy TOPSIS model is proposed to evaluate the financial performances of companies based on liquidity, solvency, efficiency, and profitability ratios to determine the companies with good financial performance for portfolio investment.

According to Table 11, the proposed model generates a portfolio mean return of 0.0225 at a portfolio risk of 0.0445. The proposed model gives a portfolio performance ratio of 0.5056. The results of this study show that the optimal MV portfolio of the proposed model is able to generate a higher mean return (0.0225) than the benchmark DJIA index return (0.0095). Therefore, it shows the effectiveness of the proposed model, which outperforms the benchmark DJIA index with a higher mean return. The proposed model provides insights to the investors in identifying and selecting the good performing companies in terms of financial performance for portfolio investment.

4. Conclusions

In this paper, an entropy-fuzzy TOPSIS model is proposed to evaluate the financial performance of companies based on liquidity, solvency, efficiency, and profitability ratios to determine the companies with good financial performance for portfolio investment. The proposed entropy-fuzzy TOPSIS model consists of two stages. The first stage involves Shannon's entropy weight method to determine the objective weights of the financial ratios, which are CR, QR, AT, DER, DAR, ROA, and ROE. In this study, ROE and DER are identified as the influential financial ratios for the financial performance evaluation of companies which are the components of the DJIA. The second stage includes the fuzzy TOPSIS model to assess and rank the companies based on their financial performance. Regarding the ranking of the companies, HD is determined to be the best company, followed by NKE, UNH, MSFT, WMT, INTC, and AAPL. The companies with good financial performance have been determined based on the proposed model for portfolio selection.

The validation of the proposed entropy-fuzzy TOPSIS model in portfolio investment is performed using the MV model. Based on the proposed model, the optimal MV portfolio is determined by the selected companies with good financial performance. The results indicate that the proposed model is able to generate an optimal MV portfolio with higher mean return than the benchmark DJIA index. This implies that the proposed model outperforms the benchmark DJIA index with a higher portfolio mean return based on the selection of well-performing companies. This study provides insights to investors in portfolio investment. The investors can determine an optimal portfolio from the well-performing companies in terms of financial performance for portfolio investment based on the proposed model. The limitation of the proposed model is that it does not allow short selling in portfolio investment.

The companies could embark on making decisions and taking initiatives to enhance the top financial ratios to improve their financial performance. The financial ratios used in this research include liquidity, solvency, efficiency, and profitability ratios. Based on the integration of fuzzy in the proposed model, uncertainties in financial data can be reduced, which is important for decision making in financing, expansion, and growth. Future studies could consider the application of the proposed entropy-fuzzy TOPSIS model for portfolio investment in other stock markets, such as developed, emerging, or developing markets.

Author Contributions: Conceptualization, W.H.L. and W.S.L.; methodology, W.H.L., W.S.L. and K.F.L.; software, W.H.L., W.S.L. and K.F.L.; validation, W.H.L., W.S.L. and P.F.L.; formal analysis, W.H.L., W.S.L., K.F.L. and P.F.L.; investigation, W.H.L., W.S.L., K.F.L. and P.F.L.; resources, W.H.L. and W.S.L.; data curation, W.H.L., W.S.L., K.F.L. and P.F.L.; writing—original draft preparation, W.H.L., W.S.L., K.F.L. and P.F.L.; writing—review and editing, W.H.L., W.S.L., K.F.L. and P.F.L.; supervision, W.H.L. and W.S.L. All authors have read and agreed to the published version of the manuscript.

Funding: This research received no external funding.

Data Availability Statement: The data presented in this study are available on request from the corresponding author.

Acknowledgments: This research is supported by the Universiti Tunku Abdul Rahman, Malaysia.

Conflicts of Interest: The authors declare no conflict of interest.

References

1. Barcellos-Paula, L.; la Vega, I.D.; Gil-Lafuente, A.M. The quintuple helix of innovation model and the SDGs: Latin-American countries' case and its forgotten effects. *Mathematics* **2021**, *9*, 416. [CrossRef]
2. Lafuente-Lechuga, M.; Cifuentes-Faura, J.; Faura-Martínez, U. Sustainability, Big Data and Mathematical Techniques: A Bibliometric Review. *Mathematics* **2021**, *9*, 2557. [CrossRef]
3. Safitri, Y.; Ningsih, R.D.; Agustianingsih, D.P.; Sukhwani, V.; Kato, A.; Shaw, R. COVID-19 Impact on SDGs and the Fiscal Measures: Case of Indonesia. *Int. J. Environ. Res. Public Health* **2021**, *18*, 2911. [CrossRef] [PubMed]
4. Suriyankietkaew, S.; Nimsai, S. COVID-19 impacts and sustainability strategies for regional recovery in Southeast Asia: Challenges and opportunities. *Sustainability* **2021**, *13*, 8907. [CrossRef]
5. International Monetary Fund. Fiscal Monitor: Policy for the Recovery. Washington, WA, USA, 2020. Available online: https://www.imf.org/en/Publications/FM/Issues/2020/09/30/october-2020-fiscal-monitor (accessed on 25 December 2021).
6. Sachs, J.; Schmidt-Traub, G.; Kroll, C.; Lafortune, G.; Fuller, G.; Woelm, F. The Sustainable Development Goals and COVID-19. In *Sustainable Development Report 2020*; Cambridge University Press: Cambridge, UK, 2020. Available online: https://s3.amazonaws.com/sustainabledevelopment.report/2020/2020_sustainable_development_report.pdf (accessed on 25 December 2021).
7. Donthu, N.; Gustafsson, A. Effects of COVID-19 on business and research. *J. Bus. Res.* **2020**, *117*, 284–289. [CrossRef]
8. Nikkei Asia. Dow Closes Down 430 Points on Omicron Fears. 2021. Available online: https://asia.nikkei.com/Business/Markets/Dow-closes-down-430-points-on-omicron-fears (accessed on 25 December 2021).
9. Bachman, D. United States Economic Forecast. 2021. Available online: https://www2.deloitte.com/us/en/insights/economy/us-economic-forecast/united-states-outlook-analysis.html (accessed on 25 December 2021).
10. Batrancea, L.M. An Econometric Approach on Performance, Assets, and Liabilities in a Sample of Banks from Europe, Israel, United States of America, and Canada. *Mathematics* **2021**, *9*, 3178. [CrossRef]
11. Batrancea, L. The Nexus between Financial Performance and Equilibrium: Empirical Evidence on Publicly Traded Companies from the Global Financial Crisis Up to the COVID-19 Pandemic. *J. Risk. Finance.* **2021**, *14*, 218. [CrossRef]
12. Achim, M.V.; Safta, I.L.; Văidean, V.L.; Mureșan, G.M.; Borlea, N.S. The impact of covid-19 on financial management: Evidence from Romania. *Econ. Res.-Ekon. Istraz.* **2022**, *35*, 1807–1832. [CrossRef]
13. Karim, M.R.; Shetu, S.A.; Razia, S. COVID-19, liquidity and financial health: Empirical evidence from South Asian economy. *Asian J. Econ. Bank.* **2021**, *5*, 307–323. [CrossRef]
14. Mirza, N.; Rahat, B.; Naqvi, B.; Rizvi, S.K.A. Impact of COVID-19 on corporate solvency and possible policy responses in the EU. *Q. Rev. Econ. Finance.* **2020**. [CrossRef]
15. Zheng, F.; Zhao, Z.; Sun, Y.; Khan, Y.A. Financial performance of China's listed firms in presence of coronavirus: Evidence from corporate culture and corporate social responsibility. *Curr. Psychol.* **2021**. [CrossRef] [PubMed]
16. Vito, A.D.; Gómez, J. Estimating the COVID-19 cash crunch: Global evidence and policy. *J. Account. Public Policy* **2020**, *39*, 106741. [CrossRef]
17. Rababah, A.; Al-Haddad, L.; Sial, M.S.; Chunmei, Z.; Cherian, J. Analyzing the effects of COVID-19 pandemic on the financial performance of Chinese listed companies. *J. Public Affairs* **2020**, *20*, e2440.
18. Ali, S.; Talha, N. During COVID-19, impact of subjective and objective financialknowledge and economic insecurity on financial managementbehavior: Mediating role of financial wellbeing. *J. Public Affairs* **2021**, *22*, e2789.
19. Stojić, G.; Stević, Ž.; Antuchevićienė, J.; Pamučar, D.; Vasiljević, M. A novel rough WASPAS approach for supplier selection in a company manufacturing PVC carpentry products. *Information* **2018**, *9*, 121. [CrossRef]
20. Shaverdi, M.; Ramezani, I.; Tahmasebi, R.; Rostamy, A.A.A. Combining fuzzy AHP and fuzzy TOPSIS with financial ratios to design a novel performance evaluation model. *Int. J. Fuzzy Syst.* **2016**, *18*, 248–262. [CrossRef]

21. Shaverdi, M.; Heshmati, M.R.; Ramezani, I. Application of fuzzy AHP approach for financial performance evaluation of Iranian petrochemical sector. *Procedia Comput. Sci.* **2014**, *31*, 995–1004. [CrossRef]
22. Monga, R.; Aggrawal, D.; Singh, J. Application of AHP in evaluating the financial performance of industries. In *Advances in Mathematics for Industry 4.0*, 1st ed.; Ram, M., Ed.; Academic Press: London, UK, 2020; pp. 319–333.
23. İç, Y.T.; Yurdakul, M.; Pehlivan, E. Development of a hybrid financial performance measurement model using AHP and DOE methods for Turkish commercial banks. *Soft Comput.* **2021**, *26*, 2959–2979. [CrossRef]
24. Chiang, J.; Chiou, C.; Doong, S.; Chang, I. Research on construction of performance indicators for the marketing alliance of catering industry and credit card issuing banks by using the Balanced Scorecard and fuzzy AHP. *Sustainability* **2020**, *12*, 9005. [CrossRef]
25. Bulgurcu, B.K. Application of TOPSIS technique for financial performance evaluation of technology firms in Istanbul Stock Exchange Market. *Procedia Soc. Behav. Sci.* **2012**, *62*, 1033–1040. [CrossRef]
26. Gayathri, C.; Kamala, V.; Gajanand, M.S.; Yamini, S. Analysis of operational and financial performance of ports: An integrated fuzzy DEMATEL-TOPSIS approach. *Benchmarking Int. J.* **2021**, *29*, 1046–1066. [CrossRef]
27. Shannon, C.E. A mathematical theory of communication. *Bell Syst. Tech.* **1948**, *27*, 379–423. [CrossRef]
28. Saraswat, S.K.; Digalwar, A.K. Evaluation of energy alternatives for sustainable development of energy sector in India: An integrated Shannon's entropy fuzzy multicriteria decision approach. *Renew. Energy* **2021**, *171*, 58–74. [CrossRef]
29. Chodha, V.; Dubey, R.; Kumar, R.; Singh, S.; Kaur, S. Selection of industrial arc welding robot with TOPSIS and Entropy MCDM techniques. *Mater. Today Proc.* **2022**, *50*, 709–715. [CrossRef]
30. Li, J.; Chen, Y.; Yao, X.; Chen, A. Risk management priority assessment of heritage sites in China based on entropy weight and TOPSIS. *J. Cult. Herit.* **2021**, *49*, 10–18. [CrossRef]
31. Yang, W.; Xu, K.; Lian, J.; Ma, C.; Bin, L. Integrated flood vulnerability assessment approach based on TOPSIS and Shannon entropy methods. *Ecol. Indic.* **2018**, *89*, 269–280. [CrossRef]
32. Huang, W.; Shuai, B.; Sun, Y.; Wang, Y.; Antwi, E. Using entropy-TOPSIS method to evaluate urban rail transit system operation performance: The China case. *Transp. Res. A* **2018**, *111*, 292–303. [CrossRef]
33. Zadeh, L.A. Fuzzy sets. *Inf. Control.* **1965**, *8*, 338–353. [CrossRef]
34. Hwang, B. Chapter 3—Methodology. In *Performance and Improvement of Green Construction Projects: Management Strategies and Innovations*; Butterworth-Heinemann: Oxford, UK, 2018; pp. 15–22.
35. Nădăban, S.; Dzitac, S.; Dzitac, I. Fuzzy TOPSIS: A general view. *Procedia Comput. Sci.* **2016**, *91*, 823–831. [CrossRef]
36. Sokolović, J.; Stanujkić, D.; Štirbanović, Z. Selection of process for aluminium separation from waste cables by TOPSIS and WASPAS methods. *Miner. Eng.* **2021**, *173*, 107186. [CrossRef]
37. Shamsuzzoha, A.; Piya, S.; Shamsuzzaman, M. Application of fuzzy TOPSIS framework for selecting complex project in a case company. *J. Glob. Oper. Strateg. Sourc.* **2021**, *14*, 528–566. [CrossRef]
38. Palczewski, K.; Sałabun, W. The fuzzy TOPSIS applications in the last decade. *Procedia Comput. Sci.* **2019**, *159*, 2294–2303. [CrossRef]
39. Sahin, B.; Yip, T.L.; Tseng, P.; Kabak, M.; Soylu, A. An application of a fuzzy TOPSIS multi-criteria decision analysis algorithm for dry bulk carrier selection. *Information* **2020**, *11*, 251. [CrossRef]
40. Kabassi, K.; Botonis, A.; Karydis, C. Evaluating websites of specialized cultural content using fuzzy multi-criteria decision making theories. *Informatica* **2020**, *44*, 45–54. [CrossRef]
41. Sharma, N.K.; Kumar, V.; Verma, P.; Luthra, S. Sustainable reverse logistics practices and performance evaluation with fuzzy TOPSIS: A study on Indian retailers. *Clean. Logist. Supply Chain* **2021**, *1*, 100007. [CrossRef]
42. Korol, T. The implementation of fuzzy logic in forecasting financial ratios. *Contemp. Econ.* **2017**, *12*, 165–188.
43. Leal, M.; Ponce, D.; Puerto, J. Portfolio problems with two levels decision-makers: Optimal portfolio selection with pricing decisions on transaction costs. *Eur. J. Oper. Res.* **2020**, *284*, 712–727. [CrossRef]
44. Lahmiri, S.; Bekiros, S. Nonlinear analysis of Casablanca Stock Exchange, Dow Jones and S&P500 industrial sectors with a comparison. *Physica A* **2020**, *539*, 122923.
45. Kamaludin, K.; Sundarasen, S.; Ibrahim, I. Covid-19, Dow Jones and equity market movement in ASEAN-5 countries: Evidence from wavelet analyses. *Heliyon* **2021**, *7*, e05851. [CrossRef] [PubMed]
46. Plastun, A.; Sibande, X.; Gupta, R.; Wohar, M.E. Evolution of price effects after one-day abnormal returns in the US stock market. *N. Am. J. Econ. Finance* **2021**, *57*, 101405. [CrossRef]
47. González, F.F.; Webb, J.; Sharmina, M.; Hannon, M.; Braunholtz-Speight, T.; Pappas, D. Local energy businesses in the United Kingdom: Clusters and localism determinants based on financial ratios. *Energy* **2022**, *239*, 122119. [CrossRef]
48. Messer, R. Common financial ratios. In *Financial Modeling for Decision Making: Using MS-Excel in Accounting and Finance*; Emerald Publishing Limited: Bingley, UK, 2020; p. 325.
49. Batrancea, L. The influence of liquidity and solvency on performance within the healthcare industry: Evidence from publicly listed companies. *Mathematics* **2021**, *9*, 2231. [CrossRef]
50. Horta, I.M.; Camanho, A.S.; da Costa, J.M. Performance assessment of construction companies: A study of factors promoting financial soundness and innovation in the industry. *Int. J. Prod. Econ.* **2012**, *137*, 84–93. [CrossRef]
51. Huang, J.; Wang, H. A data analytics framework for key financial factors. *J. Model. Manag.* **2016**, *12*, 178–189. [CrossRef]

52. Nguyen, L.T.M.; Dinh, P.H. Ex-ante risk management and financial stability during the COVID-19 pandemic: A study of Vietnamese firms. *China Finance Rev. Int.* **2021**, *11*, 349–371. [CrossRef]
53. Wieprow, J.; Gawlik, A. The Use of Discriminant Analysis to Assess the Risk of Bankruptcy of Enterprises in Crisis Conditions Using the Example of the Tourism Sector in Poland. *Risks* **2021**, *9*, 78. [CrossRef]
54. Zorn, A.; Esteves, M.; Baur, I.; Lips, M. Financial Ratios as Indicators of Economic Sustainability: A Quantitative Analysis for Swiss Dairy Farms. *Sustainability* **2018**, *10*, 2942. [CrossRef]
55. Lee, P.T.; Lin, C.; Shin, S. Financial performance evaluation of shipping companies using entropy and grey relation analysis. In *Multi-Criteria Decision Making in Maritime Studies and Logistics*; Lee, P., Yang, Z., Eds.; Springer International Publishing: New York, NY, USA, 2018; pp. 219–247.
56. Yadav, S.K.; Dharani, M. Prioritizing of banking firms in India using entropy-TOPSIS method. *Int. J. Bus. Innov. Res.* **2019**, *20*, 554–570. [CrossRef]
57. Li, Z.; Luo, Z.; Wang, Y.; Fan, G.; Zhang, J. Suitability evaluation system for the shallow geothermal energy implementation in region by Entropy Weight Method and TOPSIS method. *Renew. Energy* **2022**, *184*, 564–576. [CrossRef]
58. Chen, P. Effects of the entropy weight on TOPSIS. *Expert Syst. Appl.* **2021**, *168*, 114186. [CrossRef]
59. Mavi, R.K.; Goh, M.; Mavi, N.K. Supplier selection with Shannon entropy and fuzzy TOPSIS in the context of supply chain risk management. *Procedia Soc. Behav. Sci.* **2016**, *235*, 216–225. [CrossRef]
60. Chen, C.T. Extensions of the TOPSIS for group decision-making under fuzzy environment. *Fuzzy Sets Syst.* **2000**, *114*, 1–9. [CrossRef]
61. Solangi, Y.A.; Cheng, L.; Shah, S.A.A. Assessing and overcoming the renewable energy barriers for sustainable development in Pakistan: An integrated AHP and fuzzy TOPSIS approach. *Renew. Energy* **2021**, *173*, 209–222. [CrossRef]
62. Emovon, I.; Aibuedefe, W.O. Fuzzy TOPSIS application in materials analysis for economic production of cashew juice extractor. *Fuzzy Inf. Eng.* **2020**, *12*, 1–18. [CrossRef]
63. Mathangi, S.; Maran, J.P. Sensory evaluation of apple ber using fuzzy TOPSIS. *Mater. Today Proc.* **2021**, *45*, 2982–2986. [CrossRef]
64. Liu, P. An extended TOPSIS method for multiple attribute group decision making based on generalized interval-valued trapezoidal fuzzy numbers. *Informatica* **2011**, *35*, 185–196.
65. Markowitz, H. Mean–variance approximations to expected utility. *Eur. J. Oper. Res.* **2014**, *234*, 346–355. [CrossRef]
66. Tayali, H.A.; Tolun, S. Dimension reduction in mean-variance portfolio optimization. *Expert Syst. Appl.* **2018**, *92*, 161–169. [CrossRef]
67. Huang, X. Mean–variance models for portfolio selection subject to experts' estimations. *Expert Syst. Appl.* **2012**, *39*, 5887–5893. [CrossRef]
68. Pinasthika, N.; Surya, B.A. Optimal portfolio analysis with risk-free assets using index-tracking and Markowitz mean-variance portfolio optimization model. *J. Bus. Manag.* **2014**, *3*, 737–751.
69. Spaseski, N. Portfolio management: Mean-variance analysis in the US asset market. *Eur. J. Bus. Soc. Sci.* **2014**, *3*, 242–248.
70. Markowitz, H.M. Foundations of portfolio theory. *J. Financ.* **1991**, *46*, 469–477. [CrossRef]
71. Markowitz, H. Portfolio selection. *J. Financ.* **1952**, *7*, 77–91.
72. Xiao, H.; Ren, T.; Zhou, Z. Time-consistent strategies for the generalized multiperiod mean-variance portfolio optimization considering benchmark orientation. *Mathematics* **2019**, *7*, 723. [CrossRef]
73. Lefebvre, W.; Loeper, G.; Pham, H. Mean-variance portfolio selection with tracking error penalization. *Mathematics* **2020**, *8*, 1915–1937. [CrossRef]
74. Aljinović, Z.; Marasović, B.; Šestanović, T. Cryptocurrency portfolio selection—A multicriteria approach. *Mathematics* **2021**, *9*, 1677–1697. [CrossRef]
75. Fernandez-Navarro, F.; Martinez-Nieto, L.; Carbonero-Ruz, M.; Montero-Romero, T. Mean squared variance portfolio: A mixed-integer linear programming formulation. *Mathematics* **2021**, *9*, 223. [CrossRef]
76. Park, H. Modified mean-variance risk measures for long-term portfolios. *Mathematics* **2021**, *9*, 111. [CrossRef]
77. Corsaro, S.; De Simone, V.; Marino, Z.; Scognamiglio, S. l1-Regularization in portfolio selection with machine learning. *Mathematics* **2022**, *10*, 540. [CrossRef]
78. Novais, R.G.; Wanke, P.; Antunes, J.; Tan, Y. Portfolio optimization with a mean-entropy-mutual information model. *Entropy* **2022**, *24*, 369. [CrossRef]
79. Bodie, Z.; Kane, A.; Marcus, A. *Investments*, 12th ed.; McGraw-Hill: New York, NY, USA, 2021.

Disclaimer/Publisher's Note: The statements, opinions and data contained in all publications are solely those of the individual author(s) and contributor(s) and not of MDPI and/or the editor(s). MDPI and/or the editor(s) disclaim responsibility for any injury to people or property resulting from any ideas, methods, instructions or products referred to in the content.

Article

Performance Evaluation of the Efficiency of Logistics Companies with Data Envelopment Analysis Model

Pei Fun Lee, Weng Siew Lam and Weng Hoe Lam *

Department of Physical and Mathematical Science, Faculty of Science, Universiti Tunku Abdul Rahman, Kampar Campus, Jalan Universiti, Bandar Barat, Kampar 31900, Perak, Malaysia
* Correspondence: whlam@utar.edu.my

Abstract: Malaysia has great geo-economic advantages, especially in becoming a major logistics and investment hub. However, as operational risk events create uncertainties, logistics companies suffer from supply and demand issues which affect their bottom lines, customer satisfaction and reputations. This is a pioneer paper to propose the optimization of the efficiency of listed logistics companies in Malaysia with operational risk factor using a data envelopment analysis (DEA) model. The basic indicator approach (BIA) is used as an output indicator for the operational risk capital requirement factor in the proposed model. This paper has practical and managerial implications with the identification of potential improvements for the inefficient listed logistics companies based on the optimal solution of the DEA model. This proposed model can be applied in emerging fields such as finance and project-based construction companies, where operational risk is a high concern.

Keywords: data envelopment analysis; efficiency; operational risk; potential improvement; ranking

MSC: 90B50

1. Introduction

Malaysia has geo-economic advantages in connecting resources to markets for investments and business developments [1]. This natural privilege has increased the bilateral and multilateral trade volumes as major logistics companies make Malaysia a focal hub for their activities [2]. Nevertheless, local logistics companies also contribute to increasing the logistics performance in Malaysia because of the realization that logistics performance has significant relationships with the efficiency of a company and the outputs of the country [3]. Logistics companies typically manage a wide range of activities including transportation, inventories, warehouses, distribution, and information sharing [4]. All these activities are operational wherein an activity will affect subsequent processes in the logistics chain. Thus, logistics companies are highly prone to operational risk. Operational risk includes adverse activities from individuals, internal systems or activities, and some macroeconomic events [5–7].

Poor inventory management could lead to an inadequate number of safety stocks for sudden shift in customer demand, which cause the inability for transport planning and shipment scheduling that prolong lead time, decrease customer satisfaction, and company image, which will influence the company's bottom line. On the other hand, inventory surplus leads to high carrying cost and wastage in times of obsoletion [8]. Many operational risk events are unrecognized while the consequences are hard to be quantified. Lochan et al. [9] found that operational risks induced by demand fluctuation and lead time are the main factors that affect logistics companies financially. This study also found that natural catastrophe, such as fire or COVID-19, prompting a logistics company to shut down for a week, could cause its customer to lose more than USD 180 million in revenue. This shows that logistics companies need to manage their operational risk well because all the activities and processes are highly interdependent. Gurtu and Johny [10] stated

Citation: Lee, P.F.; Lam, W.S.; Lam, W.H. Performance Evaluation of the Efficiency of Logistics Companies with Data Envelopment Analysis Model. *Mathematics* 2023, 11, 718. https://doi.org/10.3390/math11030718

Academic Editors: Qun Li and Aihua Wood

Received: 29 December 2022
Revised: 26 January 2023
Accepted: 28 January 2023
Published: 31 January 2023

Copyright: © 2023 by the authors. Licensee MDPI, Basel, Switzerland. This article is an open access article distributed under the terms and conditions of the Creative Commons Attribution (CC BY) license (https://creativecommons.org/licenses/by/4.0/).

that operational and financial risks are the top concerns which cause major disruption in companies.

The Basel Committee on Banking Supervision (BCBS) presented the basic indicator approach (BIA) to bring down the adverse effects of operational risk [11]. Under BIA, companies could carry a capital of at least the mean of a fixed percentage (alpha) of positive gross income for the last three years [12,13]. BIA has received wide acceptance worldwide [14,15]. Operational risk has a causal relationship with the efficiency of a company, especially in terms of financial performance and should be monitored continuously [16,17]. Bai et al. [18] found that operational risk management could help shipping companies reduce financial risk exposures and increase their efficiency. Th efficiency of the logistics companies can be optimized with the data envelopment analysis (DEA) model [19,20]. DEA is non-parametric model which aims to optimize the efficiency of decision-making units (DMUs) under various inputs and outputs [21,22]. Efficiency is measured by the outputs over inputs, wherein bigger outputs or smaller inputs contribute to higher efficiency [23]. The efficiency score ranges from 0.0000 to 1.0000 under the variable return to scale (VRS) model [22,24]. This implies that the highest efficiency score is 1.0000 [17]. DMUs with this highest efficiency score is on the efficiency frontier while the distance from the frontier signals the level of inefficiency [22]. The achievement of the highest efficiency score denotes the full use of inputs for the greatest output generation under the output oriented VRS model [22].

DEA has been widely employed in the efficiency assessment in hospitals [25,26], farming [27,28], construction [29], education [30], and the power industry [31,32]. This study proposes a DEA model to optimize the efficiency of listed logistics companies in Malaysia by incorporating operational risk factor, which is the BIA. This study is the pioneer in analyzing the listed logistics companies in Malaysia over a long term with regards to operational risk factor with the DEA model. The significance of this study includes the identification of efficient and inefficient listed logistics companies in terms of operational risk factor through the proposed DEA model. Another notable contribution of this study is the ability of the DEA model for benchmarking and determining the improvement values of inefficient listed logistics companies to facilitate them to achieve efficiency score of 1.0000 and become efficient companies. Benchmarking is essential for continuous improvement especially in managerial decision-making. The flowchart of this study is presented in Figure 1.

Section 2 discusses the research method of the proposed DEA model. Section 3 presents the results and discussion. Section 4 concludes the paper with a summary of the results, limitation, and future directions.

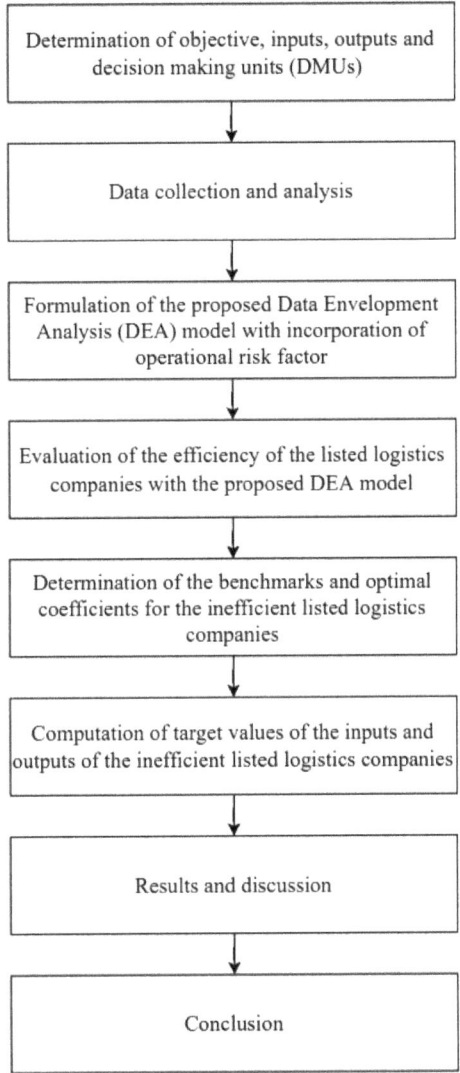

Figure 1. Research flowchart.

2. Literature Review

The DEA is a linear programming model which assesses the efficiency of the DMUs with several inputs and outputs [33–35]. One of the strengths of DEA lies in the non-parametric methodology as DEA does not require assumption in the production function or distribution [36]. DEA is also powerful in converting multiple inputs to multiple outputs when assessing the DMUs. DEA was established by Charnes et al. [37] with constant return to scale assumption [38,39]. Since the change in input does not always cause a proportional difference in the outputs, Banker et al. [24] then developed the variable return to scale (VRS) model. The efficiency is the weighted sum of outputs divided by the weighted sum of inputs [40,41]. In the DEA model, efficiency ranges from 0.0000 to 1.0000 [24,41,42]. The DMU is classified as efficient if it achieves the efficiency score of 1.0000. On the other hand, the DMU is classified as inefficient if the efficiency score is below 1.0000 [36,42].

DEA has been widely applied to assess the efficiency of companies with financial ratios. When financial ratios complement DEA, the results could serve as an early warning for inefficiencies for the companies [43–45]. DEA is able to translate the financial ratios into a single efficiency score for evaluation and comparison [46,47]. Based on the optimal solution of the DEA model, the weights of the inputs and outputs can also be determined so that the sources of inefficiency for the inefficient DMUs can be identified [42,48]. Moreover, DEA also serves as a powerful benchmarking tool as past studies have employed DEA to determine the references for the inefficient DMUs to enhance their performances and to determine the potential improvements [46,47].

DEA complements the financial ratios to assess the performances of companies in many industries. Current ratios (CTR), debt-to-asset ratio (DAR), debt-to-equity ratio (DER), and ROE, were used to study the food and beverages companies in Europe [42]. The DAR, DER, earnings per share (EPS), ROA, and ROE, were also used to determine the efficiency of manufacturing companies in Iran [43]. The oil industry has also been assessed with the DEA model using financial ratios such as ROA and ROE to determine the strengths and weaknesses of the companies [44]. Kedžo and Lukač [45] noted that financial ratios could reflect the operations of the manufacturers in Europe when complemented with DEA. CTR, DAR, DER, EPS, ROA, and ROE have also been used to study financial institutions in Iran using DEA [49]. Hospitals were also assessed with DEA and financial ratios such as ROA and ROE [50].

The DEA model has been applied to evaluate the performances of logistics companies. Chen [51] applied the DEA model to study the companies which provide transportation, warehousing, and postal services in China. Wohlgemuth et al. [52] assessed the various types of logistics operators in Brazil with DEA. Zhang and Koutmos [53] used the DEA model to evaluate the airlines in the United States and Canada with financial ratios such as weighted average cost of capital (WACC) and return on equity (ROE). Venkadasalam et al. [54] analyzed the performances of the shipping companies in Southeast Asia with financial ratios such as return on asset (ROA) and ROE. Li et al. [55] studied container terminals in China and found the areas of inefficiency to be enhanced. Port logistics efficiency has also been evaluated with the DEA model and the study found that the efficiency was low [56]. Besides, the selection of logistics partners in Vietnam was also done using the DEA model [57]. DEA has also been applied in green logistics and third-party logistics in China and France, respectively [58,59].

Operational risk, which happens in the daily operations of a company, is caused by humans, systems, and events. The basic indicator approach (BIA) can be used to determine the capital requirement needed for operational risk based on the gross income of a company [60]. WACC involves a mix of debt and equity to finance a company's operations. WACC is also the smallest return a company has to make from its operations. A small WACC indicates low cost of finance, whereas high WACC indicates high operational cost that would bring up a company's operational risk. A company that experiences operational risk event requires greater cost of capital to rectify the problem and regain shareholders' trust, which causes high volatility in the company's equity, thus greater WACC [61]. Since past studies did not incorporate operational risk factor into the DEA model, this paper intends to fill the gap by proposing a DEA model that incorporates the operational risk factor for evaluating the efficiency of logistics companies in Malaysia.

3. Materials and Methods

This study aims to propose a DEA model to optimize the efficiency of the listed logistics companies in Malaysia with the incorporation of operational risk factor via BIA. The DMUs consist of 27 listed logistics companies on Bursa Malaysia [62]. This study follows the rule of thumb developed by Bowlin [63] who noted that the number of DMUs must be at least thrice the number of inputs and outputs [64–66]. There are four inputs and four outputs in this study. The inputs and outputs contain financial ratios and financial variables [67,68]. A combination of financial ratios including liquidity, leverage and profitability ratios could sufficiently highlight a company's competitiveness. As such, this paper adopted current ratios (CTR), debt-to-asset (DAR), debt-to-equity ratios (DER) and weighted average cost of capital (WACC) as the inputs [44,50,69]. The outputs are earnings per share (EPS), return on assets (ROA), return on equity (ROE) and BIA [13,50,54]. The period of study is 12 years from 2010–2021 as this period is sufficient to include considerable business and product lifecycles [70,71]. Table 1 displays the proposed research framework to optimize the efficiency of the listed logistics companies with operational risk factor using the proposed DEA model.

Table 1. Proposed research framework.

Objective	To Optimize the Efficiency of the Listed Logistics Companies with Operational Risk Factor in Malaysia Using Proposed DEA Model		
Inputs	Current ratios (CTR) Debt-to-asset ratios (DAR) Debt-to-equity ratios (DER) Weighted average cost of capital (WACC)		
Outputs	Earnings per share (EPS) Return on asset (ROA) Return on equity (ROE) Basic indicator approach (BIA)		
Decision Making Units (DMUs)	AIRPORT	HUBLINE	PRKCORP
	BHIC	ILB	SEALINK
	BIPORT	LITRAK	SEEHUP
	CJCEN	MAYBULK	SURIA
	COMPLET	MISC	SYSCORP
	FREIGHT	MMCCORP	TAS
	GCAP	NATWIDE	TASCO
	GDEX	POS	TNLOGIS
	HARBOUR	PDZ	TOCEAN

Based on Table 1, this study aims to optimize the efficiency of the listed logistics companies with operational risk factor in Malaysia using the proposed DEA model. CTR, DAR, DER, and WACC are the inputs while EPS, ROA, ROE, and BIA are the outputs. This study includes all the 27 listed logistics companies in Malaysia from 2010 to 2021. After the identification of the objective, inputs, outputs and DMUs, this study shall evaluate and rank the efficiency of the listed logistics companies with the proposed DEA model. Then, the inefficient companies can benchmark the efficient companies based on the optimal solution of the proposed DEA model. After that, this paper shall determine the target values for the inefficient companies according to the respective optimal coefficients of the benchmarked efficient companies. Based on the target values of outputs and inputs for potential improvement, the inefficient companies can achieve the efficiency score of 1.0000 and thus, classified as efficient companies.

The efficiency is the quotient of weighted-sum of outputs to the weighted-sum of inputs, yielding efficiency of 0.0000 to 1.0000 [22,23]. The DMUs can then be ranked according to their efficiency. The highest ranking is achieved when the efficiency is 1.0000 because the DMU has garnered the greatest outcomes from its resources. When the DMU has achieved the highest ranking with 1.0000 efficiency score, this implies that the DMU is efficient. Conversely, if the efficiency score of the DMU is less than 1.0000, the DMU is inefficient and can improve based on the optimal solution of the DEA model [24]. The formulation of the proposed DEA model to optimize the efficiency of the listed logistics companies with the incorporation of operational risk factor is presented below [22,72,73].

$$\text{Maximize } E_p = \frac{\sum_{h=1}^{m} t_h y_{hp} - u_p}{\sum_{k=1}^{n} w_k x_{kp}} \qquad (1)$$

Subject to

$$\frac{\sum_{h=1}^{m} t_h y_{hp} - u_p}{\sum_{k=1}^{n} w_k x_{kp}} \leq 1, p = 1, 2, 3, \ldots, q, \quad (2)$$

$$t_h \geq \begin{cases} \varepsilon, \text{ if } h = 1, 2, 3, \ldots, m, \text{ where } h \neq BIA; \\ \alpha, \text{ if } h = BIA \end{cases} \quad (3)$$

$$w_k \geq \varepsilon, \; k = 1, 2, 3, \ldots, n \quad (4)$$

where
E_p denotes the efficiency of DMU p,
t_h denotes the weights of output h,
y_{hp} denotes the value of h output of DMU p,
m denotes the number of outputs,
w_k denotes the weights of input k,
x_{kp} denotes the value of k input of DMU p,
n denotes the number of inputs,
ε denotes positive value,
α denotes 15% as set by the Basel Committee on Banking Supervision,
q denotes the number of DMU,
u_p denotes free variable of DMU p,
BIA denotes the hth output for Basic Indicator Approach.

Equation (1) maximizes the efficiency of the DMUs wherein the efficiency is the quotient of the weighted-sum of outputs to the weighted-sum of inputs. Equation (2) constraints the efficiency from 0 to 1. t_h is the weight of output obtained from the optimal solution of DEA model for the determination of the contribution of the output among all outputs to the efficiency of the DMU. Under BIA, companies should have a capital of at least the mean of a fixed percentage (alpha) of the positive gross income over three years where alpha is 15% [14,15]. As such, t_h is set to be at least 0.15 for BIA as shown in (3). w_k is the input weight retrieved from the optimal solution of DEA model to quantify the contribution of the input among all inputs to the efficiency of the DMU. Since DEA is a linear programming model, the following transformation applies where the Equations (3) to (7) are the linear programming forms of the DEA model.

$$\text{Maximize } E_p = \sum_{h=1}^{m} t_h y_{hp} - u_p \quad (5)$$

Subject to

$$-\sum_{h=1}^{m} t_h y_{hp} + \sum_{k=1}^{n} w_k x_{kp} + u_p \geq 0, \; p = 1, 2, 3, \ldots, q, \quad (6)$$

$$\sum_{k=1}^{n} w_k x_{kp} = 1, \quad (7)$$

Equations (3) and (4).

The computational work of the proposed DEA model is solved with LINGO [74,75]. The efficient DMUs may form the reference units to be benchmarked by the inefficient DMUs. The optimal solution of the DEA model will also provide the optimal coefficient for the calculation of target values for the inefficient DMUs in terms of the outputs and inputs [76]. The potential improvements show the amount that an input should be reduced and the value that an output should be increased for the inefficient DMUs in order to achieve 1.0000 efficiency score and thus classified as efficient DMUs [77].

The target value of the output of inefficient DMU is shown below:

$$Y_{hp} = \sum_{g=1}^{z} r_g v_{hg}, \; h = 1, 2, 3, \ldots, m \quad (8)$$

where

Y_{hp} denotes the target value of output h of DMU p,
r_g denotes the optimal coefficient of benchmarked DMU g,
v_{hg} denotes the initial value of output h of benchmarked DMU g,
z denotes the number of benchmarked DMU.

The determination of the target value of the output is shown in Equation (8). The target value can be determined using the summation of the product of the optimal coefficient of the benchmarked DMU and the initial value of the output of the benchmarked DMU.

The target value of the input of inefficient DMU is shown below:

$$X_{kp} = \sum_{g=1}^{z} r_g x_{kg}, \ k = 1, 2, 3, \ldots, n \qquad (9)$$

where

X_{kp} denotes the target value of input k of DMU p,
r_g denotes the optimal coefficient of benchmarked DMU g,
x_{kg} denotes the initial value of input k of benchmarked DMU g,
z denotes the number of benchmarked DMU.

For the input, the determination of the target value is shown in Equation (9). The target value can be computed using the summation of the product of the optimal coefficient of the benchmarked DMU and the initial value of the input of the benchmarked DMU. Based on the target value of output and input as presented in the Equations (8) and (9) respectively for potential improvement, the inefficient DMU can achieve the efficiency score of 1.0000 and thus, classified as efficient DMU.

4. Results and Discussion

The efficiencies and ranks of the listed logistics companies in Malaysia with the inclusion of operational risk factor are tabulated in Table 2.

From Table 2, listed logistics companies with efficiency equals to 1.0000 are ranked first because they are efficient. Out of the 27 listed logistics companies, 15 companies achieve full efficiency of 1.0000. They are AIRPORT, COMPLET, GDEX, HUBLINE, ILB, MISC, MMCCORP, NATWIDE, POS, PDZ, PRKCORP, SEEHUP, SYSCORP, TNLOGIS, and TOCEAN. These 15 listed logistics companies have made full use of their inputs for the greatest output generation. Since these 15 companies are efficient and lie on the efficiency frontier, these companies can serve as the benchmarks and reference units for the remaining inefficient companies. On the other hand, there are 12 listed logistics companies which have not managed to achieve full efficiency. From higher ranks in descending order, these companies are SEALINK (0.9906), HARBOUR (0.9860), BIPORT (0.9737), SURIA (0.9666), BHIC (0.9649), FREIGHT (0.9400), GCAP (0.9026), TASCO (0.8966), CJCEN (0.8889), LITRAK (0.8875), MAYBULK (0.8497), and TAS (0.6725). SEALINK is very close to the efficiency frontier since its efficiency is 0.9906 while TAS, with an efficiency of 0.6725, requires more improvement since it is the furthest from the efficiency frontier. All these 12 listed logistics companies have not maximized their input utilization for the greatest outputs.

Table 3 presents the summary of the efficiency of the listed logistics companies with the incorporation of operational risk factor using DEA model.

From Table 3, the percentage of efficiency is 55.56%, which means that 55.56% of listed logistics companies have achieved full efficiency of 1.0000. This percentage of efficiency is in line with past studies where the range of efficiency is from 48.00% to 62.00% [50,78,79]. The average efficiency is 0.9600 and this also in accordance with past studies which have average efficiency of 0.9220 to 0.9710 [54,66,80,81]. Moreover, out of the 27 companies, 20 companies (74.07%) managed to achieve above average efficiency [82]. They are AIRPORT, COMPLET, GDEX, HUBLINE, ILB, MISC, MMCCORP, NATWIDE, POS, PDZ, PRKCORP, SEEHUP, SYSCORP, TNLOGIS, TOCEAN, SEALINK, HARBOUR, BIPORT, SURIA, and BHIC.

Table 2. Efficiencies of the listed logistics companies.

DMUs	Efficiency	Rank	Categorization
AIRPORT	1.0000	1	Efficient
BHIC	0.9649	20	Inefficient
BIPORT	0.9737	18	Inefficient
CJCEN	0.8889	24	Inefficient
COMPLET	1.0000	1	Efficient
FREIGHT	0.9400	21	Inefficient
GCAP	0.9026	22	Inefficient
GDEX	1.0000	1	Efficient
HARBOUR	0.9860	17	Inefficient
HUBLINE	1.0000	1	Efficient
ILB	1.0000	1	Efficient
LITRAK	0.8875	25	Inefficient
MAYBULK	0.8497	26	Inefficient
MISC	1.0000	1	Efficient
MMCCORP	1.0000	1	Efficient
NATWIDE	1.0000	1	Efficient
POS	1.0000	1	Efficient
PDZ	1.0000	1	Efficient
PRKCORP	1.0000	1	Efficient
SEALINK	0.9906	16	Inefficient
SEEHUP	1.0000	1	Efficient
SURIA	0.9666	19	Inefficient
SYSCORP	1.0000	1	Efficient
TAS	0.6725	27	Inefficient
TASCO	0.8966	23	Inefficient
TNLOGIS	1.0000	1	Efficient
TOCEAN	1.0000	1	Efficient

Table 3. Summary of efficiency.

	Efficiency
Minimum efficiency	0.6725
Maximum efficiency	1.0000
Average efficiency	0.9600
Percentage of efficiency (%)	55.56
Percentage of inefficiency (%)	44.44

From the optimal solution of the DEA model, the benchmarks which form the reference units, together with the respective optimal coefficients for the inefficient listed logistics companies are identified and shown in Table 4. The benchmarks are made up of the efficient companies.

BHIC, BIPORT, CJCEN, FREIGHT, GCAP, HARBOUR, LITRAK, MAYBULK, SEALINK, SURIA, TAS, and TASCO are the 12 inefficient listed logistics, thus require improvements. These 12 companies can benchmark the 15 efficient companies, which include AIRPORT, COMPLETE, GDEX, HUBLINE, ILB, MISC, MMCCORP, NATWIDE, POS, PDZ, PRKCORP, SEEHUP, SYSCORP, TNLOGIS, and TOCEAN. Out of the 15 efficient listed logistics companies, only 11 companies serve as benchmarks for these inefficient companies. AIRPORT, GDEX, NATWIDE, and PDZ do not form the benchmarks for any inefficient companies. POS appears the most in the reference units of the inefficient companies as POS serves as the benchmark for nine inefficient companies. This is followed by ILB, MISC and SEEHUP which are the benchmarks for seven inefficient companies, respectively. SYSCORP and TOCEAN only appear as the benchmarks for one company, which are SEALINK and MAYBULK, respectively.

Table 4. Benchmarks for inefficient DMUs.

Inefficient DMUs	Benchmarks (Efficient DMUs)										
	Complet	Hubline	ILB	MISC	Mmccorp	POS	Prkcorp	Seehup	Syscorp	Tnlogis	Tocean
BHIC		0.5682			0.1476	0.0001	0.0025			0.2816	
BIPORT				0.1580	0.1239	0.0001	0.0406	0.1368		0.5405	
CJCEN			0.0894		0.5247	0.0012		0.3847			
FREIGHT			0.2039	0.4376		0.0025		0.3560			
GCAP			0.7071				0.0857	0.2072			
HARBOUR			0.1507	0.2119		0.0021		0.6353			
LITRAK					0.1478	0.0039	0.0375			0.8108	
MAYBULK	0.4004			0.1028		0.0032	0.0003				0.4933
SEALINK		0.1194							0.8806		
SURIA	0.8525		0.0336	0.0992			0.0147				
TAS			0.0379	0.6720				0.2901			
TASCO			0.0334	0.3635		0.0022	0.0049	0.5960			

From Table 4, BIPORT has six benchmarks in the reference unit, which means that BIPORT is less efficient compared to these six companies. These six companies are MISC, MMCCORP, POS, PRKCORP, SEEHUP, and TNLOGIS. The optimal coefficients of these six companies are then used to compute the target values for the outputs and inputs of BIPORT based on Equations (8) and (9), respectively. For example, the target value of the EPS can be computed based on the sum of the product of the optimal coefficients of MISC (0.1580), MMCCORP (0.1239), POS (0.0001), PRKCORP (0.0406), SEEHUP (0.1368), and TNLOGIS (0.5405) and the initial values of the EPS of MISC, MMCCORP, POS, PRKCORP, SEEHUP, and TNLOGIS, respectively.

SEALINK, which is the closest to the efficiency frontier among all the inefficient companies because of the efficiency of 0.9906, can benchmark two companies, which are HUBLINE and SYSCORP to improve its efficiency. The target values of the outputs and inputs for SEALINK shall be based on the optimal coefficients of HUBLINE (0.1194) and SYSCORP (0.8806) and the initial values of the outputs and inputs of HUBLINE and SYSCORP, according to Equations (8) and (9), respectively.

Table 5 explains the potential improvements of the inefficient listed logistics companies based on the reference units and optimal coefficients in Table 4.

Table 5. Potential improvement for inefficient DMUs.

DMU	Output/Input	Initial Value	Target Value	Potential Improvement
BHIC	EPS	0.0690	0.0690	0.0000
	ROA	0.0192	0.0192	0.0000
	ROE	0.0414	0.0441	0.0027
	BIA	0.0545	0.0545	0.0000
	CTR	0.9947	0.9598	−0.0349
	DAR	0.5779	0.5471	−0.0308
	DER	1.8922	1.6809	−0.2113
	WACC	0.0733	0.0707	−0.0026
BIPORT	EPS	0.3648	0.3648	0.0000
	ROA	0.0689	0.0689	0.0000
	ROE	0.1501	0.1746	0.0245
	BIA	0.1102	0.1102	0.0000
	CTR	3.2174	1.2836	−1.9338
	DAR	0.5415	0.5273	−0.0142
	DER	1.2977	1.2638	−0.0339
	WACC	0.0602	0.0586	−0.0016

Table 5. *Cont.*

DMU	Output/Input	Initial Value	Target Value	Potential Improvement
CJCEN	EPS	0.1121	0.1145	0.0024
	ROA	0.0456	0.0374	−0.0082
	ROE	0.0739	0.0722	−0.0017
	BIA	0.0116	0.1768	0.1652
	CTR	1.8669	1.6569	−0.2100
	DAR	0.3959	0.5228	0.1268
	DER	0.6771	1.3977	0.7207
	WACC	0.0772	0.0612	−0.0160
FREIGHT	EPS	0.1018	0.1932	0.0914
	ROA	0.0633	0.0641	0.0008
	ROE	0.1023	0.1023	0.0000
	BIA	0.0160	0.1710	0.1550
	CTR	2.1968	2.1162	−0.0807
	DAR	0.3794	0.3513	−0.0281
	DER	0.6125	0.5900	−0.0225
	WACC	0.0731	0.0704	−0.0027
GCAP	EPS	0.0362	0.0991	0.0629
	ROA	1.1417	1.1417	0.0000
	ROE	0.0650	1.8885	1.8235
	BIA	0.0049	0.0166	0.0117
	CTR	13.9511	3.8790	−10.0721
	DAR	5.2244	0.3059	−4.9185
	DER	0.5446	0.4934	−0.0513
	WACC	0.0775	0.0702	−0.0073
HARBOUR	EPS	0.1041	0.1232	0.0191
	ROA	0.0550	0.0550	0.0000
	ROE	0.0907	0.0911	0.0003
	BIA	0.0122	0.0899	0.0777
	CTR	1.9375	1.9331	−0.0044
	DAR	0.3852	0.3755	−0.0097
	DER	0.6587	0.6572	−0.0015
	WACC	0.0657	0.0655	−0.0001
LITRAK	EPS	0.3192	0.3192	0.0000
	ROA	0.0753	0.1150	0.0398
	ROE	0.2539	0.2539	0.0000
	BIA	0.0608	0.0608	0.0000
	CTR	3.0011	1.2042	−1.7969
	DAR	0.6972	0.5896	−0.1076
	DER	2.9152	1.5080	−1.4072
	WACC	0.0603	0.0535	−0.0068
MAYBULK	EPS	0.0771	0.0771	0.0000
	ROA	0.0668	0.0730	0.0062
	ROE	0.1121	0.1121	0.0000
	BIA	0.0425	0.0425	0.0000
	CTR	2.3389	1.9873	−0.3516
	DAR	0.3433	0.2917	−0.0516
	DER	0.7257	0.4414	−0.2843
	WACC	0.0997	0.0801	−0.0195
SEALINK	EPS	0.0122	0.0286	0.0165
	ROA	0.0067	0.0129	0.0063
	ROE	0.0136	0.0208	0.0071
	BIA	0.0034	0.0081	0.0048
	CTR	1.0091	1.0004	−0.0088
	DAR	0.4391	0.4094	−0.0297
	DER	0.8154	0.8083	−0.0071
	WACC	0.0719	0.0682	−0.0037

Table 5. Cont.

DMU	Output/Input	Initial Value	Target Value	Potential Improvement
SURIA	EPS	0.1925	0.1925	0.0000
	ROA	0.0439	0.0712	0.0274
	ROE	0.0620	0.1157	0.0537
	BIA	0.0159	0.0404	0.0245
	CTR	2.8923	2.8063	−0.0861
	DAR	0.2793	0.2710	−0.0083
	DER	0.4018	0.3875	−0.0143
	WACC	0.0848	0.0822	−0.0025
TAS	EPS	0.0405	0.2532	0.2127
	ROA	0.0266	0.0303	0.0037
	ROE	0.0450	0.0477	0.0026
	BIA	0.0018	0.2577	0.2559
	CTR	2.1528	1.5306	−0.6222
	DAR	0.5080	0.3612	−0.1468
	DER	1.5783	0.6088	−0.9695
	WACC	0.1028	0.0731	−0.0297
TASCO	EPS	0.1886	0.1886	0.0000
	ROA	0.0597	0.0597	0.0000
	ROE	0.1032	0.1058	0.0026
	BIA	0.0160	0.1463	0.1303
	CTR	1.6644	1.5248	−0.1396
	DAR	0.4191	0.3840	−0.0351
	DER	0.8357	0.6753	−0.1604
	WACC	0.0734	0.0672	−0.0062

From Table 5, the inefficient logistics companies can obtain the target values based on the benchmarks and optimal coefficients as provided by the optimal solution of the DEA model. Upon obtaining the target values, the potential improvements can be calculated by the difference between the target values and the initial values. The potential improvements for the outputs should be at least zero or a positive value because the outputs should be maximized; for inputs, the potential improvements should be zero or less than zero so that there can be input reduction [77]. The inefficient listed logistics companies are BHIC, BIPORT, CJCEN, FREIGHT, GCAP, HARBOUR, LITRAK, MAYBULK, SEALINK, SURIA, TAS, and TASCO.

For BHIC, in terms of outputs, EPS, ROA and BIA can be kept at the initial values of 0.0690, 0.0192 and 0.0545, respectively. ROE can be increased by 0.0027 from 0.0414 to 0.0441. However, all the inputs should be reduced to move towards greater efficiency. CTR of BHIC should be reduced from 0.9947 to a target value of 0.9598, with a difference of −0.0349. DAR should be brought down by 0.0308 from its initial value of 0.5779 to attain the target value of 0.5471. Since BHIC has a very high DER of 1.8922, BHIC could bring down its DER by 0.2116 to 1.6809. WACC can have a reduction of 0.0026 from the initial value of 0.0733 to reach 0.0707.

TAS has the lowest efficiency of 0.6725. All the outputs should be increased while all the inputs should be reduced for higher efficiency. EPS and BIA of TAS are very low, therefore, TAS should increase its EPS by 0.2127 from 0.0405 to 0.2532 while its BIA should be increased by 0.2559 from the initial value of 0.0018 to the target value of 0.2577. The initial values of ROA and ROE of TAS are 0.0266 and 0.0450, respectively. The potential improvements of ROA and ROE of TAS are 0.0037 and 0.0026, so that the ROA and ROE can reach 0.0303 and 0.0477, respectively. Among all the inputs, TAS has a very high initial values of CTR and DER amounting to 2.1528 and 1.5783. Therefore, based on the optimal solution of DEA model, its CTR and DER can be lowered by 0.6222 and 0.9695 to arrive at the values of 1.5306 and 0.6088, respectively. DAR and WACC of TAS could be reduced from 0.5080 to 0.3612 and from 0.1028 to 0.0731, respectively.

5. Conclusions

This study has successfully optimized the efficiency of the listed logistics companies in Malaysia with the incorporation of operational risk factor, which is the BIA, using DEA model from 2010 to 2021. The percentage of efficiency is 55.56% and the efficient companies are AIRPORT, COMPLET, GDEX, HUBLINE, ILB, MISC, MMCCORP, NATWIDE, POS, PDZ, PRKCORP, SEEHUP, SYSCORP, TNLOGIS, and TOCEAN. The average efficiency is 0.9600 with 74.07% of the companies managed to achieve above average efficiency. The potential improvements of the inefficient listed logistics companies, which include BHIC, BIPORT, CJCEN, FREIGHT, GCAP, HARBOUR, LITRAK, MAYBULK, SEALINK, SURIA, TAS, and TASCO have also been obtained with the powerful benchmarking ability of the DEA model.

Based on the optimal solution of the proposed DEA model, the inefficient listed logistics companies can identify the inputs to be reduced and outputs to be raised. To increase its EPS, ROA, and ROE, the inefficient companies can reduce its expenses, such as participating in global sourcing to procure from markets with high quality materials at lower cost or by lowering its cost of goods sold and expenses through Kaizen costing for continuous improvement. Besides, the inefficient companies can set aside the respective capital for operational risk hedging based on the BIA determined by the optimal solution of the proposed model. A high CTR can reduce the company's operating capital in the short term. Therefore, the inefficient listed logistics companies can delay their capital purchases or restructure their short-term debts to reduce their CTR. For DAR and DER reduction, the inefficient companies can perform effective inventory management for better utilization of its assets and equities. It is important for companies to assess their risks as lower market risks would bring down its cost of equity, thereby lowering WACC for the inefficient logistics companies.

This paper is highly significant as the benchmarking process could facilitate the decision-making processes by the top management for financial structure and investment insights. This proposed model is also the pioneer in including BIA to optimize the efficiency of listed logistics companies in Malaysia. For the limitation of this research, the proposed model is only applicable for the efficiency evaluation of listed companies that provide the annual financial reports for data analysis. In the future, this model can be adopted in various prominent fields such as finance, project-based construction, engineering, manufacturing, and retail industries. This proposed model can also be applied in other countries to evaluate the efficiency of companies.

Author Contributions: Conceptualization, P.F.L., W.S.L. and W.H.L.; methodology, P.F.L., W.S.L. and W.H.L.; software, P.F.L.; validation, W.S.L. and W.H.L.; formal analysis, P.F.L., W.S.L. and W.H.L.; investigation, P.F.L., W.S.L. and W.H.L.; resources, P.F.L., W.S.L. and W.H.L.; data curation, P.F.L.; writing—original draft preparation, P.F.L., W.S.L. and W.H.L.; writing—review and editing, P.F.L., W.S.L. and W.H.L.; supervision, W.S.L. and W.H.L.; project administration, W.S.L. and W.H.L. All authors have read and agreed to the published version of the manuscript.

Funding: This research received no external funding.

Data Availability Statement: The data presented in this study are available on request from the corresponding author.

Acknowledgments: This research is supported by the Universiti Tunku Abdul Rahman, Malaysia.

Conflicts of Interest: The authors declare no conflict of interest.

References

1. Ramli, A.; Shakir, K.A. Current and future prospect of logistics and transportation sector in Malaysia. In *Modeling Economic Growth in Contemporary Malaysia (Entrepreneurship and Global Economic Growth)*; Sergi, B.S., Jaafar, A.R., Eds.; Emerald Publishing Limited: Bingley, UK; pp. 279–290.
2. Jeevan, J.; Othman, M.R.; Hasan, Z.R.A.; Pham, T.Q.M.; Park, G.K. Exploring the development of Malaysian seaports as a hub for tourism activities. *Marit. Bus. Rev.* **2019**, *4*, 310–327. [CrossRef]

3. Rashidi, K.; Cullinane, K. Evaluating the sustainability of national logistics performance using data envelopment analysis. *Transp. Policy* **2019**, *74*, 35–46. [CrossRef]
4. Khan, S.A.R.; Jian, C.; Zhang, Y.; Golpîra, H.; Kumar, A.; Sharif, A. Environmental, social and economic growth indicators spur logistics performance: From the perspective of South Asian Association for Regional Cooperation countries. *J. Clean. Prod.* **2019**, *214*, 1011–1023. [CrossRef]
5. Ko, C.; Lee, P.; Anandarajan, A. The impact of operational risk incidents and moderating influence of corporate governance on credit risk and firm performance. *Int. J. Account. Inf. Manag.* **2019**, *27*, 96–110. [CrossRef]
6. Xu, G.; Qiu, X.; Fang, M.; Kou, X.; Yu, Y. Data-driven operational risk analysis in E-Commerce logistics. *Adv. Eng. Inform.* **2019**, *40*, 29–35. [CrossRef]
7. Ferreira, S.; Dickason-Koekemoer, Z. A conceptual model of operational risk events in the banking sector. *Cogent Econ. Finance* **2019**, *7*, 1706394. [CrossRef]
8. Suki, N.M.; Suki, N.M.; Sharif, A.; Afshan, S. The role of logistics performance for sustainable development in top Asian countries: Evidence from advance panel estimations. *Sustain. Dev.* **2021**, *29*, 595–606. [CrossRef]
9. Lochan, S.A.; Rozanova, T.P.; Bezpalov, V.V.; Fedyunin, D.V. Supply chain management and risk management in an environment of stochastic uncertainty (retail). *Risks* **2021**, *9*, 197. [CrossRef]
10. Gurtu, A.; Johny, J. Supply chain risk management: Literature review. *Risks* **2021**, *9*, 16. [CrossRef]
11. Vasiliev, I.I.; Smelov, P.A.; Klimovskih, N.V.; Shevashkevich, M.G.; Donskaya, E.N. Operational risk management in a commercial bank. *Int. J. Eng. Technol.* **2018**, *7*, 524–529. [CrossRef]
12. Valová, I. Basel II approaches for the calculation of the regulatory capital for operational risk. *Financial Asset. Investig.* **2011**, *2*, 1–16.
13. Hasan, M.F.; Al-Dahan, N.S.; Abdulameer, H.H. Analysis of the impact of operational risk on the banking liquidity and growth using BIA method: A comparative study. *J. Xi'an Univ. Archit. Technol.* **2020**, *12*, 1363–1374.
14. Cristea, M. Operational risk management in banking activity. *J. East. Eur. Res. Bus. Econ.* **2021**, *2021*, 969612. [CrossRef]
15. Siddika, A.; Haron, R. Capital adequacy regulation. In *Banking and Finance*; Haron, R., Husin, M.M., Murg, M., Eds.; Intech Open: London, UK, 2020.
16. Chen, J.; Sohal, A.S.; Prajogo, D.I. Supply chain operational risk mitigation: A collaborative approach. *Int. J. Prod. Res.* **2013**, *57*, 2186–2199. [CrossRef]
17. Hunjra, A.I. Do firm-specific risks affect bank performance? *Int. J. Emerg. Mark.* **2022**, *17*, 664–682. [CrossRef]
18. Bai, X.; Cheng, L.; Iris, Ç. Data-driven financial and operational risk management: Empirical evidence from the global tramp shipping industry. *Transp. Res. Part E Logist. Transp. Rev.* **2022**, *158*, 102617. [CrossRef]
19. Hosseinzadeh-Bandbafha, H.; Nabavi-Pelesaraei, A.; Khanali, M.; Ghahderijani, M.; Chau, K. Application of data envelopment analysis approach for optimization of energy use and reduction of greenhouse gas emission in peanut production of Iran. *J. Clean. Prod.* **2018**, *172*, 1327–1335. [CrossRef]
20. Cavalcanti, J.H.; Kovács, T.; Kő, A. Production system efficiency optimization using sensor data, machine learning-based simulation and genetic algorithms. *Procedia CIRP* **2022**, *107*, 528–533. [CrossRef]
21. Rahimpour, K.; Shirouyehzad, H.; Asadpour, M.; Karbasian, M. A PCA-DEA method for organizational performance evaluation based on intellectual capital and employee loyalty: A case study. *J. Model. Manag.* **2020**, *15*, 1479–1513. [CrossRef]
22. Mohanta, K.K.; Sharanappa, D.S.; Aggarwal, A. Efficiency analysis in the management of COVID-19 pandemic in India based on data envelopment analysis. *Curr. Res. Behav. Sci.* **2021**, *2*, 100063. [CrossRef]
23. Shabanpour, H.; Yousefi, S.; Saen, R.F. Forecasting sustainability of supply chains in the circular economy context: A dynamic network data envelopment analysis and artificial neural network approach. *J. Enterp. Inf. Manag.* **2021**, *154*, 113357. [CrossRef]
24. Banker, R.D.; Charnes, A.; Cooper, W.W. Some models for estimating technical and scale inefficiencies in data envelopment analysis. *Manag. Sci.* **1984**, *30*, 1078–1092. [CrossRef]
25. Cinaroglu, S. Changes in hospital efficiency and size: An integrated propensity score matching with data envelopment analysis. *Socio-Econ. Plan. Sci.* **2021**, *76*, 100960. [CrossRef]
26. İlgün, G.; Sönmez, S.; Konca, M.; Yetim, B. Measuring the efficiency of Turkish maternal and child health hospitals: A two-stage data envelopment analysis. *Eval. Program Plan.* **2022**, *91*, 102023. [CrossRef] [PubMed]
27. Sefeedpari, P.; Shokoohi, Z.; Pishgar-Komleh, S.H. Dynamic energy efficiency assessment of dairy farming system in Iran: Application of window data envelopment analysis. *J. Clean. Prod.* **2020**, *275*, 124178. [CrossRef]
28. Bhunia, S.; Karmaker, S.; Bhattacharjee, S.; Roy, K.; Kanthal, S.; Pramanick, M.; Baishya, A.; Mandal, B. Optimization of energy consumption using data envelopment analysis (DEA) in rice-wheat-green gram cropping system under conservation tillage practices. *Energy* **2021**, *236*, 121499. [CrossRef]
29. Albertini, F.; Gomes, L.P.; Grondona, A.E.B.; Caetano, M.O. Assessment of environmental performance in building construction sites: Data envelopment analysis and Tobit model approach. *J. Build. Eng.* **2021**, *44*, 102994. [CrossRef]
30. Torres-Samuel, M.; Vásquez, C.L.; Luna, M.; Bucci, N.; Viloria, A.; Crissien, T.; Manosalva, J. Performance of education and research in Latin American countries through data envelopment analysis (DEA). *Procedia Comput. Sci.* **2020**, *170*, 1023–1028. [CrossRef]
31. Zeng, X.; Zhou, Z.; Gong, Y.; Liu, W. A data envelopment analysis model integrated with portfolio theory for energy mix adjustment: Evidence in the power industry. *Socio-Econ. Plan. Sci.* **2022**, *83*, 101332. [CrossRef]

32. Fathi, B.; Ashena, M.; Bahari, A.R. Energy, environmental, and economic efficiency in fossil fuel exporting countries: A modified data envelopment analysis approach. *Sustain. Prod. Consum.* **2021**, *26*, 588–596. [CrossRef]
33. Saen, R.F.; Karimi, B.; Fathi, A. Assessing the sustainability of transport supply chains by double frontier network data envelopment analysis. *J. Clean. Prod.* **2022**, *354*, 131771. [CrossRef]
34. Pascoe, S.; Cannard, T.; Dowling, N.A.; Dichmont, C.M.; Asche, F.; Little, L.R. Use of data envelopment analysis (DEA) to assess management alternatives in the presence of multiple objectives. *Mar. Policy* **2023**, *148*, 105444. [CrossRef]
35. Qi, H.; Zhou, Z.; Li, N.; Zhang, C. Construction safety performance evaluation based on data envelopment analysis (DEA) from a hybrid perspective of cross-sectional and longitudinal. *Saf. Sci.* **2022**, *146*, 105532. [CrossRef]
36. Čiković, K.F.; Martinčević, I.; Lozić, J. Application of data envelopment analysis (DEA) in the selection of sustainable suppliers: A review and bibliometric analysis. *Sustainability* **2022**, *14*, 6672. [CrossRef]
37. Charnes, A.; Cooper, W.; Rhodes, E. Measuring the efficiency of decision-making units. *Eur. J. Oper. Res.* **1978**, *2*, 429–444. [CrossRef]
38. Nong, T.N. Performance efficiency assessment of Vietnamese ports: An application of Delphi with Kamet principles and DEA model. *Asian J. Shipp. Logist.* 2022, in press. [CrossRef]
39. Wanke, P.; Rojas, F.; Tan, Y.; Moreira, J. Temporal dependence and bank efficiency drivers in OECD: A stochastic DEA-ratio approach based on generalized auto-regressive moving averages. *Expert Syst. Appl.* **2023**, *214*, 119120. [CrossRef]
40. Smętek, K.; Zawadzka, D.; Strzelecka, A. Examples of the use of data envelopment analysis (DEA) to assess the financial effectiveness of insurance companies. *Procedia Comput. Sci.* **2022**, *207*, 3924–3930. [CrossRef]
41. Ning, Y.; Zhang, Y.; Wang, G. An improved DEA prospect cross-efficiency evaluation method and its application in fund performance analysis. *Mathematics* **2023**, *11*, 585. [CrossRef]
42. Gardijan, M.; Lukač, Z. Measuring the relative efficiency of the food and drink industry in the chosen EU countries using the data envelopment analysis with missing data. *Cent. Eur. J. Oper. Res.* **2018**, *26*, 695–713. [CrossRef]
43. Karimi, A.; Barati, M. Financial performance evaluation of companies listed on Tehran Stock Exchange. A negative data envelopment analysis approach. *Int. J. Law. Manag.* **2018**, *60*, 885–900. [CrossRef]
44. Al-Mana, A.A.; Nawaz, W.; Kamal, A.; Koç, M. Financial and operational efficiencies of national and international oil companies: An empirical investigation. *Resour. Policy* **2020**, *68*, 101701. [CrossRef]
45. Kedžo, M.G.; Lukač, Z. The financial efficiency of small food and drink producers across selected European Union countries using data envelopment analysis. *Eur. J. Oper. Res.* **2020**, *291*, 586–600. [CrossRef]
46. Halkos, G.E.; Salamouris, D.S. Efficiency measurement of the Greek commercial banks with the use of financial ratios: A data envelopment analysis approach. *Manag. Account. Res.* **2004**, *15*, 201–224. [CrossRef]
47. Curtis, P.G.; Hanias, M.; Kourtis, E.; Kourtis, M. Data envelopment analysis (DEA) and financial ratios: A pro-stakeholders' view of performance measurement for sustainable value creation of the wind energy. *Int. J. Econ. Bus. Admin.* **2020**, *8*, 326–350.
48. Dahooie, J.H.; Hajiagha, S.H.R.; Farazmehr, S.; Zavadskas, E.K.; Antucheviciene. A novel dynamic credit risk evaluation method using data envelopment analysis with common weights and combination of multi-attribute decision-making methods. *Comput. Oper. Res.* **2021**, *129*, 105223. [CrossRef]
49. Mohtashami, A.; Ghiasvand, B.M. Z-ERM DEA integrated approach for evaluation of banks & financial institutes in stock exchange. *Expert Syst. Appl.* **2020**, *147*, 113218.
50. Habib, A.M.; Shahwan, T.M. Measuring the operational and financial efficiency using a Malmquist data envelopment analysis: A case of Egyptian hospitals. *Benchmarking Int. J.* **2020**, *27*, 2521–2536. [CrossRef]
51. Chen, J. A new approach to overall performance evaluation based on multiple contexts: An application to the logistics of China. *Comput. Ind. Eng.* **2018**, *122*, 170–180. [CrossRef]
52. Wohlgemuth, M.; Fries, C.E.; Sant'Anna, A.M.O.; Giglio, R.; Fettermann, D.C. Assessment of the technical efficiency of Brazilian logistic operators using data envelopment analysis and one inflated beta regression. *Ann. Oper. Res.* **2020**, *286*, 703–717. [CrossRef]
53. Zhang, Q.; Koutmos, D. Using operational and stock analytics to measure airline performance: A network DEA approach. *Decis. Sci.* **2021**, *52*, 720–748. [CrossRef]
54. Venkadasalam, S.; Mohamad, A.; Sifat, I.M. Operational efficiency of shipping companies: Evidence from Malaysia, Singapore, the Philippines, Thailand and Vietnam. *Int. J. Emerg. Mark.* **2019**, *15*, 875–897. [CrossRef]
55. Li, Z.; Wang, X.; Zheng, R.; Na, S.; Liu, C. Evaluation analysis of the operational efficiency and total factor productivity of container terminals in China. *Sustainability* **2022**, *14*, 13007. [CrossRef]
56. Li, H.; Jiang, L.; Liu, J.; Su, D. Research on the evaluation of logistics efficiency in Chinese coastal ports based on the four-stage DEA model. *J. Mar. Sci. Eng.* **2022**, *10*, 1147. [CrossRef]
57. Ho, N.; Nguyen, P.M.; Luu, T.; Tran, T. Selecting partners in strategic alliances: An application of the SBM DEA model in the Vietnamese logistics industry. *Logistics* **2022**, *6*, 64. [CrossRef]
58. Gan, W.; Yao, W.; Huang, S. Evaluation of green logistics efficiency in Jiangxi province based on three-stage DEA from the perspective of high-quality development. *Sustainability* **2022**, *14*, 797. [CrossRef]
59. Cavaignac, L.; Dumas, A.; Petiot, R. Third-party logistics efficiency: An innovative two-stage DEA analysis of the French market. *Int. J. Logist. Res.* **2020**, *24*, 581–604. [CrossRef]
60. Dziwok, E. New approach to operational risk measurement in banks. *Int. J. Trade Glob. Mark.* **2018**, *11*, 259–269. [CrossRef]

61. Oberholzer, M.; Mong, D.; van Romburgh, J. Towards a new model to benchmark firms' operating efficiency: A data envelopment analysis approach. *S. Afr. J. Account. Res.* **2017**, *31*, 223–239. [CrossRef]
62. Bursa Malaysia. Company Announcements. Available online: https://www.bursamalaysia.com/market_information/announcements/company_announcement (accessed on 10 August 2022).
63. Bowlin, W.F. Measuring performance: An introduction to data envelopment analysis (DEA). *J. Cost. Anal.* **1998**, *15*, 3–27. [CrossRef]
64. Sharif, O.; Hasan, M.Z.; Kurniasari, F.; Hermawan, A.; Gunardi, A. Productivity and efficiency analysis using DEA: Evidence from financial companies listed in Bursa Malaysia. *Manag. Sci. Lett.* **2019**, *9*, 301–312. [CrossRef]
65. Koengkan, M.; Fuinhas, J.A.; Kazemzadeh, E.; Osmani, F.; Alavijeh, M.K.; Auza, A.; Teixeira, M. Measuring the economic efficiency performance in Latin America and Caribbean countries: An empirical evidence from stochastic production frontier and data envelopment analysis. *Int. Econ.* **2022**, *169*, 43–54. [CrossRef]
66. Hsu, W.K.; Huang, S.S.; Huynh, N.T. An assessment of operating efficiency of container terminals in a port— an empirical study in Kaohsiung Port using data envelopment analysis. *Res. Transp. Bus. Manag.* 2022, in press. [CrossRef]
67. Campisi, D.; Mancuso, P.; Mastrodnato, S.L.; Morea, D. Efficiency assessment of knowledge intensive business services industry in Italy: Data envelopment analysis (DEA) and financial ratio analysis. *Meas. Bus. Excell.* **2019**, *23*, 484–495. [CrossRef]
68. Kamel, M.A.; Mousa, M.E.; Hamdy, R.M. Financial efficiency of commercial banks listed in Egyptian stock exchange using data envelopment analysis. *Int. J. Prod. Perform. Manag.* **2022**, *71*, 3683–3703. [CrossRef]
69. Shah, S.A.A.; Masood, O. Input efficiency of financial services sector: A non-parametric analysis of banking and insurance sectors of Pakistan. *Eur. J. Islamic. Finance* **2017**, *6*, 1–12.
70. Merendino, A.; Gagliardo, E.D.; Coronella, S. The efficiency of the top mega yacht builders across the world: A financial ratio-based data envelopment analysis. *Int. J. Manag. Decis. Mak.* **2018**, *17*, 125–147. [CrossRef]
71. Tamatam, R.; Dutta, P.; Dutta, G.; Lessmann, S. Efficiency analysis of Indian banking industry over the period of 2008-2017 using data envelopment analysis. *Benchmarking Int. J.* **2019**, *26*, 2417–2442. [CrossRef]
72. Raval, S.J.; Kant, R.; Shankar, R. Analyzing the lean six sigma enabled organizational performance to enhance operational efficiency. *Benchmarking Int. J.* **2020**, *27*, 2401–2434. [CrossRef]
73. Pham, T.Q.M.; Park, G.K.; Choi, K. The efficiency analysis of world top container ports using two-stage uncertainty DEA model and FCM. *Marit. Bus. Rev.* **2020**, *6*, 2–21. [CrossRef]
74. Taleb, M.; Ramli, R.; Khalid, R. Developing a two-stage approach of super efficiency slack-based measure in the presence of non-discretionary factors and mixed integer-valued data envelopment analysis. *Expert Syst. Appl.* **2018**, *103*, 14–24. [CrossRef]
75. Kouaissah, N.; Hocine, A. XOR data envelopment analysis and its application to renewable energy sector. *Expert Syst. Appl.* **2022**, *207*, 118044. [CrossRef]
76. Ng, C.Y.; Chuah, K.B.; King, A.P. An integrated approach for the benchmarking of production facilities' environmental performance: Data envelopment analysis and life cycle assessment. *Int. J. Sustain. Eng.* **2019**, *12*, 108–114. [CrossRef]
77. Raith, A.; Rouse, P.; Seiford, L.M. Benchmarking using data envelopment analysis: Application to stores of a post and banking business. In *Multiple Criteria Decision Making and Aiding: Cases on Models and Methods with Computer Implementations (International Series in Operations Research & Management Science 274*; Huber, S., Geiger, M.J., Almeida, A.T., Eds.; Springer: Cham, Switzerland, 2018.
78. Güner, S. Investigating infrastructure, superstructure, operating and financial efficiency in the management of Turkish seaports using data envelopment analysis. *Transp. Policy* **2015**, *40*, 36–48. [CrossRef]
79. Gandhi, A.V.; Sharma, D. Technical efficiency of private sector hospitals in India using data envelopment analysis. *Benchmarking Int. J.* **2018**, *25*, 3570–3591. [CrossRef]
80. Ghondaghsaz, N.; Kordnaeij, A.; Delkhah, J. Operational efficiency of plastic producing firms in Iran: A DEA approach. *Benchmarking Int. J.* **2018**, *25*, 2126–2144. [CrossRef]
81. Susanty, A.; Purwanggono, B.; Al Faruq, C. Electricity distribution efficiency analysis using data envelopment analysis (DEA) and soft system methodology. *Procedia Comput. Sci.* **2022**, *203*, 342–349. [CrossRef]
82. Malhotra, R.; Malhotra, D.K.; Lermack, H. Using data envelopment analysis to analyze the performance of North American class I freight railroads. *Financ. Model. Appl. Data Envel. Appl.* **2009**, *13*, 113–131.

Disclaimer/Publisher's Note: The statements, opinions and data contained in all publications are solely those of the individual author(s) and contributor(s) and not of MDPI and/or the editor(s). MDPI and/or the editor(s) disclaim responsibility for any injury to people or property resulting from any ideas, methods, instructions or products referred to in the content.

Numerical Simulation of the Korteweg–de Vries Equation with Machine Learning

Kristina O. F. Williams * and Benjamin F. Akers

Department of Mathematics and Statistics, Air Force Institute of Technology, Dayton, OH 45433, USA; benjamin.akers@afit.edu
* Correspondence: kristina.williams@afit.edu

Abstract: A machine learning procedure is proposed to create numerical schemes for solutions of nonlinear wave equations on coarse grids. This method trains stencil weights of a discretization of the equation, with the truncation error of the scheme as the objective function for training. The method uses centered finite differences to initialize the optimization routine and a second-order implicit-explicit time solver as a framework. Symmetry conditions are enforced on the learned operator to ensure a stable method. The procedure is applied to the Korteweg–de Vries equation. It is observed to be more accurate than finite difference or spectral methods on coarse grids when the initial data is near enough to the training set.

Keywords: machine learning; Korteweg–de Vries equation; coarse grid

MSC: 65M25

1. Introduction

Numerical methods for nonlinear wave equations have a long history, from the seminal works of Courant, Friedrichs, and Lewy [1] almost a century ago, to more recent contributions of Fornberg, Trefethen, LeVeque, and many others [2–10]. By and large, these methods are successful when a sufficiently fine discretization is used. Many classical numerical methods for partial differential equations (PDE) perform poorly on coarse grids, i.e., with few data points [11–13]. Recently, a number of authors have used machine learning to augment numerical solvers in the coarse discretization regime [14–16]. In this work, a procedure for numerically solving a nonlinear dispersive wave equation is proposed using a machine learning model to optimize stencil weights. A simple neural network is used, and the resulting numerical scheme is trained on solutions of the PDE (*The method allows for training on either exact solutions or coarse samples of a highly-resolved numerical solution*). The result is a numerical scheme that can outperform both Fourier collocation and its sister finite difference scheme when applied on the coarse grid.

The novel numerical method is developed and applied to the Korteweg–de Vries (KdV) equation. The KdV equation was originally derived as a model for waves in shallow water [17,18]. Numerous recent works have since used the KdV equation or a modified version of it in many areas where long, weakly nonlinear waves are of interest [18–29]. The KdV equation has localized traveling wave solutions, or solitons. These localized waves maintain their shape as they propagate through space and time [30]. This is due to a balance between the nonlinear and dispersive properties of the equation [31,32]. The KdV equation is integrable, and the solutions are real. Although the formula of the soliton was used for debugging, the results in this paper rely on neither the existence of solitary waves nor integrability. The form of the KdV equation in consideration is

$$u_t + u_{xxx} - 6uu_x = 0, \quad (1)$$

where the subscripts denote the derivative of the respective independent variables. The closed-form solutions of the KdV equation are

$$\tilde{u}(x,t) = -\frac{c}{2}\text{sech}^2\left(\frac{\sqrt{c}}{2}(x - ct)\right), \qquad (2)$$

where c is the speed. Figure 1 shows a plot of the wave solution in time and space, using $c = 1$, with a time interval length of 3 and spatial domain size of 40.

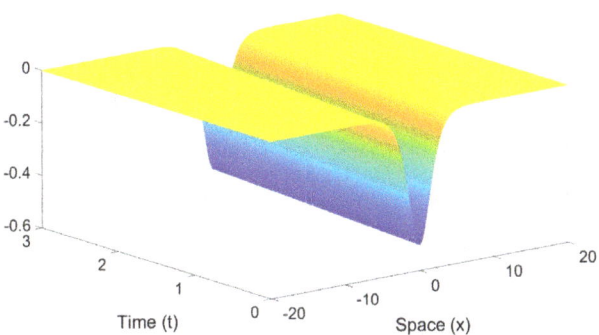

Figure 1. An example of the traveling waves solution of the Korteweg–de Vries equation, $c = 1$ in (2), is plotted as a function of space and time.

Machine learning methods have been applied to PDEs many times [33] and in numerous applications [34,35]. Several recent works have used machine learning methods to find the underlying PDE [18,20,25,26,36,37]. Many recent works have aimed to improve the accuracy of solutions to PDEs [15,19,21–25,38,39]. The machine learning models and approaches vary throughout these works such as the use of a residual network [37,40], a new proposed network called PDE-Net [36], a neural network based on Lie groups [27], a multilayer feed-forward neural network [34], and an unsupervised learning [41] approach [42]. Some approaches combine deep neural networks with other methods such as regression models [20] and Galerkin methods [43]. Several works have implemented the physics-informed neural networks (PINNs) approach [19,21,22,24,25,44,45], as proposed by Raissi et al. [39]. PINNs incorporate the PDE and boundary conditions into the objective or loss function to preserve the physics of the equation [19,22,39,46]. Variations within the PINN framework exist to include the gradient optimized [24] and parareal [47] PINNs. An important note to make about PINNs is that the machine learning models represent the solution as a neural network, which are functions of x and t. In this work, a neural network is used to model the stencil weights as a function of the unknown solution u.

Deep learning models, also known as deep neural networks, are very common machine learning models used in problems involving PDEs [15,25,33,48]. Historically, deep neural networks were defined to have more than two hidden layers [49,50]. With today's technology, the number of layers can be well into the double digits, so a neural network with three or four hidden layers may be considered "simple". Um et al. [33] use a model with 22 layers. On the lower end, Bar-Sinai et al. [15] use a three-layer neural network. Raissi et al. [25] use two deep neural networks, one with five layers and the other with only two. Raissi et al. [48] provide results using different numbers of layers in their model. The drawbacks to using deep neural networks may include having insufficient training data, slow training time, and/or overfitting [49,50]. This paper uses a single-layer neural network, which is considered a simple neural network, and which has 16 unknown coefficients.

The numerical method of this paper uses a fixed stencil width for the spatial discretization (as opposed to variable as in [15]) and bases the time-stepping algorithm on a second-order implicit-explicit scheme (IMEX2) so as to have an unbounded stability region [11]. Many recent numerical machine learning works use fourth-order Runge–Kutta (RK4) [21,23,25,39,46], presumably for its temporal accuracy, but we find the stability properties to be of greater importance for this training procedure, hence IMEX2 [11,51,52]. Other second-order time-stepping algorithms exist, such as RK2, and could be used in future studies but may lack the stability properties offered by IMEX2 [11]. In addition to choosing a time-stepper with an unbounded stability region, the machine learning network is built in such a way as to preserve the operator's anti-symmetry, guaranteeing eigenvalues which live in the stability region of the scheme. The resulting scheme is stable for all time, with no limitations on the time step size k (time step is limited in [15]).

The machine-learned numerical method is compared in performance against classical methods, here finite difference and Fourier collocation. Several other works have established methodologies that effectively use machine learning to solve various problems associated with PDEs but do not compare performance with classical methods [19,21–24,39,44]. The method in this paper is observed to outperform these two classic methods, but comes with a restriction that the initial data must be close to the training set. This is an expected trade-off based on how the scheme was designed.

Training and test data sets can be generated in various ways. In several works, an initial set of data is generated using a classical method such as from finite difference or spectral methods [20–23,25,36], and the training and test data sets are both taken from that initial set [22,23,25,43]. Another approach includes generating one set of solutions to train on and another entirely different set to test on [43]. One last approach is training and testing on data randomly sub-sampled from several different initial sets of solutions [15]. This paper first uses a short time interval of a single solution trajectory for training, then tests on both the long time dynamics of the trained trajectory and those of other initial data. Also tested were training routines that used short time intervals from two solution trajectories.

The remainder of the paper is organized as follows: Section 2 discusses the architecture of the scheme, the machine learning model, and the procedure for creating the solutions to be used for training and testing. Section 3 discusses the outcomes of using different sets of initial data when training and testing the model and the performance compared to finite difference and spectral methods. Finally, Section 4 provides conclusions about the use of this method for approximating solutions to PDEs on coarse grids and future research.

2. Numerical Method
2.1. Initial Data

Both training and testing data was generated via highly-resolved numerical simulations. The numerical method used for this data was Fourier collocation for spatial derivatives and an IMEX2 time-stepping scheme, which has the form

$$\frac{u^{n+1} - u^{n-1}}{2k} = \frac{1}{2}g(u^{n+1}) + \frac{1}{2}g(u^{n-1}) + f(u^n), \quad (3)$$

where n denotes a point in space and the superscripts denote the solutions evaluated at the point n, and k is the temporal step size [52]. This scheme uses an implicit scheme (trapezoidal) for the linear term of the KdV equation, denoted as $g(u)$ in (3), and an explicit scheme (leap frog) for the nonlinear term, denoted as $f(u)$ in (3). This method is not self-starting, so for the first time step, a first-order IMEX scheme was used with the form

$$\frac{u^{n+1} - u^n}{k} = g(u^{n+1}) + f(u^n), \quad (4)$$

which uses the backward Euler method for the linear term and the forward Euler method for the nonlinear term [52]. For a small nonlinearity, the IMEX2 scheme becomes the trapezoidal scheme, which is stable on the entire left-half of the λk-plane, to include the imaginary axis. Since the eigenvalues of the KdV equation are all pure imaginary, the IMEX2 scheme is linearly stable (with an unbounded stability region [11]).

All simulations in this work were conducted on a Windows 10 laptop computer and Mac Pro with macOS Monterey using MATLAB version R2022b. The initial data are all localized and exponentially decaying. The total number of spatial points was sampled logarithmically in powers of two. The infinite spatial domain was approximated by $L = 40, 50,$ and 60. For each domain size, the initial highly-resolved solution sets consist of 512 spatial steps and 30,001 temporal steps. Spatial and temporal data were sub-sampled from highly-resolved numerical simulations to build the training and test data sets for the machine learning model. The temporal data is sampled every 10th time step and spatial data is sampled to achieve grids with 16, 32, and 64 points for each domain size. The resulting highly-resolved, but coarsely gridded, data were used for both training and testing.

2.2. Model Set-Up

Many recent works build numerical methods with a machine learning component [18–26,36,39,43,46]. In contrast to these previous works, the machine learning model herein is applied solely to the linear spatial derivative term. In this section, we describe the construction of this model. The model is built off of a finite difference method for the third derivative term of the equation, specifically a second-order centered difference approximation [53], which has the following form:

$$(u_{xxx})_j \approx \frac{-\frac{1}{2}u_{j-2} + u_{j-1} - u_{j+1} + \frac{1}{2}u_{j+2}}{h^3}. \tag{5}$$

This approximation uses a five-point stencil with coefficients $-\frac{1}{2}, 1, 0, -1,$ and $\frac{1}{2}$. Let $b_1 = -\frac{1}{2}$ and $b_2 = 1$. Then, Equation (5) can be written as

$$(u_{xxx})_j \approx \frac{b_1 u_{j-2} + b_2 u_{j-1} - b_2 u_{j+1} - b_1 u_{j+2}}{h^3},$$

and the differentiation matrix is the matrix $\mathbf{B}_{FD}$ such that

$$\begin{bmatrix} (u_{xxx})_1 \\ (u_{xxx})_2 \\ \\ \vdots \\ \\ \\ (u_{xxx})_{N-1} \\ (u_{xxx})_N \end{bmatrix} \approx \frac{1}{h^3} \begin{bmatrix} 0 & -b_2 & -b_1 & 0 & \ldots & 0 & b_1 & b_2 \\ b_2 & 0 & -b_2 & -b_1 & 0 & \ldots & 0 & b_1 \\ b_1 & b_2 & 0 & -b_2 & -b_1 & 0 & \ldots & 0 \\ 0 & b_1 & b_2 & 0 & -b_2 & -b_1 & 0 & \ldots \\ \vdots & & \ddots & \ddots & \ddots & \ddots & \ddots & \vdots \\ \ldots & 0 & b_1 & b_2 & 0 & -b_2 & -b_1 & 0 \\ 0 & \ldots & 0 & b_1 & b_2 & 0 & -b_2 & -b_1 \\ -b_1 & 0 & \ldots & 0 & b_1 & b_2 & 0 & -b_2 \\ -b_2 & -b_1 & 0 & \ldots & 0 & b_1 & b_2 & 0 \end{bmatrix} \begin{bmatrix} u_1 \\ u_2 \\ \\ \vdots \\ \\ \\ u_{N-1} \\ u_N \end{bmatrix},$$

for j from 1 to N. $\mathbf{B}_{FD}$ is a circulant matrix, so the coefficients are the same in every row since they have no dependence on j [3]. Additionally, $\mathbf{B}_{FD}$ is anti-symmetric; that is, a matrix such that $\mathbf{B}^T = -\mathbf{B}$ where the superscript T denotes the transpose.

In this paper, the coefficients b_1 and b_2 are replaced with optimal weights found using machine learning that reduce error on coarse grids. The model function used to find the weights has the form

$$\overrightarrow{a_j(\vec{u}^n)} = \vec{b} + \mathbf{W}_1 \overrightarrow{\sigma(\mathbf{W}_2(\mathbf{X}_j \vec{u}^n))}, \tag{6}$$

which is a vector-valued function of length two, where $\vec{b}$ is a vector of length two of unknown coefficients, $\mathbf{W}_1$ and $\mathbf{W}_2$ are matrices of unknown coefficients with dimensions 2×2 and 2×5, respectively, and $\vec{\sigma}$ is an activation function which acts on the input vector component-wise. $\mathbf{X}_j$ is a $5 \times N$ matrix with entries

$$(\mathbf{X}_j)_{i,l} = \delta_{(j-3+i) \bmod N, l},$$

with mod N accounting for the periodicity, and where δ is the Kronecker delta defined as

$$\delta_{ij} = \begin{cases} 1, & \text{if } i = j, \\ 0, & \text{if } i \neq j, \end{cases}$$

so that $\mathbf{X}_j$ applied to u^n evaluates the five adjacent function values,

$$\mathbf{X}_j \vec{u}^n = \begin{pmatrix} u^n_{j-2} \\ u^n_{j-1} \\ u^n_j \\ u^n_{j+1} \\ u^n_{j+2} \end{pmatrix}, \tag{7}$$

thus the model design preserves the support of the finite difference stencil (*Equation (7) will look different when $j = 1, 2, N-1$ or N due to periodicity at the boundaries, and this change is handled explicitly in the definition of X_j*).

The differentiation matrix of the machine learning model, denoted $\mathbf{B}_{ML}$, is enforced to be anti-symmetric so that its eigenvalues lie on the imaginary axis. This gives a stable scheme, but also enforces an added consistency with the PDE. For each j from 1 to N, the output of the vector function of the machine learning model is

$$\overrightarrow{a_j(\vec{u}^n)} = \begin{bmatrix} (a_1)_j \\ (a_2)_j t \end{bmatrix}.$$

Unlike in the finite difference method, the coefficients found using the machine learning model are different for every row, since they depend on u^n_j. Therefore, $\mathbf{B}_{ML}$ has the following form:

$$\begin{bmatrix}
0 & (-a_2)_1 & (-a_1)_1 & 0 & \cdots & 0 & (a_1)_{N-1} & (a_2)_N \\
(a_2)_1 & 0 & (-a_2)_2 & (-a_1)_2 & 0 & \cdots & 0 & (a_1)_N \\
(a_1)_1 & (a_2)_2 & 0 & (-a_2)_3 & (-a_1)_3 & 0 & \cdots & 0 \\
0 & (a_1)_2 & (a_2)_3 & 0 & (-a_2)_4 & (-a_1)_4 & 0 & \cdots \\
\ddots & \ddots & \ddots & \ddots & \ddots & \ddots & \ddots & \ddots \\
\cdots & 0 & (a_1)_{N-5} & (a_2)_{N-4} & 0 & (-a_2)_{N-3} & (-a_1)_{N-3} & 0 \\
0 & \cdots & 0 & (a_1)_{N-4} & (a_2)_{N-3} & 0 & (-a_2)_{N-2} & (-a_1)_{N-2} \\
(-a_1)_{N-1} & 0 & \cdots & 0 & (a_1)_{N-3} & (a_2)_{N-2} & 0 & (-a_2)_{N-1} \\
(-a_2)_N & (-a_1)_N & 0 & \cdots & 0 & (a_1)_{N-2} & (a_1)_{N-1} & 0
\end{bmatrix}.$$

This results in a machine learning approximation for the third derivative term as follows:

$$(u_{xxx})_j \approx \frac{(a_1)_{j-2} u_{j-2} + (a_2)_{j-1} u_{j-1} + (-a_2)_j u_{j+1} + (-a_1)_j u_{j+2}}{h^3}. \tag{8}$$

This approximation is substituted into the IMEX2 scheme, replacing the finite difference approximation for the third derivative term, which gives

$$\frac{u^{n+1} - u^{n-1}}{2k} = -\frac{1}{2h^3} \mathbf{B}_{ML}(u^n) u^{n+1} - \frac{1}{2h^3} \mathbf{B}_{ML}(u^n) u^{n-1} + f(u^n). \tag{9}$$

This scheme differs from the IMEX2 scheme in Equation (3) since g now depends on u at two different time steps. Since this scheme is not self-starting, the following time-stepping scheme is used for the first time step:

$$\frac{u^{n+1} - u^n}{k} = -\frac{1}{h^3}\mathbf{B}_{ML}(u^n)u^{n+1} + f(u^n).$$

2.3. Objective Function and Error

The objective function used for training is the truncation error of Equation (9), evaluated by using the highly-resolved numerical simulations as a proxy for the exact solution. The nonlinear function f is approximated using a second-order finite difference approximation for first derivatives. Minimization techniques are then applied to the scheme to optimize the model's truncation error.

Gradient-based optimization algorithms for the objective function are commonly used to include stochastic gradient descent [19,24,43], Adam optimizer [19,20,23,42], Broyden–Fletcher–Goldfarb–Shanno (BFGS) [27], and Limited-memory BFGS [19,21,22,26,28,39,44]. For this paper, the gradient-based method used to minimize the truncation error is the steepest descent algorithm. The tolerance for the algorithm is one-tenth of the truncation error of the corresponding finite difference method (where $\vec{b} = [-\frac{1}{2}; 1]$ and $\mathbf{W}_1$ and $\mathbf{W}_2$ are matrices whose entries are all zeros). This finite difference method was also used as an initial guess in the optimization routines.

In addition to the truncation error, the forward error is also used as a measure of performance. The forward error is calculated by taking the 2-norm of the difference between the approximated solutions found using each method and the highly-resolved Fourier solution, u_F:

$$\text{Forward error} = ||u - u_F||_2.$$

To summarize, the training data from the highly-resolved Fourier simulations is used as a proxy for the exact solution, then the truncation error of (9) is minimized. The weights (i.e., the entries of $\vec{b}$, $\mathbf{W}_1$, and $\mathbf{W}_2$) are optimized via steepest descent. Once these weights are found, they are used in Equation (9) to evolve new initial data. The results are compared to finite difference and Fourier collocation using the same time-stepper and spatial discretization.

3. Results

Two training routines were evaluated. One training method used a single solution trajectory over a short time interval. The second used two solution trajectories (again over a short time interval). In both scenarios, the trained numerical method was evaluated against the parent finite difference method and Fourier collocation both at and near the training initial data, for short and long times.

In both training routines, the set of initial data trained and tested on is of the form

$$u(x,0) = -A\left[\frac{c}{2}\text{sech}^2\left(\frac{\sqrt{c}}{2}x\right)\right], \tag{10}$$

where A is a changeable parameter. When $A = 1$, this is a soliton solution of the KdV equation traveling at speed c. For $A \neq 1$, the solution is not a traveling wave, and has a more complicated trajectory. The model was trained and tested using both traveling wave and non-traveling wave initial data.

The activation function used in simulations in this paper was the hyperbolic tangent function, which resulted in the machine learning model function

$$\overrightarrow{a_j(\vec{u}^n)} = \vec{b} + \mathbf{W}_1 \overrightarrow{\tanh(\mathbf{W}_2(\mathbf{X}_j \vec{u}^n))}. \tag{11}$$

This is a common activation function [50] and is used in several other recent works involving PDEs [15,19–22,25,43–45].

Figure 2 shows an example plot of the truncation error through the training time using the trained speed $c = 1$ and trained $A = 1$. For larger h values, the method converged to below the threshold of one-tenth the truncation error value for the finite difference method. For smaller h, the method is unable to converge below this threshold. For these values, the model may need to be amended by adding more layers or by using a broader stencil. For the remaining figures shown in this paper, a step size of $h = 2.5$ is used, which uses a grid of 16 data points.

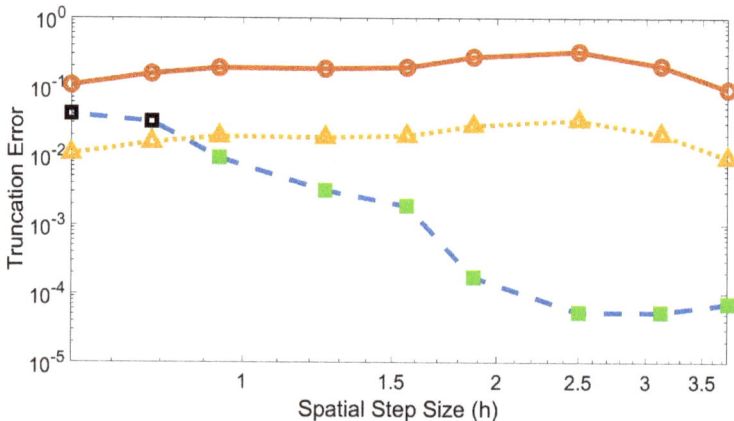

Figure 2. Truncation error for the machine learning and finite difference methods at each spatial step size through training time using trained speed $c = 1$ and trained $A = 1$. Blue dashed line with square markers is the machine learned error with green solid denoting convergence of minimization algorithm and black outline denoting non-convergence; solid red line with circle markers is the finite difference error; yellow dotted line with triangle markers is one-tenth the finite difference error.

In Figure 2, the trained scheme significantly outperforms the finite difference method on coarse grids, but the gains decrease with step size. There is no gain in using this methodology as $h \to 0$ (nor is any convergence study conducted in the small h limit). The remainder of the paper considers a fixed model with fixed step size, where the machine-learned procedure outperforms Fourier collocation and classic finite difference. To decrease errors beyond those presented, one could consider a convergence study in the number of layers or the breadth of the layers in the machine learning model. Generally, more layers in neural networks can provide more accurate approximations [49]; however, the training cost increases with layer width and depth. The effect of more or broader layers is a future research avenue.

Figure 3 shows the forward error over time using the trained speed $c = 1$ and $A = 1$, with Figure 3a showing the error through time $t = 3$. The forward error of the machine learned model is less than that of the finite difference method for the entire time interval, even though the method was only trained on a very small portion of the entire time interval, as shown in Figure 3b.

3.1. Single Solution Trajectory

When the model was trained on a single solution trajectory, one A, c pair from (10), the training set was the the first 12 consecutive time steps (t_0 to t_{11}) of a coarse sampling of the highly-resolved solution. The model was tested using other initial data (nearby A, c pairs) and for longer times.

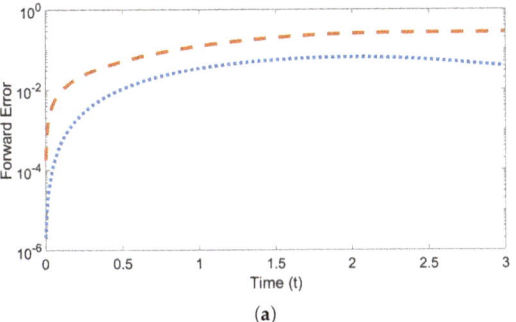 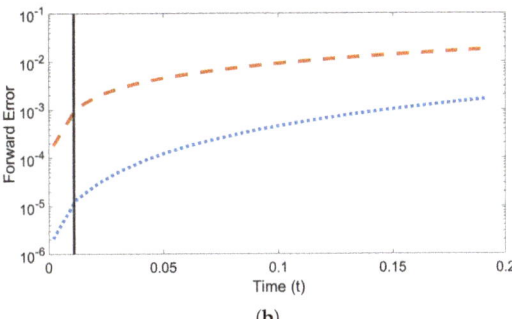

Figure 3. Forward error over time training and testing on speed $c = 1$ and $A = 1$. Red dashed line is the finite difference error; blue dotted line is the machine learned error. Dark gray vertical line indicates the end of the training time interval (**a**) Error through time $t = 3$. (**b**) Error through time $t = 0.2$.

Discussion

The model was trained on an initial highly-resolved solution set using a non-solitary wave, with $c = 1$ and $A = 1.5$. Figure 4 shows the forward error rates for each c and A that were trained and tested on. The forward error rate was calculated by taking the logarithm of the absolute maximum forward error of the machine learning model over the entire time interval divided by the absolute maximum forward error of the finite difference model over the time interval. In Figure 4, the solutions with c and A values within the region surrounded by the solid black lines performed 10 times better than the finite difference method. From Figure 4a, a range of solutions found by testing on varying c and A values around the solution that was trained on, which is indicated by the '+', also have lower forward errors when using the optimal coefficients found during minimization. The only areas shown where the machine learning model did not outperform finite difference methods were for most A values used in combination with speeds less than 0.75.

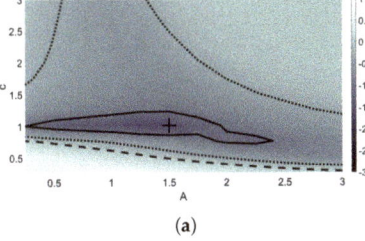 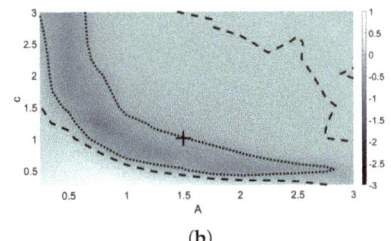

Figure 4. Forward error rate plots comparing performance of finite different methods and the machine learning model. Model trained using $c = 1$ and $A = 1.5$, indicated by "+". Model tested using c and A values ranging from 0.25 to 3. Contours indicate initial data where the machine learning model performs 10 times better than (solid), 2 times better than (dotted), and equivalent to (dashed) finite difference methods. (**a**) Maximum forward error rate through training time interval. (**b**) Maximum forward error rate through time $t = 3$.

At time $t = 3$, the machine learning model continued to outperform finite difference methods for most A, c pairs plotted in Figure 4b; however, the region of solutions that performed 10 times better than finite difference methods has essentially become non-existent. A region of A, c pairs still performed at least two times better than the finite difference method, as indicated by the dotted contours.

Figure 5 shows the wave solution at time $t = 3$ using test values $c = 1$ and $A = 0.75$ comparing the highly-resolved Fourier method, finite difference method, the machine learning model, and an under-resolved Fourier model. The machine learning model outperformed both classical methods in predicting the behavior of the wave solution at a time well beyond the interval it was trained on and on a coarse grid. The approximate computation time for each method is as follows: 0.352 s for machine-learned; 0.344 s for finite difference; and 0.037 s for under-resolved Fourier. Several other initial data were used for training and testing, both on solitary and non-solitary waves, with similar results.

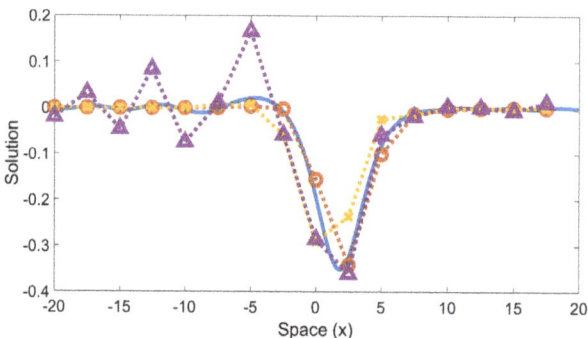

Figure 5. Time evolution of a wave trained on a non-solitary wave ($c = 1$ and $A = 1.5$) and tested on a different non-solitary wave ($c = 1$ and $A = 0.75$). Solution at time $t = 3$. Solid blue line is the highly-resolved Fourier; dotted red line with "o" markers is the machine learning model; dotted yellow line with "x" markers is finite difference; dotted purple line with "△" markers is Fourier on coarse grid. The machine-learned model relative forward error is 0.1322. The finite difference relative forward error is 0.3934. The coarse Fourier relative forward error is 0.5663.

It is important to note that the methodology in this paper has been set up so that the truncation error of the machine learning model will always be less than that of the finite difference method when the minimization method converges. By the Lax Equivalence Theorem, the forward error of a method is bounded by the sum of the accumulated truncation error of that method [2,11,12], e.g.,

$$\|\tilde{u} - u^n\| \leq \sum_{j=0}^{n-1} \sigma^j k \tau_k(t_j). \tag{12}$$

In (12), σ is the maximal growth rate of errors from one step to the next (stable schemes have $\sigma \leq 1$), $\tilde{u}$ is the exact solution, u^n is the numerical solution at time t_n, and $\tau_k(t_j)$ is the truncation error at time t_j. As a consequence of (12), the forward error of the machine learning model must be less than the accumulated truncation error of the model, and the forward error of the finite difference method must be less than the accumulated truncation error of the finite difference method; however, nothing can be said about the ordering of the forward error of the two methods. In other words, the methodology does not guarantee that the forward error of the machine learning model will be less than the forward error of the finite difference method. That said, the spectrum of the linear operators in all cases (machine learned model, finite difference, and Fourier) lie exactly on the boundary of the linear stability region of IMEX2, so the growth rates of truncation errors from step to step are exactly one ($\sigma = 1$), and there is no difference in the temporal stability of these schemes. The proof of the Lax Equivalence Theorem uses the triangle inequality, so in principle there could be more cancellation in one scheme than another. We, however, observe that the forward error and the accumulated truncation error are matched closely for all methods. Even though the machine learned model is trained using the truncation error as the objective function, it effectively also minimizes the forward error (*Direct minimization* of the forward error would be significantly more expensive as it would require running the scheme (with its matrix inversions) during each evaluation of the objective function in the training).

3.2. Two Sets of Initial Data

In addition to training on a single solution trajectory, we tested models that were trained on two sets of initial data simultaneously. The results of this training algorithm presented here used pairs $(A, c) = (1, 1)$ and $(A, c) = (1, 2)$, so the model is training on two solitary waves of different speeds. The data from the first seven time steps (t_0 to t_6) of each set of solutions were used to train the model. To create the objective function for two sets of solutions, the truncation error for each is combined to create a multi-objective minimization problem. The error using each solution is calculated individually then normalized by dividing by the square of the largest absolute solution from the respective training data set before being added together to create the objective function. In the steepest descent algorithm, the threshold is one-tenth of the minimum finite difference truncation error between the two solutions. This minimization process allows the algorithm to find the optimal coefficients that minimize both initial sets of data simultaneously.

Discussion

Figure 6 shows the forward error rate plots for training on the two solutions. In Figure 6a, by training on two initial solutions with different speeds, a larger range of speeds used in combination with varying A values were able to outperform the finite difference method by at least 10 times through the training time, as compared to training using only one solution with one speed, as was performed in Figure 4. As the wave propagates to time $t = 3$, there were no areas where the machine learning model outperformed the finite difference method by 10 times or more, although a majority of (A, c) pairs shown in Figure 6b resulted in a method that outperformed the classical method.

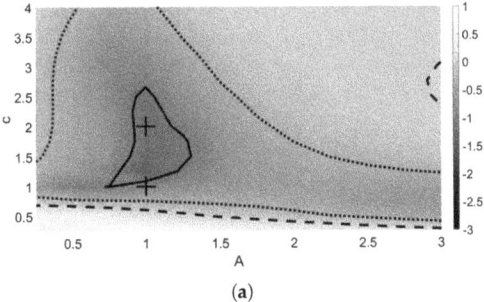
(a)

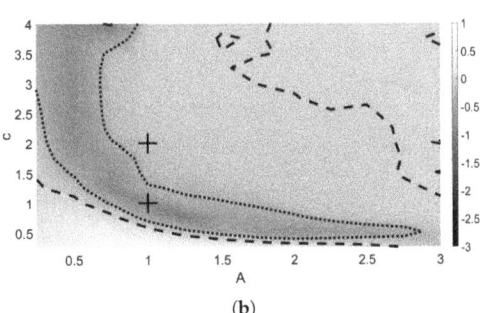
(b)

Figure 6. Forward error rate plots comparing performance of finite different methods and the machine learning model. Model trained using speeds $c_1 = 1$ and $c_2 = 2$ and $A = 1$, indicated by "+". Model tested using c and A values ranging from 0.25 to 3. Contours indicate initial data where the machine learning model performs 10 times better than (solid), 2 times better than (dotted), and equivalent to (dashed) finite difference methods. (**a**) Maximum forward error rate through end of training time interval. (**b**) Maximum forward error rate through time $t = 3$.

A wave solution is shown in Figure 7 at time $t = 3$, which tests the model using $c = 1$ and $A = 0.75$. The model outperformed both the finite difference and under-resolved Fourier methods in predicting the behavior of the highly-resolved solution.

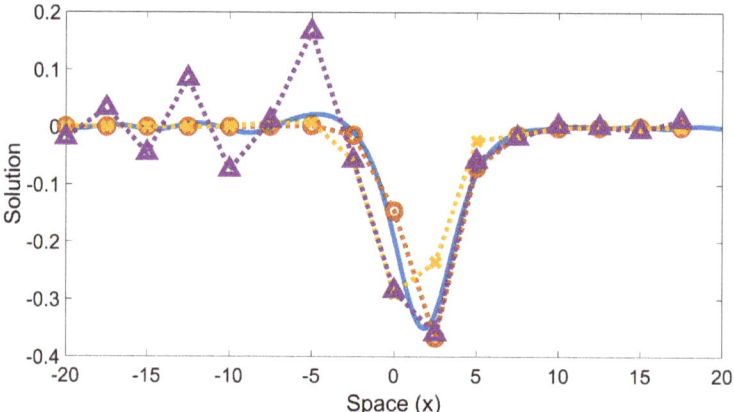

Figure 7. Time evolution of a wave trained using $c_1 = 1$ and $c_2 = 2$ and $A = 1$ and tested on a wave using $c = 1$ and $A = 0.75$. Solution at time $t = 3$. Solid blue line is the highly-resolved Fourier collocation method; dotted red line with "o" markers is the machine learning model; dotted yellow line with "x" markers is the finite difference result; dotted purple line with "Δ" markers are a Fourier collocation on the coarse grid. The machine-learned model relative forward error is 0.0452. The finite difference relative forward error is 0.1003. The coarse Fourier relative forward error is 0.1444.

The optimal coefficients found by training on the previous two initial data were tested using two different sets of data, where $(A, c) = (1, 2.25)$ and $(A, c) = (1, 0.75)$. Figure 8b shows the collision of the two solitons as they propagate through space and time using the machine learned model on a coarse grid. Despite the model not being trained on a collision, it is still able to pick up on the overall dynamics, displaying the new trajectories of each wave after the collision occurs. Figure 9 shows the time evolution of the waves, comparing the machine-learned solution to the highly-resolved Fourier at different times throughout the interval. The model is a bit slow at picking up the trajectories of the waves, but is able to recognize the collision between the solitons.

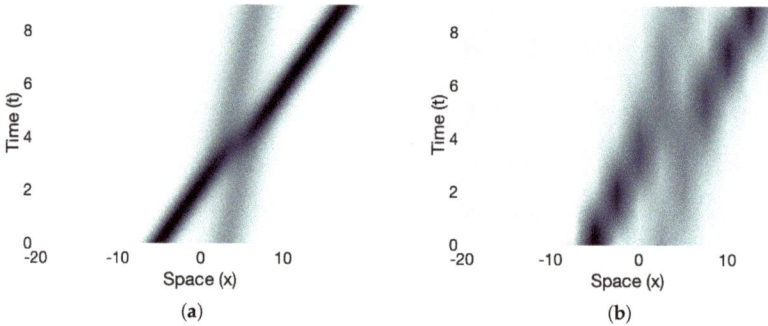

Figure 8. Simulation of a collision between solitons with speeds $c = 2.25$ and $c = 0.75$. (**a**) Highly-resolved Fourier dynamics. (**b**) Machine learned dynamics. Coefficients found by training on initial data $(A, c) = (1, 1)$ and $(A, c) = (1, 2)$; tested using $(A, c) = (1, 2.25)$ and $(A, c) = (1, 0.75)$.

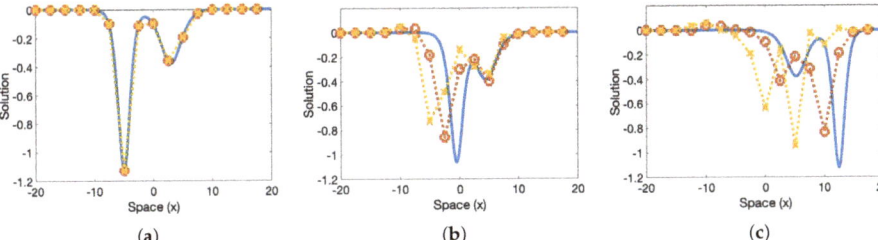

Figure 9. The collision of two solitary waves is depicted. The machine learned model was trained using two single solitary wave trajectories at $(A, c) = (1, 1)$ and $(A, c) = (1, 2)$; the colliding waves in this test had different amplitudes from the trained trajectories, $(A, c) = (1, 2.25)$ and $(A, c) = (1, 0.75)$, and the training did not include a collision. The solid blue line is the highly-resolved Fourier; the dotted red line with "o" markers is the machine learning model; the dotted yellow line with "x" markers is the finite difference result. The solution at time $t = 0$ is in panel (**a**), at $t = 2$ in panel (**b**), and at $t = 7$ in panel (**c**).

4. Conclusions

In this paper, machine learning was utilized to optimize the coefficients of a numerical differencing scheme for the KdV equation. This scheme was trained on a coarse grid and outperformed two classical methods (finite difference and Fourier). Training procedures using a single solution trajectory and a pair of trajectories were implemented. The model was tested on a variety of nearby initial data, both solitary and non-solitary trajectories. A solitary wave collision was also tested. The methodology is expected to be applicable to other nonlinear wave equations. Future work could include using the forward error as the objective function instead of the truncation error; however, this will be more expensive as a matrix inversion will be required for the time-stepping scheme for each iteration in the steepest descent algorithm. Other future work could include training the model on non-consecutive time steps by randomly sampling the initial data to obtain the training and test data sets as has been carried out in several recent works [19,21–23,25,36,37,39]. This could also include randomly sampling from several initial data sets. Additionally, more layers could be added to the model. A different activation function could be used, e.g., leaky or standard rectified linear unit [15,44–46]. The method also naturally generalizes to broader stencils.

Author Contributions: Conceptualization, B.F.A.; methodology, K.O.F.W. and B.F.A.; software, K.O.F.W.; validation, K.O.F.W. and B.F.A.; formal analysis, K.O.F.W. and B.F.A.; writing—original draft preparation, K.O.F.W. and B.F.A.; writing—review and editing, K.O.F.W. and B.F.A.; visualization, K.O.F.W.; supervision, B.F.A.; project administration, B.F.A.; funding acquisition, B.F.A. All authors have read and agreed to the published version of the manuscript.

Funding: B.F.A. acknowledges funding from the APTAWG, under the program "Simulation of laser propagation in reactive media".

Data Availability Statement: MATLAB code is available upon request.

Acknowledgments: The authors would like to thank Jonah Reeger for helpful conversations.

Conflicts of Interest: This report was prepared as an account of work sponsored by an agency of the United States Government. Neither the United States Government nor any agency thereof, nor any of their employees, make any warranty, express or implied, or assume any legal liability or responsibility for the accuracy, completeness, or usefulness of any information, apparatus, product, or process disclosed, or represent that its use would not infringe privately owned rights. Reference herein to any specific commercial product, process, or service by trade name, trademark, manufacturer, or otherwise does not necessarily constitute or imply its endorsement, recommendation, or favoring by the United States Government or any agency thereof. The views and opinions of authors expressed herein do not necessarily state or reflect those of the United States Government or any agency thereof.

References

1. Thomée, V. From finite differences to finite elements: A short history of numerical analysis of partial differential equations. In *Numerical Analysis: Historical Developments in the 20th Century*; Elsevier: Amsterdam, The Netherlands, 2001; pp. 361–414.
2. Fornberg, B. *A Practical Guide to Pseudospectral Methods*; Number 1; Cambridge University Press: Cambridge, UK, 1998.
3. Trefethen, L.N. *Spectral Methods in MATLAB*; SIAM: Philadelphia, PA, USA, 2000.
4. LeVeque, R.J. *Finite Difference Methods for Ordinary and Partial Differential Equations: Steady-State and Time-Dependent Problems*; SIAM: Philadelphia, PA, USA, 2007.
5. Milewski, P.A.; Tabak, E.G. A pseudospectral procedure for the solution of nonlinear wave equations with examples from free-surface flows. *SIAM J. Sci. Comput.* **1999**, *21*, 1102–1114. [CrossRef]
6. Jin, S.; Xin, Z. The relaxation schemes for systems of conservation laws in arbitrary space dimensions. *Commun. Pure Appl. Math.* **1995**, *48*, 235–276. [CrossRef]
7. Dutykh, D.; Pelinovsky, E. Numerical simulation of a solitonic gas in KdV and KdV–BBM equations. *Phys. Lett. A* **2014**, *378*, 3102–3110. [CrossRef]
8. Akers, B.; Liu, T.; Reeger, J. A radial basis function finite difference scheme for the Benjamin–Ono equation. *Mathematics* **2020**, *9*, 65. [CrossRef]
9. Akers, B.F.; Ambrose, D.M. Efficient computation of coordinate-free models of flame fronts. *ANZIAM J.* **2021**, *63*, 58–69.
10. Akers, B. The generation of capillary-gravity solitary waves by a surface pressure forcing. *Math. Comput. Simul.* **2012**, *82*, 958–967. [CrossRef]
11. Novak, K. *Numerical Methods for Scientific Computing*; Lulu Press: Morrisville, NC, USA, 2017.
12. Smith, G.D. *Numerical Solution of Partial Differential Equations: Finite Difference Methods*; Oxford University Press: Oxford, UK, 1985.
13. Quarteroni, A.; Sacco, R.; Saleri, F. *Numerical Mathematics*; Springer Science & Business Media: Berlin/Heidelberg, Germany, 2010; Volume 37.
14. Pathak, J.; Mustafa, M.; Kashinath, K.; Motheau, E.; Kurth, T.; Day, M. Using machine learning to augment coarse-grid computational fluid dynamics simulations. *arXiv* **2020**, arXiv:2010.00072.
15. Bar-Sinai, Y.; Hoyer, S.; Hickey, J.; Brenner, M.P. Learning data-driven discretizations for partial differential equations. *Proc. Natl. Acad. Sci. USA* **2019**, *116*, 15344–15349. [CrossRef]
16. Nordström, J.; Ålund, O. Neural network enhanced computations on coarse grids. *J. Comput. Phys.* **2021**, *425*, 109821. [CrossRef]
17. Korteweg, D.J.; De Vries, G. XLI. On the change of form of long waves advancing in a rectangular canal, and on a new type of long stationary waves. *Lond. Edinb. Dublin Philos. Mag. J. Sci.* **1895**, *39*, 422–443. [CrossRef]
18. Rudy, S.H.; Brunton, S.L.; Proctor, J.L.; Kutz, J.N. Data-driven discovery of partial differential equations. *Sci. Adv.* **2017**, *3*, e1602614. [CrossRef] [PubMed]
19. Guo, Y.; Cao, X.; Liu, B.; Gao, M. Solving partial differential equations using deep learning and physical constraints. *Appl. Sci.* **2020**, *10*, 5917. [CrossRef]
20. Xu, H.; Chang, H.; Zhang, D. DL-PDE: Deep-learning based data-driven discovery of partial differential equations from discrete and noisy data. *arXiv* **2019**, arXiv:1908.04463.
21. Bai, Y.; Chaolu, T.; Bilige, S. Physics informed by deep learning: Numerical solutions of modified Korteweg-de Vries equation. *Adv. Math. Phys.* **2021**, *2021*, 1–11. [CrossRef]
22. Zhang, Y.; Dong, H.; Sun, J.; Wang, Z.; Fang, Y.; Kong, Y. The new simulation of quasiperiodic wave, periodic wave, and soliton solutions of the KdV-mKdV Equation via a deep learning method. *Comput. Intell. Neurosci.* **2021**, *2021*, 8548482. [CrossRef] [PubMed]
23. Li, J.; Chen, Y. A deep learning method for solving third-order nonlinear evolution equations. *Commun. Theor. Phys.* **2020**, *72*, 115003. [CrossRef]
24. Li, J.; Chen, J.; Li, B. Gradient-optimized physics-informed neural networks (GOPINNs): A deep learning method for solving the complex modified KdV equation. *Nonlinear Dyn.* **2022**, *107*, 781–792. [CrossRef]
25. Raissi, M. Deep hidden physics models: Deep learning of nonlinear partial differential equations. *J. Mach. Learn. Res.* **2018**, *19*, 932–955.
26. Raissi, M.; Karniadakis, G.E. Hidden physics models: Machine learning of nonlinear partial differential equations. *J. Comput. Phys.* **2018**, *357*, 125–141. [CrossRef]
27. Wen, Y.; Chaolu, T. Learning the nonlinear solitary wave solution of the Korteweg-de Vries equation with novel neural network algorithm. *Entropy* **2023**, *25*, 704. [CrossRef]
28. Gurieva, J.; Vasiliev, E.; Smirnov, L. Improvements of accuracy and convergence speed of AI-based solution for the Korteweg-De Vries equation. ББК 22.18 я43 М34 **2022**, *5*, 49336041.
29. Wu, H.; Xu, H. Studies of wave interaction of high-order Korteweg-de Vries equation by means of the homotopy strategy and neural network prediction. *Phys. Lett. A* **2021**, *415*, 127653. [CrossRef]
30. Remoissenet, M. *Waves Called Solitons: Concepts and Experiments*; Springer Science & Business Media: Berlin/Heidelberg, Germany, 2013.
31. Markowski, P.; Richardson, Y. *Mesoscale Meteorology in Midlatitudes*; John Wiley & Sons: Hoboken, NJ, USA, 2011; Volume 2.
32. Holton, J. *An Introduction to Dynamic Meteorology*; International Geophysics; Elsevier Science: Amsterdam, The Netherlands, 2004.

33. Um, K.; Brand, R.; Fei, Y.R.; Holl, P.; Thuerey, N. Solver-in-the-loop: Learning from differentiable physics to interact with iterative pde-solvers. *Adv. Neural Inf. Process. Syst.* **2020**, *33*, 6111–6122.
34. Khodadadian, A.; Parvizi, M.; Teshnehlab, M.; Heitzinger, C. Rational Design of Field-Effect Sensors Using Partial Differential Equations, Bayesian Inversion, and Artificial Neural Networks. *Sensors* **2022**, *22*, 4785. [CrossRef] [PubMed]
35. Noii, N.; Khodadadian, A.; Ulloa, J.; Aldakheel, F.; Wick, T.; Francois, S.; Wriggers, P. Bayesian inversion with open-source codes for various one-dimensional model problems in computational mechanics. *Arch. Comput. Methods Eng.* **2022**, *29*, 4285–4318. [CrossRef]
36. Long, Z.; Lu, Y.; Ma, X.; Dong, B. Pde-net: Learning pdes from data. In Proceedings of the International Conference on Machine Learning, PMLR, Stockholm, Sweden, 10–15 July 2018; pp. 3208–3216.
37. Wu, K.; Xiu, D. Data-driven deep learning of partial differential equations in modal space. *J. Comput. Phys.* **2020**, *408*, 109307. [CrossRef]
38. Yang, X.; Wang, Z. Solving Benjamin–Ono equation via gradient balanced PINNs approach. *Eur. Phys. J. Plus* **2022**, *137*, 864. [CrossRef]
39. Raissi, M.; Perdikaris, P.; Karniadakis, G.E. Physics-informed neural networks: A deep learning framework for solving forward and inverse problems involving nonlinear partial differential equations. *J. Comput. Physics* **2019**, *378*, 686–707. [CrossRef]
40. He, K.; Zhang, X.; Ren, S.; Sun, J. Deep residual learning for image recognition. In Proceedings of the IEEE Conference on Computer Vision and Pattern Recognition, Las Vegas, NV, USA, 26 June–1 July 2016; pp. 770–778.
41. James, G.; Witten, D.; Hastie, T.; Tibshirani, R. *An Introduction to Statistical Learning*; Springer: Berlin/Heidelberg, Germany, 2013; Volume 112.
42. Bar, L.; Sochen, N. Unsupervised deep learning algorithm for PDE-based forward and inverse problems. *arXiv* **2019**, arXiv:1904.05417.
43. Sirignano, J.; Spiliopoulos, K. DGM: A deep learning algorithm for solving partial differential equations. *J. Comput. Phys.* **2018**, *375*, 1339–1364. [CrossRef]
44. Kadeethum, T.; Jørgensen, T.M.; Nick, H.M. Physics-informed neural networks for solving nonlinear diffusivity and Biot's equations. *PLoS ONE* **2020**, *15*, e0232683. [CrossRef]
45. Beck, C.; Hutzenthaler, M.; Jentzen, A.; Kuckuck, B. An overview on deep learning-based approximation methods for partial differential equations. *arXiv* **2020**, arXiv:2012.12348.
46. Blechschmidt, J.; Ernst, O.G. Three ways to solve partial differential equations with neural networks—A review. *GAMM-Mitt.* **2021**, *44*, e202100006. [CrossRef]
47. Meng, X.; Li, Z.; Zhang, D.; Karniadakis, G.E. PPINN: Parareal physics-informed neural network for time-dependent PDEs. *Comput. Methods Appl. Mech. Eng.* **2020**, *370*, 113250. [CrossRef]
48. Raissi, M.; Perdikaris, P.; Karniadakis, G.E. Physics informed deep learning (part i): Data-driven solutions of nonlinear partial differential equations. *arXiv* **2017**, arXiv:1711.10561.
49. Goodfellow, I.; Bengio, Y.; Courville, A. *Deep Learning*; Adaptive Computation and Machine Learning Series; MIT Press: Cambridge, MA, USA, 2017; pp. 321–359.
50. Géron, A. *Hands-on Machine Learning with Scikit-Learn, Keras, and TensorFlow: Concepts, Tools, and Techniques to Build Intelligent Systems*; O'Reilly Media, Inc.: Newton, MA, USA, 2019.
51. Ascher, U.M.; Ruuth, S.J.; Spiteri, R.J. Implicit-explicit Runge-Kutta methods for time-dependent partial differential equations. *Appl. Numer. Math.* **1997**, *25*, 151–167. [CrossRef]
52. Ascher, U.M.; Ruuth, S.J.; Wetton, B.T.R. Implicit-explicit methods for time-dependent partial differential equations. *SIAM J. Numer. Anal.* **1995**, *32*, 797–823. [CrossRef]
53. Fornberg, B. Generation of finite difference formulas on arbitrarily spaced grids. *Math. Comput.* **1988**, *51*, 699–706. [CrossRef]

Disclaimer/Publisher's Note: The statements, opinions and data contained in all publications are solely those of the individual author(s) and contributor(s) and not of MDPI and/or the editor(s). MDPI and/or the editor(s) disclaim responsibility for any injury to people or property resulting from any ideas, methods, instructions or products referred to in the content.

Article

A Bibliometric Analysis of Digital Twin in the Supply Chain

Weng Siew Lam *, Weng Hoe Lam and Pei Fun Lee

Department of Physical and Mathematical Science, Faculty of Science, Universiti Tunku Abdul Rahman, Kampar Campus, Jalan Universiti, Bandar Barat, Kampar 31900, Perak, Malaysia; whlam@utar.edu.my (W.H.L.); pflee@utar.edu.my (P.F.L.)
* Correspondence: lamws@utar.edu.my

Abstract: Digital twin is the digital representation of an entity, and it drives Industry 4.0. This paper presents a bibliometric analysis of digital twin in the supply chain to help researchers, industry practitioners, and academics to understand the trend, development, and focus of the areas of digital twin in the supply chain. This paper found several key clusters of research, including the designing of a digital twin model, integration of a digital twin model, application of digital twin in quality control, and digital twin in digitalization. In the embryonic stage of research, digital twin was tested in the production line with limited optimization. In the development stage, the importance of digital twin in Industry 4.0 was observed, as big data, machine learning, Industrial Internet of Things, blockchain, edge computing, and cloud-based systems complemented digital twin models. Digital twin was applied to improve sustainability in manufacturing and production logistics. In the current prosperity stage with high annual publications, the recent trends of this topic focus on the integration of deep learning, data models, and artificial intelligence for digitalization. This bibliometric analysis also found that the COVID-19 pandemic drove the start of the prosperity stage of digital twin research in the supply chain. Researchers in this field are slowly moving towards applying digital twin for human-centric systems and mass personalization to prepare to transit to Industry 5.0.

Keywords: digital twin; machine learning; Industry 4.0; supply chain; bibliometric analysis; subject area

MSC: 00A06

Citation: Lam, W.S.; Lam, W.H.; Lee, P.F. A Bibliometric Analysis of Digital Twin in the Supply Chain. *Mathematics* 2023, *11*, 3350. https://doi.org/10.3390/math11153350

Academic Editors: Aihua Wood and Qun Li

Received: 13 June 2023
Revised: 17 July 2023
Accepted: 24 July 2023
Published: 31 July 2023

Copyright: © 2023 by the authors. Licensee MDPI, Basel, Switzerland. This article is an open access article distributed under the terms and conditions of the Creative Commons Attribution (CC BY) license (https://creativecommons.org/licenses/by/4.0/).

1. Introduction

Many industries are red oceans, hypercompetitive, and oversaturated [1,2]. Shorter product lifecycles means that companies are placing more efforts in innovating new ideas for market launch [3]. Consumers have increased purchasing power as they are offered a large pool of product and service choices. Meanwhile, consumers are also given greater empowerment because they can obtain information online easily. Many companies often rely on market research when developing their products or services. However, market research is insufficient to bring success to a company as this process only helps companies to understand consumer demand. To increase sales and revenues, companies have to satisfy the demand by creating the right products and delivering astonishing services. Typically, companies can only test their new or upgraded offerings after creating and displaying them for sampling. This may be a long process as errors and faults could happen during production and the final product may not meet consumer expectations.

Digital twin shows the virtual representation of a physical entity that changes instantaneously with the actual object, process, or system [4,5]. This emerging technology allows companies to create a virtual manufacturing process to identify defects before the actual process is conducted [6]. Digital twin also helps to provide various results concurrently as inputs are manipulated when testing a product, process, or system [7,8]. Even as the production process is ongoing, the production team can halt the process to perform simulations with various ideas to examine the potential outcomes [9]. This enhances the risk assessment process and development of risk mitigation plan [10]. Moreover, the digital twin allows financial data to be incorporated so that the cost of the entire supply chain can be adjusted from time to time. As such, companies can save time and cost to deliver their products [11].

After obtaining data on consumer demands and expectations, the first step of developing a product is designing. The production trend has changed from make to stock to make to order as consumers are becoming more empowered. Thus, the process of designing is also becoming more complex to match the individual preferences. Digital twin then facilitates the translation of the needs of the customers to the product designs where the parameters, structures, and geometry of the product can be conceptualized in a virtual setting [12]. With constant data generation, the virtual product can be improved and optimized [13]. Zhang et al. [14] proposed a digital twin manufacturing cell framework for smart manufacturing that includes replicas for work in process items, devices, processes, and environments to simulate and optimize production. Cheng et al. [15] explained that the concept of smart manufacturing is data-driven to connect the physical and cyber worlds. Onaji et al. [16] proposed a digital twin framework for manufacturing. This framework consists of the integration of physical assets and virtual models, creating an intelligent layer to allow supportive decision making to take place.

The history of digital twin can be traced back to the 1960s when the National Aeronautics and Space Administration (NASA) created a representation of space vehicles to reflect their performances and identify faults when on a mission [17]. Then, in the early 2000s, Professor Michael Grieves presented the digital twin concept in his course [18]. This means that the research of digital twin in the supply chain only began after Professor Michael Grieves presented the white paper of digital twin in 2002 with the proposal to develop a product lifecycle management center [18,19]. This digital twin concept has three components, namely, the real spaces, virtual spaces, and a linking system to transfer data and information between the real and virtual spaces [20]. This was then called the "Mirrored Spaces Model" [21]. A year later, Kary Främling suggested an architecture where physical items would have a virtual representation for more efficient information flow in manufacturing [22]. In 2006, Hribernik et al. [23] also proposed a similar concept known as "product avatar". In the same year, the initial model of Professor Michael Greives was renamed to the "Information Mirroring Model" to emphasize the importance of two-way information flow and the availability of more than one virtual space for an individual real space [24].

The name "digital twin" was only widely applied from 2010 when NASA introduced digital twin in their roadmap. From the first presentation of a digital twin by Professor Grieves in 2002 until 2010, the application of digital twin was not widely explored as the concept of digital twin was still in its infancy. In 2012, NASA simulated vehicle management systems and maintenance to increase the safety and reliability of transportation [25]. Since then, the aerospace industry has been employing digital twin in research and development. As Industry 4.0 took place, Internet of Things then drove the advancement of digital twin in other fields, as large multinational companies such as IBM, Siemens, and General Electric implemented digital twin for optimization and prediction [4,26–28]. The global market for digital twin is expected to exceed USD 73 billion by 2027, with a compounded annual growth rate of greater than 60% [28]. The rapid growth of the digital twin industry will continue as this industry becomes one of the main drivers for Industry 4.0 [29].

Digital twin was also reflected in the planning, ordering, making, delivering, returning, and enabling in the supply chain operations reference (SCOR) model, which is a supply chain performance measurement model [30]. Planning in the supply chain requires past data for forecasting. Digital twin reduces the time between target setting, data collection from a large pool of sources, big data analytics, data processing, deriving inferences, and taking actions for future planning. Researchers can plan instantaneously by using the synchronized data and making changes in the virtual model with higher accuracy [31]. The longer the digital twin model runs, the more data it collects, the higher the precision of the model. Thus, product designs, inventory management, material usage, transportation, and lead time can be streamlined and optimized with ease and accuracy for profit maximization and cost reduction [32]. In the supply chain, digital twin can be found in the designing, manufacturing, and servicing phases [33]. In designing, digital twin provides information that could be used for decision making in various design processes. Digital twin can be used for geometry assurance in the design process for optimization in manufacturing variation [34]. Each design and dimension will be listed and formed into a locator or datum position. Digital twin can also provide information on the tolerances of each part in the design process before they are moved into production. Tao et al. [12] explained that the virtual model consists of the geometric and physical models of products, consumers, and the environments. This allows the designers to observe the behaviors of products and consumer interactions. After that, data from the behaviors, environmental data, or Internet data can be integrated into the virtual model to be analyzed and visualized using digital twin's cognitive abilities. Then, a simulation can take place to observe how the product would function in the real world. Besides creating a prototype, using virtual reality, consumers or designers can also interact with the virtual product. At the later stage, based on the outcomes of the digital twin model, sensors and actuators will be equipped on the physical item to allow the physical item to adjust itself to changes in the consumers and environment. Finally, networking technologies and cloud computing allow information transfer between the physical and virtual models. In short, product designs with digital twin begin with planning, conceptual designs, embodiment designs, detail designs, and virtual verifications. Digital twin can also be used for risk management to identify areas of hazard using the virtual model, especially for events such as natural disasters during shipping and accidents in ports [35–38].

Zhu et al. [39] reviewed production logistics activities such as transportation, packaging, warehousing, material distribution, and information processing with digital twin. In transportation, past data embedded in the production logistics of digital twin were used to highlight the bottlenecks in the entire transport process [40]. A digital twin model of the transportation system also allows for real-time tracking of the location and condition of cargoes during transit [41]. Pan et al. [42] proposed a digital twin control architecture to simulate, analyze, and optimize the production logistics in industrial parks in China. This digital twin solved the sudden surge in order volume, which could not be handled with the usual transportation and storage in the industrial parks because the digital twin model helped in arranging vehicles with optimal routing at the lowest cost. Wu et al. [43] developed an Industrial Internet of Things and Digital Twin model for finished goods logistics. This model helped to reduce picking time, detect emergency orders, and optimize waiting time in packaging. Marmolejo-Saucedo [44] optimized bin-packing issues with digital twin. This model reduced packaging volumes, lowered operation cost, and minimized servers. Leng et al. [45] used the digital twin system to optimize stacked packing and storage in a warehouse. A prototype was developed and applied in a tobacco warehouse that successfully maximized the utilization and efficiency of automated high-rise warehouse product service systems. Perez and Korth [46] adopted digital twin to establish a database for compliance in the handling and storage of dangerous goods in warehouses. Petković et al. [47] proposed a human intention prediction algorithm to estimate a worker's path in a warehouse. A very important benefit of digital twin is the ability to integrate all the production logistics activities for parallel monitoring [48].

Liu et al. [33] reviewed the applications of digital twin and found that digital twin helps in iterative optimization by integrating past product design with potential improvements for configuration and execution as digital twin could forecast the outcomes of the products and allow designers to take preventive measures [49]. This could also help in careful planning when selecting materials [50]. As virtual prototypes can be created with digital twin, designers are able to test various product designs under different conditions to find the best fit and balance between the expected and real functions. Therefore, digital twin is important to produce an effective product design within a shorter time frame. Currently, monitoring of the manufacturing process is performed in the physical floor. Digital twin allows monitoring with the virtual model as all data are integrated into the virtual model.

It combines past, current, and future data for real-time monitoring and forecasting of the future outcomes for informed decision making [51,52]. The importance of digital twin in manufacturing is the ability to visualize the production process and to compare the physical item with the virtual model to match expectations with realities as personalized production takes over the traditional manufacturing process [53]. Moreover, as unexpected events such as slight discrepancies of raw materials and underperformance of machines might happen, digital twin can adjust the entire manufacturing process quickly to produce similar results [54]. This reduces manufacturing defects and increases quality consistency of the produced items. After manufacturing and upon usage, digital twin can detect faults and perform predictive maintenance for issues that were not identified during the product design phase. For a large and complex product such as a vessel, digital twin can detect performance deviations and predict damages [55].

Digital twin is an important advancement in the supply chain during industrialization and digitalization. Liu et al. [33] reviewed the status, technologies, and application of digital twin. Holler et al. [56] reviewed 38 papers on digital twin until 2016 to clarify the status of digital twin during that time. Negri et al. [57] reviewed the definitions of digital twin and explored smart manufacturing with digital twin. Shekarian et al. [58] reviewed sustainable supply chain management in manufacturing, design, logistics, procurement, management information systems, quality assurance, safety, social responsibility, financial management, structural management, and promotional activities. This current paper aims to present a bibliometric analysis of digital twin in the supply chain. This bibliometric analysis is distinct and differs from past publications in which this analysis considers the application of digital twin in the entire supply chain, including product design, manufacturing, shipping, warehousing, logistics, port, packaging, distribution, and transportation. This bibliometric analysis also studied the impact of digital twin in Industry 4.0 and the future research and application of digital twin in Industry 5.0.

Bibliometric analysis includes performance analysis and science mapping [59]. Performance analysis studies the contributions of each research component such as authorship, publication title, keyword, and region [60,61]. Performance analysis includes performance metrics such as total publication (TP) and citation metrics such as number of cited publications (NCPs), total citations (TCs), average citation per paper (C/P), average citation per cited paper (C/CP), h-index, and g-index [62,63]. Science mapping examines the relationships that exist in each research component such as co-citation, co-occurrence, and co-authorship [64]. Science mapping visualizes the scientific links and systematic patterns within the research area to find connected research themes [65–67]. The main focus of a bibliometric analysis is to identify the scientific research contribution of the authors and countries [68]. This paper also determined the reputable publication titles for digital twin publications. Moreover, this paper underlined the topics of digital twin to uncover the hot topics in this area for potential future studies [69]. Moreover, this paper studied the evolvement of the research on digital twin over the years. This paper can be a reference to help researchers, governments, and industry leaders in developing a proper digitalization framework by including digital twin technology.

Section 2 presents the materials and methods for this bibliometric analysis. Section 3 discusses the findings of this bibliometric analysis. Section 4 concludes the paper with potential future studies.

2. Materials and Methods

This paper aims to present a bibliometric analysis of digital twin in the supply chain. The database used was the Web of Science. Owned by Thomson and Reuters, Web of Science has comprehensive and high-quality multidisciplinary journals and is becoming the most preferred database for bibliometric analysis [70–72]. Figure 1 presents the flowchart of the bibliometric analysis of digital twin in supply chain.

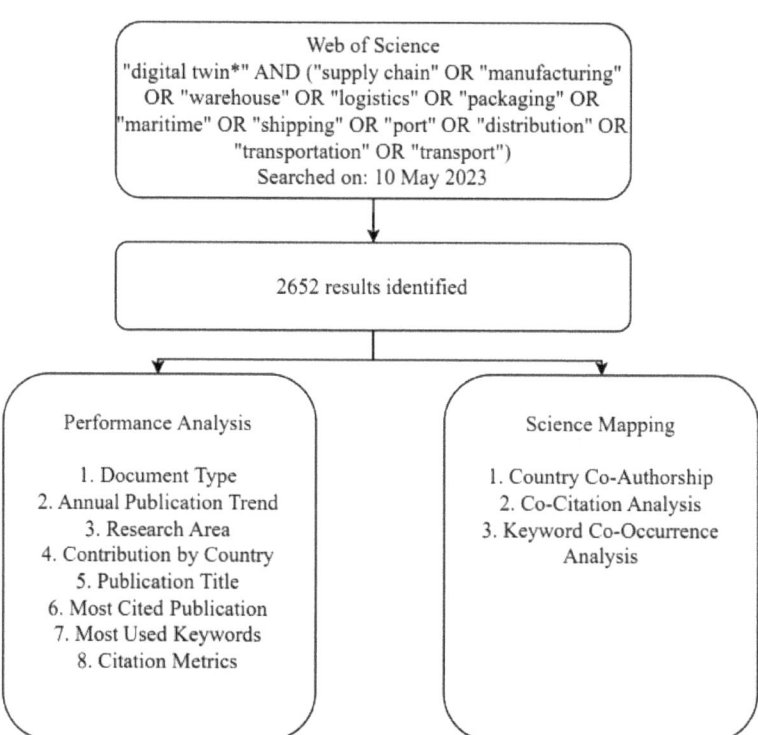

Figure 1. Flowchart of bibliometric analysis of digital twin in the supply chain.

Figure 1 presents the flowchart of the bibliometric analysis of digital twin in the supply chain. After identifying the keywords, the Web of Science database was queried, and 2652 documents were found to match the criteria for bibliometric analysis. The publication period was from 2014 to 2023. The data were exported on 10 May 2023. About 60.98% (or 1708 documents) of the 2652 documents are articles, followed by proceeding papers (29.95%), review articles (7.64%), editorial materials (0.86%), and book chapters (0.57%). The document types are described in Table 1.

Table 1. Document types.

Document Types	Total Publications (TP)	Percentage (%)
Article	1708	60.98
Proceeding paper	839	29.95
Review article	214	7.64
Editorial material	24	0.86
Book chapters	16	0.57

Performance analysis is then performed using Harzing's Publish or Perish 8 [73–75]. This paper then evaluated the contributions by year, research area, country, and publication title while identifying the impacts of the most cited publications. VOSviewer, one of the most popular bibliometric tools, is used to present the visual graphs of the research elements. The country co-authorship analysis was performed to understand the collaboration among researchers across countries. Then, to identify the hotspots and trends of research, the keyword co-authorship diagram was generated. The co-citation analysis was also conducted to identify the classical publication of digital twin in the supply chain [76–78]. Data processing was carried out using Microsoft Excel 365 [79].

3. Results

3.1. Publication Trend Analysis

The trends and growth of digital twin can be observed from the total number of publications (TP) and total citations (TC). From 2014 to 10 May 2023, there was a collection of 2652 documents on digital twin in the supply chain, with 40,768 total citations. Table 2 tabulates the publication trends of digital twin in the supply chain. Figure 2 demonstrates the trends of publication and citation for digital twin in the supply chain.

Table 2. Publication trend.

Year	TP [1]	Percentage (%)	Cumulative Percentage (%)	NCP [2]	TC [3]	C/P [4]	C/CP [5]	h-Index	g-Index
2014	2	0.08	0.08	2	71	35.50	35.50	2	2
2015	2	0.08	0.15	2	547	273.50	273.50	2	2
2016	6	0.23	0.38	6	393	65.50	65.50	5	6
2017	34	1.28	1.66	31	3555	104.56	114.68	20	34
2018	101	3.81	5.47	95	5652	55.96	59.49	29	74
2019	244	9.20	14.67	227	8561	35.09	37.71	48	86
2020	399	15.05	29.71	357	9349	23.43	26.19	51	83
2021	654	24.66	54.37	556	8614	13.17	15.52	42	68
2022	880	33.18	87.56	539	3683	4.19	6.83	24	40
2023	330	12.44	100.00	94	343	1.04	3.65	9	13

[1] Total publication; [2] number of cited publications; [3] total citations; [4] citations per publication; [5] citations per cited publication.

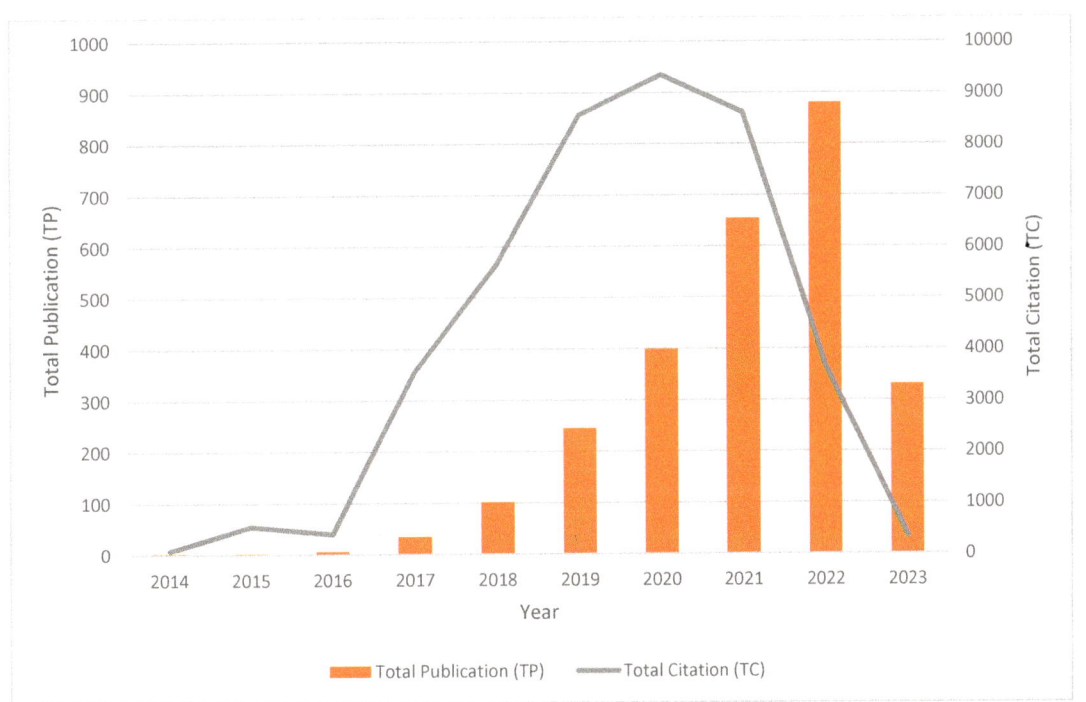

Figure 2. Publication and citation trend.

As shown in Table 2, the first publications listed on the Web of Science database were produced in 2014. One of the papers was published by Cerrone et al. [80], which modelled the as-manufactured component geometry, which is a part of the digital twin. This paper obtained 69 citations. Another paper published in 2014 was by Scott-Emuakpor et al. [81]. This paper received two citations and the discussed process of obtaining part-specific geometry and material performance to create a digital twin model for gas turbine engines. The total number of publications and citations have increased tremendously since 2018. The number of publications exceeded 100 in 2018, up to 880 in 2022. The number of citations also crossed 3000 for the publications in 2017, up to 9349 for the publications in 2020. This indicates that digital twin in the supply chain is becoming more popular.

The highest citation per paper (C/P) and citation per cited paper (C/CP) were recorded in 2015. There were two listed papers with 547 citations in 2015. The paper by Rosen et al. [82] titled "About the importance of autonomy and digital twins for the future of manufacturing" has received 531 citations. This paper then contributed to the high C/P and C/CP over the years. The highest h-index of 51 was in 2020. This implies that in 2020, there were 51 publications receiving at least 51 total citations. The highest g-index of 86 was in 2019. This implies that 86 documents have received an average of 86^2 or 7396 citations.

3.2. Research Area

There were more than 70 research areas on digital twin in the supply chain. The top 10 research areas were engineering (1681), computer science (847), automation control systems (345), operations research/management science (265), materials science (249), telecommunications (198), chemistry (189), science technology other topics (159), physics (145), and energy fuels (109). Table 3 shows the top 20 research areas on digital twin in the supply chain.

Table 3. Research area.

Research Areas	Total Publication
Engineering	1681
Computer Science	847
Automation Control Systems	345
Operations Research/Management Science	265
Materials Science	249
Telecommunications	198
Chemistry	189
Science Technology Other Topics	159
Physics	145
Energy Fuels	109
Instruments Instrumentation	92
Environmental Sciences Ecology	82
Business Economics	66
Robotics	59
Transportation	59
Mathematics	47
Construction Building Technology	41
Remote Sensing	37
Imaging Science Photographic Technology	25
Metallurgy Metallurgical Engineering	25
Mechanics	23
Thermodynamics	23

3.3. Country Contribution

China had the most publications, with 648 documents on digital twin in the supply chain. China also had 15,058 total citations, 23.24 citations per publication, and 30.92 citations per cited publication. This makes China the most productive and impactful country in terms of digital twin in the supply chain publications. China had a h-index of 59 and g-index of 110. This implies that 59 documents had at least 59 citations while 110 documents had an average of at least 110^2 or 12,100 citations. Table 4 displays the top 10 countries contributing to digital twin in the supply chain. The top 10 countries contributed more than 87% of the total publications.

Table 4. Top 10 countries contributing to digital twin in the supply chain.

Country	TP [1]	NCP [2]	TC [3]	C/P [4]	C/CP [5]	h-Index	g-Index
China	648	487	15,058	23.24	30.92	59	110
Germany	384	270	5771	15.03	21.37	29	69
United States	366	272	5822	15.91	21.40	40	66
Italy	220	150	3305	15.02	22.03	27	53
England	198	149	3105	15.68	20.84	27	51
France	114	86	2288	20.07	26.60	21	47
Spain	112	81	940	8.39	11.60	16	28
Sweden	112	95	1884	16.82	19.83	21	41
South Korea	91	67	1045	11.48	15.60	16	30
India	81	59	1418	17.51	24.03	20	36

[1] Total publication; [2] number of cited publications; [3] total citations; [4] citations per publication; [5] citations per cited publication.

Collaboration between countries is important in order to develop a research domain. This is reflected in the country co-authorship diagram generated from VOSviewer. Table 5 presents the top 10 countries with the highest collaboration between countries. China (300) had the highest total link strength, which means that China had the highest collaboration between countries. This was followed by the United States (241), Germany (209), England (186), Italy (173), France (122), Sweden (122), Spain (103), India (77), and Switzerland (75). Figure 3 demonstrates the country co-authorship diagram.

Table 5. Country co-authorship.

Country	Total Publication	Total Link Strength
China	648	300
United States	366	241
Germany	384	209
England	198	286
Italy	220	173
France	114	122
Sweden	112	122
Spain	112	103
India	81	77
Switzerland	64	75

Figure 3 displays the country co-authorship diagram. China has the largest node size because China had the highest number of publications. The line between China and the United States is the thickest, indicating the strongest collaboration between China and the United States, with a link strength of 49. China and Sweden also have a strong collaborative relationship, with a link strength of 33. China and England also work well, with a link strength of 31.

There are six clusters in total. Australia, Bangladesh, Canada, Egypt, India, Iran, Malaysia, New Zealand, Pakistan, China, Saudi Arabia, Singapore, South Korea, Taiwan, United Arab Emirates, and Wales make up the largest cluster in red. The second cluster (green) is formed by Austria, the Czech Republic, Finland, Germany, Japan, Latvia, the Netherlands, Norway, Poland, Romania, Scotland, Slovakia, Sweden, and Ukraine. Argentina, Croatia, Greece, Israel, Italy, Northern Ireland, Serbia, Slovenia, Spain, and Switzerland form the third cluster in blue. The fourth cluster is in yellow and has countries such as England, Estonia, Hungary, Portugal, Russia, the United States, and Vietnam. The fifth cluster is in purple with countries such as Brazil, Columbia, Denmark, France, Luxembourg, and Morocco. The last cluster (light blue) consists of Belgium, Ireland, Mexico, South Africa, and Turkey.

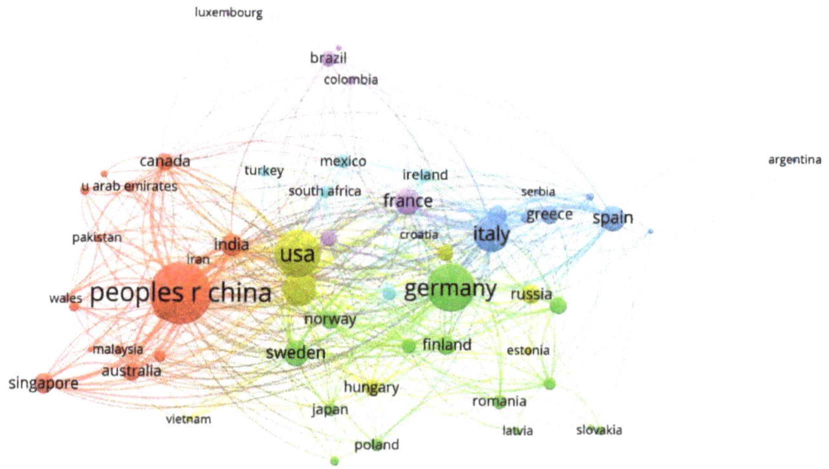

Figure 3. Country co-authorship.

3.4. Publication Title

The top 10 publication titles are listed in Table 6. Applied Science (impact factor, IF = 2.838) was the journal with the highest publication for digital twin in the supply chain, with 100 total publications. IEEE Access (IF = 3.476) was the highest cited publication title, with 2979 total citations. The highest cited publication under IEEE Access was written by Qi and Tao [83], which compared big data and digital twin in Industry 4.0. Journal of Manufacturing Systems (IF = 9.498) and International Journal of Production Research (IF = 9.018) had the highest impact factors among the top 10 publication titles.

3.5. Citation Analysis

Table 7 reveals the top 10 highly cited publications of digital twin in the supply chain. The paper "Digital twin-driven product design, manufacturing and service with big data" published by Tao et al. [13] received 1002 citations since its publication in 2018. This paper investigated the application methods and frameworks of digital-twin-driven product design, manufacturing, and service. It is important to implement the digital twin in the supply chain, particularly in terms of material intelligent tracking and distribution technology. The second most cited paper is titled "Digital twin in industry: state-of-the-art" authored by Tao et al. [84], which received 814 citations. This paper reviewed the development and application of digital twin in industry. In supply chain management, the digital twin provides more accurate planning and efficient dispatching. The scheduling scheme can be analyzed, evaluated, and optimized through self-organizing and self-learning. The third most cited paper by Kritzinger et al. [85] provided a categorical literature review of the digital twin in manufacturing. The authors found that the main focus of digital twin research in the supply chain is dealing with production planning and control. Ivanov [86] studied the impacts of epidemic outbreaks on global supply chain with the example of the coronavirus COVID-19. The study showed that lead time, speed of epidemic propagation, and the upstream and downstream disruption durations in the supply chain were major factors that determined the epidemic outbreak impact on the performance of supply chain based on the simulation results. The next most cited paper by Qi and Tao [83] studied big data and digital twin in manufacturing as well as their applications in product design, production planning, manufacturing, and predictive maintenance. Digital twin could optimize the whole process in the supply chain based on the cyber–physical closed loop system.

Table 6. Publication titles.

Publication Title	TP [1]	Percentage (%)	TC [2]	Publisher	JIF [3]	JCI [4]	Cite Score	SJR [5]	SNIP [6]	h-Index
Applied Sciences	100	3.76	1103	MDPI	2.838	0.59	3.7	0.507	1.026	101
IFAC-PapersOnLine	100	3.76	1942	ELSEVIER	N/A	N/A	1.5	0.324	0.442	86
Journal of Manufacturing Systems	76	2.86	2181	ELSEVIER SCI LTD	9.498	1.81	15.0	2.950	3.439	92
International Journal of Advanced Manufacturing Technology	72	2.71	1855	SPRINGER LONDON LTD	3.563	0.67	6.4	0.924	1.368	145
IEEE Access	67	2.52	2979	IEEE-INST ELECTRICAL ELECTRONICS ENGINEERS INC	3.476	0.93	6.7	0.927	1.326	204
Procedia Manufacturing	60	2.26	1640	ELSEVIER	N/A	N/A	N/A	N/A	N/A	69
Sensors	58	2.18	416	MDPI	3.847	0.90	6.4	0.803	1.420	219
International Journal of Production Research	47	1.77	1656	TAYLOR & FRANCIS LTD	9.018	1.51	14.6	2.780	2.901	170
International Journal of Computer Integrated Manufacturing	43	1.62	968	TAYLOR & FRANCIS LTD	4.420	0.81	7.2	1.095	1.409	63
Processes	43	1.62	451	MDPI	3.352	0.48	3.5	0.474	0.889	54

[1] Total publication; [2] total citation; [3] journal impact factor 2021; [4] journal citation indicator 2021; [5] SCImago journal rank 2021; [6] source normalized impact per paper 2021.

Table 7. Most cited publications.

Title	Year	Total Citation	Publication Title
Digital twin-driven product design, manufacturing and service with big data [13]	2018	1002	International Journal of Advanced Manufacturing Technology
Digital Twin in Industry: State-of-the-Art [84]	2019	814	IEEE Transactions on Industrial Informatics
Digital twin in manufacturing: A categorical literature review and classification [85]	2018	711	IFAC Papersonline
Predicting the impacts of epidemic outbreaks on global supply chains: A simulation-based analysis on the coronavirus outbreak (COVID-19/SARS-CoV-2) case [86]	2020	660	Transportation Research Part E-Logistics and Transportation Review
Digital twin and big data towards smart manufacturing and Industry 4.0: 360 degree comparison [83]	2018	569	IEEE Access
A review of the roles of digital twin in CPS-based production systems [57]	2017	534	27th International Conference on Flexible Automation and Intelligent Manufacturing, FAIM2017
About the importance of autonomy and digital twins for the future of manufacturing [82]	2015	531	IFAC Papersonline
The future of manufacturing industry: a strategic roadmap toward Industry 4.0 [87]	2018	498	Journal of Manufacturing Technology Management
Digital twin shop-floor: a new shop-floor paradigm towards smart manufacturing [88]	2017	479	IEEE Access
Shaping the digital twin for design and production engineering [89]	2017	470	CIRP Annals-Manufacturing Technology

The sixth most cited paper by Negri et al. [57] explored digital twin in the scientific literature and identified the role of digital twin for manufacturing in the Industry 4.0 era. This paper reviewed the concept of digital twin in industrial engineering and the supply chain. The seventh most cited paper by Rosen et al. [82] focused on the importance of modularity, connectivity, autonomy, and digital twin in the design of products and production. This paper addressed the opportunities to apply simulation for improving the production planning in the supply chain. The next most cited paper by Ghobakhloo [87] reviewed the Industry 4.0 phenomenon, determined its key design principles and technology trends, and offered a strategic roadmap as a guide for the process of Industry 4.0 transition. Industry 4.0 enabled an automated creation of products, services, supply, and product delivery. Tao and Zhang [88] discussed the digital twin shop-floor based on digital twin and its key components, namely, physical shop-floor, virtual shop-floor, shop-floor service system, and shop-floor digital twin data. This paper addressed the needs of application of digital twin in smart manufacturing to improve the supply chain management. The 10th most cited paper by Schleich et al. [89] presented a comprehensive reference model that serves as a digital twin of the physical product in design and manufacturing. Model conceptualization, implementation, and application along the product life-cycle in the supply chain were addressed.

Based on the most cited publications described above, the supply chain management system tends to be intelligent with the development of information technology. The use of technology in the supply chain is enhanced by emerging technologies such as artificial intelligence, digital twin, and big data. According to Xue et al. [90], the future development of the supply chain should study the impact of emerging technologies for continuous improvement. Xue et al. [90] conducted a review of supply chain management and suggested that emerging technologies can be integrated into the supply chain model. Moreover, the application of block chain and Industry 4.0 in the supply chain has received great attention. According to Fang et al. [91], the research of intelligent supply chain driven by new technologies includes block-chain-technology-driven as well as big-data-analysis-technology-driven research. In line with our study on technology-driven research, our paper presents a bibliometric analysis of digital twin in the supply chain to help researchers, industry practitioners, and academics to understand the trend, development, and focus of the areas of digital twin in the supply chain.

Co-citation analysis studies at least two publications cited by another article. The co-cited references show the classical research area in the field [79]. The top 10 co-cited references are listed in Table 8. Among them, eight articles are among the top 10 cited papers. Figure 4 depicts the reference co-citation analysis diagram.

Table 8. Top 10 co-cited references.

Co-Cited References	Total Link Strength
Digital twin-driven product design, manufacturing and service with big data [13]	5911
Digital twin in industry: state-of-the-art [84]	4467
Digital twin shop-floor: a new shop-floor paradigm towards smart manufacturing [88]	4276
Digital twin in manufacturing: a categorical literature review and classification [85]	4222
Digital twin and big data towards smart manufacturing and Industry 4.0: 360 degree comparison [83]	3811
A review of the roles of digital twin in CPS-based production systems [57]	3718
Digital twin: mitigating unpredictable, undesirable emergent behavior in complex systems [92]	3699
Shaping the digital twin for design and production engineering [89]	3548
About the importance of autonomy and digital twins for the future of manufacturing [82]	3493
Digital twin-driven smart manufacturing: connotation, reference model, applications, and research issues [93]	3293

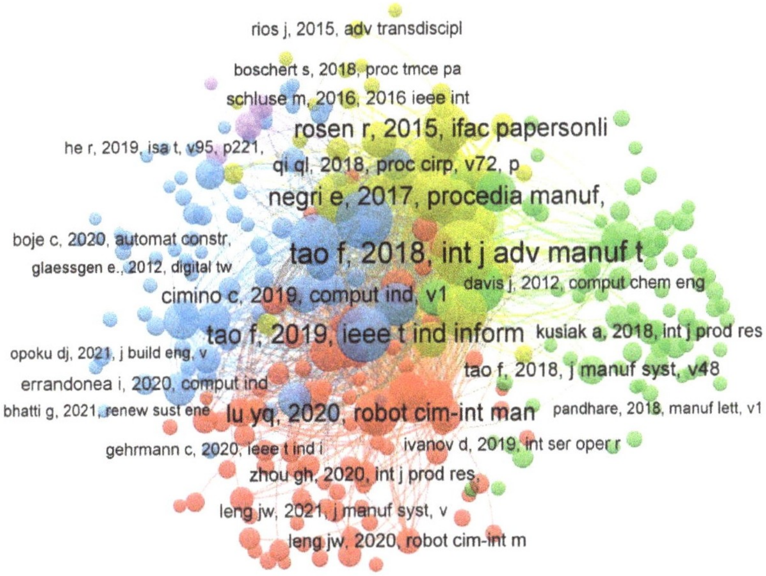

Figure 4. Co-citation analysis of references.

The top 10 co-cited authors are shown in Table 9, while Figure 5 describes the author co-citation network. It is worth to note that Tao, F., is an expert in intelligent manufacturing and authored the papers "Digital twin-driven product design, manufacturing and service with big data" [13], "Digital twin in industry: state-of-the-art" [84], "Digital twin and big data towards smart manufacturing and Industry 4.0: 360 degree comparison" [83], and "Digital twin shop-floor: a new shop-floor paradigm towards smart manufacturing" [88], which received 1002, 814, 569, and 479 citations, respectively. Grieves, M., whose expertise is in product life cycle management, authored the book chapter "Digital twin: mitigating unpredictable, undesirable emergent behavior in complex systems" [92], with 1033 citations on Scopus and 2010 citations on Google Scholar. J. W. Leng's work focuses on blockchain, mass individualization, smart manufacturing, and Industry 5.0. He wrote the paper "A digital twin-based approach for designing and multi-objective optimization of hollow glass production line" [94], with 208 citations on the Web of Science database.

Table 9. Top 10 co-cited authors.

Co-Cited Authors	Affiliations
Tao, F.	Beihang University, Beijing, China
Grieves, M.	University of Central Florida, Florida, United States
Leng, J. W.	Guangdong University of Technology, Guangzhou, China
Qi, Q. L.	Beihang University, Beijing, China
Lu, Y. Q.	The University of Auckland, Auckland, New Zealand
Negri, E.	Politecnico di Milano, Milan, Italy
Schleich, B.	University of Erlangen-Nuremberg, Erlangen, Germany
Uhlemann, T. H. J.	Bayreuth University, Bayreuth, Germany
Kritzinger, W.	Fraunhofer Austria Research GmbH, Vienna, Austria
Glaessgen, E.	NASA Langley Research Center Hampton, Virginia, United States

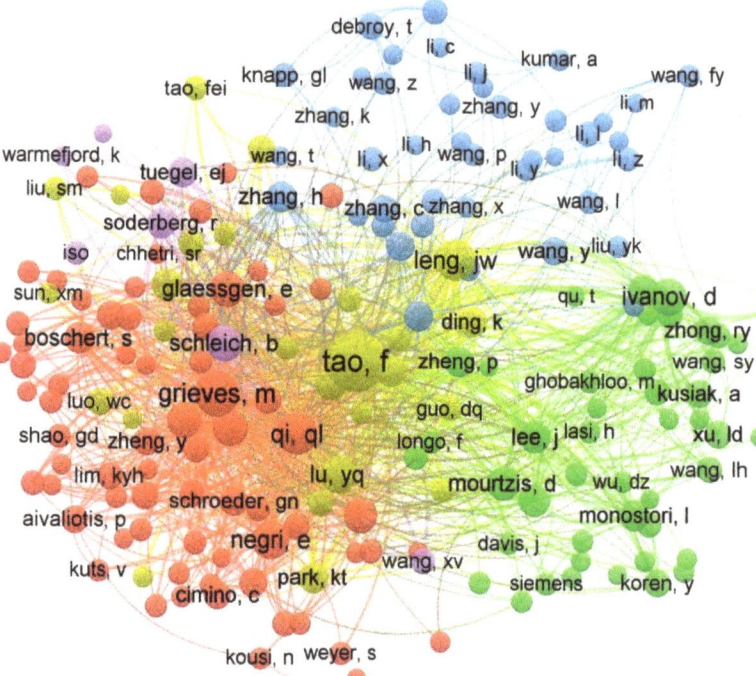

Figure 5. Co-citation analysis of authors.

The co-citation of publication title is presented in Figure 6. The *International Journal of Advanced Manufacturing Technology* (IF = 3.563, Q2); *International Journal of Production Research* (IF = 9.018, Q1); *Journal of Manufacturing Systems* (IF = 9.498, Q1); *IEEE Access* (IF = 3.476, Q2); *Procedia CIRP, CIRP Annals—Manufacturing Technology* (IF = 4.482, Q2); *Procedia Manufacturing, Robotics and Computer-Integrated Manufacturing* (IF = 10.103, Q1); *Journal of Cleaner Production* (IF = 11.072, Q1); and *IFAC Papers-Online* are the top 10 co-cited sources.

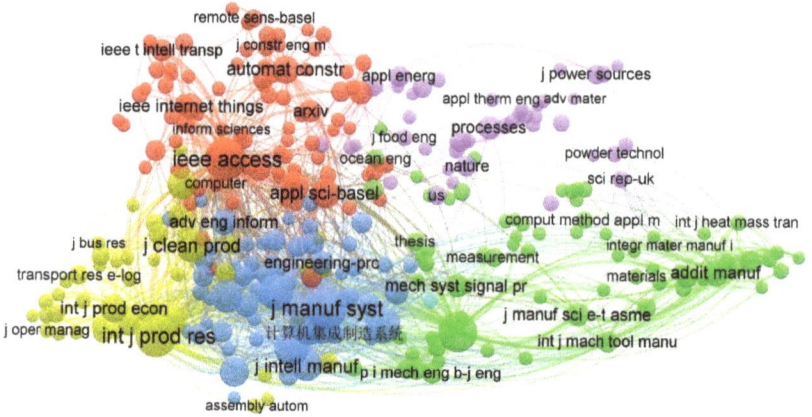

Figure 6. Co-citation analysis of publication titles.

3.6. Keyword Analysis

Table 10 shows the top 10 keywords regarding digital twin in the supply chain. Figure 7 describes the keyword co-occurrence map. As shown in Figure 7, the first cluster in red focuses on the process of designing and building a digital twin model, where the keywords are made up of architecture, artificial intelligence, big data, blockchain, cloud computing, cyber–physical system, data models, edge computing, Internet of Things, security, and sensors. The second cluster, which is green, involves the implementation and integration of digital twin to increase the efficiency in industrial uses, with keywords such as augmented reality, building information modeling (BIM), decision-making, discrete event simulation, industry, integration, logistics, manufacturing system, performance, resilience, supply chain, sustainability, and virtual reality. The third cluster is in blue and focuses on digital twin in quality controls and improvements. The keywords in this cluster are data analytics, deep learning, fault diagnosis, genetic algorithm, intelligent manufacturing, machine learning, optimization, prediction, predictive maintenance, and quality. The fourth cluster is in yellow and highlights the contribution of digital twin in digitalization and industrialization. The keywords are automation, digital manufacturing, digital transformation, Industry 4.0, modeling, and smart factory.

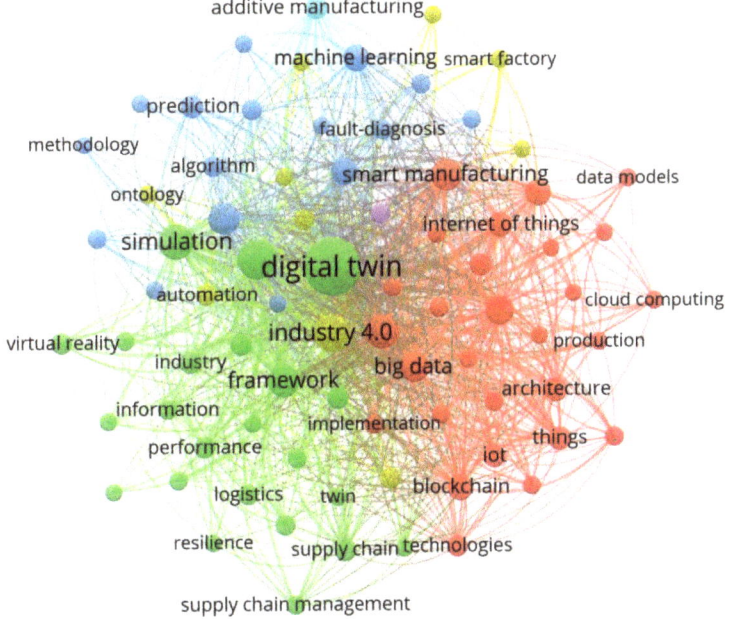

Figure 7. Keyword co-occurrence analysis.

Figure 8 displays the trends and developments of the keywords in recent years. The lighter colors show the recent study areas of researchers in digital twin in the supply chain. They include deep learning, machine learning, data models, edge computing, artificial intelligence, and supply chain management. Nowadays, researchers are engaging in integrating digital twin with machine and deep learning. Fischer et al. [95] used the artificial neural network, which was a part of deep learning, for activity recognition, which was then used to perform discrete-event simulation. The digital twin technology and functional block has an application domain for data visualization and analytics, which is a part of machine learning [96]. The digital twin of an entity is also able to train deep learning algorithms [97]. There is also a potential research gap for the application of digital twin in a deep learning architecture for mobile edge computing. Moreover, Yang et al. [98] proposed a model with model reduction and deep neural network as a basic to develop digital twin for nuclear power system but noted that there was still a research gap to increase the efficiency of the model. Moreover, digital twin is also seen as a driver to speed up the realization of Industry 5.0 in the future [99].

Table 10. Top 10 keywords.

Keywords	Occurrences	Total Link Strength
Digital twin	1546	4340
Design	413	1769
Industry 4.0	319	1360
Framework	218	1165
Big data	166	1011
Simulation	289	996
Smart manufacturing	193	848
Optimization	193	806
Cyber–physical systems	140	779
Blockchain	91	523

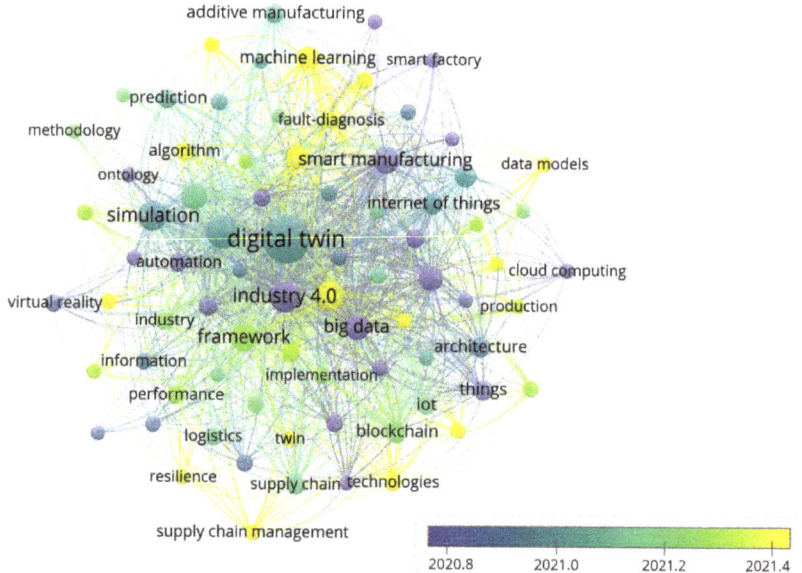

Figure 8. Keyword overlay analysis.

As the world is moving towards human-centric industrialization, there are also huge research gaps with the application of digital twin and deep learning, machine learning, and artificial intelligence to achieve mass personalization through intelligent transformation [100,101]. In the supply chain where all the logistics processes are interconnected and would largely impact the next step of operation, there exists a gap between digital twin applications, deep learning, machine learning, and artificial intelligence for occupational safety and health to prevent accidents and hazards for the wellbeing of the workers [102]. Digital twin could analyze the potential areas and degree of severity of accidents and help the companies to visualize a proper floor plan to minimize the adverse effects and losses due to the potential hazards [103]. Digital twin can also study the movement and interaction of humans in the workplace to reduce their risk of accident [104,105]. For better personalized working experience, digital twin can help workers visualize the outcomes of their actions and design mitigation strategies to enhance their own productivity. All these are still in the development phase, and there are boundless prospects.

The sustainable development goals (SDGs) focus on smart yet sustainable industrialization and manufacturing. Therefore, digital twin can be applied for sustainable intelligent transformation [106–108]. This involves transformation in the equipment, systems, and services that interconnect with each other. When broken down, the equipment consists of units and lines; systems start from designing, producing, logistics, and selling, while services range from innovating, manufacturing, and post-purchase assistances [109]. Meanwhile, digital twin could also help with the maintenance, overhauls, and repairs of complex systems, products, and equipment [110–112]. Moreover, for optimization in resource allocation, digital twin can complement edge computing, improve efficiency, and reduce wastage [113,114]. Various digital twin infrastructures could be explored to support different phases in sustainable intelligent transformation with the integration of deep learning, machine learning, and artificial intelligence.

3.7. Research Evolution

Based on the bibliometric analysis above, the evolution of research trends can be divided into three stages, namely, the embryonic, developmental, and prosperity stages [90]. In the Web of Science, the research on digital twin in the supply chain began in 2014. Therefore, the embryonic stage of the research of digital twin in the supply chain is from 2014 to 2017, since the number of publications listed on the Web of Science was still low. Then, the developmental stage of the research was from 2018 to 2020. The prosperity stage of the research is from 2021 onwards.

3.7.1. Embryonic Stage (2014–2017)

The embryonic stage of the research of digital twin in the supply chain on the Web of Science database began years after NASA introduced digital twin in their roadmap. During this period, about 66% (29 documents) were proceeding papers. In this first stage, several papers tested out the digital twin concept in the production line. Vachálek et al. [115] proposed the digital twin concept for the production of pneumatic cylinders by creating a virtual model of the hydraulic pistons. The changes in the virtual model were almost instantaneous with a difference of one second. This proposed digital twin model was still basic with limited optimization, proactive maintenance, and sensors for big data analysis. Zhang et al. [94] developed a digital twin for the hollow glass production line. Digital twin started to be involved in the cyber–physical system in the supply chain during this period. Realizing that small and medium enterprises were not aware of digital twin, Uhlemann et al. [116] presented a CPS learning concept for real-time data acquisition, automated optimization, and data capturing. Cai et al. [117] developed a CPS system for a three-axis vertical milling machine. The digital twin produced was limited to a single milling machine and only two sensors and low sensory data. For shopfloor planning, Brenner and Hummel [118] started to build a learning factory and noted that artificial intelligence such as self-calibrating localizations were part of the future of digital twin. Blum and Schuh [119] developed a digital twin that was limited to real-time order processing with potential improvements for big data analytics and integration with other production logistics activities. In this stage, ideas have also slowly been proposed and explored to apply digital twin in wider areas of the supply chain such as additive manufacturing and 3D printing [120,121].

3.7.2. Developmental Stage (2018–2020)

This stage highlights the connection of digital twin with components of Industry 4.0. Tao et al. [13] and Qi and Tao [83] started to emphasize the combination of digital twin and big data to create cyber–physical data for designs, production, and service in the supply chain. These papers noted that big data analysis could help users detect the causes of problems and find solutions in the virtual model that were significant in smart manufacturing. Integration of digital twin with machine learning also started in this stage, as Xu et al. [122] developed a digital twin for fault diagnosis with deep transfer learning. Several machine learning techniques had also been incorporated into digital twin [123–125]. Industrial Internet of Things, edge computing, and cloud-based systems were also introduced in digital twin [126–131]. The security awareness while using digital twin was enhanced with the application of blockchain for cryptographic hashing algorithms, decentralization, and immutability [132–135]. In this stage, the need for more sensitive and efficient sensors for digital twin modeling arose. Jin et al. [136] developed triboelectric nanogenerator sensors for a soft-robotic gripper system for digital twin models for assembly lines and automated warehouses. Research in this stage also started to move towards sustainable digital twin applications [137]. Sustainable designs, productions, logistics, sales, and services made up the sustainable closed loop for sustainable intelligent manufacturing in a study by He and Bai [106]. Kaewunruen and Lian [138] constructed a 6D building information system with digital twin for sustainable railway turnout for economy and sustainability. Digital twin was also used to develop a sustainable business model for a comprehensive network that focused on several product life cycles [139]. Digital twin was also used for sustainable performance assessment of the production system [140]. Wang et al. [141] developed a big-data-driven digital twin to configure sustainable products and remanufacture processes. Optimal selection of green materials using digital twin was also established [50].

3.7.3. Prosperity Stage (2021–Present)

The spike in the number of papers in this stage was mainly driven by the COVID-19 pandemic, where industries realized that resiliency was important to manage operating cost and profit for sustainability during an emergency [142–144]. Digital twin was also used to perform impact analysis for the food retail supply chain to help the companies cope with the adverse impacts of COVID-19 [145]. Digital twin as a service started to become a highlight in this stage as mass individualization became important in manufacturing [101,146,147]. The research of digital twin in the supply chain became more specific as digital twin was implemented in actual environments such as ports and other maritime operations [148–151]. Big data, deep Q-learning, and generative adversarial networks were also used in digital twin for traffic prediction [152]. The research on production logistics was also enhanced with deep neural network and Internet of Things [153]. Sustainability is also a part of the digital twin research in the supply chain to reduce raw material consumption [154]. In this stage, research highlighting digital twin as an enabler of Industry 5.0 has started to emerge, as digital twin is a supporting technology for Industry 5.0 [155–157]. Digital twin as an enabler in Industry 5.0 consists of seven elements, namely, technologies, humans, management, organizations, scopes, tasks, and modelling, while the types of digital twin in the supply chain involve product, process, organization, supply chain, and network-of-networks [158]. In using digital twin for Industry 5.0, the cyber–physical manufacturing system has now been shifted to cyber–physical human-centered systems for smart and sustainable manufacturing [159,160].

3.8. Citation Metrics

Table 11 presents the citation metrics of the publications of digital twin in the supply chain. A total of 2652 documents have been published from 2014 to 2023 as of 10 May 2023. In total, 40,768 citations have been obtained from these publications, with a h-index of 87 and a g-index of 153.

Table 11. Citation metrics of digital twin publications in the supply chain.

Items	Metrics
Extraction date	10 May 2023
Total publication	2652
Total citation	40,768
Number of years	10

Table 11. Cont.

Items	Metrics
Citation per year	4076.80
Citation per paper	15.37
Citation per author	12,295.62
Papers per author	781.8
Authors per paper	4.33
h-index	87
g-index	153

4. Conclusions

In this bibliometric analysis, 2652 documents published from 2014 to 2023 were extracted to study the research trend, development, and focus of digital twin in the supply chain. Digital twin in the supply chain is an emerging field in the midst of Industry 4.0. As Industry 5.0 is still in its infancy, the development and implementation of digital twin will accelerate the connection of the physical and digital environments. As such, this bibliometric analysis serves as an important reference for researchers, academics, and industry practitioners to understand the development of digital twin in the supply chain.

The total annual publication has been low from 2014 to 2017. From 2018 onwards, the number of publications rose quickly and reached its peak at 880 publications in 2022. The citation per publication (273.50) and citation per cited publication (273.50) were the highest in 2015 as they were contributed to by the paper by Rosen et al. [82] titled "About the importance of autonomy and digital twins for the future of manufacturing", which has received 531 citations. The highest h-index (51) was in 2020, which means that 51 publications in 2020 received at least 51 citations until 10 May 2023.

The publications were mostly articles, proceeding papers, and review articles in the subjects of engineering, computer science, and automation control systems. China (650) had the most publications on digital twin in the supply chain. China also had the highest number of citations, which amounted to about 36% of the total citations of the 2652 publications. China also had the highest h-index (59) and g-index (110). The strongest country collaborations existed between China and the United States (49), followed by China and Sweden (33), and China and England (31).

The top publication titles were Applied Science (IF = 2.838, Q2), IFAC PapersOnLine, and Journal of Manufacturing Systems (IF = 9.498, Q1). IEEE Access (IF = 3.476, Q2) had the highest total citations for publications on digital twin in the supply chain. The paper "Digital twin-driven product design, manufacturing and service with big data" published by Tao et al. [13] was the top cited publication, with 1002 total citations. This paper was also the highest co-cited reference, while the main author, Tao, F., was also the top co-cited author, followed by Grieves, M., and Leng, J. W. The International Journal of Advanced Manufacturing Technology (IF = 3.563, Q2), International Journal of Production Research (IF = 9.018, Q1), and Journal of Manufacturing Systems (IF = 9.498, Q1) journals were the top three co-cited publication titles.

In the initial stage of research, the documents revolve around conceptualizing digital twin in the production line. However, the advantages of digital twin in application were low as the models could only handle limited data and optimization. Digital twin was introduced into the cyber–physical system in this initial stage, with prospectives in smart manufacturing. Then, during the development of digital twin research, the capabilities of digital twin expanded as some limitations were removed with the integration of the components of Industry 4.0 such as big data, Industrial Internet of Things, cloud computing, edge computing, blockchain, and machine learning technologies. Digital twin also helped to visualize sustainable intelligent manufacturing. After the outbreak of the COVID-19 pandemic, companies realized that resiliency in the supply chain was important for survival and sustainability during emergency and digital twin was a potential solution. This drove the spike in the number of research on digital twin in the supply chain. Recently, several researchers have begun to explore the application of digital twin in the supply chain for the future in Industry 5.0.

This bibliometric analysis has several limitations. Firstly, the Web of Science database is updated regularly. Hence, this bibliometric analysis may be revisited in the future for the understanding of evolving trends. Secondly, this study focused on the Web of Science database. Therefore, future studies may consider other databases for the bibliometric analysis of digital twin in the supply chain.

Author Contributions: Conceptualization, W.S.L. and W.H.L.; methodology, W.S.L., W.H.L. and P.F.L.; software, W.S.L. and P.F.L.; validation, W.S.L. and W.H.L.; formal analysis, W.S.L., W.H.L. and P.F.L.; investigation, W.S.L., W.H.L. and P.F.L.; resources, W.S.L., W.H.L. and P.F.L.; data curation, W.S.L., W.H.L. and P.F.L.; writing—original draft preparation, W.S.L., W.H.L. and P.F.L.; writing—review and editing, W.S.L., W.H.L. and P.F.L.; visualization, W.S.L., W.H.L. and P.F.L.; supervision, W.S.L. and W.H.L.; project administration, W.S.L. and W.H.L. All authors have read and agreed to the published version of the manuscript.

Funding: This research received no external funding.

Data Availability Statement: The data presented in this study are available on request from the corresponding author.

Acknowledgments: This research is supported by the Universiti Tunku Abdul Rahman, Malaysia.

Conflicts of Interest: The authors declare no conflict of interest.

References

1. Caballero-Morales, S.-O. Innovation as Recovery Strategy for SMEs in Emerging Economies during the COVID-19 Pandemic. *Res. Int. Bus. Financ.* **2021**, *57*, 101396. [CrossRef] [PubMed]
2. Donnelly, S.; Gee, L.; Silva, E.S. UK Mid-Market Department Stores: Is Fashion Product Assortment One Key to Regaining Competitive Advantage? *J. Retail. Consum. Serv.* **2020**, *54*, 102043. [CrossRef]
3. Fu, W.; Jing, S.; Liu, Q.; Zhang, H. Resilient Supply Chain Framework for Semiconductor Distribution and an Empirical Study of Demand Risk Inference. *Sustainability* **2023**, *15*, 7382. [CrossRef]
4. Hu, W.; Zhang, T.; Deng, X.; Liu, Z.; Tan, J. Digital Twin: A State-of-the-Art Review of Its Enabling Technologies, Applications and Challenges. *J. Intell. Manuf. Spec. Equip.* **2021**, *2*, 1–34. [CrossRef]
5. Holopainen, M.; Saunila, M.; Rantala, T.; Ukko, J. Digital Twins' Implications for Innovation. *Technol. Anal. Strateg. Manag.* **2022**, 1–13. [CrossRef]
6. Qi, Q.; Tao, F.; Zuo, Y.; Zhao, D. Digital Twin Service towards Smart Manufacturing. *Procedia CIRP* **2018**, *72*, 237–242. [CrossRef]
7. Kuo, Y.-H.; Pilati, F.; Qu, T.; Huang, G.Q. Digital Twin-Enabled Smart Industrial Systems: Recent Developments and Future Perspectives. *Int. J. Comput. Integr. Manuf.* **2021**, *34*, 685–689. [CrossRef]
8. Fukawa, N.; Rindfleisch, A. Enhancing Innovation via the Digital Twin. *J. Prod. Innov. Manag.* **2023**, *40*, 391–406. [CrossRef]
9. Li, H.; Yang, Y.; Zhang, C.; Zhang, C.; Chen, W. Visualization Monitoring of Industrial Detonator Automatic Assembly Line Based on Digital Twin. *Sustainability* **2023**, *15*, 7690. [CrossRef]
10. Sreenivasan, A.; Ma, S.; Rehman, A.U.; Muthuswamy, S. Assessment of Factors Influencing Agility in Start-Ups Industry 4.0. *Sustainability* **2023**, *15*, 7564. [CrossRef]
11. Yildiz, E.; Møller, C.; Bilberg, A. Demonstration and Evaluation of a Digital Twin-Based Virtual Factory. *Int. J. Adv. Manuf. Technol.* **2021**, *114*, 185–203. [CrossRef]
12. Tao, F.; Sui, F.; Liu, A.; Qi, Q.; Zhang, M.; Song, B.; Guo, Z.; Lu, S.C.-Y.; Nee, A.Y.C. Digital Twin-Driven Product Design Framework. *Int. J. Prod. Res.* **2019**, *57*, 3935–3953. [CrossRef]
13. Tao, F.; Cheng, J.; Qi, Q.; Zhang, M.; Zhang, H.; Sui, F. Digital Twin-Driven Product Design, Manufacturing and Service with Big Data. *Int. J. Adv. Manuf. Technol.* **2018**, *94*, 3563–3576. [CrossRef]
14. Zhang, C.; Zhou, G.; He, J.; Li, Z.; Cheng, W. A Data- and Knowledge-Driven Framework for Digital Twin Manufacturing Cell. *Procedia CIRP* **2019**, *83*, 345–350. [CrossRef]
15. Cheng, Y.; Zhang, Y.; Ji, P.; Xu, W.; Zhou, Z.; Tao, F. Cyber-Physical Integration for Moving Digital Factories Forward towards Smart Manufacturing: A Survey. *Int. J. Adv. Manuf. Technol.* **2018**, *97*, 1209–1221. [CrossRef]
16. Onaji, I.; Tiwari, D.; Soulatiantork, P.; Song, B.; Tiwari, A. Digital Twin in Manufacturing: Conceptual Framework and Case Studies. *Int. J. Comput. Integr. Manuf.* **2022**, *35*, 831–858. [CrossRef]
17. Allen, B.D. *Digital Twins and Living Models at NASA*; US Government: Washington, DC, USA, 2021.
18. Grieves, M. Origins of the Digital Twin Concept. Available online: https://www.researchgate.net/publication/307509727_Origins_of_the_Digital_Twin_Concept (accessed on 14 July 2023).

19. Huang, S.; Wang, G.; Yan, Y.; Fang, X. Blockchain-Based Data Management for Digital Twin of Product. *J. Manuf. Syst.* **2020**, *54*, 361–371. [CrossRef]
20. Yao, J.-F.; Yang, Y.; Wang, X.-C.; Zhang, X.-P. Systematic Review of Digital Twin Technology and Applications. *Vis. Comput. Ind. Biomed. Art.* **2023**, *6*, 10. [CrossRef] [PubMed]
21. Singh, M.; Fuenmayor, E.; Hinchy, E.P.; Qiao, Y.; Murray, N.; Devine, D. Digital Twin: Origin to Future. *Appl. Syst. Innov.* **2021**, *4*, 36. [CrossRef]
22. Främling, K.; Holmström, J.; Ala-Risku, T.; Kärkkäinen, M. *Product Agents for Handling Information about Physical Objects*; Helsinki University of Technology: Espoo, Finland, 2003; Volume 153.
23. Hribernik, K.A.; Rabe, L.; Thoben, K.-D.; Schumacher, J. The Product Avatar as a Product-Instance-Centric Information Management Concept. *Int. J. Prod. Lifecycle Manag.* **2006**, *1*, 367–379. [CrossRef]
24. Grieves, M. Back to the Future: Product Lifecycle Management and the Virtualization of Product Information. In *Product Realization: A Comprehensive Approach*; Tomovic, M., Wang, S., Eds.; Springer: Boston, MA, USA, 2009; pp. 1–13, ISBN 978-0-387-09482-3.
25. Glaessgen, E.H.; Stargel, D.S. The Digital Twin Paradigm for Future NASA and U.S. Air Force Vehicles. In Proceedings of the 53rd AIAA/ASME/ASCE/AHS/ASC Structures, Structural Dynamics and Materials Conference, Honolulu, HI, USA, 23–26 April 2012.
26. Jacoby, M.; Usländer, T. Digital Twin and Internet of Things—Current Standards Landscape. *Appl. Sci.* **2020**, *10*, 6519. [CrossRef]
27. Khalyasmaa, A.I.; Stepanova, A.I.; Eroshenko, S.A.; Matrenin, P.V. Review of the Digital Twin Technology Applications for Electrical Equipment Lifecycle Management. *Mathematics* **2023**, *11*, 1315. [CrossRef]
28. Attaran, M.; Celik, B.G. Digital Twin: Benefits, Use Cases, Challenges, and Opportunities. *Decis. Anal. J.* **2023**, *6*, 100165. [CrossRef]
29. Khandare, A.D.; Jadhav, V.S.; Deshmukh, S.P.; Rane, K.K. Digital Twins for Manufacturing Process and System: A State of the Art Review. *ECS Trans.* **2022**, *107*, 15497. [CrossRef]
30. Reddy, K.J.M.; Rao, A.N.; Krishnanand, L. A Review on Supply Chain Performance Measurement Systems. *Procedia Manuf.* **2019**, *30*, 40–47. [CrossRef]
31. Wang, Y.; Wang, X.; Liu, A. Digital Twin-Driven Supply Chain Planning. *Procedia CIRP* **2020**, *93*, 198–203. [CrossRef]
32. Abideen, A.Z.; Sundram, V.P.K.; Pyeman, J.; Othman, A.K.; Sorooshian, S. Digital Twin Integrated Reinforced Learning in Supply Chain and Logistics. *Logistics* **2021**, *5*, 84. [CrossRef]
33. Liu, M.; Fang, S.; Dong, H.; Xu, C. Review of Digital Twin about Concepts, Technologies, and Industrial Applications. *J. Manuf. Syst.* **2021**, *58*, 346–361. [CrossRef]
34. Söderberg, R.; Wärmefjord, K.; Carlson, J.S.; Lindkvist, L. Toward a Digital Twin for Real-Time Geometry Assurance in Individualized Production. *CIRP Ann.* **2017**, *66*, 137–140. [CrossRef]
35. Madusanka, N.S.; Fan, Y.; Yang, S.; Xiang, X. Digital Twin in the Maritime Domain: A Review and Emerging Trends. *J. Mar. Sci. Eng.* **2023**, *11*, 1021. [CrossRef]
36. Lv, Z.; Lv, H.; Fridenfalk, M. Digital Twins in the Marine Industry. *Electronics* **2023**, *12*, 2025. [CrossRef]
37. Mauro, F.; Kana, A.A. Digital Twin for Ship Life-Cycle: A Critical Systematic Review. *Ocean. Eng.* **2023**, *269*, 113479. [CrossRef]
38. Wang, K.; Hu, Q.; Zhou, M.; Zun, Z.; Qian, X. Multi-Aspect Applications and Development Challenges of Digital Twin-Driven Management in Global Smart Ports. *Case Stud. Transp. Policy* **2021**, *9*, 1298–1312. [CrossRef]
39. Zhu, Y.; Cheng, J.; Liu, Z.; Cheng, Q.; Zou, X.; Xu, H.; Wang, Y.; Tao, F. Production Logistics Digital Twins: Research Profiling, Application, Challenges and Opportunities. *Robot. Comput. Integr. Manuf.* **2023**, *84*, 102592. [CrossRef]
40. Lei, W.; Yong, W.; Haigen, Y.; Hongyan, Y.; Wenting, X.; Longbao, H.; Kejia, J. Research on Application of Virtual-Real Fusion Technology in Smart Manufacturing. In Proceedings of the 2018 IEEE 9th International Conference on Software Engineering and Service Science (ICSESS), Beijing, China, 23–25 November 2018; pp. 1066–1069.
41. Hauge, J.; Zafarzadeh, M.; Jeong, Y.; Li, Y.; Khilji, W.; Larsen, C.; Wiktorsson, M. Digital Twin Testbed and Practical Applications in Production Logistics with Real-Time Location Data. *Int. J. Ind. Eng. Manag.* **2021**, *12*, 129–140. [CrossRef]
42. Pan, Y.H.; Wu, N.Q.; Qu, T.; Li, P.Z.; Zhang, K.; Guo, H.F. Digital-Twin-Driven Production Logistics Synchronization System for Vehicle Routing Problems with Pick-up and Delivery in Industrial Park. *Int. J. Comput. Integr. Manuf.* **2021**, *34*, 814–828. [CrossRef]
43. Wu, B.; Zhiheng, Z.; Shen, L.; Kong, X.; Guo, D.; Zhong, R.; Huang, G.Q. Just Trolley: Implementation of Industrial IoT and Digital Twin-Enabled Spatial-Temporal Traceability and Visibility for Finished Goods Logistics. *Adv. Eng. Inform.* **2022**, *52*, 101571. [CrossRef]
44. Marmolejo-Saucedo, J.A. Digital Twin Framework for Large-Scale Optimization Problems in Supply Chains: A Case of Packing Problem. *Mob. Netw. Appl.* **2022**, *27*, 2198–2214. [CrossRef]
45. Leng, J.; Yan, D.; Liu, Q.; Zhang, H.; Zhao, G.; Wei, L.; Zhang, D.; Yu, A.; Chen, X. Digital Twin-Driven Joint Optimisation of Packing and Storage Assignment in Large-Scale Automated High-Rise Warehouse Product-Service System. *Int. J. Comput. Integr. Manuf.* **2021**, *34*, 783–800. [CrossRef]
46. Perez, G.C.; Korth, B. Digital Twin for Legal Requirements in Production and Logistics Based on the Example of the Storage of Hazardous Substances. In Proceedings of the 2020 IEEE International Conference on Industrial Engineering and Engineering Management (IEEM), Singapore, 14–17 December 2020; pp. 1093–1097.

47. Petković, T.; Puljiz, D.; Marković, I.; Hein, B. Human Intention Estimation Based on Hidden Markov Model Motion Validation for Safe Flexible Robotized Warehouses. *Robot. Comput. Integr. Manuf.* **2019**, *57*, 182–196. [CrossRef]
48. Andronie, M.; Lăzăroiu, G.; Ștefănescu, R.; Uță, C.; Dijmărescu, I. Sustainable, Smart, and Sensing Technologies for Cyber-Physical Manufacturing Systems: A Systematic Literature Review. *Sustainability* **2021**, *13*, 5495. [CrossRef]
49. Liu, Q.; Zhang, H.; Leng, J.; Chen, X. Digital Twin-Driven Rapid Individualised Designing of Automated Flow-Shop Manufacturing System. *Int. J. Prod. Res.* **2019**, *57*, 3903–3919. [CrossRef]
50. Xiang, F.; Zhang, Z.; Zuo, Y.; Tao, F. Digital Twin Driven Green Material Optimal-Selection towards Sustainable Manufacturing. *Procedia CIRP* **2019**, *81*, 1290–1294. [CrossRef]
51. Zhu, Z.; Liu, C.; Xu, X. Visualisation of the Digital Twin Data in Manufacturing by Using Augmented Reality. *Procedia CIRP* **2019**, *81*, 898–903. [CrossRef]
52. Zheng, Y.; Yang, S.; Cheng, H. An Application Framework of Digital Twin and Its Case Study. *J. Ambient. Intell. Hum. Comput.* **2019**, *10*, 1141–1153. [CrossRef]
53. Park, K.T.; Nam, Y.W.; Lee, H.S.; Im, S.J.; Noh, S.D.; Son, J.Y.; Kim, H. Design and Implementation of a Digital Twin Application for a Connected Micro Smart Factory. *Int. J. Comput. Integr. Manuf.* **2019**, *32*, 596–614. [CrossRef]
54. Lee, J.; Lapira, E.; Bagheri, B.; Kao, H. Recent Advances and Trends in Predictive Manufacturing Systems in Big Data Environment. *Manuf. Lett.* **2013**, *1*, 38–41. [CrossRef]
55. Coraddu, A.; Oneto, L.; Baldi, F.; Cipollini, F.; Atlar, M.; Savio, S. Data-Driven Ship Digital Twin for Estimating the Speed Loss Caused by the Marine Fouling. *Ocean. Eng.* **2019**, *186*, 106063. [CrossRef]
56. Holler, M.; Uebernickel, F.; Brenner, W. Digital Twin Concepts in Manufacturing Industries: A Literature Review and Avenues for Further Research. In Proceedings of the IJIE 2016: The 18th International Conference on Industrial Engineering, Seoul, South Korea, 10–12 October 2016; Volume 2016.
57. Negri, E.; Fumagalli, L.; Macchi, M. A Review of the Roles of Digital Twin in CPS-Based Production Systems. *Procedia Manuf.* **2017**, *11*, 939–948. [CrossRef]
58. Shekarian, E.; Ijadi, B.; Zare, A.; Majava, J. Sustainable Supply Chain Management: A Comprehensive Systematic Review of Industrial Practices. *Sustainability* **2022**, *14*, 7892. [CrossRef]
59. Garcia-Buendia, N.; Moyano-Fuentes, J.; Maqueira-Marín, J.M.; Cobo, M.J. 22 Years of Lean Supply Chain Management: A Science Mapping-Based Bibliometric Analysis. *Int. J. Prod. Res.* **2021**, *59*, 1901–1921. [CrossRef]
60. Banshal, S.K.; Verma, M.K.; Yuvaraj, M. Quantifying Global Digital Journalism Research: A Bibliometric Landscape. *Libr. Hi Tech.* **2022**, *40*, 1337–1358. [CrossRef]
61. Farooq, R. Knowledge Management and Performance: A Bibliometric Analysis Based on Scopus and WOS Data (1988–2021). *J. Knowl. Manag.* **2022**, *27*, 1948–1991. [CrossRef]
62. Borgohain, D.J.; Bhardwaj, R.K.; Verma, M.K. Mapping the Literature on the Application of Artificial Intelligence in Libraries (AAIL): A Scientometric Analysis. *Libr. Hi Tech.* **2022**. ahead-of-print. [CrossRef]
63. Bakır, M.; Özdemir, E.; Akan, Ş.; Atalık, Ö. A Bibliometric Analysis of Airport Service Quality. *J. Air Transp. Manag.* **2022**, *104*, 102273. [CrossRef]
64. Gouda, G.K.; Tiwari, B. Mapping Talent Agility: A Bibliometric Analysis and Future Research Agenda. *Manag. Decis.* **2022**, *60*, 3165–3187. [CrossRef]
65. Rashed, A.; Mutis, I. Trends of Integrated Project Delivery Implementations Viewed from an Emerging Innovation Framework. *Eng. Constr. Archit. Manag.* **2021**, *30*, 989–1014. [CrossRef]
66. Donthu, N.; Kumar, S.; Mukherjee, D.; Pandey, N.; Lim, W.M. How to Conduct a Bibliometric Analysis: An Overview and Guidelines. *J. Bus. Res.* **2021**, *133*, 285–296. [CrossRef]
67. Tiwari, S. Smart Warehouse: A Bibliometric Analysis and Future Research Direction. *Sustain. Manuf. Serv. Econ.* **2023**, *2*, 100014. [CrossRef]
68. Degila, J.; Tognisse, I.S.; Honfoga, A.-C.; Houetohossou, S.C.A.; Sodedji, F.A.K.; Avakoudjo, H.G.G.; Tahi, S.P.G.; Assogbadjo, A.E. A Survey on Digital Agriculture in Five West African Countries. *Agriculture* **2023**, *13*, 1067. [CrossRef]
69. Sahoo, S. Big Data Analytics in Manufacturing: A Bibliometric Analysis of Research in the Field of Business Management. *Int. J. Prod. Res.* **2022**, *60*, 6793–6821. [CrossRef]
70. Xu, S.; Zhang, X.; Feng, L.; Yang, W. Disruption Risks in Supply Chain Management: A Literature Review Based on Bibliometric Analysis. *Int. J. Prod. Res.* **2020**, *58*, 3508–3526. [CrossRef]
71. Zhang, L.; Ling, J.; Lin, M. Artificial Intelligence in Renewable Energy: A Comprehensive Bibliometric Analysis. *Energy Rep.* **2022**, *8*, 14072–14088. [CrossRef]
72. Liu, W.; Wu, J.; Zhang, N.; Chen, G.; Li, J.; Shen, Y.; Li, F. Postural Deformities in Parkinson's Disease: A Bibliometric Analysis Based on Web of Science. *Heliyon* **2023**, *9*, e14251. [CrossRef] [PubMed]
73. Anugerah, A.R.; Muttaqin, P.S.; Trinarningsih, W. Social Network Analysis in Business and Management Research: A Bibliometric Analysis of the Research Trend and Performance from 2001 to 2020. *Heliyon* **2022**, *8*, e09368. [CrossRef] [PubMed]
74. Hassan, S.A.; Amlan, H.A.; Alias, N.E.; Ab-Kadir, M.A.; Sukor, N.S.A. Vulnerability of Road Transportation Networks under Natural Hazards: A Bibliometric Analysis and Review. *Int. J. Disaster Risk Reduct.* **2022**, *83*, 103393. [CrossRef]
75. Donthu, N.; Marc Lim, W.; Kumar, S.; Pandey, N. Tribute to a Marketing Legend: Commemorating the Contributions of Shelby D. Hunt with Implications for the Future of Marketing. *J. Bus. Res.* **2023**, *164*, 113954. [CrossRef]

76. Chaudhuri, R.; Apoorva, A.; Vrontis, D.; Siachou, E.; Trichina, E. How Customer Incivility Affects Service-Sector Employees: A Systematic Literature Review and a Bibliometric Analysis. *J. Bus. Res.* **2023**, *164*, 114011. [CrossRef]
77. Abdelwahab, S.I.; Taha, M.M.E.; Moni, S.S.; Alsayegh, A.A. Bibliometric Mapping of Solid Lipid Nanoparticles Research (2012–2022) Using VOSviewer. *Med. Novel. Technol. Device* **2023**, *17*, 100217. [CrossRef]
78. Tamala, J.K.; Maramag, E.I.; Simeon, K.A.; Ignacio, J.J. A Bibliometric Analysis of Sustainable Oil and Gas Production Research Using VOSviewer. *Clean. Eng. Technol.* **2022**, *7*, 100437. [CrossRef]
79. Ying, H.; Zhang, X.; He, T.; Feng, Q.; Wang, R.; Yang, L.; Duan, J. A Bibliometric Analysis of Research on Heart Failure Comorbid with Depression from 2002 to 2021. *Heliyon* **2023**, *9*, e13054. [CrossRef] [PubMed]
80. Cerrone, A.; Hochhalter, J.; Heber, G.; Ingraffea, A. On the Effects of Modeling As-Manufactured Geometry: Toward Digital Twin. *Int. J. Aerosp. Eng.* **2014**, *2014*, e439278. [CrossRef]
81. Scott-Emuakpor, O.; George, T.; Beck, J.; Schwartz, J.; Holycross, C.; Shen, M.H.H.; Slater, J. *Material Property Determination of Vibration Fatigued DMLS and Cold-Rolled Nickel Alloys*; American Society of Mechanical Engineers: New York, NY, USA, 2014.
82. Rosen, R.; von Wichert, G.; Lo, G.; Bettenhausen, K.D. About The Importance of Autonomy and Digital Twins for the Future of Manufacturing. *IFAC-Pap.* **2015**, *48*, 567–572. [CrossRef]
83. Qi, Q.; Tao, F. Digital Twin and Big Data Towards Smart Manufacturing and Industry 4.0: 360 Degree Comparison. *IEEE Access* **2018**, *6*, 3585–3593. [CrossRef]
84. Tao, F.; Zhang, H.; Liu, A.; Nee, A.Y.C. Digital Twin in Industry: State-of-the-Art. *IEEE Trans. Industr. Inform.* **2019**, *15*, 2405–2415. [CrossRef]
85. Kritzinger, W.; Karner, M.; Traar, G.; Henjes, J.; Sihn, W. Digital Twin in Manufacturing: A Categorical Literature Review and Classification. *IFAC-Pap.* **2018**, *51*, 1016–1022. [CrossRef]
86. Ivanov, D. Predicting the Impacts of Epidemic Outbreaks on Global Supply Chains: A Simulation-Based Analysis on the Coronavirus Outbreak (COVID-19/SARS-CoV-2) Case. *Transp. Res. E: Logist. Transp. Rev.* **2020**, *136*, 101922. [CrossRef] [PubMed]
87. Ghobakhloo, M. The Future of Manufacturing Industry: A Strategic Roadmap toward Industry 4.0. *J. Manuf. Technol. Manag.* **2018**, *29*, 910–936. [CrossRef]
88. Tao, F.; Zhang, M. Digital Twin Shop-Floor: A New Shop-Floor Paradigm Towards Smart Manufacturing. *IEEE Access* **2017**, *5*, 20418–20427. [CrossRef]
89. Schleich, B.; Anwer, N.; Mathieu, L.; Wartzack, S. Shaping the Digital Twin for Design and Production Engineering. *CIRP Ann.* **2017**, *66*, 141–144. [CrossRef]
90. Xue, J.; Zhang, W.; Rasool, Z.; Zhou, J. A Review of Supply Chain Coordination Management Based on Bibliometric Data. *Alex. Eng. J.* **2022**, *61*, 10837–10850. [CrossRef]
91. Fang, H.; Fang, F.; Hu, Q.; Wan, Y. Supply Chain Management: A Review and Bibliometric Analysis. *Processes* **2022**, *10*, 1681. [CrossRef]
92. Grieves, M.; Vickers, J. Digital Twin: Mitigating Unpredictable, Undesirable Emergent Behavior in Complex Systems. In *Transdisciplinary Perspectives on Complex Systems*; Kahlen, F.-J., Flumerfelt, S., Alves, A., Eds.; Springer International Publishing: Cham, Switzerland, 2017; pp. 85–113. ISBN 978-3-319-38754-3.
93. Lu, Y.; Liu, C.; Wang, K.I.-K.; Huang, H.; Xu, X. Digital Twin-Driven Smart Manufacturing: Connotation, Reference Model, Applications and Research Issues. *Robot. Comput. Integr. Manuf.* **2020**, *61*, 101837. [CrossRef]
94. Zhang, H.; Liu, Q.; Chen, X.; Zhang, D.; Leng, J. A Digital Twin-Based Approach for Designing and Multi-Objective Optimization of Hollow Glass Production Line. *IEEE Access* **2017**, *5*, 26901–26911. [CrossRef]
95. Fischer, A.; Beiderwellen Bedrikow, A.; Tommelein, I.D.; Nübel, K.; Fottner, J. From Activity Recognition to Simulation: The Impact of Granularity on Production Models in Heavy Civil Engineering. *Algorithms* **2023**, *16*, 212. [CrossRef]
96. Fuller, A.; Fan, Z.; Day, C.; Barlow, C. Digital Twin: Enabling Technologies, Challenges and Open Research. *IEEE Access* **2020**, *8*, 108952–108971. [CrossRef]
97. Dong, R.; She, C.; Hardjawana, W.; Li, Y.; Vucetic, B. Deep Learning for Hybrid 5G Services in Mobile Edge Computing Systems: Learn From a Digital Twin. *IEEE Trans. Wirel. Commun.* **2019**, *18*, 4692–4707. [CrossRef]
98. Yang, J.; Huang, Y.; Wang, D.; Sui, X.; Li, Y.; Zhao, L. Fast Prediction of Compressor Flow Field in Nuclear Power System Based on Proper Orthogonal Decomposition and Deep Learning. *Front. Energy Res.* **2023**, *11*, 1163043. [CrossRef]
99. Lv, Z. Digital Twins in Industry 5.0. *Research* **2023**, *6*, 0071. [CrossRef]
100. Li, L.; Mao, C.; Sun, H.; Yuan, Y.; Lei, B. Digital Twin Driven Green Performance Evaluation Methodology of Intelligent Manufacturing: Hybrid Model Based on Fuzzy Rough-Sets AHP, Multistage Weight Synthesis, and PROMETHEE II. *Complexity* **2020**, *2020*, e3853925. [CrossRef]
101. Aheleroff, S.; Zhong, R.Y.; Xu, X. A Digital Twin Reference for Mass Personalization in Industry 4.0. *Procedia CIRP* **2020**, *93*, 228–233. [CrossRef]
102. Park, J.-S.; Lee, D.-G.; Jimenez, J.A.; Lee, S.-J.; Kim, J.-W. Human-Focused Digital Twin Applications for Occupational Safety and Health in Workplaces: A Brief Survey and Research Directions. *Appl. Sci.* **2023**, *13*, 4598. [CrossRef]
103. Wang, H.; Lv, L.; Li, X.; Li, H.; Leng, J.; Zhang, Y.; Thomson, V.; Liu, G.; Wen, X.; Sun, C.; et al. A Safety Management Approach for Industry 5.0′s Human-Centered Manufacturing Based on Digital Twin. *J. Manuf. Syst.* **2023**, *66*, 1–12. [CrossRef]
104. Hou, L.; Wu, S.; Zhang, G.K.; Tan, Y.; Wang, X. Literature Review of Digital Twins Applications in Construction Workforce Safety. *Appl. Sci.* **2021**, *11*, 339. [CrossRef]

105. Caputo, F.; Greco, A.; Fera, M.; Macchiaroli, R. Digital Twins to Enhance the Integration of Ergonomics in the Workplace Design. *Int. J. Ind. Ergon.* **2019**, *71*, 20–31. [CrossRef]
106. He, B.; Bai, K.-J. Digital Twin-Based Sustainable Intelligent Manufacturing: A Review. *Adv. Manuf.* **2021**, *9*, 1–21. [CrossRef]
107. Corallo, A.; Del Vecchio, V.; Lezzi, M.; Morciano, P. Shop Floor Digital Twin in Smart Manufacturing: A Systematic Literature Review. *Sustainability* **2021**, *13*, 12987. [CrossRef]
108. Warke, V.; Kumar, S.; Bongale, A.; Kotecha, K. Sustainable Development of Smart Manufacturing Driven by the Digital Twin Framework: A Statistical Analysis. *Sustainability* **2021**, *13*, 10139. [CrossRef]
109. Zhang, X.; Zhu, W. Application Framework of Digital Twin-Driven Product Smart Manufacturing System: A Case Study of Aeroengine Blade Manufacturing. *Int. J. Adv. Robot. Syst.* **2019**, *16*, 1729881419880663. [CrossRef]
110. Zhang, C.; Dong, L.; Wang, Y. Design-Manufacturing-Operation & Maintenance (O&M) Integration of Complex Product Based on Digital Twin. *Appl. Sci.* **2023**, *13*, 1052. [CrossRef]
111. Zhong, D.; Xia, Z.; Zhu, Y.; Duan, J. Overview of Predictive Maintenance Based on Digital Twin Technology. *Heliyon* **2023**, *9*, e14534. [CrossRef]
112. Lünnemann, P.; Fresemann, C.; Richter, F. The Digital Twin for Operations, Maintenance, Repair and Overhaul. In *The Digital Twin*; Crespi, N., Drobot, A.T., Minerva, R., Eds.; Springer International Publishing: Cham, Switzerland, 2023; pp. 661–675. ISBN 978-3-031-21343-4.
113. Qiu, S.; Zhao, J.; Lv, Y.; Dai, J.; Chen, F.; Wang, Y.; Li, A. Digital-Twin-Assisted Edge-Computing Resource Allocation Based on the Whale Optimization Algorithm. *Sensors* **2022**, *22*, 9546. [CrossRef]
114. Protner, J.; Pipan, M.; Zupan, H.; Resman, M.; Simic, M.; Herakovic, N. Edge Computing and Digital Twin Based Smart Manufacturing. *IFAC-Pap.* **2021**, *54*, 831–836. [CrossRef]
115. Vacháleh, J.; Bartalský, L.; Rovný, O.; Šišmišová, D.; Morháč, M.; Lokšík, M. The Digital Twin of an Industrial Production Line within the Industry 4.0 Concept. In Proceedings of the 2017 21st International Conference on Process Control (PC), Strbske Pleso, Slovakia, 6–9 June 2017; pp. 258–262.
116. Uhlemann, T.H.-J.; Schock, C.; Lehmann, C.; Freiberger, S.; Steinhilper, R. The Digital Twin: Demonstrating the Potential of Real Time Data Acquisition in Production Systems. *Procedia Manuf.* **2017**, *9*, 113–120. [CrossRef]
117. Cai, Y.; Starly, B.; Cohen, P.; Lee, Y.-S. Sensor Data and Information Fusion to Construct Digital-Twins Virtual Machine Tools for Cyber-Physical Manufacturing. *Procedia Manuf.* **2017**, *10*, 1031–1042. [CrossRef]
118. Brenner, B.; Hummel, V. Digital Twin as Enabler for an Innovative Digital Shopfloor Management System in the ESB Logistics Learning Factory at Reutlingen—University. *Procedia Manuf.* **2017**, *9*, 198–205. [CrossRef]
119. Blum, M.; Schuh, G. Towards a Data-Oriented Optimization of Manufacturing Processes—A Real-Time Architecture for the Order Processing as a Basis for Data Analytics Methods. In Proceedings of the 19th International Conference on Enterprise Information Systems, Porto, Portugal, 26–29 April 2017; pp. 257–264.
120. DebRoy, T.; Zhang, W.; Turner, J.; Babu, S.S. Building Digital Twins of 3D Printing Machines. *Scr. Mater.* **2017**, *135*, 119–124. [CrossRef]
121. Knapp, G.L.; Mukherjee, T.; Zuback, J.S.; Wei, H.L.; Palmer, T.A.; De, A.; DebRoy, T. Building Blocks for a Digital Twin of Additive Manufacturing. *Acta Mater.* **2017**, *135*, 390–399. [CrossRef]
122. Xu, Y.; Sun, Y.; Liu, X.; Zheng, Y. A Digital-Twin-Assisted Fault Diagnosis Using Deep Transfer Learning. *IEEE Access* **2019**, *7*, 19990–19999. [CrossRef]
123. Wang, Q.; Jiao, W.; Zhang, Y. Deep Learning-Empowered Digital Twin for Visualized Weld Joint Growth Monitoring and Penetration Control. *J. Manuf. Syst.* **2020**, *57*, 429–439. [CrossRef]
124. Zhang, C.; Zhou, G.; Hu, J.; Li, J. Deep Learning-Enabled Intelligent Process Planning for Digital Twin Manufacturing Cell. *Knowl. Based Syst.* **2020**, *191*, 105247. [CrossRef]
125. Franciosa, P.; Sokolov, M.; Sinha, S.; Sun, T.; Ceglarek, D. Deep Learning Enhanced Digital Twin for Closed-Loop In-Process Quality Improvement. *CIRP Ann.* **2020**, *69*, 369–372. [CrossRef]
126. Hofmann, W.; Branding, F. Implementation of an IoT- and Cloud-Based Digital Twin for Real-Time Decision Support in Port Operations. *IFAC-Pap.* **2019**, *52*, 2104–2109. [CrossRef]
127. Borangiu, T.; Trentesaux, D.; Thomas, A.; Leitão, P.; Barata, J. Digital Transformation of Manufacturing through Cloud Services and Resource Virtualization. *Comput. Ind.* **2019**, *108*, 150–162. [CrossRef]
128. Hu, L.; Nguyen, N.-T.; Tao, W.; Leu, M.C.; Liu, X.F.; Shahriar, M.R.; Al Sunny, S.M.N. Modeling of Cloud-Based Digital Twins for Smart Manufacturing with MT Connect. *Procedia Manuf.* **2018**, *26*, 1193–1203. [CrossRef]
129. Qi, Q.; Tao, F. A Smart Manufacturing Service System Based on Edge Computing, Fog Computing, and Cloud Computing. *IEEE Access* **2019**, *7*, 86769–86777. [CrossRef]
130. Urbina Coronado, P.D.; Lynn, R.; Louhichi, W.; Parto, M.; Wescoat, E.; Kurfess, T. Part Data Integration in the Shop Floor Digital Twin: Mobile and Cloud Technologies to Enable a Manufacturing Execution System. *J. Manuf. Syst.* **2018**, *48*, 25–33. [CrossRef]
131. Park, Y.; Woo, J.; Choi, S. A Cloud-Based Digital Twin Manufacturing System Based on an Interoperable Data Schema for Smart Manufacturing. *Int. J. Comput. Integr. Manuf.* **2020**, *33*, 1259–1276. [CrossRef]
132. Yaqoob, I.; Salah, K.; Uddin, M.; Jayaraman, R.; Omar, M.; Imran, M. Blockchain for Digital Twins: Recent Advances and Future Research Challenges. *IEEE Netw.* **2020**, *34*, 290–298. [CrossRef]
133. Hasan, H.R.; Salah, K.; Jayaraman, R.; Omar, M.; Yaqoob, I.; Pesic, S.; Taylor, T.; Boscovic, D. A Blockchain-Based Approach for the Creation of Digital Twins. *IEEE Access* **2020**, *8*, 34113–34126. [CrossRef]

134. Zhang, C.; Zhou, G.; Li, H.; Cao, Y. Manufacturing Blockchain of Things for the Configuration of a Data- and Knowledge-Driven Digital Twin Manufacturing Cell. *IEEE Internet Things J.* **2020**, *7*, 11884–11894. [CrossRef]
135. Mazzei, D.; Baldi, G.; Fantoni, G.; Montelisciani, G.; Pitasi, A.; Ricci, L.; Rizzello, L. A Blockchain Tokenizer for Industrial IOT Trustless Applications. *Future Gener. Comput. Syst.* **2020**, *105*, 432–445. [CrossRef]
136. Jin, T.; Sun, Z.; Li, L.; Zhang, Q.; Zhu, M.; Zhang, Z.; Yuan, G.; Chen, T.; Tian, Y.; Hou, X.; et al. Triboelectric Nanogenerator Sensors for Soft Robotics Aiming at Digital Twin Applications. *Nat. Commun.* **2020**, *11*, 5381. [CrossRef]
137. Pham, A.-D.; Ahn, H.-J. High Precision Reducers for Industrial Robots Driving 4th Industrial Revolution: State of Arts, Analysis, Design, Performance Evaluation and Perspective. *Int. J. Precis. Eng. Manuf.-Green. Tech.* **2018**, *5*, 519–533. [CrossRef]
138. Kaewunruen, S.; Lian, Q. Digital Twin Aided Sustainability-Based Lifecycle Management for Railway Turnout Systems. *J. Clean. Prod.* **2019**, *228*, 1537–1551. [CrossRef]
139. Li, X.; Cao, J.; Liu, Z.; Luo, X. Sustainable Business Model Based on Digital Twin Platform Network: The Inspiration from Haier's Case Study in China. *Sustainability* **2020**, *12*, 936. [CrossRef]
140. Li, L.; Qu, T.; Liu, Y.; Zhong, R.Y.; Xu, G.; Sun, H.; Gao, Y.; Lei, B.; Mao, C.; Pan, Y.; et al. Sustainability Assessment of Intelligent Manufacturing Supported by Digital Twin. *IEEE Access* **2020**, *8*, 174988–175008. [CrossRef]
141. Wang, Y.; Wang, S.; Yang, B.; Zhu, L.; Liu, F. Big Data Driven Hierarchical Digital Twin Predictive Remanufacturing Paradigm: Architecture, Control Mechanism, Application Scenario and Benefits. *J. Clean. Prod.* **2020**, *248*, 119299. [CrossRef]
142. Lv, Z.; Qiao, L.; Mardani, A.; Lv, H. Digital Twins on the Resilience of Supply Chain Under COVID-19 Pandemic. *IEEE Trans. Eng. Manag.* **2022**, 1–12. [CrossRef]
143. Longo, F.; Mirabelli, G.; Padovano, A.; Solina, V. The Digital Supply Chain Twin Paradigm for Enhancing Resilience and Sustainability against COVID-like Crises. *Procedia Comput. Sci.* **2023**, *217*, 1940–1947. [CrossRef]
144. Attaran, M.; Attaran, S.; Celik, B.G. The Impact of Digital Twins on the Evolution of Intelligent Manufacturing and Industry 4.0. *Adv. Comp. Int.* **2023**, *3*, 11. [CrossRef] [PubMed]
145. Burgos, D.; Ivanov, D. Food Retail Supply Chain Resilience and the COVID-19 Pandemic: A Digital Twin-Based Impact Analysis and Improvement Directions. *Transp. Res. E: Logist. Transp. Rev.* **2021**, *152*, 102412. [CrossRef] [PubMed]
146. Mourtzis, D.; Angelopoulos, J.; Panopoulos, N. Personalized PSS Design Optimization Based on Digital Twin and Extended Reality. *Procedia CIRP* **2022**, *109*, 389–394. [CrossRef]
147. Ramesh, A.; Qin, Z.; Lu, Y. *Digital Thread Enabled Manufacturing Automation towards Mass Personalization*; American Society of Mechanical Engineers: New York, NY, USA, 2021.
148. Yang, W.; Bao, X.; Zheng, Y.; Zhang, L.; Zhang, Z.; Zhang, Z.; Li, L. A Digital Twin Framework for Large Comprehensive Ports and a Case Study of Qingdao Port. *Int. J. Adv. Manuf. Technol.* **2022**, 1–18. [CrossRef]
149. Zhou, Y.; Fu, Z.; Zhang, J.; Li, W.; Gao, C. A Digital Twin-Based Operation Status Monitoring System for Port Cranes. *Sensors* **2022**, *22*, 3216. [CrossRef]
150. Pang, T.Y.; Pelaez Restrepo, J.D.; Cheng, C.-T.; Yasin, A.; Lim, H.; Miletic, M. Developing a Digital Twin and Digital Thread Framework for an 'Industry 4.0' Shipyard. *Appl. Sci.* **2021**, *11*, 1097. [CrossRef]
151. Zhou, C.; Xu, J.; Miller-Hooks, E.; Zhou, W.; Chen, C.-H.; Lee, L.H.; Chew, E.P.; Li, H. Analytics with Digital-Twinning: A Decision Support System for Maintaining a Resilient Port. *Decis. Support. Syst.* **2021**, *143*, 113496. [CrossRef]
152. Nie, L.; Wang, X.; Zhao, Q.; Shang, Z.; Feng, L.; Li, G. Digital Twin for Transportation Big Data: A Reinforcement Learning-Based Network Traffic Prediction Approach. *IEEE Trans. Intell. Transp. Syst.* **2023**, 1–11. [CrossRef]
153. Zhao, Z.; Zhang, M.; Chen, J.; Qu, T.; Huang, G.Q. Digital Twin-Enabled Dynamic Spatial-Temporal Knowledge Graph for Production Logistics Resource Allocation. *Comput. Ind. Eng.* **2022**, *171*, 108454. [CrossRef]
154. Li, D.; Li, J. Big Data of Enterprise Supply Chain under Green Financial System Based on Digital Twin Technology. *Kybernetes* **2023**, *ahead-of-print*. [CrossRef]
155. Maddikunta, P.K.R.; Pham, Q.-V.; Prabadevi, B.; Deepa, N.; Dev, K.; Gadekallu, T.R.; Ruby, R.; Liyanage, M. Industry 5.0: A Survey on Enabling Technologies and Potential Applications. *J. Ind. Inf. Integr.* **2022**, *26*, 100257. [CrossRef]
156. Mincă, E.; Filipescu, A.; Cernega, D.; Șolea, R.; Filipescu, A.; Ionescu, D.; Simion, G. Digital Twin for a Multifunctional Technology of Flexible Assembly on a Mechatronics Line with Integrated Robotic Systems and Mobile Visual Sensor—Challenges towards Industry 5.0. *Sensors* **2022**, *22*, 8153. [CrossRef] [PubMed]
157. Raja Santhi, A.; Muthuswamy, P. Industry 5.0 or Industry 4.0S? Introduction to Industry 4.0 and a Peek into the Prospective Industry 5.0 Technologies. *Int. J. Interact. Des. Manuf.* **2023**, *17*, 947–979. [CrossRef]
158. Ivanov, D. Conceptualisation of a 7-Element Digital Twin Framework in Supply Chain and Operations Management. *Int. J. Prod. Res.* **2023**, 1–13. [CrossRef]
159. Fraga-Lamas, P.; Barros, D.; Lopes, S.I.; Fernández-Caramés, T.M. Mist and Edge Computing Cyber-Physical Human-Centered Systems for Industry 5.0: A Cost-Effective IoT Thermal Imaging Safety System. *Sensors* **2022**, *22*, 8500. [CrossRef]
160. Adel, A. Future of Industry 5.0 in Society: Human-Centric Solutions, Challenges and Prospective Research Areas. *J. Cloud Comput.* **2022**, *11*, 40. [CrossRef]

Disclaimer/Publisher's Note: The statements, opinions and data contained in all publications are solely those of the individual author(s) and contributor(s) and not of MDPI and/or the editor(s). MDPI and/or the editor(s) disclaim responsibility for any injury to people or property resulting from any ideas, methods, instructions or products referred to in the content.

Article

Graph Convolutional-Based Deep Residual Modeling for Rumor Detection on Social Media

Na Ye [1], Dingguo Yu [2,3,*], Yijie Zhou [3,4], Ke-ke Shang [5,*] and Suiyu Zhang [3]

[1] School of Journalism and Communication, Communication University of Zhejiang, Hangzhou 310018, China
[2] College of Media Engineering, Communication University of Zhejiang, Hangzhou 310018, China
[3] Key Lab of Film and TV Media Technology of Zhejiang Province, Hangzhou 310018, China
[4] Institute of Intelligent Media Technology, Communication University of Zhejiang, Hangzhou 310018, China
[5] Computational Communication Collaboratory, Nanjing University, Nanjing 210023, China
* Correspondence: yudg@cuz.edu.cn (D.Y.); kekeshang@nju.edu.cn (K.-k.S.)

Abstract: The popularity and development of social media have made it more and more convenient to spread rumors, and it has become especially important to detect rumors in massive amounts of information. Most of the traditional rumor detection methods use the rumor content or propagation structure to mine rumor characteristics, ignoring the fusion characteristics of the content and structure and their interaction. Therefore, a novel rumor detection method based on heterogeneous convolutional networks is proposed. First, this paper constructs a heterogeneous map that combines both the rumor content and propagation structure to explore their interaction during rumor propagation and obtain a rumor representation. On this basis, this paper uses a deep residual graph convolutional neural network to construct the content and structure interaction information of the current network propagation model. Finally, this paper uses the Twitter15 and Twitter16 datasets to verify the proposed method. Experimental results show that the proposed method has higher detection accuracy compared to the traditional rumor detection method.

Keywords: false information detection; residual structure; graph neural network

MSC: 68T09

1. Introduction

An important feature of the information age is the emergence of information, which includes a great deal of disinformation. This disinformation influences people's decision making and can trigger social conflict. With the spread of the internet, disinformation often comes in the form of online rumors. Online rumors usually refer to words spread through online communication media (such as Weibo, WeChat, forums, etc.), which have no basis in fact and have an offensive and purposeful nature [1]. Online rumors are often used for fraud and phishing, which pose a significant threat to the safety and interests of individuals and society, making the detection of false information increasingly important.

The application scenarios of false information detection are extensive, involving multiple fields such as news media, social networks, and e-commerce. In the news media field, false information detection can help news organizations and reporters distinguish and block fake news, improving the credibility of news reporting. In the social network field, false information detection can help social network platforms discover and remove false information in a timely manner, thereby maintaining the health and order of the network space. In the e-commerce field, false information detection can help consumers identify fake goods and false advertising and safeguard the rights and interests of consumers.

In false information detection tasks, there are many research results available for reference. Traditional content-based approaches, which analyze the credibility of individual tweets or claims separately, ignore the high correlation between tweets and events and do

not consider information from human–content interaction data. In recent years, many methods based on deep learning and methods based on novel feature fusion have also emerged. For example, Ma proposed a method for rumor detection using a tree-structured recursive neural network, and the results show that the proposed method can achieve excellent early detection of rumors [2]. However, this method may have some difficulties in processing long texts and complex syntax structures. Vu proposed a new model based on graph convolutional networks and propagation embedding for rumor detection in social media and conducted sufficient experiments on real datasets to prove the effectiveness of the method [3]. However, this method is aimed at text propagation in social networks and may not be suitable for cases involving visual or other non-textual information in the propagation process. In addition, Monti proposed a new type of automatic fake news detection model based on geometric deep learning, and experiments showed that social network propagation and structure are important features for the highly accurate detection of fake news [4]. However, this method may be affected by the sparseness and incompleteness of the data. Social media data often have high dynamicity and noise and lack complete information labels, which may lead to a decline in the performance of the model. In addition, since different news data are often interrelated, they are naturally interactive. Graph neural networks that are good at processing graph structures are also applied to rumor detection tasks. For example, Lotfi proposed a model that uses graph convolutional networks to detect rumor conversations, which extracts reply trees and user graphs for each conversation, achieving better performance compared to the baseline method [5]. Bian proposed a bidirectional graph model called a bidirectional graph convolutional network (Bi-GCN) to explore both features through top-down and bottom-up rumor propagation. It uses a GCN with a top-down directed graph of rumor propagation to learn the patterns of rumor propagation, and a GCN with a rumor propagation graph in the opposite direction to capture the structure of rumor propagation, which empirically demonstrated the superiority of this method over state-of-the-art methods [6]. Qian proposed a hierarchical multimodal contextual attention network (HMCAN) that uses the Resnet and Bert models to learn the features of images and text, respectively, and designed a hierarchical coding network to capture hierarchical semantics for fake news detection [7].

In contrast to existing methods, this article proposes a rumor detection method for the interaction characteristics of both the content and structure named GCRES, which can combine content and propagation patterns to characterize rumors. The residual structure, based on a graph convolutional network, is used to model the content structure correlations of heterogeneous graphs, thus overcoming the problem of the indistinguishable effects of adjacent neighbor nodes in the rumor propagation process and effectively realizing rumor classification. Specifically, the main contributions of this article include the following three points:

(1) This article constructs a heterogeneous graph to obtain a representation of rumors by combining post content and rumor propagation patterns, which includes the textual information of rumors and the initial propagation information.
(2) This article proposes a residual structure based on a graph convolutional network. This structure uses a skip connection method to effectively overcome the problem of the indistinguishable effects of adjacent nodes in the rumor propagation process and obtain the interaction characteristics of heterogeneous graphs.
(3) This article uses the Twitter15 and Twitter16 datasets, which are widely used in rumor detection for experimental verification. The experimental results show that, compared with traditional rumor monitoring methods, the proposed GCRES method can achieve a higher rumor detection accuracy.

2. Related Works

Traditional methods for detecting fake information can be categorized into two types: rule-based methods and machine learning-based methods. Rule-based methods classify real and fake information using the differences between them, including features like keywords, sentence structures, and sentiment polarities in the text [8]. On the other hand, machine learning-based methods classify real and fake information by building models, such as using support vector machines, random forests, or other algorithms to train and classify data. Ma et al. first used deep learning models to detect rumors on Weibo [9]. In subsequent studies, they proposed two recursive neural network models based on top-down and bottom-up tree structures to better capture rumor structures and text features. The results showed that this model achieved high accuracy in detecting early propagating rumors [2].

Since introducing deep learning methods, the accuracy and efficiency of fake information detection have significantly improved. Among them, graph neural networks, as a powerful representation learning method, have a wide range of applications in fake information detection. Graph neural network-based fake information detection methods usually fall into two categories: node-based methods and graph-based methods.

Node-based methods mainly focus on node features and contextual information, whereas graph-based methods use the entire graph as input and utilize graph neural networks to learn graph representations. In node-based methods, the most commonly used approach is to use the social and content attributes of nodes for fake information detection, for example, by using features such as user information, text content [2,10], and time information to determine whether the node is spreading fake information. Y Liu et al. used recurrent and convolutional networks to construct a time-series classifier to capture global and local variations in user features on the propagation path, thus detecting fake news [11]. This method is the first to model the news dissemination path on social media as multi-dimensional time series and practice fake news detection through a sequence classifier. Ling Sun et al. discussed a novel joint learning model called HG-SL for the early detection of fake news. This model uses a hyper-GNN to embed the global relationships of users, and multi-head self-attention modules to simultaneously learn local contexts (local context in specific news) during propagation in order to comprehensively capture the differences between true and false news. The introduction of global node centrality and local propagation status further highlights user influence and news dissemination ability. The experiments show that HG-SL is significantly better than the SOTA models in the early detection of fake news [12]. In addition, some studies have also considered the propagation behavior of nodes as one of the node features, such as the forwarding and like counts of nodes [13,14].

In graph-based methods, the main approach is to learn the representation of the entire graph through graph neural networks and then perform fake information detection. For example, Tian Bian et al. proposed a novel bidirectional graph convolutional network (Bi-GCN) model, which uses a rumor propagation-directed graph with a top-down structure to learn the propagation patterns of rumors, and a rumor propagation graph with a reverse direction to capture the structure of rumor propagation. The influence of the original post of the rumor is enhanced in the graph structure, and the model achieved excellent results in fake information detection [6]. K Tu et al. proposed a framework for rumor representation learning and detection. This framework uses combined text and propagation structure representation learning to improve rumor detection performance. The authors proposed a joint graph concept to integrate the propagation structure of all tweets to alleviate the sparsity issue of the propagation structure in the early stage [15]. Some researchers have also combined graph neural networks with attention mechanisms to learn graph representations more accurately. For instance, Qi Huang et al. proposed a meta-path-based heterogeneous graph attention network framework. The heterogeneous graph is decomposed into tweet word and user subgraphs according to tweet words and tweet user paths, and node representations are learned using subgraph attention networks to capture the global semantic relationships of text content and fuse information involved in source tweet propagation for rumor detection [16]. Chunyuan Yuan et al. proposed a novel global-local attention network (GLAN) for rumor detection on social media. Their method combines local semantic relationships with global structural information, uses multi-head attention mechanisms to integrate the semantic information of relevant retweets into the source tweet, generates a better-integrated representation, establishes a heterogeneous graph using global structural information to capture the complex global information between different source tweets, and uses global attention for rumor detection. Experimental results show that the GLAN is significantly better than existing models in rumor detection and early detection [17]. In addition, Ma et al. used statistical features in three aspects, including rumor content language characteristics, user characteristics participating in rumor transmission, and the propagation network structure to build a feature graph. The authors integrated entity recognition, sentence reconstruction, and ordinary differential equation networks into a unified framework called ESODE, which improved the performance of rumor detection [18].

3. Solution Design

3.1. System Model

A rumor detection dataset $X = \{x_1, x_2, \ldots x_n\}$, where x_i represents the i-th event, and n represents the total number of events. Each event x_i contains two independent sets: content and propagation structure. In addition, $x_i = \{P_i, G_i\}$, where P_i and G_i represent the content and propagation structure of x_i, respectively. The propagation structure G_i is composed of a set of nodes $C_i = \{c_{i0}, c_{i1}, \ldots, c_{iN}\}$ and a set of connections $E_i = \{e_{st} \mid s, t = 0, 1, \ldots, N\}$, where c_{i0} represents the original post, and c_{ij} represents the j-th response post. Let $A \in \{0,1\}^{N \times N}$ be the adjacency matrix, where $A_{st} = 1$ if there exists an edge from node c_{is} to node c_{it}, and $A_{st}=0$ otherwise. Moreover, Let A' be the adjacency matrix of the heterogeneous graph that combines both the content and propagation structure. In this paper, we model the rumor detection task as a supervised classification problem, where each event has a true label y_i, with a value set of $\{NR, FR, TR, UR\}$, representing non-rumors, falsehood rumors, true rumors, and unverified rumors, respectively. Our goal is to train a classifier $f : x_i \rightarrow y_i$ to accurately predict the label of the content and the propagation structure of a given post.

3.2. Rumor Detection Framework

A heterogeneous graph is a graph in which there are multiple different types of nodes and multiple types of edges between the different types of nodes. Compared with traditional homogeneous graphs, heterogeneous graphs have richer structures and more associated information. In heterogeneous graphs, nodes are divided into different types, and there is a clear distinction between node types. For example, the heterogeneous composition of a social network may include user nodes, post nodes, and tag nodes. The edges between the different node types can represent the follow relationship between users, the interaction relationship between users and posts, and the association relationship between posts and tags. Such heterogeneous graphs can more accurately simulate the complex relationship network in the real world and capture rich correlation information between different nodes.

As shown in Figures 1 and 2, we propose a rumor detection framework based on the interaction characteristics of heterogeneous graphs, named GCRES. The framework consists of three parts: rumor representation, interaction representation learning, and rumor classification. Firstly, we construct a graph model based on the content and propagation structure for rumor representation. Specifically, we first use the TF-IDF model to extract the representation information of the rumor content [19]. Then, we encode the propagation node vectors using the adjacency matrix, combine the content and propagation information, and finally embed the joint graph into a low-dimensional space. Secondly, we use a graph convolutional network (GCN) to learn the initial state of the heterogeneous graph. At the same time, we use interaction representation learning technology to obtain the interaction features of the heterogeneous graph. Finally, we use an average pooling layer to cascade the features of heterogeneous maps and make predictions of rumor categories.

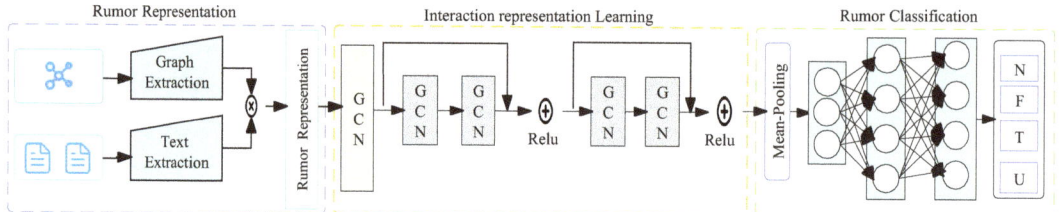

Figure 1. Rumordetection framework.

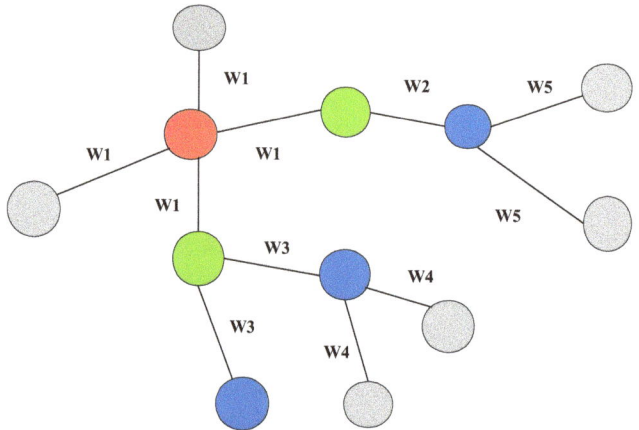

Figure 2. Heterogeneousgraph combining rumor content and propagation structure. The red circles represent the original nodes, and the other colored circles represent the nodes in the propagation path

3.3. Rumor Representation

As shown in Figure 1, we constructed a heterogeneous graph to characterize rumors by combining the content and propagation structure. Specifically, we used the TF-IDF method to obtain the representation of the content in each post. First, we filtered out stop words and constructed a corpus. Then, the word frequency can be represented as:

$$tf_{ij} = \frac{n_{ij}}{\sum_k n_{ik}} \quad (1)$$

In the equation, n_{ij} represents the number of times the i-th vocabulary appears in the j-th post. At the same time, inverse document frequency can be represented as:

$$idf_i = \frac{\log |D|}{1 + |k : t_i \in p_k|} \quad (2)$$

where $|D|$ represents the total number of posts in the corpus, and $|k : t_i \in p_k|$ represents the number of posts containing the vocabulary t_i. Then, the weight of the vocabulary t_i can be represented as:

$$t_i = tf_{ij} \times idf_i \quad (3)$$

Therefore, the content representation of the j-th post is $p_j = \left[t_1, t_2, \ldots, t_{|W|}\right]$, where $|W|$ is the total number of vocabulary in the corpus.

On the other hand, since the representation of p_j is high dimensional and sparse, we use an embedding layer to map it to a low-dimensional space to obtain dense real-valued vectors as the content representation of the j-th post:

$$v_j = W_j p_j \quad (4)$$

where W_j represents the weight of the embedding layer.

Based on the above framework, we further construct the propagation structure of the rumor $G_j = \{C_j, E_j, A\}$. Since the adjacency matrix $A \in \{0,1\}^{N \times N}$ reflects the transmission path of the rumor, the adjacency matrix of the joint rumor content and propagation path can be obtained from A and v_j:

$$A'_{st} = A_{st} v_j \tag{5}$$

where A_{st} represents the weight of the edge from node c_{js} to node c_{jt}. Based on this, the initial representation of the rumor r_j can be represented as:

$$r_j = \frac{1}{M} \sum_{c_{js}, c_{jt} \in C_j} A'_{st} \tag{6}$$

where M is the number of edges occupied by the j-th post in the propagation structure.

3.4. Acquiring the Initial State

After obtaining the representation of the rumor, we use a GCN to obtain the initial state of the heterogeneous graph. Specifically, we first construct the operator $\tilde{A}$ of the GCN, defined as:

$$\Phi = \tilde{D}^{-\frac{1}{2}} \tilde{A} \tilde{D}^{-\frac{1}{2}} \tag{7}$$

$$\tilde{A} = A' + I \tag{8}$$

where A' and I are the adjacency matrix and identity matrix of the heterogeneous graph, respectively, and $\tilde{D}$ is the degree matrix of $\tilde{A}$. Then, the initial state representation of the joint graph can be represented as:

$$H^{(0)} = \sigma\left(\Phi r_j W^{(0)}\right) \tag{9}$$

where $H^{(0)}$ represents the initial state of the rumor propagation, $W^{(0)}$ is the weight matrix of the filter, and $\sigma(\cdot)$ is the ReLU activation function.

3.5. Interaction Representation Learning

In order to obtain the interaction feature information of the rumor content and propagation graph, we use interaction representation learning to learn the continuous temporal correlation in the propagation process.

First, we assume that the hidden representations of all nodes are correlated, and we combine the GCN and residual network (ResNet) methods to learn the embedding representations of the nodes. Specifically, we use a two-layer GCN network model to learn the representation of the propagation graph and extract potential relationships through the feature information of the nodes themselves, as well as the adjacent nodes. Each GCN layer first obtains the features of the current node and the adjacent nodes, then uses aggregation functions to obtain local feature relationships, and finally trains through shallow learning to obtain high-dimensional features. The propagation relationship between layers can be represented as:

$$H^{(l+1)} = \sigma\left(\tilde{D}^{-\frac{1}{2}} \tilde{A} \tilde{D}^{-\frac{1}{2}} H^{(l)} W^{(l)}\right) \tag{10}$$

where $\tilde{A} = A + I$, I is the identity matrix, $\tilde{D}$ is the degree matrix of $\tilde{A}$, and $\sigma(\cdot)$ is the ReLU activation function.

On the other hand, we use a structure based on residual networks to cascade four GCN networks. As the number of model layers in the GCN increases, it is prone to the problem of over-smoothing, which makes the differentiation of neighboring nodes' effects in the rumor propagation process unclear. Therefore, a graph neural network incorporating residual networks is designed, adopting skip connection to improve and avoid this problem. As shown in Figure 1, the output of each residual block can be represented as:

$$y^{(l+1)} = h^{(l)}\left(x^{(l)}\right) + F\left(x^{(l)}, H^{(l)}\right) \tag{11}$$

3.6. Rumor Classification

We further use the average pooling operation to aggregate the output of all GCNs, that is,

$$H = \frac{1}{L}\sum_{l=0}^{L} H^{(l)} \tag{12}$$

where L is the number of GCNs. Then, we use fully connected layers and a softmax layer for rumor classification, which is:

$$\hat{y} = \text{softmax}(W_{FC}H + b_{FC}) \tag{13}$$

where W_{FC} and b_{FC} are the weight and bias of the last hidden layer, and $\hat{y}$ represents the predicted probability vector of rumors belonging to each category, which is also the label for predicting rumor events. Finally, we train the model by minimizing the cross-entropy between $\hat{y}$ and the true distribution y and adding L2 regularization to prevent overfitting.

4. Experiment

4.1. Dataset

We conducted experimental validation of the proposed method using two open source datasets, Twitter15 and Twitter16. Both datasets consist of social media data, each with 1490 and 818 propagation graphs. The labeling of the propagation graphs includes four types: non-rumor, true rumor, false rumor, and unverified rumor. In addition, the nodes in the graph represent users, and the edges represent replies and forwarding. Table 1 provides statistical information on the two datasets.

Table 1. Twitter15 and Twitter16 datasets.

Statistical Information	Twitter15	Twitter16
Total number of posts	331,612	204,820
Original post count	1490	818
Non-rumor count	372	205
True rumor count	374	203
False rumor count	370	205
Unverified rumor count	374	205

4.2. Baseline Methods

We used the following seven baseline methods for rumor detection:

(1) DTC [10]: This method uses decision tree classifiers and manually designed features to extract and analyze tweet information.
(2) RFC [20]: This method uses a random forest classifier to detect rumors by combining user features, language features, and news structure features.
(3) SVM-TS [12]: This method is based on an SVM classifier, using manually designed features to form a time-series kernel to identify rumors.
(4) SVM-HK [21] : This method uses a graph kernel to measure the similarity of propagation structures combined with an SVM classifier for rumor detection.
(5) GRU-RNN [9]: This method relies on a recurrent neural network with GRUs to capture the contextual changes in relevant posts over time for rumor detection.
(6) BU-RvNNand TD-RvNN [22]: This method adopts a bidirectional tree-structured recursive neural model, which includes top-down and bottom-up tree-structured neural networks combined with GRUs to learn and analyze rumor information.

(7) Rumor2vec [15]: This method uses a CNN-based model to combine the textual content with the propagation structure to achieve joint representation learning for rumor detection.

4.3. Experimental Setup

We used a TF-IDF model based on a 5000-word vocabulary to represent the content of the post. The node and hidden layer embedding sizes were searched in $\{32, 64, 128, 256\}$. The embedding size of the model and the number of samples selected for each training were both set to 64. At the same time, we divided each dataset into five parts and performed fivefold cross-validation to ensure the robustness and fairness of the experimental results. We used the accuracy values for the four categories and the F1 value for each category as performance indicators. In addition, we used the Adam algorithm for model optimization. The learning rate was 0.005, and the number of iterations was 100 epochs. Finally, to prevent overfitting, we stopped training early when the validation stopped decreasing for 10 epochs.

4.4. Analysis of the Results

We used the accuracy and F1 values to evaluate the performance of our proposed classification model. The accuracy rate helps us understand the accuracy of the classification, whereas the F1 value takes into account the accuracy and recall, allowing us to more comprehensively evaluate the classification effect of the model on different classes. In Table 2, Acc. represents accuracy, and NR F1, TR F1, FR F1, and UR F1 represent the F1 values of the non-rumor, true rumor, false rumor, and unverified rumor categories.

Table 2. Comparison experiment results.

Method	Acc.	NR F1	FR F1	TR F1	UR F1
Twitter15 dataset					
DTC	0.454	0.733	0.355	0.317	0.415
RFC	0.565	0.810	0.422	0.401	0.543
SVM-TS	0.544	0.796	0.472	0.404	0.483
SVM-HK	0.493	0.650	0.439	0.342	0.336
GRU-RNN	0.641	0.684	0.634	0.688	0.571
BU-RvNN	0.708	0.695	0.728	0.759	0.653
TD-RvNN	0.723	0.682	0.758	0.821	0.654
Rumor2vec	0.796	0.883	0.746	0.836	0.723
GCRES	0.853	0.855	0.858	0.903	0.746
Twitter16 dataset					
DTC	0.473	0.254	0.080	0.190	0.482
RFC	0.585	0.752	0.415	0.547	0.563
SVM-TS	0.574	0.755	0.420	0.571	0.526
SVM-HK	0.511	0.648	0.434	0.473	0.451
GRU-RNN	0.633	0.617	0.715	0.577	0.527
BU-RvNN	0.718	0.723	0.712	0.779	0.659
TD-RvNN	0.737	0.662	0.743	0.835	0.708
Rumor2vec	0.852	0.857	0.769	0.927	0.850
GCRES	0.888	0.801	0.877	0.912	0.919

Table 2 shows the test results of the proposed method and the seven baseline methods on Twitter15 and Twitter16. In the table, it can be seen that compared with methods using manually designed features (DTC, RFC, SVM-TS, and SVM-HK), methods based on deep learning (GRU-RNN, BU-RvNN, Rumor2vec) and the proposed method achieved higher accuracy and F1 values. This is because deep learning technology can learn effective high-dimensional features of rumors. These results prove that deep learning technology can effectively improve the performance of rumor detection.

On the other hand, the proposed method achieved the highest accuracy on both datasets. Specifically, the proposed method achieved accuracies of 85.3% and 88.8% on Twitter15 and Twitter16, respectively, which were 5.7% and 3.6% higher than the baseline method Rumor2vec. This is because CNNs cannot handle data with dynamic features, making it difficult for Rumor2vec to capture the interaction characteristics of rumor propagation. These results demonstrate that incorporating interaction features can effectively improve the performance of rumor detection. It is worth noting that for the non-rumor category, Rumor2vec outperformed the proposed method. This is because non-rumor posts are often posted or replied to by more authoritative and credible users, so the propagation path and content of non-rumor posts are more fixed. Therefore, the interaction characteristics of non-rumor posts have little impact on the detection performance.

Figures 3 and 4 depict the confusion matrices of the experimental results for the Twitter15 and Twitter16 datasets, respectively. As shown in Figure 3, for the Twitter15 dataset, the accuracy of our method was high for data that were identified as true rumors or false rumors. But the accuracy achieved for unverified rumors was only 0.746 due to the peculiarities of the data in this category. As they were unverified, the samples in this category could be both true or false, which is very confusing. Therefore, our method is more suitable for only facticity and falsehood identification of known data, and for unidentified rumors, there are no features that can be relied on from the data.

As shown in Figure 4, for the Twitter16 dataset, true rumors, false rumors, and unverified rumors were more accurately identified compared to non-rumors. The reason for this may lie in the correlation between the rumor sample data and whether a sample was a true rumor or a false rumor, as some characteristics can be discerned from a textual point of view (unverified rumors may be true or false). However, for the non-rumor sample, it was less related to the other three categories, so its classification accuracy was low.

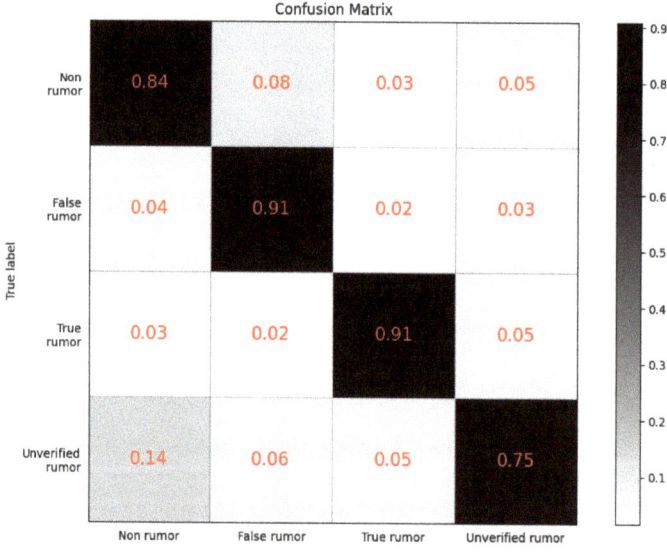

Figure 3. Confusion matrix of Twitter15.

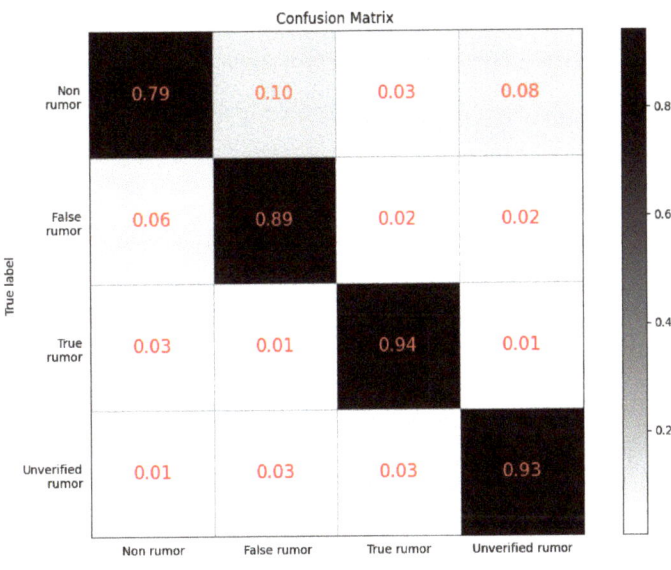

Figure 4. Confusion matrix of Twitter16.

5. Conclusions

By utilizing the dynamic changes in rumor content, propagation structure, and propagation heterogeneous graph, this paper proposes a novel interaction rumor detection method based on a graph convolutional network called GCRES. Firstly, a novel heterogeneous graph is proposed by combining the rumor content and propagation structure to obtain accurate rumor representation. Secondly, a residual module consisting of four cascaded graph convolutional networks is designed using the powerful ability of graph convolutional networks in dealing with heterogeneous graphs for representation learning, thus fully mining the interaction characteristics of the heterogeneous graph. Experimental results show that compared with traditional rumor detection methods, the GCRES method exhibits better detection performance on both the Twitter15 and Twitter16 datasets.

Author Contributions: Conceptualization, D.Y. and Y.Z.; methodology, Y.Z. and N.Y.; software, N.Y. and S.Z.; validation, S.Z. and Y.Z.; formal analysis, N.Y. and S.Z.; writing—original draft preparation, N.Y., Y.Z., and D.Y.; writing—review and editing, Y.Z. and K.-k.S.; visualization, N.Y. and K.-k.S.; supervision, K.-k.S.; funding acquisition, D.Y. All authors have read and agreed to the published version of the manuscript.

Funding: This work is supported by the National Social Science Funds of China (Grant No. 22BSH025), National Natural Science Foundation of China (Grant No. 61803047), Major Project of The National Social Science Foundation of China (19ZDA149, 19ZDA324) and Fundamental Research Funds for the Central Universities (14370119, 14390110). Ke-ke Shang is supported by Jiangsu Qing Lan Project.

Institutional Review Board Statement: Not applicable.

Informed Consent Statement: Not applicable.

Data Availability Statement: Not applicable.

Acknowledgments: College of Media Engineering, Communication University of Zhejiang; Institute of Intelligent Media Technology, Communication University of Zhejiang; Key Lab of Film and TV Media Technology of Zhejiang Province; Computational Communication Collaboratory, Nanjing University.

Conflicts of Interest: The authors declare no conflict of interest

References

1. Jia, J.W.; Wu, W.J. A rumor transmission model with incubation in social networks. *Phys. A Stat. Mech. Its Appl.* **2018**, *491*, 453–462. [CrossRef]
2. Ma, J.; Gao, W.; Wong, K.-F. *Rumor Detection on Twitter with Tree-Structured Recursive Neural Networks*; Association for Computational Linguistics: Melbourne, Australia, 2018.
3. Vu, D.T.; Jung, J.J. Rumor Detection by Propagation Embedding Based on Graph Convolutional Network. *Int. J. Comput. Intell. Syst.* **2021**, *14*, 1053–1065. [CrossRef]
4. Monti, F.; Frasca, F.; Eynard, D.; Mannion, D.; Bronstein, M.M. Fake News Detection on Social Media Using Geometric Deep Learning. *arXiv* **2019**, arXiv:1902.06673.
5. Lotfi, S.; Mirzarezaee, M.; Hosseinzadeh, M.; Seydi, V. Detection of rumor conversations in Twitter using graph convolutional networks. *Appl. Intell.* **2021**, *51*, 4774–4787. [CrossRef]
6. Bian, T.; Xiao, X.; Xu, T.; Zhao, P.; Huang, W.; Rong, Y.; Huang, J. Rumor detection on social media with bi-directional graph convolutional networks. In Proceedings of the AAAI Conference on Artificial Intelligence, New York, NY, USA, 7–12 February 2020; Volume 34, pp. 549–556.
7. Qian, S.; Wang, J.; Hu, J.; Fang, Q.; Xu, C. Hierarchical multi-modal contextual attention network for fake news detection. In Proceedings of the 44th International ACM SIGIR Conference on Research and Development in Information Retrieval, Virtual Event, Canada, 11–15 July 2021; pp. 153–162.
8. Andreevskaia, A.; Bergler, S. Sentiment Tag Extraction from WordNet Glosses. In Proceedings of the 5th Conference on Language Resources and Evaluation (LREC'06), Genoa, Italy, 22–28 May 2006.
9. Ma, J.; Gao, W.; Mitra, P.; Kwon, S.; Jansen, B.J.; Wong, K.-F.; Cha, M. Detecting Rumors from Microblogs with Recurrent Neural Networks. In Proceedings of the Proceedings of the Twenty-Fifth International Joint Conference on Artificial Intelligence (IJCAI-16), New York, NY, USA, 9–15 July 2016.
10. Castillo, C.; Mendoza, M.; Poblete, B. Information Credibility on Twitter. In Proceedings of the 20th International Conference on World Wide Web, Hyderabad, India, 28 March–1 April 2011; pp. 675–684.
11. Liu, Y.; Wu, Y.-F. Early Detection of Fake News on Social Media through Propagation Path Classification with Recurrent and Convolutional Networks. In Proceedings of the AAAI Conference on Artificial Intelligence, New Orleans, LA, USA, 2–7 February 2018; Volume 32.
12. Sun, L.; Rao, Y.; Lan, Y.; Xia, B.; Li, Y. HG-SL: Jointly Learning of Global and Local User Spreading Behavior for Fake News Early Detection. *Proc. AAAI Conf. Artif. Intell.* **2023**, *37*, 5248–5256. [CrossRef]
13. Jin, Z.; Cao, J.; Jiang, Y.-G.; Zhang, Y. News Credibility Evaluation on Microblog with a Hierarchical Propagation Model. In Proceedings of the 2014 IEEE International Conference on Data Mining, Shenzhen, China, 14–17 December 2014; pp. 230–239.
14. Ruchansky, N.; Seo, S.; Liu, Y. Csi: A Hybrid Deep Model for Fake News Detection. In Proceedings of the 2017 ACM on Conference on Information and Knowledge Management, Singapore, 6–10 November 2017; pp. 797–806.
15. Tu, K.; Chen, C.; Hou, C.; Yuan, J.; Li, J.; Yuan, X. Rumor2vec: A Rumor Detection Framework with Joint Text and Propagation Structure Representation Learning. *Inf. Sci.* **2021**, *560*, 137–151. [CrossRef]
16. Huang, Q.; Yu, J.; Wu, J.; Wang, B. Heterogeneous Graph Attention Networks for Early Detection of Rumors on Twitter. In Proceedings of the 2020 International Joint Conference on Neural Networks (IJCNN), Glasgow, UK, 19–24 July 2020; pp. 1–8.
17. Yuan, C.; Ma, Q.; Zhou, W.; Han, J.; Hu, S. Jointly Embedding the Local and Global Relations of Heterogeneous Graph for Rumor Detection. In Proceedings of the 2019 IEEE international conference on data mining (ICDM), Beijing, China, 8–11 November 2019; pp. 796–805.
18. Ma, T.; Zhou, H.; Tian, Y.; Al-Nabhan, N. A Novel Rumor Detection Algorithm Based on Entity Recognition, Sentence Reconfiguration, and Ordinary Differential Equation Network. *Neurocomputing* **2021**, *447*, 224–234. [CrossRef]
19. Ramos, J. Using Tf-Idf to Determine Word Relevance in Document Queries. In Proceedings of the First Instructional Conference on Machine Learning, Piscataway, NJ, USA, 3–8 December 2003; Volume 242, pp. 29–48.
20. Kwon, S.; Cha, M.; Jung, K. Rumor Detection over Varying Time Windows. *PLoS ONE* **2017**, *12*, e0168344. [CrossRef] [PubMed]
21. Wu, K.; Yang, S.; Zhu, K.Q. False Rumors Detection on Sina Weibo by Propagation Structures. In Proceedings of the 2015 IEEE 31st International Conference on Data Engineering, Seoul, Korea, 13–17 April 2015; pp. 651–662.
22. Ma, J.; Gao, W.; Wong, K.-F. *Detect Rumors in Microblog Posts Using Propagation Structure via Kernel Learning*; Association for Computational Linguistics: Melbourne, Australia, 2017.

Disclaimer/Publisher's Note: The statements, opinions and data contained in all publications are solely those of the individual author(s) and contributor(s) and not of MDPI and/or the editor(s). MDPI and/or the editor(s) disclaim responsibility for any injury to people or property resulting from any ideas, methods, instructions or products referred to in the content.

Article

Anomaly Detection in the Molecular Structure of Gallium Arsenide Using Convolutional Neural Networks

Timothy Roche *, Aihua Wood *, Philip Cho and Chancellor Johnstone

Department of Mathematics & Statistics, Air Force Institute of Technology, 2950 Hobson Way, Wright-Patterson AFB, OH 45433, USA
* Correspondence: timothy.roche@afit.edu (T.R.); aihua.wood@afit.edu (A.W.)

Abstract: This paper concerns the development of a machine learning tool to detect anomalies in the molecular structure of Gallium Arsenide. We employ a combination of a CNN and a PCA reconstruction to create the model, using real images taken with an electron microscope in training and testing. The methodology developed allows for the creation of a defect detection model, without any labeled images of defects being required for training. The model performed well on all tests under the established assumptions, allowing for reliable anomaly detection. To the best of our knowledge, such methods are not currently available in the open literature; thus, this work fills a gap in current capabilities.

Keywords: electron microscope; convolutional neural networks (CNNs); anomaly detection; principal component analysis (PCA); machine learning; deep learning; neural networks; Gallium Arsenide (GaAs)

MSC: 68U10

Citation: Roche, T.; Wood, A.; Cho, P.; Johnstone, C. Anomaly Detection in the Molecular Structure of Gallium Arsenide Using Convolutional Neural Networks. *Mathematics* **2023**, *11*, 3428. https://doi.org/10.3390/math11153428

Academic Editor: Huawen Liu

Received: 21 June 2023
Revised: 28 July 2023
Accepted: 2 August 2023
Published: 7 August 2023

Copyright: © 2023 by the authors. Licensee MDPI, Basel, Switzerland. This article is an open access article distributed under the terms and conditions of the Creative Commons Attribution (CC BY) license (https://creativecommons.org/licenses/by/4.0/).

1. Introduction

Electron microscopes use electrons to "take pictures" of incredibly small areas; these areas so small that one can see the atomic structure of the material. Gallium Arsenide (GaAs) is a semiconductive material extensively used in a wide variety of modern day technology, such as cell phones, solar panels, and much more [1]. Minor flaws and imperfections at the molecular scale can impact the properties of GaAs [2]. However, it is difficult to detect these defects, as they happen at an incredibly small scale. Ref. [3] developed a machine learning technique to detect defects within GaAs using simulated data, as real data were not available. This paper aims to extend the work of [3] with the construction of a machine learning classifier trained on actual images of GaAs.

The GaAs images used in this work were collected with a Titan 80–300 image spherical aberration-corrected transmission electron microscope operated at 300 kV, hereby referred to as "the Titan". Similar to [3], we employ a combination of principle component analysis (PCA) and convolutional neural networks (CNNs) to detect defects within GaAs images. CNNs are a type of neural network that has been shown to perform well on defect detection tasks across a variety of fields [4–6].

PCA is a method frequently used to reduce the dimensionality of data [7]. In the data sciences, large data sets often have correlated or redundant factors. When utilizing PCA, the principle components are calculated with linear combinations of covariates; these principle components are then used as new features in the analysis. While there is a slight loss of information, increasing the number of principle components reduces the percentage of information lost. Once a PCA is trained, it can be used to calculate the principle components for a specific sample of data. From this point, a PCA reconstruction of an image can be created. The idea is that the PCA reconstruction resembles the general pattern of the original data while removing or ignoring anomalies in the data set [8].

The rest of the paper is organized as follows: First, we discuss the data used in this project, how they are obtained, and certain limitations that we must address. Section 3 explains the methodology implemented to create, train, and test the model, with the results being discussed in Section 4. The paper is concluded in Section 5.

2. Data

All the data used in the training of our model are created from a single picture taken by the Titan. This image is of a "defect free" sample of GaAs (hereby referred to as the substrate image). While not 100% defect-free, the sample was grown in a way that made it as close to defect-free as possible. For training, we use the 40-square-nanometer GaAs image shown in Figure 1. To provide a sense of scale, a single human hair is generally between 40,000- and 120,000-nanometer-thick.

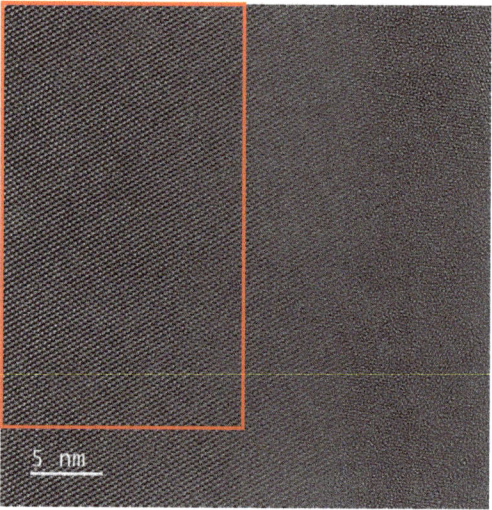

Figure 1. Example of image from the Titan. The section used to generate data is highlighted in red.

A myriad of issues arise in the electron microscope images of GaAs samples. Even the "defect free" samples created are not fully defect-free; the number of defects is far lower than what would usually be seen, but it is likely that there are still defects present in the samples. Other issues can be caused when the samples are prepared for imaging. The samples must be ground down to very small thickness, and this process can cause a minor warping of the samples.

Yet another issue is alignment. In simulated data, the alignment of samples can be fully controlled and aligned to a precise, preferable angle. With real-world images, this level of control is not possible. It is important to remember that we are dealing with images of atoms; while the structure of GaAs is quite consistent, there is very little indication of the alignment of the atoms before the images are captured. This often leads to the data being slightly rotated or skewed when compared with the simulated data.

The state of the Titan also impacts image quality, as the characteristics of the electron beam affect the quality of the image. Also, due to the small scale, the Titan is very sensitive to outside interference. People walking nearby and even the operator breathing can affect the quality of the image. Due to these factors, obtaining high-quality images is difficult.

These issues render parts of the training image unusable, with warping from the sample preparation process and the scale in the corner being the main contributors. Therefore, only part of the full image is used. The 1800-by-1024-pixel section identified with the red bounding box in Figure 1 is the substrate section used for the remainder of this paper.

Samples from this subsection are then taken to create the data set used to train the model. These samples are 118-by-84-pixel rectangles chosen at random from the 1800-by-1024 substrate section, allowing over 1.5 million unique samples to be created from a single electron microscope image. An example of one of these samples is shown in the top-left corner of Figure 2.

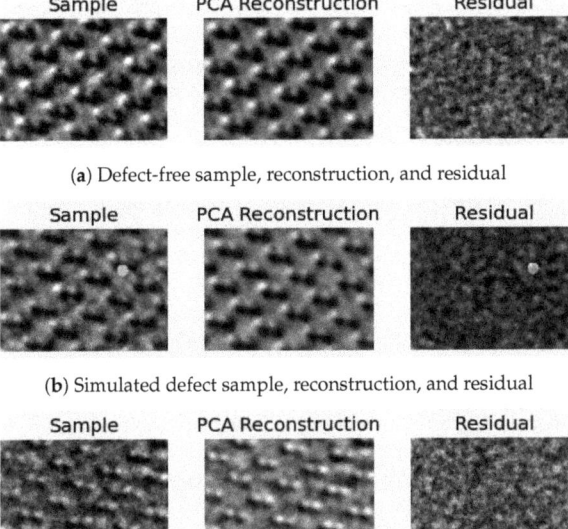

(a) Defect-free sample, reconstruction, and residual

(b) Simulated defect sample, reconstruction, and residual

(c) Actual defect sample, reconstruction, and residual

Figure 2. Examples of the data used in training and testing the model. From right to left: section taken from microscope image, PCA reconstruction of section, and residual.

During the training of the model, these samples are chosen to be either a defect sample or a non-defect sample, with a specified probability. For defects, a simulated defect is added to the section at a random location. The process for simulating defects and further data preparations are discussed in further detail in Section 3.

The reliance on simulated defects is due to the fact that we do not have any labeled images of actual defects. The best we have is an image that we know has defects in it but with no idea how many or where they are. Not only does this force us to generate simulated data for training the model, but it also makes validating the model nearly impossible, because there is no way to tell if the predictions are correct.

To overcome this issue, the assumption followed for this paper is that each 84-by-118 section from the defect image has at least one defect in it. Based on information gathered when the sample was grown, the subject matter experts are confident this assumption is true. An example of one of these defect samples can be seen in the bottom left of Figure 2.

Testing Data

Once the model is trained, we perform three different tests, each using a different data set. The first of these tests is a model validation test and uses defect-free, or substrate, samples with and without simulated defects. Generators are used to create this test set, and about 30% of the data contain simulated defects.

The second test is to ensure that the model actually detects defects and does not just detect samples taken from a different image. The data for this test do not contain any defects, neither simulated nor real. Half the samples for this are taken from the original data set, and the other half is taken from a different picture of "defect free" GaAs. Ideally, the models predict most of these as defect-free, but they may find a few defects, as even the "defect free" images may still contain some defects.

The third test is to determine if the model can find actual defects. We currently do not have a way of detecting and labeling real defects in images, so we do not have a labeled set of defects for this test. Instead, we have an image of GaAs that definitely contains defects, we just do not know where. Based off information gathered when the GaAs sample was created, the subject matter experts are confident that each 84-by-118 section from this image contains at least one defect. These images comprise half of the data for the third test, and ideally, the model predicts all of these samples as containing defects. The other half of the data are original defect-free samples without simulated defects.

3. Methodology

The prior work on this project using simulated data [3] performed well but was never applied to real-world data. The actual data collected with the electron microscope suffered minor distortion from sample preparation and other sources. This caused the models trained on the simulated data to detect this distortion as defects rather than random noise. The models had to be retrained using real data to compensate for these other non-defect-related imperfections. Regardless, the methodology is quite similar to the prior work by [3], with changes to incorporate the recently available data.

The three main pieces are a CNN, PCA, and a data generator. The CNN used is a standard AlexNet CNN [9], which is a type of neural network commonly used for defect detection. A summary of the model can be found in Figure 3a, with loss and accuracy graphs from training in Figure 3b and Figure 3c, respectively. While this style of CNN is commonly used for defect detection tasks, our CNN is trained on an unusual set of data. The samples discussed in the previous section are not directly used in training. Before the samples can be used in training, they go through a process involving a PCA reconstruction.

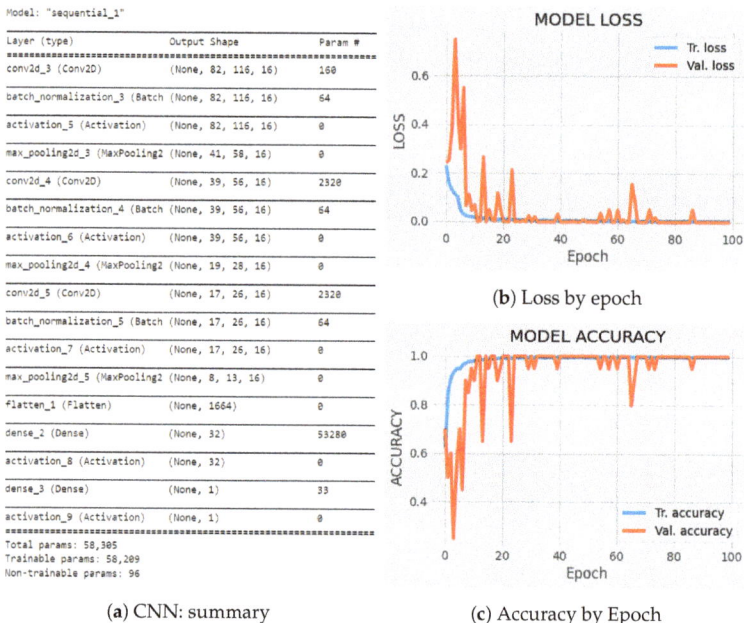

(a) CNN: summary (b) Loss by epoch (c) Accuracy by Epoch

Figure 3. Neural network structure and training results.

The PCA used for this reconstruction is trained on the same 84-by-118-pixel samples that are discussed in the previous section of this paper. Once trained, this PCA model has

200 components and accounts for over 90% of the variance (see Figure 4). This PCA is then used in the last piece: the data generator.

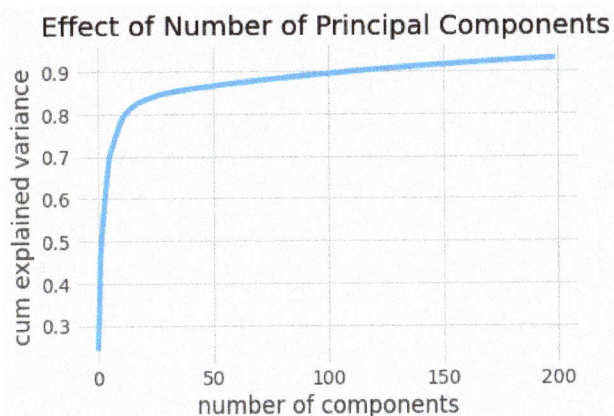

Figure 4. Training PCA: variance explained per number of components.

The data generator is the piece that produces the data used to train the model. This is where the simulated defects are added and a PCA reconstruction is used to generate a batch of training samples. Section 3.1 covers the data generation process in further detail.

The rest of this section is divided into two subsections. First, we will discuss the training of the neural network and how the simulated defects are created. The second subsection will cover how the model is tested and validated.

3.1. Model Training

The neural network is trained for 100 epochs containing 100 batches of 100 samples. Unlike many neural networks, our CNN is not trained using a conventional training set. Instead, a data generator is used, due to the nature of the data available. Pseudo-code for the generator is provided in Algorithm 1 and is discussed further below.

Algorithm 1: Data Generator

1 function Generator(*substrate_array*, *pca*);
   Input : 1800 by 1024 section from substrate image, trained PCA
   Output: Batch of 100 training images
2 **for** *i = 1 to 100* **do**
3   sample = Random 84 by 118 section of substrate image;
4   **if** *rand() > defect_rate* **then**
5   reconstruction = PCA reconstruction of sample;
6   residual = sample - reconstruction;
7   Add residual to data set, labeled as "non-defect";
8   **else**
9   Add simulated defect in a random location on the sample;
10   reconstruction = PCA reconstruction of sample;
11   residual = sample - reconstruction;
12   Add residual to data set, labeled as "defect";
13   **end**
14 **end**
15 Yield batch of 100 training samples

The generator requires inputs of the substrate section and the training PCA and yields a batch of 100 samples. First, a random 84-by-118-pixel sample is taken from the substrate image. From there, the sample is randomly chosen to be either a defect image or a defect-free image. The probability of choosing a defect can be changed but is set at 50% for training. If the sample is chosen to be defect-free, its PCA reconstruction is created and subtracted from the sample, providing the residual, which is then added to the training set and labeled as defect-free.

However, if the sample is chosen to contain a defect, a simulated defect is added at a random location. For this model, the simulated defects are circles of three to five pixels in radius, with a gray-scale color value of 0.8 (light gray), but the size, shape, and color of the defects can be changed at will. A PCA reconstruction of the simulated defect sample is then created and subtracted from the simulated defect image. The resulting residual is then added to the training set and labeled as a defect. A sample with a simulated defect, its PCA reconstruction, and the residual can be seen in the middle row of Figure 2. These residual images are what is used to train the CNN.

This process is repeated 100 times to create a batch of 100 residual images. For each epoch of training, 100 of these random batches are generated, and the model is trained for 100 epochs. The validation data are generated in the same way, except the validation batch size contains 20 samples.

3.2. Model Testing and Validation

Three different criteria are used to evaluate the performance of the model, using data from three separate pictures taken with the Titan. The first test is to ensure the model trains properly. This test uses data simulated in the same way as the training set. The second test uses data from a different image of the substrate (defect-free) GaAs to ensure that other defect-free samples are not predicted as containing defects. The final test uses samples from an image of GaAs containing defects, under the assumption that each sample taken from the image contains at least one defect. This is the test to determine whether or not we can detect actual defects. The results of these tests are discussed in the next section.

Originally, the PCA calculated on the training substrate image was used to create reconstructions for all the data used in the testing of the model. However, when the models were tested, all samples taken from any set other than the training set were predicted to contain defects. This indicated that the training PCA was not applicable to the other data sets. In response to this discovery, a PCA model is trained for each different set of data used in the testing process. The second substrate PCA explains about 90% of the total variance, while the defect PCA explains about 80%. The variance explained versus the number of components graphs for these additional PCA models are shown in Figure 5.

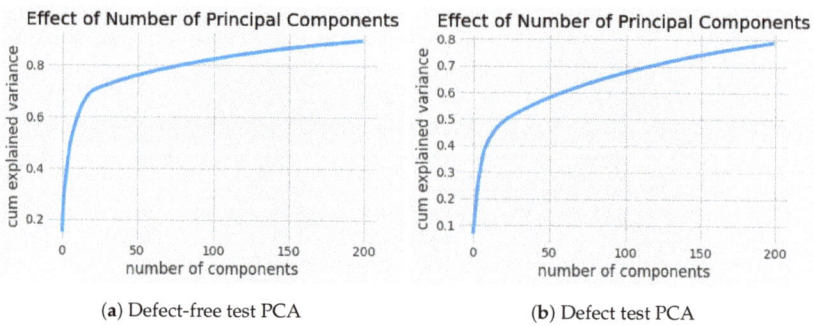

Figure 5. Test PCAs: variance explained per number of components.

4. Results

As discussed in Section Testing Data, three tests were performed on the model, with each test using a different data set and checking different things. The first test was a model validation test. Data similar to the training data, that is, data with simulated defects, were fed into the trained model. The purpose of this test was to ensure that the model trained properly. The defect ratio was also lowered for this test set to ensure that it had no impact on model accuracy. As seen in the confusion matrix shown in Figure 6a, the model performed well in this test, predicting only one simulated defect as not a defect. The distribution of the predicted defect probabilities is shown in Figure 6b.

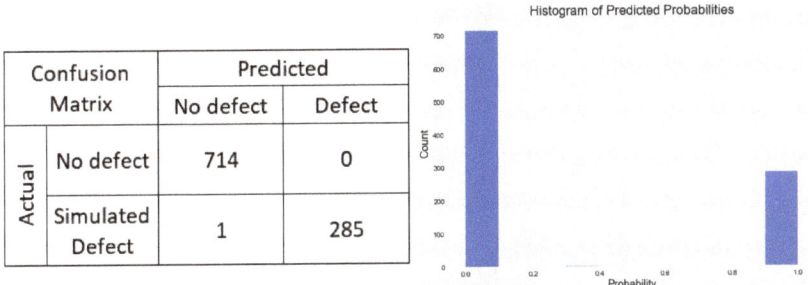

(a) Validation test: confusion matrix (b) Validation test: prediction distribution

Figure 6. Outputs from the validation test. (**a**) Confusion matrix: This test had 99.9% accuracy, with only one simulated defect being classified incorrectly. The cause of this is not clear, but it is not a major concern. (**b**) Distribution of predicted probabilities: A histogram showing the number of samples with the predicted probability of a defect. Probabilities above 0.5 were predicted as defects.

The next test checked for false positives. The data for this test were from a different substrate sample, meaning that there should have been few to no defects in the sample. This test was to check if the model actually predicted defects or if it detected something else. Thus, the "confusion matrix" (shown in Figure 7a) for this test is not a typical confusion matrix. The top row concerns samples from the original "defect free" substrate image used in training, while the second row concerns samples from a different "defect free" image. The model performed well in this test, only predicting eleven samples from the second substrate image as having defects. These predictions could even be true, since the sample, while as close to perfect as possible, may still have contained some defects. The distribution of the predicted probabilities is shown in Figure 7b.

We note that in this test, there were multiple instances of high estimated probabilities of defects, i.e., estimated probabilities greater than 0.5. The exploration of the substrate images resulting in these high estimated probabilities is of interest to us. However, this is out of the scope of the current work.

The final test was performed on samples from the test image containing defects. Recall that the assumption for this test set was that each sample contained at least one defect. Under this assumption, the model performed perfectly. To confirm this, the test was performed ten times, each on a different random set of samples. All ten tests had 100% accuracy. A confusion matrix and a prediction distribution histogram from one of these tests are shown in Figure 8.

Confusion Matrix		Predicted	
		No defect	Defect
Actual	Training Substrate	489	0
	Test Substrate	491	11

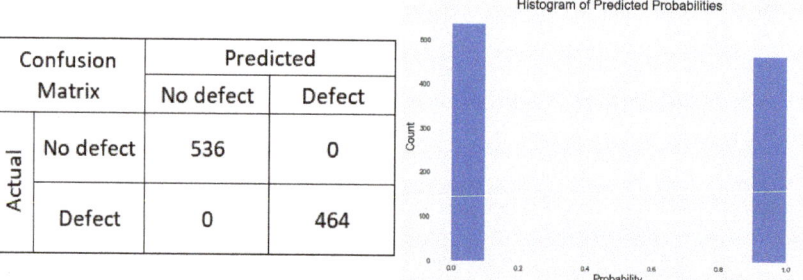

(**a**) Substrate test: confusion matrix

(**b**) Substrate test: prediction distribution

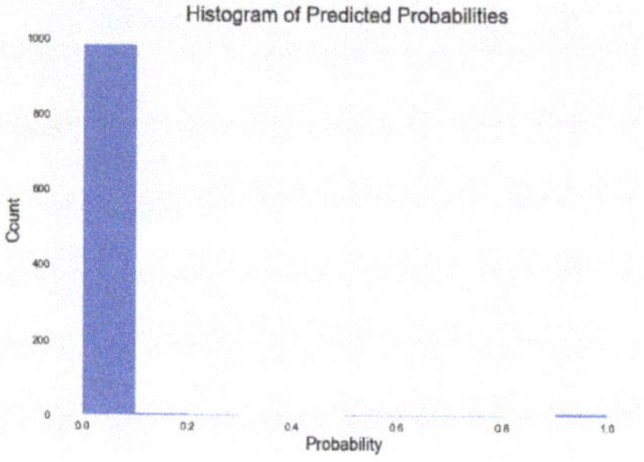

Figure 7. Results of the substrate test. (**a**) Confusion matrix: The expected result was no defects for both sets. However, it is likely that both "defect free" images had some defects, so the predicted defects could be true defects. No defects were detected in the training substrate image because it was used in training. (**b**) Distribution of predicted probabilities: A histogram showing the number of samples with the predicted probability of a defect. Probabilities above 0.5 were predicted as defects.

Confusion Matrix		Predicted	
		No defect	Defect
Actual	No defect	536	0
	Defect	0	464

(**a**) Defect test: confusion matrix

(**b**) Defect test: prediction distribution

Figure 8. Results of the defect test. (**a**) Confusion matrix: This test had 100% accuracy, correctly predicting all samples from the defect sample as defects and all samples from the defect-free image as no defects. (**b**) Distribution of predicted probabilities: A histogram showing the number of samples with the predicted probability of a defect. For this test, all non-defect samples had a predicted probability under 0.1, and all defect samples had a predicted probability above 0.9.

4.1. Discussion

The results from this set of tests are promising, and the model performed as we hoped. However, there are certain gaps in our validation process that we cannot currently fill. The first issue is the lack of a baseline model. As this is the first attempt to accomplish this specific task, there does not exist another model to use as a comparison. As work continues in this area, this model can be used as a baseline in the future. The other issue is the lack of labeled data, thus certain assumptions must be made, as must be done for most real-world applications. The two main assumptions we made were that the substrate images were defect-free and that other images of GaAs contained many defects. The subject experts are confident that our assumption that every 118-by-84 section from the "defect" image contains at least one defect is correct.

That being said, the model performed well in all tests under our assumptions. It is still possible that the model detected something other than defects in the defect test data, leading to these results. As we acquire more data, this will allow for more options for testing and validating the model. Other validation methods are currently being explored and will be reported in a subsequent paper.

4.2. Calibration

Given that the output of our CNN is an estimated probability of a defect on a particular substrate image, it is also helpful to explore the performance of these probability estimates further than with accuracy only (or even other metrics like sensitivity, specificity, or F1). Ideally, probability estimates should be well *calibrated*. Perfect calibration occurs when

$$E_{\hat{p}}\left[\left|\mathbb{P}\left(\hat{z}=z|\hat{p}=p\right)-p\right|\right]=0, \tag{1}$$

where E_X is the expectation of some random variable X and $\mathbb{P}$ is a (conditional) probability mass function. In our case, z is the observed class, i.e., defect-free or defected, while $\hat{z}$ is the predicted class. $\hat{p}$ is a probability estimate for the predicted class, and p is the true class probability. With Equation (1), the implication for defect identification in our substrate images is that our estimated probabilities are reflective of the true underlying probabilities of a defect. As an example, we should observe defects, say, in 10% of our observations ("relative frequency") where we estimate a 10% defect probability. We can assess calibration in practice with the use of metrics like empirical calibration error (ECE) or with the use of reliability plots. We point the interested reader to [10] for more details on these approaches. We include reliability plots for our two test sets in Figure 9.

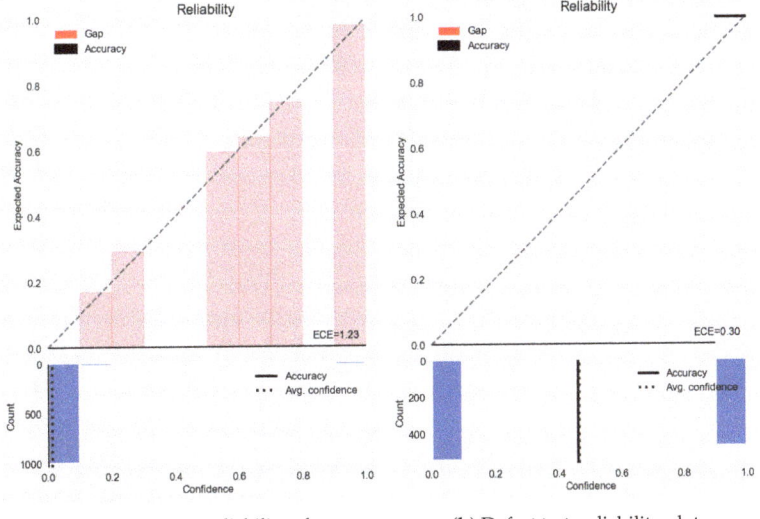

(a) Substrate test: reliability plot (b) Defect test: reliability plot

Figure 9. Reliability plots. (a) Reliability for substrate test. (b) Reliability for defect test.

We note the two plots in Figure 9 provide very contrasting results. The poor calibration performance of the substrate test set is inherently due to its lack of defects; we have a range of estimated probabilities but only defect-free substrate images. Thus, the images for which we estimate higher probabilities of defects are never defected, resulting in relative frequencies of zero. Figure 9b, corresponding to the defect test set, shows near-perfect calibration, i.e., the points lie exactly along the diagonal. This results from our perfect classification performance on this test set, as well as the high confidence on whether images were defect-free or defected; recall from Figure 8b that our collection of estimated probabilities for this test set were massed near zero and one.

5. Conclusions

We developed a machine learning method for detecting anomalies in the molecular structure of Gallium Arsenide. Additionally, this method can be successfully trained without access to a training set containing labeled defects. This allows us to create a model to find defects in a substance without any prior knowledge as to what a defect actually looks like. This method could also be effective in detecting defects in the atomic structure of other materials, with appropriate alterations to accommodate new data structures.

We note that our results are based on the assumption that each 118-by-84-pixel sample from the defect image contains at least one defect. Based on the conditions in which the samples are created, we are confident in this assumption, yet we currently do not have a way to verify this. With the understanding that a test set with 100%-accurate labels may never be possible, work on developing alternative ways to validate the results is underway and will be reported in a follow-on paper.

Although this work mainly constitutes the proof of concept, it demonstrates that it is possible to detect *if* a defect is present in a section of Gallium Arsenide, thus filling a capability gap. The natural next step is to actually locate where the defects are: the *where* problem. This will surely be more challenging in the absence of accurate test data and the lack of educated assumptions.

Author Contributions: Conceptualization, A.W. and P.C.; Methodology, T.R. and P.C.; Software, T.R. and P.C.; Validation, P.C. and C.J.; Resources, A.W.; Writing—original draft, T.R. and C.J.; Writing—review & editing, T.R., A.W., P.C. and C.J.; Visualization, P.C. and C.J.; Supervision, A.W.; Project administration, A.W. All authors have read and agreed to the published version of the manuscript.

Funding: This research received no external funding.

Data Availability Statement: Not applicable.

Conflicts of Interest: The authors declare no conflict of interest.

References

1. Moss, S.J.; Ledwith, A. *Chemistry of the Semiconductor Industry*; Springer Science & Business Media: Cham, Switzerland, 1989.
2. McCluskey, M.D.; Haller, E.E. *Dopants and Defects in Semiconductors*; CRC Press: Boca Raton, FL, USA, 2018.
3. Cho, P.; Wood, A.; Mahalingam, K.; Eyink, K. Defect detection in atomic resolution transmission electron microscopy images using machine learning. *Mathematics* **2021**, *9*, 1209. [CrossRef]
4. Zhang, M.; Wu, J.; Lin, H.; Yuan, P.; Song, Y. The application of one-class classifier based on CNN in image defect detection. *Procedia Comput. Sci.* **2017**, *114*, 341–348. [CrossRef]
5. Chen, X.; Chen, J.; Han, X.; Zhao, C.; Zhang, D.; Zhu, K.; Su, Y. A light-weighted CNN model for wafer structural defect detection. *IEEE Access* **2020**, *8*, 24006–24018. [CrossRef]
6. Shi, J.; Li, Z.; Zhu, T.; Wang, D.; Ni, C. Defect detection of industry wood veneer based on NAS and multi-channel mask R-CNN. *Sensors* **2020**, *20*, 4398. [CrossRef] [PubMed]
7. Roweis, S. EM algorithms for PCA and SPCA. *Adv. Neural Inf. Process. Syst.* **1997**, *10*, 626–632.
8. Malagon-Borja, L.; Fuentes, O. Object detection using image reconstruction with PCA. *Image Vis. Comput.* **2009**, *27*, 2–9. [CrossRef]
9. Alom, M.Z.; Taha, T.M.; Yakopcic, C.; Westberg, S.; Sidike, P.; Nasrin, M.S.; Van Esesn, B.C.; Awwal, A.A.S.; Asari, V.K. The history began from alexnet: A comprehensive survey on deep learning approaches. *arXiv* **2018**, arXiv:1803.01164.
10. Guo, C.; Pleiss, G.; Sun, Y.; Weinberger, K.Q. On calibration of modern neural networks. In Proceedings of the 34th International Conference on Machine Learning, PMLR, Sydney, Australia, 6–11 August 2017; pp. 1321–1330.

Disclaimer/Publisher's Note: The statements, opinions and data contained in all publications are solely those of the individual author(s) and contributor(s) and not of MDPI and/or the editor(s). MDPI and/or the editor(s) disclaim responsibility for any injury to people or property resulting from any ideas, methods, instructions or products referred to in the content.

Article

The Hybrid Modeling of Spatial Autoregressive Exogenous Using Casetti's Model Approach for the Prediction of Rainfall

Annisa Nur Falah [1,*], Budi Nurani Ruchjana [2], Atje Setiawan Abdullah [3] and Juli Rejito [3]

1 Doctoral Program of Mathematics, Faculty of Mathematics and Natural Sciences, Universitas Padjadjaran, Sumedang 45363, Indonesia
2 Department of Mathematics, Faculty of Mathematics and Natural Sciences, Universitas Padjadjaran, Sumedang 45363, Indonesia; budi.nurani@unpad.ac.id
3 Department of Computer Science, Faculty of Mathematics and Natural Sciences, Universitas Padjadjaran, Sumedang 45363, Indonesia; atje.setiawan@unpad.ac.id (A.S.A.); juli.rejito@unpad.ac.id (J.R.)
* Correspondence: annisa15046@mail.unpad.ac.id

Abstract: Spatial Autoregressive (SAR) models are used to model the relationship between variables within a specific region or location, considering the influence of neighboring variables, and have received considerable attention in recent years. However, when the impact of exogenous variables becomes notably pronounced, an alternative approach is warranted. Spatial Expansion, coupled with the Casetti model approach, serves as an extension of the SAR model, accommodating the influence of these exogenous variables. This modeling technique finds application in the realm of rainfall prediction, where exogenous factors, such as air temperature, humidity, solar irradiation, wind speed, and surface pressure, play pivotal roles. Consequently, this research aimed to combine the SAR and Spatial Expansion models through the Casetti model approach, leading to the creation of the Spatial Autoregressive Exogenous (SAR-X) model. The SAR-X was employed to forecast the rainfall patterns in the West Java region, utilizing data obtained from the National Aeronautics and Space Administration Prediction of Worldwide Energy Resources (NASA POWER) dataset. The practical execution of this research capitalized on the computational capabilities of the RStudio software version 2022.12.0. Within the framework of this investigation, a comprehensive and integrated RStudio script, seamlessly incorporated into the RShiny web application, was developed so that it is easy to use.

Keywords: SAR-X; Casetti's model; climate variables; prediction; RShiny

MSC: 9004; 62M30

1. Introduction

Water is very important for all living organisms, including humans, thereby ranking as one of the most indispensable resources in the environment [1]. The phenomenon of climate change and global warming has significantly reshaped numerous environmental aspects across multiple countries. This transformation carries the potential for profound consequences, imperiling the populace, agriculture, ecosystems, economy, and industry. Alterations in precipitation patterns exert a direct impact on the management of water resources, agricultural practices, hydrological systems, and ecological balance [2]. It is crucial to acknowledge that the entirety of life-sustaining water on Earth originates from rainfall. Consequently, comprehending the spatial distribution and fluctuations in this rainfall is very important. This understanding is pivotal for efficient water resource management and also for devising strategies for addressing challenges such as anticipating natural hazards triggered by intense rainfall events [1,3,4]. Delving into the spatial arrangement and variances of rainfall can play a pivotal role in shaping perspective notions concerning water resources. Furthermore, it aids in formulating measures for upholding stable environmental circumstances. It is imperative to acknowledge that trends in rainfall constitute a pivotal climate determinant with far-reaching implications, encompassing future factors such as population growth, economic expansion, and enduring climatic shifts. These factors collectively impact both the temporal and spatial availability of water [1,5,6].

In various spheres of life, the anticipation of rainfall yields indispensable advantages, encompassing agriculture, water resource management, disaster preparedness, infrastructure planning, renewable energy, and transportation. Forecasts of rainfall assist farmers in coordinating their planting and harvesting schedules, allowing for effective irrigation planning, suitable crop selection according to weather conditions, and a decreased risk of crop failure [7–9]. Moreover, these predictions contribute to the proficient handling of water resources, encompassing the regulation of river flow and reservoir management [10,11]. The availability of accurate rainfall information empowers optimal water utilization and mitigates flood and drought hazards, as well as plays a pivotal role in the management of natural calamities such as floods and landslides [12–14]. Informed by projected rainfall data, authorities can implement preventive measures such as early evacuation, timely alerts, and the construction of robust infrastructure. Additionally, rainfall prediction has proved vital in the realm of infrastructure planning, guiding the construction of structures including dams, drainage networks, and irrigation channels [15–17]. By leveraging rainfall insights, engineers and planners are equipped to devise designs resilient to extreme weather conditions. Rainfall profoundly affects renewable energy industries, namely hydropower and solar energy [18]. Forecasts of rainfall facilitate the strategic planning and management of renewable energy production, thereby optimizing energy potential [19]. The influence of rainfall extends to transportation planning as well [20]. Intense rainfall impacts road traffic, transportation speeds, and driver safety. By leveraging rainfall predictions, transportation schedules can be organized more efficiently, ultimately reducing accident risks. The availability of accurate rainfall information empowers sound decision making and aids in mitigating the risks and repercussions arising from unforeseen weather fluctuations [21]. Therefore, the precision and accuracy of rainfall prediction are said to be important.

Based on previous research, diverse rainfall predictions have been undertaken, including projections of rainfall variability, particularly focusing on the winter and pre-monsoon rainfall across Pakistan [22]. In Turkey, monthly and seasonal rainfall trend predictions were calculated through a comparison of three interpolation methods, namely Inverse Distance Weighted, Completely Regularized Spline, and Ordinary Kriging [23]. A Spatial Autoregressive model was employed to predict seasonal legume yields for non-irrigated croplands in the semi-arid region of Mexico, categorized by regular rainy and dry seasons [24]. The rainfall and groundwater patterns along the northeastern coast of Brazil were predicted, and the monthly rainfall patterns were characterized to mitigate their impacts during heavy rainfall periods and significant floods, utilizing the Kriging method and a clustering analysis [25]. Additionally, short-term rainfall forecasts were derived using a Hierarchical Bayesian model for spatiotemporal data [26]. It is important to note that the scope of these predictions exclusively pertains to rainfall variability and does not encompass other climate variables.

One of the outcomes of climate phenomena is La Niña, which triggers heightened rainfall in the western Pacific region. Based on empirical data from BMKG, La Niña can amplify the rainfall in West Java by anywhere from 20% to 70% [27]. Rainfall is intertwined with other climatic factors such as air temperature, humidity, solar irradiation, wind speed, and surface pressure, all of which fluctuate across different areas [28]. The climate variables pertinent to specific regions or locations can be effectively modeled using a spatial analysis approach. Among the spatial models commonly employed, the Spatial Autoregressive (SAR) model stands out. This is frequently referred to as a mixed regressive spatial autoregressive model or a spatial lag model [29]. The SAR model, a statistical tool, is harnessed to depict the relationships between variables within a given region or location, considering the impacts of surrounding variables. However, the model falls short in capturing the spatial disparities between locations. To address this gap,

Casetti [30] developed the Spatial Expansion model, which extends the SAR to encompass exogenous variables through a linear regression approach. The amalgamation of the SAR and spatial expansion models, in line with the approach of Casetti, culminates in the Spatial Autoregressive Exogenous (SAR-X) model. The SAR-X introduces spatial heterogeneity, thereby enabling the description of distinct parameter values for each spatial observation, determined by the geographical distances between locations. A notable application of the SAR-X is evident in gauging the repercussions of climate change on the ecosystem of a region. For example, when analyzing flood risk prediction within the SAR-X framework, it becomes imperative to incorporate climate variable factors. In this scenario, the model serves as a valuable tool, facilitating an elevated spatial perspective of climate effects and accounting for the spatial influences that shape relationships. In essence, SAR-X modeling has emerged as a valuable instrument for comprehending the ramifications of climate change and supporting decision making to tackle these consequences.

The current research on rainfall prediction entails observations across 13 climate-monitoring stations in the West Java region, utilizing data sourced from the Meteorology, Climatology, and Geophysics Agency (BMKG) with location indexing. The research variables comprised rainfall as the responsive parameter, coupled with exogenous variables encompassing air temperature, humidity, solar irradiation, wind speed, and surface pressure. These climate data were procured from the National Aeronautics and Space Administration Prediction of Worldwide Energy Resources (NASA POWER) dataset. The application study in this research is supported by computing using the R programming language. R is a statistical and graphical programming language; currently, R is widely known as one of the programming languages used for data analysis and data science. R has advantages, including being open source, having many packages available, finding it easy to transform and process data, and being able to create interactive applications/web-based dashboards. In this research, the RStudio software is used, which is an Integrated Development Environment (IDE) for R [31]. The custom-built RStudio script can be further evolved into a web application employing RShiny version 1.7.4, one of the packages of software specifically designed for creating interactive web interfaces [32]. These web applications, once deployed, offer a user-friendly platform for data processing. Users can conveniently upload data for analysis, and the ensuing results are promptly presented on the RShiny web application interface. In this research endeavor, integrated commands within R script enable the utilization of the SAR-X model through the RShiny web application, rendering the process effortlessly accessible.

2. Materials and Methods

2.1. Inverse Distance Weight Matrix

The spatial weight matrix is a matrix that states the proximity relationship between locations. In this study, the inverse distance weight matrix, also called the distance weight, is used, which describes the actual distance between locations. The distance between locations is calculated using the latitude and longitude coordinates of the center point of the observed location. It is known that a location $x_{ij}(u_{ij}, v_{ij})$ with x_{ij} is the symbol of the location i and j, with $i = 1, 2, 3 \ldots, N$ and $j = 1, 2, 3 \ldots, N$, while u and v indicate the latitude and longitude coordinates. If d_{ij} is the distance between location i and location j, and W_{ij} is the inverse value of d_{ij}, we use the Euclidean distance and the equation is as follows [33]:

$$d_{ij} = \sqrt{\left(x_i(u_i) - x_j(u_j)\right)^2 + \left(x_i(v_i) - x_j(v_j)\right)^2} \quad (1)$$

$$w_{ij} = \begin{cases} \frac{1}{d_{ij}}, i \neq j \\ 0, i = j \end{cases} \quad (2)$$

Next, if the sum of the distance weights of a row in the inverse distance weight matrix is not equal to 1, then the distance weights must be standardized, so as to obtain $\sum_{j=1}^{N} w_{ij} = 1, \forall i = 1, 2, 3, \ldots, N$, where:

$$w_{ij}^* = \frac{w_{ij}}{\sum_{j=1}^{N} w_{ij}}, \forall i = 1, 2, 3, \ldots, N. \tag{3}$$

In detail:
x_{ij}: the symbol of location i and j, with $i = 1, 2, 3 \ldots, N$ and $j = 1, 2, 3 \ldots, N$
u_i: latitude $i -$ th for $i = 1, 2, 3, \ldots, N$
v_i: longitude $i -$ th for $i = 1, 2, 3, \ldots, N$
u_j: latitude $j -$ th for $j = 1, 2, 3, \ldots, N$
v_j: longitude $j -$ th for $j = 1, 2, 3, \ldots, N$
d_{ij}: the distance between location i and location j

In this investigation, the inverse distance weight matrix was employed to calculate the climate variable data across 13 climate observation stations in the West Java region. The input coordinates for each location, expressed as latitude and longitude, served to establish the proximity relationship between these locations.

2.2. Moran Index

One approach to assessing the spatial dependencies among locations is through a spatial autocorrelation test using the Moran Index statistic. Spatial autocorrelation gauges the correlation between observation values concerning the location of the same variable. When a systematic pattern emerges in the distribution of a variable, spatial autocorrelation is present. This phenomenon underscores the interdependence of the spatial data between different locations, influenced by their proximity or intersection [29].

$$I = \frac{n \sum_{i=1}^{n} \sum_{j=1}^{n} w_{ij}(x_i - \bar{x})(x_j - \bar{x})}{\sum_{i=1}^{n} \sum_{j=1}^{n} w_{ij} \sum_{i=1}^{n} (x_i - \bar{x})^2} \tag{4}$$

The hypothesis formulation in this test is as follows:
$H_0 : I = 0$ There is no spatial autocorrelation between locations.
$H_1 : I \neq 0$ There is spatial autocorrelation between locations.
The test statistic employed is expressed below:

$$Z(I) = \frac{I - E(I)}{\sqrt{Var(I)}} \approx N(0, 1) \tag{5}$$

with,

$$E(I) = -\frac{1}{n-1} \tag{6}$$

$$Var(I) = \frac{n^2 S_1 - n S_2 + 3 S_0^2}{(n^2 - 1) S_0^2} - [E(I)]^2 \tag{7}$$

$$S_0 = \sum_{i=1}^{n} \sum_{j=1}^{n} w_{ij} \quad S_1 = \frac{1}{2} \sum_{1 \neq j}^{n} (w_{ij} + w_{ji})^2 \quad S_2 = \sum_{i \neq j}^{n} \left(\sum_{i=1}^{n} w_{ij} + \sum_{j=1}^{n} w_{ji} \right)^2$$

where:
I: the Moran Index value
n: the number of observation locations

x_i: the value of the observation variable at location $i-$th
x_j: the value of the observation variable at location $j-$th
$\bar{x}$: the average of the number of variables
w_{ij}: the elements of the standardized weight matrix between regions i and j
Decision:
Reject H_0 at the significance level α if $-Z_{score} \leq -Z_{\frac{\alpha}{2}}$ or $-Z_{score} \geq Z_{\frac{\alpha}{2}}$.
The Moran Index was in the range of $[-1, 1]$. A negative value signified a negative spatial autocorrelation, while a positive value implied a positive spatial autocorrelation [34].

2.3. Spatial Autoregressive Exogenous (SAR-X)

Spatial regression is a method tailored for data with spatial effects, encompassing spatial dependency and heterogeneity. Spatial dependence pertains to observations at one location being influenced by those at another, while spatial heterogeneity arises due to random location effects. The foundation of spatial regression lies in the classical linear regression method, evolving to consider the influence of space on the data under scrutiny. The first Law of Geography by Tobler emphasizes interconnectedness and the greater influence of nearby entities [29]. The general model of spatial regression can be written as follows:

$$\mathbf{y} = \rho \mathbf{W}\mathbf{y} + \mathbf{X}\boldsymbol{\beta} + \mathbf{u}$$
$$\mathbf{u} = \lambda \mathbf{W}\mathbf{u} + \boldsymbol{\varepsilon} \text{ with } \boldsymbol{\varepsilon} \overset{iid}{\sim} N(0, \sigma^2 \mathbf{I}) \tag{8}$$

In [29], an alternative model derived from Equation (8) was developed. When $\rho \neq 0$ and $\lambda = 0$, then the Spatial Autoregressive (SAR) model can be formed as follows:

$$\mathbf{y} = \rho \mathbf{W}\mathbf{y} + \mathbf{X}\boldsymbol{\beta} + \boldsymbol{\varepsilon} \text{ with } \boldsymbol{\varepsilon} \overset{iid}{\sim} N(0, \sigma^2 \mathbf{I}) \tag{9}$$

The SAR model, an area-based spatial model, encompasses the impact of spatial lag on the dependent variable [29].

The introduction of the Spatial Expansion model (Casetti, 1972) [30] addresses spatial heterogeneity, which characterizes diverse parameter values for each spatial observation based on the distance between locations. The Euclidean distance, such as location coordinates, quantifies the separation between two locations. The Spatial Expansion model, adopting a linear regression approach, can be formulated as follows:

$$\mathbf{y} = \mathbf{X}\boldsymbol{\beta} + \boldsymbol{\varepsilon} \text{ with } \boldsymbol{\varepsilon} \overset{iid}{\sim} N(0, \sigma^2 \mathbf{I})$$
$$\boldsymbol{\beta} = \mathbf{Z}\mathbf{J}\boldsymbol{\beta}_0 \tag{10}$$

In this research, a fusion of the SAR and Spatial Expansion models was executed, utilizing the approach of Casetti on exogenous variables, called the Spatial Autoregressive Exogenous (SAR-X) model. The SAR-X model could be said to be an extension of SAR, which encompasses exogenous variables. Referring to [35], the SAR-X model served to describe and predict independent variables, considering location effects and exogenous variables. Mathematically, the SAR-X model prediction with the Casetti's model approach was derived by substituting Equation (10) into (9), in order to produce the following:

$$\mathbf{y} = \rho \mathbf{W}\mathbf{y} + \mathbf{X}\boldsymbol{\beta} + \boldsymbol{\varepsilon} \text{ with } \boldsymbol{\beta} = \mathbf{Z}\mathbf{J}\boldsymbol{\beta}_0 \tag{11}$$

Equation (11) is subsequently written as:

$$\mathbf{y} = \rho \mathbf{W}\mathbf{y} + \mathbf{X}\mathbf{Z}\mathbf{J}\boldsymbol{\beta}_0 + \boldsymbol{\varepsilon} \text{ with } \boldsymbol{\varepsilon} \overset{iid}{\sim} N(0, \sigma^2 \mathbf{I}) \tag{12}$$

with:
$\mathbf{y}$: the vector of the dependent variables of size $(n \times 1)$
ρ: the spatial lag parameter coefficient of the independent variable
$\mathbf{W}$: a spatial weight matrix of size $(n \times n)$

X: the matrix of the independent variables of size $(n \times nk)$

Z: location information that contains elements Z_{xi}, Z_{yi} with $i = 1, \ldots, n$, representing the latitude and longitude of each observation, of size $(nk \times 2nk)$

J: the expansion of the identity matrix of size $(2nk \times 2k)$

β: a matrix of size $(nk \times 1)$, containing parameter estimators for all the explanatory k variables at each observation

β₀: parameter expressed by $\boldsymbol{\beta}_{latitude}, \boldsymbol{\beta}_{longitude}$ of size $(2k \times 1)$

$\otimes$: the Kronecker product

ε: an error vector of size $(n \times 1)$

sᵢ: the location matrix with $i = 1, \ldots, n$

The matrix form in the model can be written as follows:

$$\mathbf{y} = \begin{pmatrix} y(s_1) \\ y(s_2) \\ \vdots \\ y(s_n) \end{pmatrix}, \mathbf{W} = \begin{pmatrix} 0 & w_{12} & \cdots & w_{1n} \\ w_{21} & 0 & \cdots & w_{2n} \\ \vdots & \vdots & \ddots & \vdots \\ w_{n1} & w_{n2} & \cdots & 0 \end{pmatrix}, \mathbf{X} = \begin{pmatrix} x_{11} & \cdots & x_{1k} & 0 & \cdots & 0 & \cdots & 0 & \cdots & 0 \\ 0 & \cdots & 0 & x_{21} & \cdots & x_{2k} & 0 & \vdots & \cdots & \vdots \\ \vdots & \ddots & \vdots & 0 & \ddots & 0 & \ddots & 0 & \ddots & 0 \\ 0 & \cdots & 0 & 0 & \cdots & 0 & 0 & x_{n1} & \cdots & x_{nk} \end{pmatrix}$$

$$\boldsymbol{\beta} = \begin{pmatrix} \beta_1(s_1) \\ \beta_1(s_2) \\ \vdots \\ \beta_k(s_n) \end{pmatrix}, \boldsymbol{\varepsilon} = \begin{pmatrix} \varepsilon(s_1) \\ \varepsilon(s_2) \\ \vdots \\ \varepsilon(s_n) \end{pmatrix}, \boldsymbol{\beta}_0 = \begin{pmatrix} \boldsymbol{\beta}_{latitude} \\ \boldsymbol{\beta}_{longitude} \end{pmatrix}$$

$$\mathbf{Z} = \begin{pmatrix} Z_{x1} \otimes \mathbf{I}_k & Z_{y1} \otimes \mathbf{I}_k & 0 & 0 & 0 & 0 \\ 0 & 0 & \ddots & \ddots & 0 & 0 \\ 0 & 0 & 0 & 0 & Z_{xn} \otimes \mathbf{I}_k & Z_{yn} \otimes \mathbf{I}_k \end{pmatrix}, \mathbf{J} = \begin{pmatrix} \mathbf{I}_k & 0 \\ 0 & \mathbf{I}_k \\ \vdots & \vdots \\ 0 & \mathbf{I}_k \end{pmatrix}$$

2.4. Estimation

The random error variable in the SAR-X model assumed a normal distribution. Therefore, the parameter estimation in this model followed the SAR parameter estimation method, employing the Maximum Likelihood Estimation (MLE) technique. The observed sources for this approach included Ord [36], Smirnov and Anselin [37], Robinson and Rossi [38], and Feng [39]. Equation (12) can be written as the following equation:

$$\mathbf{y} = \rho \mathbf{W} \mathbf{y} + \mathbf{A} \boldsymbol{\beta}_0 + \boldsymbol{\varepsilon} \text{ with } \mathbf{A} = \mathbf{XZJ} \tag{13}$$

$$\mathbf{y} = \rho \mathbf{W} \mathbf{y} + \mathbf{A} \boldsymbol{\beta}_0 + \boldsymbol{\varepsilon} \text{ with } \boldsymbol{\varepsilon} \overset{iid}{\sim} N(0, \sigma^2 \mathbf{I}) \tag{14}$$

The probability density function used is expressed below:

$$f(\mathbf{y}) = \left(\frac{1}{2\pi\sigma^2}\right)^{\frac{n}{2}} \exp\left[-\frac{(\mathbf{y} - \rho \mathbf{W}\mathbf{y} - \mathbf{A}\boldsymbol{\beta}_0)^T (\mathbf{y} - \rho \mathbf{W}\mathbf{y} - \mathbf{A}\boldsymbol{\beta}_0)}{2\sigma^2}\right] \tag{15}$$

The likelihood function of the dependent variable **y** is formulated as follows:

$$\begin{aligned} L(\rho, \boldsymbol{\beta}_0 | \mathbf{y}) &= f(\mathbf{y} | \rho, \boldsymbol{\beta}_0) \\ &= \left(\frac{1}{2\pi\sigma^2}\right)^{\frac{n}{2}} \exp\left[-\frac{(\mathbf{y} - \rho \mathbf{W}\mathbf{y} - \mathbf{A}\boldsymbol{\beta}_0)^T (\mathbf{y} - \rho \mathbf{W}\mathbf{y} - \mathbf{A}\boldsymbol{\beta}_0)}{2\sigma^2}\right] \end{aligned} \tag{16}$$

Furthermore, the log-likelihood function is obtained as:

$$\begin{aligned}\ln L(\rho, \boldsymbol{\beta}_0|\boldsymbol{\varepsilon}) &= \ln\left(\frac{1}{2\pi\sigma^2}\right)^{\frac{n}{2}} \exp\left[-\frac{(\mathbf{y}-\rho\mathbf{W}\mathbf{y}-\mathbf{A}\boldsymbol{\beta}_0)^T(\mathbf{y}-\rho\mathbf{W}\mathbf{y}-\mathbf{A}\boldsymbol{\beta}_0)}{2\sigma^2}\right] \\ &= -\frac{n}{2}\ln(2\pi) - \frac{n}{2}\ln\sigma^2 - \frac{(\mathbf{y}-\rho\mathbf{W}\mathbf{y}-\mathbf{A}\boldsymbol{\beta}_0)^T(\mathbf{y}-\rho\mathbf{W}\mathbf{y}-\mathbf{A}\boldsymbol{\beta}_0)}{2\sigma^2}\end{aligned} \quad (17)$$

A parameter estimation ρ, $\boldsymbol{\beta}_0$ is obtained by maximizing the log-likelihood function. To obtain the MLE estimation of the parameters $\hat{\rho}$, the first derivative of Equation (17) for the parameters ρ was expressed as:

$$\begin{aligned}\frac{\partial \ln L(\rho, \boldsymbol{\beta}_0|\boldsymbol{\varepsilon})}{\partial \boldsymbol{\beta}_0} &= -\frac{(\mathbf{y}-\rho\mathbf{W}\mathbf{y}-\mathbf{A}\boldsymbol{\beta}_0)^T(-\mathbf{W}\mathbf{y})}{2\sigma^2} \\ &= \frac{(\mathbf{y}-\rho\mathbf{W}\mathbf{y}-\mathbf{A}\boldsymbol{\beta}_0)^T(\mathbf{W}\mathbf{y})}{2\sigma^2}\end{aligned} \quad (18)$$

$\left.\frac{\partial \ln L(\rho, \boldsymbol{\beta}_0|\boldsymbol{\varepsilon})}{\partial \rho}\right|_{\rho=\hat{\rho}} = 0$, this is further expressed as follows:

$$\frac{(\mathbf{y}-\rho\mathbf{W}\mathbf{y}-\mathbf{A}\boldsymbol{\beta}_0)^T(\mathbf{W}\mathbf{y})}{2\sigma^2} = 0 \quad (19)$$

In Equation (19), multiply by $2\sigma^2(\mathbf{W}\mathbf{y})^T$ to obtain:

$$(\mathbf{y}-\rho\mathbf{W}\mathbf{y}-\mathbf{A}\boldsymbol{\beta}_0)^T\left(\mathbf{W}\mathbf{y}(\mathbf{W}\mathbf{y})^T\right) = 0 \quad (20)$$

Multiply Equation (20) by $\left(\mathbf{W}\mathbf{y}(\mathbf{W}\mathbf{y})^T\right)^{-1}$ to obtain:

$$(\mathbf{y}-\rho\mathbf{W}\mathbf{y}-\mathbf{A}\boldsymbol{\beta}_0)^T = 0 \quad (21)$$

Transpose Equation (21) to obtain:

$$\mathbf{y}-\mathbf{A}\boldsymbol{\beta}_0 = \rho\mathbf{W}\mathbf{y} \quad (22)$$

In Equation (22), multiply both segments by $(\mathbf{W}\mathbf{y})^T$, thus obtaining:

$$(\mathbf{y}-\mathbf{A}\boldsymbol{\beta}_0)(\mathbf{W}\mathbf{y})^T = \rho\mathbf{W}\mathbf{y}(\mathbf{W}\mathbf{y})^T \quad (23)$$

From Equation (23), multiply both segments by $\left(\mathbf{W}\mathbf{y}(\mathbf{W}\mathbf{y})^T\right)^{-1}$ to further obtain:

$$(\mathbf{y}-\mathbf{A}\boldsymbol{\beta}_0)(\mathbf{W}\mathbf{y})^T\left(\mathbf{W}\mathbf{y}(\mathbf{W}\mathbf{y})^T\right)^{-1} = \rho\left(\mathbf{W}\mathbf{y}(\mathbf{W}\mathbf{y})^T\right)\left(\mathbf{W}\mathbf{y}(\mathbf{W}\mathbf{y})^T\right)^{-1} \quad (24)$$

$$\hat{\rho} = (\mathbf{y}-\mathbf{A}\boldsymbol{\beta}_0)(\mathbf{W}\mathbf{y})^T\left(\mathbf{W}\mathbf{y}(\mathbf{W}\mathbf{y})^T\right)^{-1} \quad (25)$$

Substitute the equation $\mathbf{A} = \mathbf{XZJ}$ into Equation (13), in order to determine $\hat{\rho}$ the following:

$$\hat{\rho} = (\mathbf{y}-(\mathbf{XZJ})\boldsymbol{\beta}_0)(\mathbf{W}\mathbf{y})^T\left(\mathbf{W}\mathbf{y}(\mathbf{W}\mathbf{y})^T\right)^{-1} \quad (26)$$

To obtain the MLE estimation of the parameters $\hat{\boldsymbol{\beta}}_0$, first determine the first derivative of Equation (17) for the parameters $\boldsymbol{\beta}_0$ as follows:

$$\begin{aligned}\frac{\partial \ln L(\rho, \boldsymbol{\beta}_0|\boldsymbol{\varepsilon})}{\partial \boldsymbol{\beta}_0} &= -\frac{(\mathbf{y}-\rho\mathbf{W}\mathbf{y}-\mathbf{A}\boldsymbol{\beta}_0)^T(-\mathbf{A})}{2\sigma^2} \\ &= \frac{(\mathbf{y}-\rho\mathbf{W}\mathbf{y}-\mathbf{A}\boldsymbol{\beta}_0)^T(\mathbf{A})}{2\sigma^2}\end{aligned} \quad (27)$$

$\frac{\partial \ln L(\rho, \boldsymbol{\beta}_0 | \boldsymbol{\varepsilon})}{\partial \boldsymbol{\beta}_0}\bigg|_{\boldsymbol{\beta}_0 = \hat{\boldsymbol{\beta}}_0} = 0$. This leads to the equation below:

$$\frac{(\mathbf{y} - \rho \mathbf{W} \mathbf{y} - \mathbf{A} \boldsymbol{\beta}_0)^T \mathbf{A}}{2\sigma^2} = 0 \tag{28}$$

In Equation (28), multiply with $2\sigma^2 \mathbf{A}^T$, in order to obtain:

$$(\mathbf{y} - \rho \mathbf{W} \mathbf{y} - \mathbf{A} \boldsymbol{\beta}_0)^T \mathbf{A} \mathbf{A}^T = 0 \tag{29}$$

Multiply Equation (29) by $\left(\mathbf{A} \mathbf{A}^T\right)^{-1}$ to obtain:

$$(\mathbf{y} - \rho \mathbf{W} \mathbf{y} - \mathbf{A} \boldsymbol{\beta}_0)^T = 0 \tag{30}$$

Transpose Equation (30), in order to obtain the expression below:

$$\mathbf{A} \boldsymbol{\beta}_0 = \mathbf{y} - \rho \mathbf{W} \mathbf{y} \tag{31}$$

In Equation (31), multiply both segments by $\mathbf{A}^T$ to obtain:

$$(\mathbf{A} \boldsymbol{\beta}_0) \mathbf{A}^T = (\mathbf{y} - \rho \mathbf{W} \mathbf{y}) \mathbf{A}^T \tag{32}$$

From Equation (32), multiply both segments by $\left(\mathbf{A} \mathbf{A}^T\right)^{-1}$ to obtain the following expression:

$$\boldsymbol{\beta}_0 \left(\mathbf{A} \mathbf{A}^T\right) \left(\mathbf{A} \mathbf{A}^T\right)^{-1} = (\mathbf{y} - \rho \mathbf{W} \mathbf{y}) \mathbf{A}^T \left(\mathbf{A} \mathbf{A}^T\right)^{-1} \tag{33}$$

$$\hat{\boldsymbol{\beta}}_0 = (\mathbf{y} - \rho \mathbf{W} \mathbf{y}) \mathbf{A}^T \left(\mathbf{A} \mathbf{A}^T\right)^{-1} \tag{34}$$

Substitute the equation $\mathbf{A} = \mathbf{XZJ}$ into Equation (13) and derive $\hat{\boldsymbol{\beta}}_0$ as follows:

$$\hat{\boldsymbol{\beta}}_0 = (\mathbf{y} - \rho \mathbf{W} \mathbf{y})(\mathbf{XZJ})^T \left((\mathbf{XZJ})(\mathbf{XZJ})^T\right)^{-1} \tag{35}$$

Based on the estimated parameter $\hat{\boldsymbol{\beta}}_0$ in Equation (35), the value $\boldsymbol{\beta}$ can be obtained by substituting into Equation (11):

$$\boldsymbol{\beta} = \mathbf{ZJ} \left((\mathbf{y} - \rho \mathbf{W} \mathbf{y})(\mathbf{XZJ})^T \left((\mathbf{XZJ})(\mathbf{XZJ})^T\right)^{-1}\right) \tag{36}$$

3. Real Data Application

3.1. Data Description

In this research, secondary data from 13 climate observation stations in West Java were utilized. These data were sourced from the Meteorology, Climatology, and Geophysics Agency (BMKG), while climate variable data were extracted from the National Aeronautics and Space Administration Prediction of Worldwide Energy Resources (NASA POWER) satellite observations. The climate variable dataset included rainfall, air temperature, humidity, solar irradiation, wind speed, and surface pressure shown on Table 1.

Table 1. Climate variable data at 13 climate observation stations in West Java.

No.	Locations	Latitude	Longitude	Rainfall (mm)	Air Temperature (°C)	Humidity (%)	Solar Irradiation (W/m^2)	Wind Speed (m/s)	Surface Pressure (kPa)
1	Balitpa Sukamandi	−6.3	107.65	186.36	25.3	83.45	415.2	1.76	97.86
2	Lanud Atang Sanjaya Semplak	−6.9	106.77	200.74	23.72	87.25	411.23	1.71	95.52
3	LPHP Tasikmalaya	−7.28	108.16	228.2	23.68	89.15	398.29	2.1	96.46
4	SMPK Cirebon	−6.72	108.58	189.71	27.7	78.58	418.72	3.67	100.86
5	SMPK Maranginan Sukabumi	−7.25	106.25	191.42	25.79	84.61	415.46	3.12	98.84
6	SMPK Nariewattie	−7.25	108	194.57	22.59	87.85	398.29	1.57	93.62
7	SMPK Pacet Cianjur	−6.73	107	176.28	24.7	85.19	415.2	1.46	96.82
8	SMPK Pasir Sarongge	−6.75	107	176.28	24.7	85.19	415.2	1.46	96.82
9	Stage of Bandung	−6.92	107.6	203.29	21.41	88.29	415.2	1.51	90.93
10	Stage of Lembang	−6.83	107.62	203.29	21.41	88.29	415.2	1.51	90.93
11	Staklim Darmaga	−6.55	106.75	176.28	24.7	85.19	411.23	1.46	96.82
12	Stamet Citeko Bogor	−6.7	106.93	176.28	24.7	85.19	411.23	1.46	96.82
13	Stamet Jatiwangi	−6.75	108.27	181.08	26.45	80.97	418.72	2.49	99.66

3.2. RShiny Web Application for SAR-X Model

At this stage, an R script was developed to process the data using the SAR-X model through the RShiny web application.

A. The process of building an R script for the SAR-X model

The SAR-X modeling process, employing the Casetti model approach, entailed the following steps:

1. Importing the climate data used for the SAR-X modeling, encompassing 13 climate observation stations in the West Java region.
2. Constructing vectors and matrices based on the climate data, including:
   a. Vector **y**: defines the rainfall variable at each location.
   b. Matrix **X**: represents the exogenous variables, such as air temperature, humidity, solar irradiation, wind speed, and surface pressure.
   c. Matrix **Z**: consists of location coordinate entries in latitude and longitude.
   d. Matrix **J**: identity matrix with the size of as many as five exogenous variables, according to matrix **X**.
   e. Matrix **W**: the result of calculating the inverse distance weight matrix using the equation with input location coordinates (latitude and longitude).
   f. Kronecker **Z**: the expression obtained from the multiplication of the kronecker with the identity matrix of the five exogenous variables ($\mathbf{Z} \otimes \mathbf{I}_k$)
   g. Matrix **A**: the product of matrix **X**, **Z**, and **J**
3. The Moran Index calculation using function "moran.test" and Moran Scatterplot using function "moran.plot".

4. The calculation of parameter estimation $\hat{\rho}$ and $\hat{\beta}_0$, obtaining the prediction results $\hat{y}$, absolute error, and MAPE of the SAR-X model prediction with the Casetti model approach.
5. The SAR-X model prediction data with the Casetti model approach in the form of $\hat{y}$

B. Creating and publishing the RShiny web application with the developed script.

At this stage, the R script explicitly built for the SAR-X model was transformed into an RShiny web application following these steps:

1. Installing packages and call libraries, specifically "shiny" and "shinythemes", to set up RShiny.
2. Creating a User Interface (UI) and Server for the Web Application UI scripts managed the appearance of the web, incorporating headers, images, panel tabs, and more. Furthermore, the previously crafted R script for the SAR-X model was integrated into the server script. Running the application involved clicking "Run App." Successful execution prompted progression, while errors in the console necessitated troubleshooting.
3. Publishing the RShiny Web Application

At this stage, the designed application was published on the https://www.shinyapps.io platform, accessed on 5 July 2023. The account creation on the site was followed by token activation. The provided token was copied and inserted into RStudio. The application could be published by clicking the designated icon.

3.3. Calculation Result of Inverse Distance Weight Matrix

The inverse distance weight was computed by taking into account the actual distances between each location. The standardized inverse distance weight matrix for the SAR-X model was then obtained using Equation (2), which produced the following:

$$W = \begin{pmatrix}
0 & 0.049832 & 0.046317 & 0.054288 & 0.019748 & 0.055151 & 0.093068 & 0.090447 & 0.146109 & 0.200602 & 0.06479 & 0.083328 & 0.096319 \\
0.015477 & 0 & 0.008455 & 0.005307 & 0.044687 & 0.010736 & 0.214639 & 0.232858 & 0.025472 & 0.024137 & 0.14286 & 0.267645 & 0.007726 \\
0.016001 & 0.009405 & 0 & 0.039857 & 0.005352 & 0.736974 & 0.01185 & 0.012007 & 0.044065 & 0.039526 & 0.007747 & 0.010561 & 0.066655 \\
0.050697 & 0.015956 & 0.107736 & 0 & 0.009246 & 0.085519 & 0.021146 & 0.021139 & 0.05277 & 0.056539 & 0.015629 & 0.019388 & 0.544235 \\
0.034948 & 0.254618 & 0.027416 & 0.017521 & 0 & 0.032666 & 0.12011 & 0.123126 & 0.051796 & 0.048721 & 0.135189 & 0.130788 & 0.023102 \\
0.018078 & 0.01133 & 0.699231 & 0.030017 & 0.00605 & 0 & 0.014586 & 0.014824 & 0.068909 & 0.057761 & 0.009028 & 0.012802 & 0.057385 \\
0.000609 & 0.004519 & 0.000224 & 0.000148 & 0.000444 & 0.000291 & 0 & 0.924044 & 0.000933 & 0.000937 & 0.003895 & 0.063727 & 0.000229 \\
0.0006 & 0.00497 & 0.00023 & 0.00015 & 0.000461 & 0.0003 & 0.936838 & 0 & 0.000964 & 0.000959 & 0.003656 & 0.05064 & 0.000232 \\
0.018523 & 0.010397 & 0.01617 & 0.007164 & 0.003711 & 0.026651 & 0.018093 & 0.018428 & 0 & 0.843116 & 0.008339 & 0.014411 & 0.014999 \\
0.025362 & 0.009825 & 0.014464 & 0.007654 & 0.003481 & 0.022278 & 0.018121 & 0.018288 & 0.84081 & 0 & 0.008556 & 0.014497 & 0.016663 \\
0.021581 & 0.153208 & 0.007469 & 0.005574 & 0.025445 & 0.009174 & 0.198412 & 0.1837 & 0.02191 & 0.022542 & 0 & 0.342974 & 0.008011 \\
0.004212 & 0.043556 & 0.001545 & 0.001049 & 0.003735 & 0.001974 & 0.492634 & 0.386119 & 0.005746 & 0.005796 & 0.052045 & 0 & 0.001589 \\
0.065939 & 0.01703 & 0.132081 & 0.398967 & 0.008937 & 0.119851 & 0.023988 & 0.023994 & 0.080996 & 0.09023 & 0.016465 & 0.021523 & 0
\end{pmatrix}$$

3.4. Calculation Result of Moran's Index and Scatterplot Moran

The calculation of the Moran Index was employed to assess the existence of spatial autocorrelation among the observation locations. The Moran Index for each climate variable was calculated using Equation (4). The results of the Moran index calculations are shown on Table 2.

Aside from the computation of the Moran Index on Table 2, a Moran Scatterplot was also utilized to visualize the overall clustering tendency and distinctive attributes of each region. This visual representation took the form of a four-quadrant graph for each unit of analysis. The four quadrants showed potential groupings, bounded by mean and average lines. Areas were considered to have high attributes when their values exceeded the average, while values below the average indicated low characteristics. The complete results of the Moran Scatterplot for each climate variable can be seen in Figure 1.

Table 2. Spatial autocorrelation test using Moran's Index.

No.	Climate Variable	p-Value	Description
1	y (Rainfall)	0.0168	There is spatial autocorrelation
2	X_1 (Air Temperature)	0.0061	There is spatial autocorrelation
3	X_2 (Humidity)	0.0163	There is spatial autocorrelation
4	X_3 (Solar Irradiation)	0.0013	There is spatial autocorrelation
5	X_4 (Wind Speed)	0.0487	There is spatial autocorrelation
6	X_5 (Surface Pressure)	0.0044	There is spatial autocorrelation

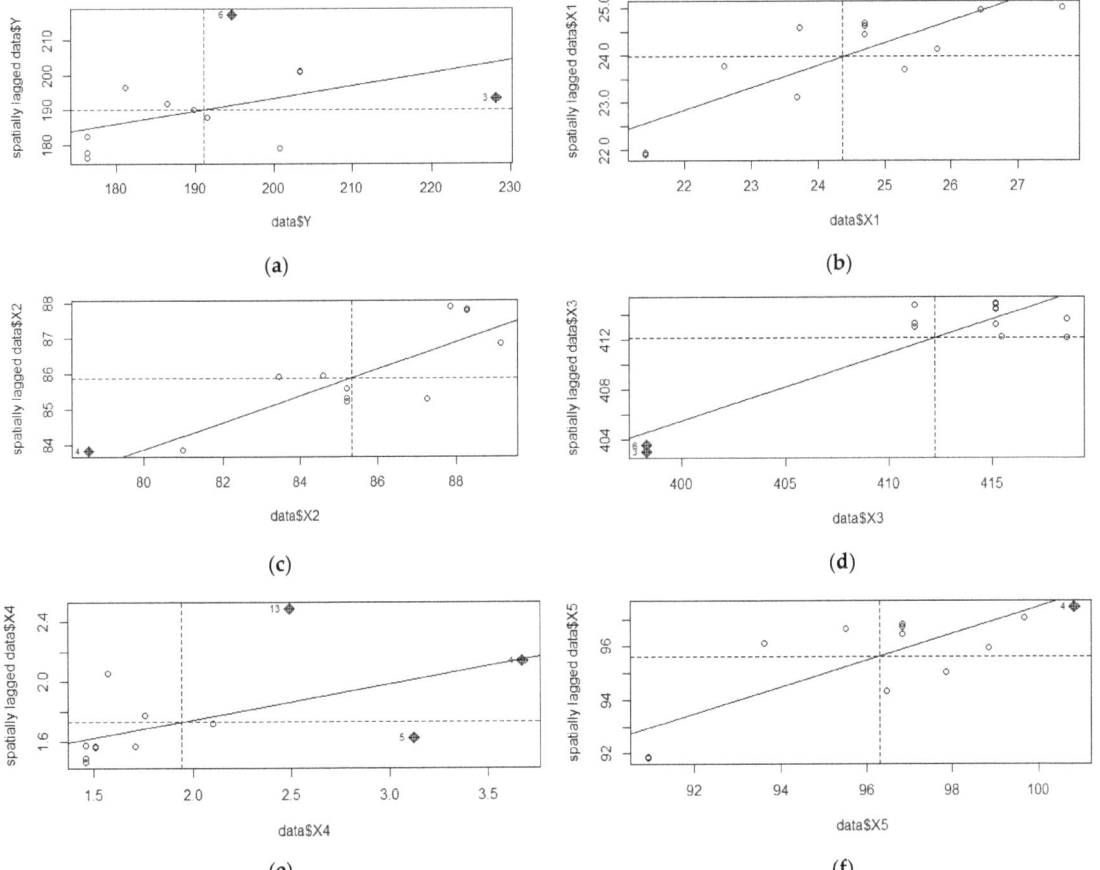

Figure 1. Moran's scatterplot of climate variables: (**a**) rainfall, (**b**) air temperature, (**c**) humidity, (**d**) solar ir-radiation, (**e**) wind speed, and (**f**) surface pressure.

3.5. Prediction Result of SAR Model

The estimation of the prediction parameters $\hat{\rho}$ and $\hat{\beta}$ in the SAR model was conducted using R version 4.2.2. An estimated $\hat{\rho}$ value of 0.744 was obtained, indicating spatial lag dependence. This signified the influence of adjacent locations within the West Java region on the rainfall prediction data. The results of the calculation of the parameter estimate for $\hat{\beta}$ are shown in Table 3.

Table 3. Parameter estimated value $\hat{\beta}$.

No.	$\hat{\beta}$	Parameter Estimated Value
1	β_1	−89.56
2	β_2	−12.21
3	β_3	−0.63
4	β_4	27.50
5	β_5	36.49

The SAR model equation for each location is presented and can be found in Appendix A. The predictions of rainfall and absolute errors at each location are shown in Table 4.

Table 4. Prediction results and error prediction of SAR model.

No.	Locations	y	$\hat{y}$	Absolute Error
1	Balitpa Sukamandi	186.36	214.49	15.09
2	Lanud Atang Sanjaya Semplak	200.74	215.98	7.59
3	LPHP Tasikmalaya	228.20	260.09	13.98
4	SMPK Cirebon	189.71	217.49	14.64
5	SMPK Maranginan Sukabumi	191.42	226.58	18.37
6	SMPK Nariewattie	194.57	273.16	40.39
7	SMPK Pacet Cianjur	176.28	189.40	7.44
8	SMPK Pasir Sarongge	176.28	189.41	7.45
9	Stage of Bandung	203.29	250.93	23.44
10	Stage of Lembang	203.29	250.81	23.38
11	Staklim Darmaga	176.28	196.39	11.41
12	Stamet Citeko Bogor	176.28	192.96	9.46
13	Stamet Jatiwangi	181.08	228.85	26.38

Based on the results of the absolute error calculation in Table 4, the MAPE (Mean Absolute Percentage Error) value for prediction using the SAR model amounted to 16.85%. According to Lewis (1982) in [40], the prediction accuracy level is accurate, as the MAPE was less than 20%.

3.6. Prediction Result of SAR-X Model

The estimation of the prediction parameters $\hat{\rho}$ and $\hat{\beta}_0$ in the SAR-X model was conducted using R software through a web application powered by RShiny. An estimated $\hat{\rho}$ value of 1.001973 was obtained, indicating spatial lag dependence. This signified the influence of adjacent locations within the West Java region on the rainfall prediction data. The results of the parameter estimate calculation of $\hat{\beta}_0$ for each $\hat{\beta}_{latitude}$ and $\hat{\beta}_{longitude}$ are shown in Table 5.

Table 5. Parameter estimated value $\hat{\beta}_0$ for each $\hat{\beta}_{latitude}$ and $\hat{\beta}_{longitude}$.

No.	$\hat{\beta}_0$	Parameter Estimated Value
1	$\hat{\beta}_{latitude(x_1)}$	−539.33
2	$\hat{\beta}_{longitude(x_1)}$	−96.53
3	$\hat{\beta}_{latitude(x_2)}$	2.93
4	$\hat{\beta}_{longitude(x_2)}$	139.34
5	$\hat{\beta}_{latitude(x_3)}$	207.11
6	$\hat{\beta}_{longitude(x_3)}$	−33.57
7	$\hat{\beta}_{latitude(x_4)}$	−5.94
8	$\hat{\beta}_{longitude(x_4)}$	0.17
9	$\hat{\beta}_{latitude(x_5)}$	8.96
10	$\hat{\beta}_{longitude(x_5)}$	12.86

Based on the estimated value of $\hat{\beta}_0$ in Table 5, the value of $\hat{\beta}$ was determined using Equation (38). The calculated values of $\hat{\beta}$ are shown in Table 6.

Table 6. Parameter estimated value of $\hat{\beta}$.

No.	Locations	Parameter Estimated Value of $\hat{\beta}$				
		$\hat{\beta}_1$	$\hat{\beta}_2$	$\hat{\beta}_3$	$\hat{\beta}_4$	$\hat{\beta}_5$
1	Balitpa Sukamandi	−215.93	−45.51	58.56	−21.52	−0.73
2	Lanud Atang Sanjaya Semplak	−31.14	−116.44	−2.56	120.40	43.66
3	LPHP Tasikmalaya	0.16	−20.48	−42.76	29.06	16.71
4	SMPK Cirebon	86.59	3.91	−112.28	−1.67	24.16
5	SMPK Maranginan Sukabumi	80.12	−0.91	38.00	−0.32	11.79
6	SMPK Nariewattie	137.49	36.36	14.27	−49.03	−1.14
7	SMPK Pacet Cianjur	32.06	5.04	−1.21	71.15	24.35
8	SMPK Pasir Sarongge	−1.75	343.87	20.79	20.24	−12.06
9	Stage of Bandung	−4.98	68.96	−17.38	−1.40	6.13
10	Stage of Lembang	−55.57	−2.87	48.79	12.41	8.65
11	Staklim Darmaga	295.90	−58.45	16.20	−30.12	−1.05
12	Stamet Citeko Bogor	60.51	−134.81	−1.27	−50.76	29.39
13	Stamet Jatiwangi	−2.62	285.08	18.01	−1.64	−5.17

The SAR-X model equation for each location can be found in Appendix B. The predictions of the rainfall and corresponding errors at each location are shown in Table 7.

Based on the results of the absolute error calculation in Table 7, the MAPE value for prediction using the SAR-X model amounted to 1.95%. According to Lewis (1982) in [40], the prediction accuracy level is very accurate, as the MAPE value was less than 10%.

Table 7. Prediction results and absolute error prediction of SAR-X Model.

No.	Locations	y	$\hat{y}$	Absolute Error
1	Balitpa Sukamandi	186.36	189.49	1.68
2	Lanud Atang Sanjaya Semplak	200.74	200.78	0.02
3	LPHP Tasikmalaya	228.20	222.30	2.59
4	SMPK Cirebon	189.71	190.80	0.57
5	SMPK Maranginan Sukabumi	191.42	193.36	1.01
6	SMPK Nariewattie	194.57	202.01	3.82
7	SMPK Pacet Cianjur	176.28	175.13	0.65
8	SMPK Pasir Sarongge	176.28	176.62	0.19
9	Stage of Bandung	203.29	193.78	4.68
10	Stage of Lembang	203.29	210.81	3.70
11	Staklim Darmaga	176.28	171.90	2.48
12	Stamet Citeko Bogor	176.28	179.17	1.64
13	Stamet Jatiwangi	181.08	176.87	2.32

3.7. Cross-Validation

In this research, for a cross-validation study, the data collection stage was carried out through a parameter selection process in the form of climate variable data. Those used were rainfall, solar irradiance, and wind speed in the West Java region, consisting of 11 regencies/cities shown on Table 8.

Table 8. Climate variable data from 11 regencies/cities in West Java.

No.	Locations	Latitude	Longitude	Rainfall (mm)	Solar Irradiation (W/m^2)	Wind Speed (m/s)
1	Bandung City	−6.91486	107.6082	203.29	415.2	1.511
2	Bekasi City	−6.24159	106.9924	172.32	411.2	2.492
3	Cirebon City	−6.73725	108.5507	189.71	418.7	3.674
4	Sukabumi City	−6.9237	106.9287	200.74	411.2	1.706
5	Tasikmalaya City	−7.31956	108.203	228.2	398.3	2.099
6	Pangandaran Regency	−7.61506	108.4988	210.14	1.816	398.3
7	Bogor Regency	−6.59504	106.8166	176.28	411.2	1.456
8	Majalengka Regency	−6.83638	108.2274	194.57	418.7	1.575
9	Indramayu Regency	−6.32758	108.3249	181.08	418.7	2.495
10	Purwakarta Regency	−6.53868	107.4499	186.36	415.2	1.76
11	Kuningan Regency	−7.01381	108.5701	184.64	398.3	1.781

An estimated $\hat{\rho}$ value of 0.8055492 was obtained, indicating spatial lag dependence. This signified the influence of adjacent locations within the West Java region on the rainfall prediction data. The results of the parameter estimate calculations of $\hat{\beta}_0$ for each $\hat{\beta}_{latitude}$ and $\hat{\beta}_{longitude}$ are shown in Table 9.

The results of calculating the estimated value of $\hat{\beta}$ are shown in Table 10.

The results of predictions of the rainfall and absolute errors at each location are shown in Table 11.

Based on the results of the absolute error calculation in Table 11, the MAPE value for prediction with the SAR-X model in the cross-validation dataset was 7.09% and the prediction accuracy level was very accurate, as the MAPE value was less than 10%.

Table 9. Parameter estimated value $\hat{\beta}_0$ for cross-validation dataset.

No.	$\hat{\beta}_0$	Parameter Estimated Value
1	$\hat{\beta}_{latitude(x_1)}$	−0.08
2	$\hat{\beta}_{longitude(x_1)}$	4.04
3	$\hat{\beta}_{latitude(x_2)}$	−0.01
4	$\hat{\beta}_{longitude(x_2)}$	0.35

Table 10. Parameter estimated value of $\hat{\beta}$ for cross-validation dataset.

No.	Locations	Parameter Estimated Value of $\hat{\beta}$	
		$\hat{\beta}_1$	$\hat{\beta}_2$
1	Bandung City	0.11	−0.06
2	Bekasi City	2.72	0.08
3	Cirebon City	0.03	3.88
4	Sukabumi City	5.48	0.10
5	Tasikmalaya City	0.08	3.26
6	Pangandaran Regency	3.79	0.03
7	Bogor Regency	0.12	5.51
8	Majalengka Regency	2.48	0.07
9	Indramayu Regency	0.16	4.32
10	Purwakarta Regency	1.14	0.12
11	Kuningan Regency	0.20	2.59

Table 11. Prediction results and MAPE Prediction of SAR-X Model for cross-validation dataset.

No.	Locations	y	$\hat{y}$	Absolute Error
1	Bandung City	203.29	206.08	2.79
2	Bekasi City	172.32	177.63	5.31
3	Cirebon City	189.71	203.23	13.52
4	Sukabumi City	200.74	201.40	0.66
5	Tasikmalaya City	228.20	223.60	4.60
6	Pangandaran Regency	210.14	140.21	69.93
7	Bogor Regency	176.28	191.01	14.73
8	Majalengka Regency	194.57	203.28	8.71
9	Indramayu Regency	181.08	183.86	2.78
10	Purwakarta Regency	186.36	190.22	3.86
11	Kuningan Regency	184.64	211.11	26.47

4. Discussion

The procedure for predicting rainfall in West Java, utilizing the SAR-X model with the Casetti Model approach, was conducted based on data from 13 climate observation stations. The entire process was carried out within the RStudio software environment, leveraging the capabilities of the RShiny web application. The R script constructed for this purpose encompassed various stages of the SAR-X modeling procedure, ranging from data import, vector, matrix construction, Moran index, Moran scatterplot calculation, parameter estimation, prediction result calculation, and MAPE assessment to the publication of the RShiny web application. It should be noted that the execution time of the script ranged from 1 to 5 min. The source code is stored in the GitHub directory and the link is included in Appendix C, which could be valuable for facilitating the replication and verification of the model and its results by other researchers [41,42].

The result of the Moran index calculation, presented in Table 2, showed a positive spatial autocorrelation across the 13 observation stations within the West Java region. In addition, it concurred with the descriptive analysis, indicating that the areas exhibiting high rainfall tended to be situated in proximity to other high-rainfall areas, and vice versa. The results of the identification, parameter estimation, and prediction of rainfall, involving five other climate variable factors in Tables 4 and 7, showed that the MAPE value of the SAR-X model prediction results was smaller than the MAPE of the SAR model, with the calculation of the rainfall prediction providing very high results based on the MAPE value of 1.95%. This shows that the prediction of rainfall using NASA POWER data from 13 observation stations in the West Java region using the SAR-X model was better than prediction with the SAR model, because the SAR-X model obtained $\hat{\beta}$ parameters that varied for each exogenous variable at each location. This research aligned with the discovery of Hermawan [28], highlighting the influential role of five climate variable factors in shaping rainfall patterns, namely air temperature, humidity, solar irradiation, wind speed, and surface pressure.

5. Conclusions

In conclusion, the SAR-X model using Casetti's approach was applied to analyze the rainfall data and climate variables in West Java, utilizing information from 13 climate observation stations. These data showed a positive spatial autocorrelation among different regions. The results highlighted the remarkable accuracy of the prediction outcomes obtained through the SAR-X model at each observation location. This accuracy was attributed to the distinct estimated parameter values assigned to each climate variable, contributing to the high precision of the prediction results.

The summary of this research underscored that the level of rainfall in each region, based on the data from 13 climate observation stations in West Java, was significantly influenced by five other climate variable factors. It should be noted that these factors collectively exhibited a positive spatial autocorrelation across various areas. Therefore, the recommendation for relevant institutions engaged in rainfall prediction is to thoroughly consider the diverse aspects of climate variables. This approach enables a comprehensive understanding of how each climate variable exerts its influence within distinct locations.

6. Patents

Granted Copy Right: Copy Right for Computer Program, number 000484465.

Entitled "Application of RShiny Program for SAR-X with Casetti Model Approach to Climate Data in West Java", Ministry of Law and Human Rights of the Republic of Indonesia (Falah, A. N., Ruchjana, B. N., Abdullah, A. S., Rejito, J.), 2023. https://annisanurfalah.shinyapps.io/SAR-X-Model/, accessed on 5 July 2023.

Author Contributions: Conceptualization, A.N.F., B.N.R. and A.S.A.; methodology, A.N.F.; software, A.N.F.; validation, A.N.F. and B.N.R.; formal analysis, A.N.F., B.N.R. and A.S.A.; investigation, A.S.A. and J.R.; resources, B.N.R.; data curation A.N.F.; writing—original draft preparation, A.N.F.; writing—review and editing, A.N.F., B.N.R., A.S.A. and J.R.; supervision, B.N.R., A.S.A. and J.R.; project administration A.N.F. and B.N.R.; funding acquisition, B.N.R. All authors have read and agreed to the published version of the manuscript.

Funding: The APC was funded by Academic Leadership Grant Universitas Padjadjaran with contract number: 1549/UN6.3.1/PT.00/2023.

Data Availability Statement: Not applicable.

Acknowledgments: The authors thank to the Rector, Directorate of Research and Community Service (DRPM), and Studies Center of Modeling and Computation Faculty of Mathematics and Natural Sciences, Universitas Padjadjaran. The authors thank to the Commission Developing Country (CDC)—International Mathematical Union (IMU) Breakout Graduate Fellowship 2020–2023, Academic Leadership Grant (ALG) with contract number 1549/UN6.3.1/PT.00/2023, and International Consortium RISE_SMA project 2019–2024.

Conflicts of Interest: The authors declare no conflict of interest.

Appendix A

- SAR model for predicting rainfall in Balitpa Sukamandi:

$$\hat{y}_{(s_1)} = 0.744 \sum_{i=1}^{13} w_{1i} y_{(s_i)} - 89.56 X_1 - 12.21 X_2 - 0.63 X_3 + 27.50 X_4 + 36.49 X_5$$

- SAR model for predicting rainfall in Lanud Atang Sanjaya Semplak:

$$\hat{y}_{(s_2)} = 0.744 \sum_{i=1}^{13} w_{2i} y_{(s_i)} - 89.56 X_1 - 12.21 X_2 - 0.63 X_3 + 27.50 X_4 + 36.49 X_5$$

- SAR model for predicting rainfall in LPHP Tasikmalaya:

$$\hat{y}_{(s_3)} = 0.744 \sum_{i=1}^{13} w_{3i} y_{(s_i)} - 89.56 X_1 - 12.21 X_2 - 0.63 X_3 + 27.50 X_4 + 36.49 X_5$$

- SAR model for predicting rainfall in SMPK Cirebon:

$$\hat{y}_{(s_4)} = 0.744 \sum_{i=1}^{13} w_{4i} y_{(s_i)} - 89.56 X_1 - 12.21 X_2 - 0.63 X_3 + 27.50 X_4 + 36.49 X_5$$

- SAR model for predicting rainfall in SMPK Maranginan Sukabumi:

$$\hat{y}_{(s_5)} = 0.744 \sum_{i=1}^{13} w_{5i} y_{(s_i)} - 89.56 X_1 - 12.21 X_2 - 0.63 X_3 + 27.50 X_4 + 36.49 X_5$$

- SAR model for predicting rainfall in SMPK Nariewattie:

$$\hat{y}_{(s_6)} = 0.744 \sum_{i=1}^{13} w_{6i} y_{(s_i)} - 89.56 X_1 - 12.21 X_2 - 0.63 X_3 + 27.50 X_4 + 36.49 X_5$$

- SAR model for predicting rainfall in SMPK Pacet Cianjur:

$$\hat{y}_{(7)} = 0.744 \sum_{i=1}^{13} w_{7i} y_{(s_i)} - 89.56 X_1 - 12.21 X_2 - 0.63 X_3 + 27.50 X_4 + 36.49 X_5$$

- SAR model for predicting rainfall in SMPK Pasir Sarongge:

$$\hat{y}_{(s_8)} = 0.744 \sum_{i=1}^{13} w_{8i} y_{(s_i)} - 89.56 X_1 - 12.21 X_2 - 0.63 X_3 + 27.50 X_4 + 36.49 X_5$$

- SAR model for predicting rainfall in Stage of Bandung:

$$\hat{y}_{(s_9)} = 0.744 \sum_{i=1}^{13} w_{9i} y_{(s_i)} - 89.56 X_1 - 12.21 X_2 - 0.63 X_3 + 27.50 X_4 + 36.49 X_5$$

- SAR model for predicting rainfall in Stage of Lembang:

$$\hat{y}_{(10)} = 0.744 \sum_{i=1}^{13} w_{10i} y_{(s_i)} - 89.56 X_1 - 12.21 X_2 - 0.63 X_3 + 27.50 X_4 + 36.49 X_5$$

- SAR model for predicting rainfall in Staklim Darmaga:

$$\hat{y}_{(s_{11})} = 0.744 \sum_{i=1}^{13} w_{11i} y_{(s_i)} - 89.56 X_1 - 12.21 X_2 - 0.63 X_3 + 27.50 X_4 + 36.49 X_5$$

- SAR model for predicting rainfall in Stamet Citeko Bogor:

$$\hat{y}_{(s_{12})} = 0.744 \sum_{i=1}^{13} w_{12i} y_{(s_i)} - 89.56 X_1 - 12.21 X_2 - 0.63 X_3 + 27.50 X_4 + 36.49 X_5$$

- SAR model for predicting rainfall in Stamet Jatiwangi:

$$\hat{y}_{(s_{13})} = 0.744 \sum_{i=1}^{13} w_{13i} y_{(s_i)} - 89.56 X_1 - 12.21 X_2 - 0.63 X_3 + 27.50 X_4 + 36.49 X_5$$

Appendix B

- SAR-X model for predicting rainfall in Balitpa Sukamandi:

$$\hat{y}_{(s_1)} = 1.001973 \sum_{i=1}^{13} w_{1i} y_{(s_i)} - 215.93 X_1 - 45.51 X_2 + 58.56 X_3 - 21.52 X_4 - 0.73 X_5$$

- SAR-X model for predicting rainfall in Lanud Atang Sanjaya Semplak:

$$\hat{y}_{(s_2)} = 1.001973 \sum_{i=1}^{13} w_{2i} y_{(s_i)} - 31.14 X_1 - 116.44 X_2 - 2.56 X_3 + 120.40 X_4 + 43.66 X_5$$

- SAR-X model for predicting rainfall in LPHP Tasikmalaya:

$$\hat{y}_{(s_3)} = 1.001973 \sum_{i=1}^{13} w_{3i} y_{(s_i)} + 0.16 X_1 - 20.48 X_2 - 42.76 X_3 + 29.06 X_4 + 16.71 X_5$$

- SAR-X model for predicting rainfall in SMPK Cirebon:

$$\hat{y}_{(s_4)} = 1.001973 \sum_{i=1}^{13} w_{4i} y_{(s_i)} + 86.59 X_1 + 3.91 X_2 - 112.28 X_3 - 1.67 X_4 + 24.16 X_5$$

- SAR-X model for predicting rainfall in SMPK Maranginan Sukabumi:

$$\hat{y}_{(s_5)} = 1.001973 \sum_{i=1}^{13} w_{5i} y_{(s_i)} + 80.12 X_1 - 0.91 X_2 + 38.00 X_3 - 0.32 X_4 + 11.79 X_5$$

- SAR-X model for predicting rainfall in SMPK Nariewattie:

$$\hat{y}_{(s_6)} = 1.001973 \sum_{i=1}^{13} w_{6i} y_{(s_i)} + 137.49 X_1 + 36.36 X_2 + 14.27 X_3 - 49.03 X_4 - 1.14 X_5$$

- SAR-X model for predicting rainfall in SMPK Pacet Cianjur:

$$\hat{y}_{(s_7)} = 1.001973 \sum_{i=1}^{13} w_{7i} y_{(s_i)} + 32.06 X_1 + 5.04 X_2 - 1.21 X_3 + 71.15 X_4 + 24.35 X_5$$

- SAR-X model for predicting rainfall in SMPK Pasir Sarongge:

$$\hat{y}_{(s_8)} = 1.001973 \sum_{i=1}^{13} w_{8i} y_{(s_i)} - 1.75 X_1 + 343.87 X_2 + 20.79 X_3 + 20.24 X_4 - 12.06 X_5$$

- SAR-X model for predicting rainfall in Stage of Bandung:

$$\hat{y}_{(s_9)} = 1.001973 \sum_{i=1}^{13} w_{9i} y_{(s_i)} - 4.98 X_1 + 68.96 X_2 - 17.38 X_3 - 1.40 X_4 + 6.13 X_5$$

- SAR-X model for predicting rainfall in Stage of Lembang:

$$\hat{y}_{(s_{10})} = 1.001973 \sum_{i=1}^{13} w_{10i} y_{(s_i)} - 55.57 X_1 - 2.87 X_2 + 48.79 X_3 + 12.41 X_4 + 8.65 X_5$$

- SAR-X model for predicting rainfall in Staklim Darmaga:

$$\hat{y}_{(s_{11})} = 1.001973 \sum_{i=1}^{13} w_{11i} y_{(s_i)} + 295.90 X_1 - 58.45 X_2 + 16.20 X_3 - 30.12 X_4 - 1.05 X_5$$

- SAR-X model for predicting rainfall in Stamet Citeko Bogor:

$$\hat{y}_{(s_{12})} = 1.001973 \sum_{i=1}^{13} w_{12i} y_{(s_i)} + 60.51 X_1 - 134.81 X_2 - 1.27 X_3 - 50.76 X_4 + 29.39 X_5$$

- SAR-X model for predicting rainfall in Stamet Jatiwangi:

$$\hat{y}_{(s_{13})} = 1.001973 \sum_{i=1}^{13} w_{13i} y_{(s_i)} - 2.62 X_1 + 285.08 X_2 + 18.01 X_3 - 1.64 X_4 - 5.17 X_5$$

Appendix C

The source code is stored in the GitHub directory and can be accessed at the following link: https://github.com/annisanurfalah02/SAR-X-Model, accessed on 15 August 2023.

References

1. Shoji, T.; Kitaura, H. Statistical and geostatistical analysis of rainfall in central Japan. *Comput. Geosci.* **2006**, *32*, 1007–1024. [CrossRef]
2. Bostan, P.A.; Zuhal, A. *Exploring The Mean Annual Precipitation and Temperature Values over Turkey by Using Environmental Variables*; University of Applied Sciences: Stuttgart, Germany, 2006; pp. 1–6.
3. Cannarozzo, M.; Noto, L.V.; Viola, F. Spatial distribution of rainfall trends in Sicily (1921–2000). *Phys. Chem. Earth* **2006**, *31*, 1201–1211. [CrossRef]
4. Diodato, N.; Tartari, G.; Bellocchi, G. Geospatial Rainfall Modelling at Eastern Nepalese Highland from Ground Environmental Data. *Water Resour. Manag.* **2010**, *24*, 2703–2720. [CrossRef]
5. Basistha, A.; Arya, D.S.; Goel, N.K. Spatial distribution of rainfall in Indian Himalayas—A case study of Uttarakhand Region. *Water Resour. Manag.* **2008**, *22*, 1325–1346. [CrossRef]
6. Yilmaz, B.; Harmancioglu, N.B. An Indicator Based Assessment for Water Resources Management in Gediz River Basin, Turkey. *Water Resour. Manag.* **2010**, *24*, 4359–4379. [CrossRef]
7. Zimit, A.Y.; Jibril, M.M.; Azimi, M.S.; Abba, S.I. Hybrid predictive based control of precipitation in a water-scarce region: A focus on the application of intelligent learning for green irrigation in agriculture sector. *J. Saudi Soc. Agric. Sci.* **2023**. [CrossRef]
8. Hussain, A.; Jadoon, K.Z.; Rahman, K.U.; Shang, S.; Shahid, M.; Ejaz, N.; Khan, H. Analyzing the impact of drought on agriculture: Evidence from Pakistan using standardized precipitation evapotranspiration index. *Nat. Hazards* **2023**, *115*, 389–408. [CrossRef]

9. Ali, U.; Jing, W.; Zhu, J.; Omarkhanova, Z.; Fahad, S.; Nurgazina, Z.; Khan, Z.A. Climate change impacts on agriculture sector: A case study of Pakistan. *Cienc. Rural* **2021**, *51*, e20200110. [CrossRef]
10. Duncan, J.M.A.; Biggs, E.M.; Dash, J.; Atkinson, P.M. Spatio-temporal trends in precipitation and their implications for water resources management in climate-sensitive Nepal. *Appl. Geogr.* **2013**, *43*, 138–146. [CrossRef]
11. Hartmann, H.; Snow, J.A.; Su, B.; Jiang, T. Seasonal predictions of precipitation in the Aksu-Tarim River basin for improved water resources management. *Glob. Planet. Chang.* **2016**, *147*, 86–96. [CrossRef]
12. Li, L.; Hong, Y.; Wang, J.; Adler, R.F.; Policelli, F.S.; Habib, S.; Irwn, D.; Korme, T.; Okello, L. Evaluation of the real-time TRMM-based multi-satellite precipitation analysis for an operational flood prediction system in Nzoia Basin, Lake Victoria, Africa. *Nat. Hazards* **2009**, *50*, 109–123. [CrossRef]
13. Sharma, S.; Khadka, N.; Hamal, K.; Baniya, B.; Luintel, N.; Joshi, B.B. Spatial and Temporal Analysis of Precipitation and Its Extremities in Seven Provinces of Nepal. *Appl. Ecol. Environ. Sci.* **2020**, *8*, 64–73.
14. Wei, N.; Sun, X.; Bi, X.; Wang, J.M.; Li, X. The spatial characteristics of precipitation and water-logging disaster during rainy season for urban planning in Xi'an. *Indoor Built Environ.* **2019**, *28*, 1263–1271. [CrossRef]
15. Cheng, L.; Aghakouchak, A. Nonstationary precipitation intensity-duration-frequency curves for infrastructure design in a changing climate. *Sci. Rep.* **2014**, *4*, 7093. [CrossRef] [PubMed]
16. Rosenberg, E.A.; Keys, P.W.; Booth, D.B.; Hartley, D.; Burkey, J.; Steinemann, A.C.; Lettenmaier, D.P. Precipitation extremes and the impacts of climate change on stormwater infrastructure in Washington State. *Clim. Chang.* **2010**, *102*, 319–349. [CrossRef]
17. Nissen, K.M.; Ulbrich, U. Increasing frequencies and changing characteristics of heavy precipitation events threatening infrastructure in Europe under climate change. *Nat. Hazards Earth Syst. Sci.* **2017**, *17*, 1177–1190. [CrossRef]
18. Ibrahim, N.A.; Alwi, S.R.W.; Manan, Z.A.; Mustaffa, A.A.; Kidam, K. Risk matrix approach of extreme temperature and precipitation for renewable energy systems in Malaysia. *Energy* **2022**, *254*, 124471. [CrossRef]
19. Bezirgiannidis, A.; Chatzopoulos, P.; Tsakali, A.; Ntougias, S.; Melidis, P. Renewable energy recovery from sewage sludge derived from chemically enhanced precipitation. *Renew. Energy* **2020**, *162*, 1811–1818. [CrossRef]
20. Black, A.W.; Mote, T.L. Characteristics of winter-precipitation-related transportation fatalities in the United States. *Weather Clim. Soc.* **2015**, *7*, 133–145. [CrossRef]
21. Bucar, R.C.B.; Hayeri, Y.M. Quantitative assessment of the impacts of disruptive precipitation on surface transportation. *Reliab. Eng. Syst. Saf.* **2020**, *203*, 107105. [CrossRef]
22. Safdar, F.; Khokhar, M.F.; Mahmood, F.; Khan, M.Z.A.; Arshad, M. Observed and predicted precipitation variability across Pakistan with special focus on winter and pre-monsoon precipitation. *Environ. Sci. Pollut. Res.* **2023**, *30*, 4510–4530. [CrossRef] [PubMed]
23. Yavuz, H.; Erdoğan, S. Spatial Analysis of Monthly and Annual Precipitation Trends in Turkey. *Water Resour. Manag.* **2012**, *26*, 609–621. [CrossRef]
24. Gonzalez-Gonzalez, M.A.; Guertin, D.P. Seasonal bean yield forecast for non-irrigated croplands through climate and vegetation index data: Geospatial effects. *Int. J. Appl. Earth Obs. Geoinf.* **2021**, *105*, 102623. [CrossRef]
25. da Silva, M.V.; Pandorfi, H.; da Rosa Ferraz Jardim, A.M.; de Oliveira-Júnior, J.F.; da Divincula, J.S.; Giongo, P.R.; da Silva, T.G.F.; de Almeida, G.L.P.; de Albuquerque Moura, G.B.; Lopes, P.M.O. Spatial modeling of rainfall patterns and groundwater on the coast of northeastern Brazil. *Urban Clim.* **2021**, *38*, 100911. [CrossRef]
26. Sigrist, F.; Künsch, H.R.; Stahel, W.A. A dynamic nonstationary spatio-temporal model for short term prediction of precipitation. *Ann. Appl. Stat.* **2012**, *6*, 1452–1477. [CrossRef]
27. BMKG. Analisis Dinamika Atmosfer Dasarian III Mei 2022. 2022. Available online: https://www.bmkg.go.id/iklim/dinamika-atmosfir.bmkg (accessed on 1 May 2022).
28. Hermawan, E.; Lubis, S.W.; Harjana, T.; Purwaningsih, A.; Risyanto; Ridho, A.; Andarini, D.F.; Ratri, D.N.; Widyaningsih, R. Large-Scale Meteorological Drivers of the Extreme Precipitation Event and Devastating Floods of Early-February 2021 in Semarang, Central Java, Indonesia. *Atmosphere* **2022**, *13*, 1092. [CrossRef]
29. Anselin, L. *Spatial Econometrics: Methods and Models*; Springerl: Berlin/Heidelberg, Germany, 1988; Volume 85.
30. LeSage, J. Spatial Econometrics Toolbox. In *Introduction to Spatial Econometrics*; CRC Press: Boca Raton, FL, USA, 1999; p. 273. Available online: http://www.spatial-econometrics.com/ (accessed on 1 May 2022).
31. Pebesma, E.; Graler, B. *Introduction to Spatio-Temporal Variography*; ifgi: Munster, Germany, 2017.
32. Gio, P.U.; Effendie, A.R. *Belajar Bahasa Pemrograman R*; USU Press: Denver, CO, USA, 2018.
33. Lu, G.Y.; Wong, D.W. An adaptive inverse-distance weighting spatial interpolation technique. *Comput. Geosci.* **2008**, *34*, 1044–1055. [CrossRef]
34. Kopczewska, K. *Applied Spatial Statistics and Econometric*; Routledge: Abingdon-on-Thames, UK, 2021.
35. Abdullah, A.S.; Ruchjana, B.N.; Toharudin, T.; Rosadi, R. Model SAR, Ekspansi SAR dan Plot Moran untuk Pemetaan Hasil Akreditasi Sekolah di Provinsi Jawa Barat. In *Prosiding Seminar Nasional Matematika dan Pendidikan Matematika*; UMS: Kota Kinabalu, Malaysia, 2015; pp. 935–943.
36. Ord, K. Estimation methods for models of spatial interaction. *J. Am. Stat. Assoc.* **1975**, *70*, 120–126. [CrossRef]
37. Smirnov, O.; Anselin, L. Fast maximum likelihood estimation of very large spatial autoregressive models: A characteristic polynomial approach. *Comput. Stat. Data Anal.* **2001**, *35*, 301–319. [CrossRef]

38. Robinson, P.M.; Rossi, F. Refinements in maximum likelihood inference on spatial autocorrelation in panel data. *J. Econom.* **2015**, *189*, 447–456. [CrossRef]
39. Qiu, F.; Ding, H.; Hu, J. Asymptotic Properties of Quasi-Maximum Likelihood Estimators for Heterogeneous Spatial Autoregressive Models. *Symmetry* **2022**, *14*, 1894. [CrossRef]
40. Lawrence, K.D.; Klimberg, R.K.; Lawrence, S.M. *Fundamentals of Forecasting Using Excel*; Industrial Press Inc.: New York, NY, USA, 2009.
41. Zhang, C.; Hu, C.; Wu, T.; Zhu, L.; Liu, X. Achieving Efficient and Privacy-Preserving Neural Network Training and Prediction in Cloud Environments. *IEEE Trans. Dependable Secur. Comput.* **2022**, *20*, 4245–4257. [CrossRef]
42. Hu, C.; Zhang, C.; Lei, D.; Wu, T.; Liu, X.; Zhu, L. Achieving Privacy-Preserving and Verifiable Support Vector Machine Training in the Cloud. *IEEE Trans. Inf. Forensics Secur.* **2023**, *18*, 3476–3491. [CrossRef]

Disclaimer/Publisher's Note: The statements, opinions and data contained in all publications are solely those of the individual author(s) and contributor(s) and not of MDPI and/or the editor(s). MDPI and/or the editor(s) disclaim responsibility for any injury to people or property resulting from any ideas, methods, instructions or products referred to in the content.

Article

Dynamically Meaningful Latent Representations of Dynamical Systems

Imran Nasim [1,2,*] and Michael E. Henderson [3]

[1] IBM Research Europe, Winchester SO21 2JN, UK
[2] Department of Mathematics, University of Surrey, Guildford GU2 7XH, UK
[3] IBM Research—Thomas J. Watson Research Center, New York, NY 10598, USA; mhender@us.ibm.com
* Correspondence: imran.nasim@ibm.com

Abstract: Dynamical systems are ubiquitous in the physical world and are often well-described by partial differential equations (PDEs). Despite their formally infinite-dimensional solution space, a number of systems have long time dynamics that live on a low-dimensional manifold. However, current methods to probe the long time dynamics require prerequisite knowledge about the underlying dynamics of the system. In this study, we present a data-driven hybrid modeling approach to help tackle this problem by combining numerically derived representations and latent representations obtained from an autoencoder. We validate our latent representations and show they are dynamically interpretable, capturing the dynamical characteristics of qualitatively distinct solution types. Furthermore, we probe the topological preservation of the latent representation with respect to the raw dynamical data using methods from persistent homology. Finally, we show that our framework is generalizable, having been successfully applied to both integrable and non-integrable systems that capture a rich and diverse array of solution types. Our method does not require any prior dynamical knowledge of the system and can be used to discover the intrinsic dynamical behavior in a purely data-driven way.

Keywords: dynamical systems; autoencoders; latent representation; manifold learning

MSC: 68T99

Citation: Nasim, I.; Henderson, M.E. Dynamically Meaningful Latent Representations of Dynamical Systems. *Mathematics* **2024**, *12*, 476. https://doi.org/10.3390/math12030476

Academic Editor: Qun Li and Aihua Wood

Received: 18 December 2023
Revised: 24 January 2024
Accepted: 26 January 2024
Published: 2 February 2024

Copyright: © 2024 by the authors. Licensee MDPI, Basel, Switzerland. This article is an open access article distributed under the terms and conditions of the Creative Commons Attribution (CC BY) license (https://creativecommons.org/licenses/by/4.0/).

1. Introduction

Nonlinear partial differential equations (PDEs) are prevalent in physics and engineering, serving as powerful tools for describing complex phenomena that exhibit nonlinear behaviors and spatiotemporal chaos. These equations are often very difficult to probe due to the formally infinite dimensional solution space. Practically, this high dimensionality often obscures the underlying behavior of a dynamical system, leading to the model being both difficult to analyze and prohibitively expensive to use for predictions. However, learning a faithful lower-dimensional representation of the high-dimensional data is not a trivial task.

Due to the rapid progress in the field of deep learning, the construction of neural network-based models such as autoencoders has become a popular and powerful technique for non-linear manifold-based dimensionality reduction of PDEs [1,2]. Consequently, such progress has spurred significant endeavors to develop techniques that directly learn low-dimensional dynamical models from time series data [3–7]. Very recently, there has been some effort to use autoencoder-based architectures to estimate the intrinsic dimensionality of a dynamical system [8–10]. The motivation for this is largely based on the so-called *Manifold Hypothesis*, which posits that high-dimensional data often lie on or near low-dimensional manifolds [11]. The rigorous analysis of a number of physical systems seems to support this hypothesis [12,13]. Despite the formal infinite dimensionality of the PDE state space, dissipative systems are hypothesized to exhibit long-term behavior that converges to a finite-dimensional invariant manifold [14,15]. Clearly, understanding this invariant manifold is of critical importance as it plays a crucial role in determining the system's overall dynamics over time. However, studying and classifying the long time dynamics of a dynamical system is a challenging task. In the case of comparatively simple and deterministic ordinary differential equations (ODEs), the dynamics may exhibit complicated behavior with strong random features commonly referred to as *deterministic chaos* [16–18]. This has prompted the development of many methods to investigate the cause of such behavior including, but not limited to, hyperbolic theory, bifurcation, and attractor theory [19–21]. PDEs are even more complex due to the presence of infinite-dimensional dynamics and require careful and sophisticated analysis methods [15,22,23]. This has led to the production of advanced analysis tools to probe the behavior of dynamical systems [24–26]. Although these tools offer great utility, they necessitate a prerequisite understanding of the underlying dynamics in order to effectively achieve the objective of 'finding what you are looking for'. In this study, we aim to provide a hybrid approach using the autoencoder architecture and validating the inherent latent representations using mathematical representations derived from the numerical simulations of the system. We show that our approach captures the nature of the underlying dynamics for a variety of solution types. Additionally, we probe the question of what topological features are preserved in the latent representation with respect to the raw data using methods from persistent homology. A key part of our framework is that it is purely data-driven, enabling the technique to be used to discover the intrinsic dynamical behavior of systems without the need to have prerequisite knowledge about the underlying dynamics.

The structure of the paper is as follows. In Section 2, we introduce the mathematical models we consider in this study. In Section 3, we probe the long time dynamics of these models using numerical experiments. In Section 4, we introduce the autoencoder model architecture and present our results. Finally, in Section 6, we present our discussion.

2. Models

2.1. fKdV Equation

The forced Korteweg–de Vries (fKdV) is used, for example, to model weakly non-linear flow in a channel with a bump or disturbance in the channel depth [27]. There exists a number of possible solutions for a given type of disturbance. For simplicity, we will assume here no disturbance, which is equivalent to setting the forcing term to zero. Under this assumption, the fKdV can be written as [28]:

$$6u_t + u_{xxx} + (9u - 6(F-1))u_x = 0, \tag{1}$$

where F is the depth-based Froude number.

Let us assume an initial condition that takes the form $u(x,0) = A\cos(kx + \phi)$. Here, A, k, and ϕ are amplitude, wavenumber, and phase shift parameters, respectively.

Consider a transformation where $v(X, T) = Au(x, t)$ and where $X = kx$ and $T = kt$. We can now re-write the original fKdV in terms of our function v using the chain rule. This results in:

$$6v_T + k^2 v_{XXX} + (9Av - 6(F-1))v_X = 0, \tag{2}$$

where $v(X,0) = \cos(X + \phi)$. From Equation (2), we can see that the amplitude parameter A acts as a direct measure of the strength of the non-linear operator (vv_X), whereas the wavenumber parameter squared (k^2) is a measure with the strength of the third-order linear dispersive term (v_{XXX}). We can define a relative non-linearity term κ where $\kappa = A/k^2$ from the reformulation given in Equation (2). We expect to be in a dispersive regime for small values of $\kappa < 1$ and to be in a nonlinear regime for $\kappa \gtrsim 1$. The importance of this reformulation is that it allows us to consider a physically motivated set of initial conditions rather than some generic functional form. Note that Equation (2) is invariant to phase shifts. If $v(x,t)$ is a trajectory, so is $v(x + \phi, t)$.

2.2. Kuramoto–Sivashinksy Equation

The Kuramoto–Sivashinsky (KS hereafter) equation is a non-integrable, nonlinear PDE that can be used to model the evolution of surface waves and pattern formation for a number of physical systems [29]. The equation can be written as:

$$u_t + uu_x + u_{xx} + \nu u_{xxxx} = 0,\qquad(3)$$

where ν is a coefficient of viscosity. The KS equation captures the dynamics of spatio-temporal instabilities, such as those seen in flame fronts and fluid flows, and, due to non-integrability, gives rise to a rich array of long time dynamics for different values of ν. For example, in the case where $\nu = \frac{16}{71}$, the KS equation exhibits bursting dynamics [30], whereas for $\nu = \frac{16}{337}$, the KS equation exhibits beating traveling wave dynamics [31].

3. Long Time Dynamics

3.1. fKdV: Effects of Amplitude and Wavenumber

To investigate the nature of the long-term dynamics, we considered the fKdV under periodic boundary conditions with the domain of $-2\pi \leq x \leq 2\pi$ ($L = 4\pi$), and we considered an initial condition of the form $u(x,0) = A\cos(kx + \phi)$, where we fixed $A = 0.5$, $k = 1.0$ and $\phi = 1.0$. We fixed the value of the Froude number $F = 1.5$. All integrations were performed on a grid of 128 points using an explicit RK finite-difference scheme with a tolerance of 10^{-6}, which was compared to a pseudo-spectral method to ensure accuracy. To assess the effects of the amplitude and wavenumber, we chose two setups: (i) varying the amplitude and keeping the wavenumber and phase fixed (varying the phase under periodic conditions corresponds to a phase shift of the periodic domain and hence does not affect the dynamics; we also observed this within our simulations); and (ii) varying the wavenumber and keeping the amplitude and phase fixed. The integrations were performed for $T = 400$ units for amplitudes $A \in (0,1]$.

To visualize the trajectories, we consider the evolution of both the speed and distance as plotted in Figure 1. Interestingly, we observe that, for smallest amplitude case $A = 0.25$, the evolution closely resembles a closed orbit, which is expected for a purely periodic motion (this was verified by running numerical integrations with smaller amplitudes). However, this characteristic changes significantly with increasing amplitude, where we observe quasi-periodic motion in speed–distance space. This behavior appears to correlate with the strength of the amplitude parameter, with larger amplitude initial conditions leading to non-periodicity. The quasi-periodic motion arises where two or more soliton frequencies are incommensurate [32]. We note that, for the transformed equation in Equation (2), the strength of this characteristic appears to correlate with the relative non-linearity term κ.

To further investigate this behavior, we proceeded to fix the amplitude and phase, then vary the value of the wavenumber k. The results for those numerical simulations are presented in Figure 2. Here, we observe that, when we increase the wavenumber by a factor of two, the initial quasi-periodic behavior quickly forms into a more pure periodic motion resembling circular motion in distance–speed space. This characteristic further supports the observation that the relative non-linearity essentially measures the strength of the quasi-periodicity, with weak relative non-linearity leading to pure periodic motion.

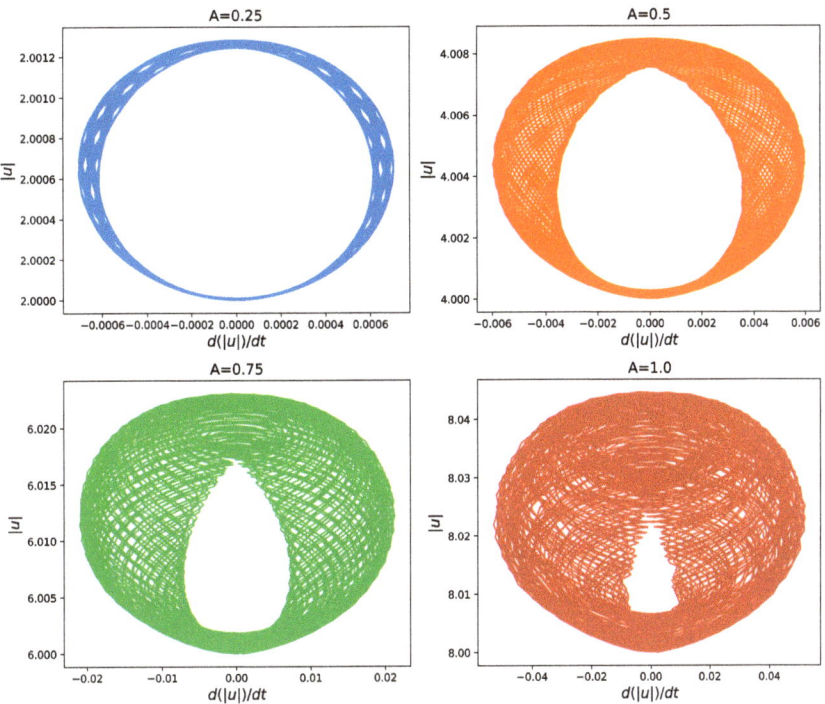

Figure 1. Evolutions of trajectories in distance–speed space for initial conditions evolved under the fKdV equation for different initial amplitude values. $A = 0.25$ (**upper left panel**), $A = 0.50$ (**upper right panel**), $A = 0.75$ (**lower left panel**), $A = 1.00$ (**lower right panel**).

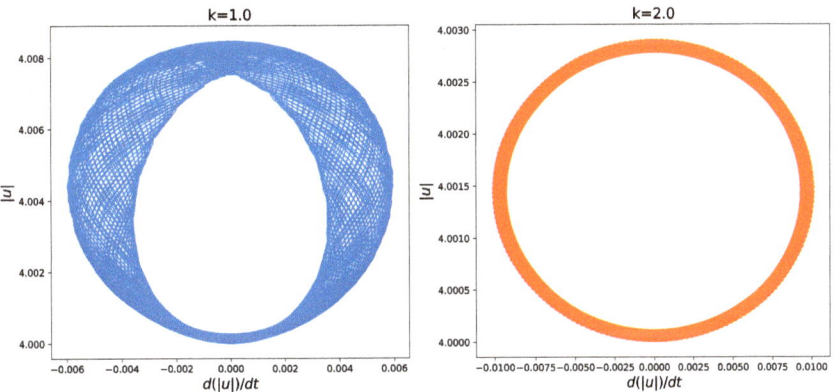

Figure 2. Evolutions of trajectories in distance–speed space for initial conditions evolved under the fKdV equation for different initial wavenumber values. $k = 1.0$ (**left panel**), $k = 2.0$ (**right panel**).

3.2. KS: Long Time Dynamics

We simulate the KS equation on a discretized grid with 64 grid points on a periodic domain $-\pi \leq x \leq \pi$ ($L = 2\pi$). As with the fKdV setup, we considered an initial condition of the form $u(x, 0) = A\cos(kx + \phi)$, where we fixed $A = 0.5$, $k = 1.0$, and $\phi = 1.0$. As we are interested in the long time dynamics, we evolved all models for $T = 400$ units to ensure all of the transients have died out. We consider two setups to reproduce the bursting dynamics and the beating traveling dynamics of the KS equation, setting $\nu = \frac{16}{71}$ and $\nu = \frac{16}{337}$, respectively. We plot the long time evolution of the wave profiles in Figure 3.

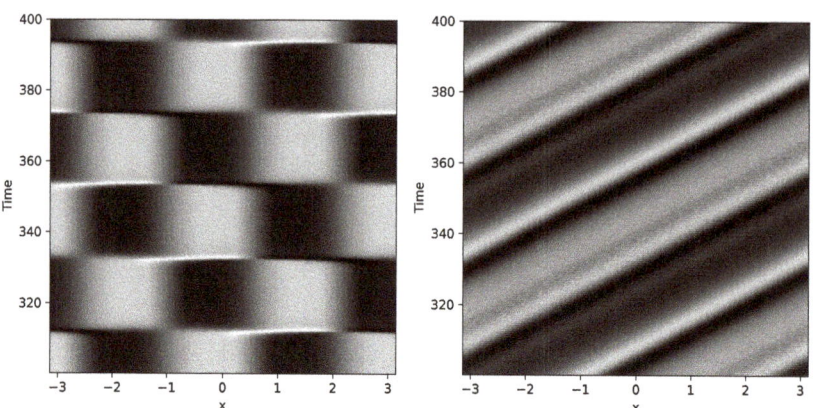

Figure 3. Long time wave profiles for the KS equation. Bursting dynamics (**left panel**) where $\nu = \frac{16}{71}$, and beating traveling wave dynamics (**right panel**) where $\nu = \frac{16}{337}$.

From dynamical systems theory, we know that the bursting dynamics in the KS equation arise as the state appears to switch between two saddle points that are connected by four heteroclinic orbits [33]. This can be observed if we project the trajectory onto the two dominant Fourier modes, which is shown in the left panel of Figure 4. Here, we observe that this representation indeed captures the two saddle points and four heteroclinic connections. We observe that the trajectories tend to spend a majority of the time around the saddle points and appear to travel quickly on the heteroclinic connections pseudo-randomly, which supports the sudden bursting transitions seen in the wave profiles in Figure 3.

In the case of the beating traveling wave dynamics exhibited by the KS equation, we know that this dynamical behavior arises as the traveling period and beating period are out of phase [31]. This causes the orbit to follow quasi-periodic motion. To see if we are able to extract a low-dimensional representation that captures this characteristic, we project the trajectory into the two dominant Fourier modes, as shown in right panel of Figure 4. We clearly observe a quasi-periodic structure within this Fourier representation, which is supportive of the fact that the periodic orbit and beating period are incommensurate.

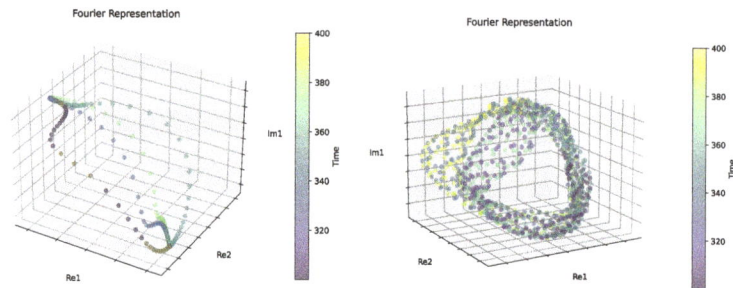

Figure 4. Fourier representation of the long time dynamics on the two leading spatial modes. Bursting dynamics (**left panel**) where $\nu = \frac{16}{71}$, and beating traveling wave dynamics (**right panel**) where $\nu = \frac{16}{337}$. Re1 and Re2 represent the real component of the first and second most dominant Fourier modes, respectively, while Im1 represents the imaginary component of the first dominant mode.

4. Interpretable Deep Learning-Based Reduced Order Model

Autoencoders have become a popular method for dimensionality reduction within the scientific community as a technique to obtain reduced order models. Autoencoders are incredibly versatile architectures. A single-layer autoencoder with a linear activation function is equivalent to Principal Component Analysis (PCA); however, multi-layered architectures with non-linear activations can perform complex non-linear dimensionality reduction. Fundamentally, autoencoders are composed of two deep neural networks, called the *encoder* and *decoder*, which are connected by a latent layer commonly referred to as the *latent space*. A schematic of a classical autoencoder is given in Figure 5.

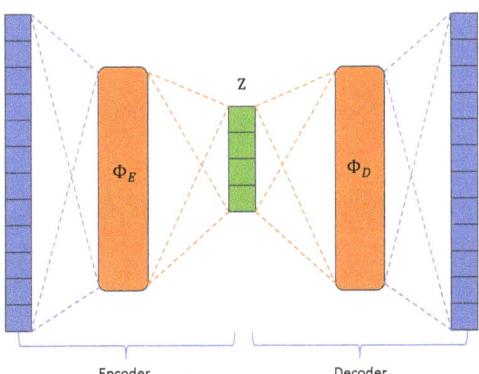

Figure 5. Schematic of the classical autoencoder architecture highlighting the encoder, decoder, and latent space (green) components.

This latent space is a bottleneck that sets the number of dimensions available to represent the input data. The encoder maps the inputs to the smaller latent space $d_z < d_i$,

$$\Phi_E(u; \theta_E) : \mathbb{R}^{d_i} \to \mathbb{R}^{d_z}, \tag{4}$$

where θ_E represents the parameters defining the encoder. The decoder maps the latent space back to: $\mathbb{R}^{d_i}$

$$\Phi_D(z; \theta_D) : \mathbb{R}^{d_z} \to \mathbb{R}^{d_i}. \tag{5}$$

The encoder reduces the dimension, and if the composition of these two mappings is the identity mapping, the decoder is the inverse of the encoder, and the encoding is one-to-one. For PCA, θ_E is an orthonormal $d_z \times (d_i + 1)$ matrix, $\Phi_E(u) = \theta_E[u\ 1]^T$, and $\Phi_D(u) = [u\ 1]\theta_E^T$. The extra dimension and the vector $[u\ 1]$ center the fit by adding a shift. Training the autoencoder on input/output pairs (u, u) minimizes the loss function in Equation (6) and forces Φ_E and Φ_D to be approximate inverses:

$$\mathcal{L}(u; \theta_E; \theta_D) = \|u - \Phi_D(\Phi_E(u; \theta_E); \theta_D)\|_2^2, \tag{6}$$

where $\|\cdot\|_2$ is the l_2 norm.

While autoencoders have obtained many impressive results, they are inherently data-driven, often leading to poor interpretability of the latent space. To probe the latent representation, we adopt a classical autoencoder architecture where the input data are the wave profile from our numerical simulation at each time interval t_i. In the case of the fKdV models, this corresponds to input data $u \in \mathbb{R}^{128}$, where we consider a latent dimension $d_z = 3$ that can be used to visualize the representation. For further details about the autoencoder model architecture and network parameters, please refer to Appendix A.

4.1. fKdV Latent Representation

A clear characteristic we inferred from the numerical simulations of the fKdV models presented in Section 3.1 was that the relative non-linearity term κ significantly influenced the type of long time dynamics, from purely periodic to strongly quasi-periodic. An important open question we aim to answer is whether the latent space of the autoencoder is able to capture and hence represent such qualitatively different dynamics. To this end, we construct the latent representation obtained from the suite of numerical simulations for the fKdV models with varying amplitudes. To focus on the representation of the long time dynamics, we train the autoencoder on the simulation data between $T = 300$ and $T = 400$. We plot the original wave profile data with the corresponding latent representations in Figure 6. To our surprise, the representations obtained from the autoencoder appear to capture the qualitatively different dynamics, with the representations showing periodic motion for small amplitude models and quasi-periodic tori for larger amplitude cases (we confirmed this characteristic was present for the entire suite of numerical simulations we performed). This result is in direct agreement with the results obtained from analyzing the numerical simulations directly using the representation in distance–speed space. It is important to state that our autoencoder model is completely data-driven and has no prior information about the model being considered, yet it is able to extract representations that are dynamically meaningful.

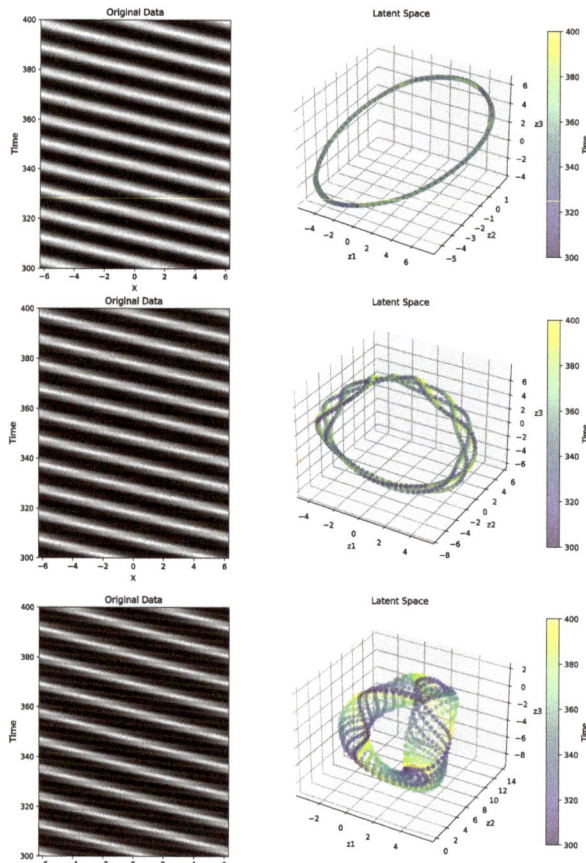

Figure 6. Original wave profiles (**left column**) obtained from the numerical simulations of the fKdV and their corresponding latent space representations (**right column**) obtained using the autoencoder. Upper to lower plot: $A = 0.11$, $A = 0.26$, $A = 0.47$.

4.2. KS Latent Representation

In Section 3.2, we described two dynamically distinct solution types to the KS equation, namely, the bursting dynamics and beating traveling dynamics. Using a projection onto the first few Fourier modes, we were able to obtain a low-dimensional representation that captured the dynamical characteristics of the full order numerical simulation in a dynamically interpretable way. A natural question we aim to answer in this section is whether we are able to extract an interpretable latent representation of these more complex dynamics using our autoencoder architecture. To tackle this question, we consider a similar approach to that which we used in the case of the fKdV. As we are focused on the long time dynamics, we train the autoencoder on the simulation data between $T = 300$ and $T = 400$. The wave profiles from the numerical simulation with the corresponding latent space representations for the bursting and beating traveling dynamics are presented in Figure 7. Strikingly, we observe that the latent representation from the autoencoder trained on the bursting dynamics data almost perfectly resembles that of the Fourier representation we showed in Figure 4. This latent representation obtained from the autoencoder has captured the characteristics of the two saddle points in addition to the four heteroclinic connections, which is in direct agreement with the results obtained from the full numerical simulation. For the case of the beating traveling wave dynamics, the latent representation obtained from the autoencoder extracts a quasi-periodic representation in the latent space, which can be observed in the lower right panel of Figure 7. This quasi-periodic latent representation is in agreement with the dynamical theory and the numerically derived results in Section 3.2. It is important to note that, although the autoencoder is purely data-driven, the representation is clearly dynamically interpretable.

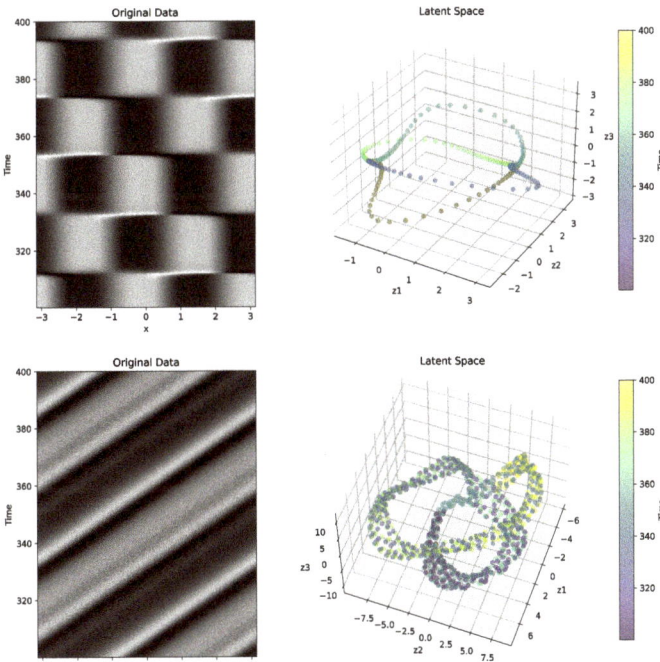

Figure 7. Original wave profiles from the numerical simulation (**left panels**) and their corresponding latent representations obtained from the autoencoder. Bursting dynamics (**upper panels**) where $\nu = \frac{16}{71}$ and beating traveling wave dynamics (**lower panels**) where $\nu = \frac{16}{337}$.

5. Topology Preservation

In the previous section, we have shown how we can use an autoencoder to obtain dynamically interpretable latent space embeddings, motivating the use of this architecture as a tool to probe the intrinsic dynamics in a purely data-driven way. However, while we have demonstrated the interpretability, we have not investigated the qualitative properties captured in the latent space with respect to the raw high-dimensional data. To address this question, we probe the nature of the topological features in both the raw data and latent representations using persistent homology. In the following subsection, we provide a very brief overview of the concepts used in this section to probe the topological features. For a deeper overview, we refer the reader to [34].

5.1. Persistent Homology

Topological data analysis gives away of classifying point clouds by connecting points across a range of scales and studying how the topology of the result changes. We give a broad overview of the technique below. A more detailed overview may be found in [35].

A classical way to represent the topology of discrete structures such as point clouds P is via simplicial complexes, which are a collection of smaller components called simplices. A 0-simplex is a single point, a 1-simplex an edge, and a 2-simplex a triangle with higher-order simplices having well-defined structures. Homology provides topologists with a formalized method for quantifying the presence of n-dimensional holes within a space [36]. The ith homology group $H_i(P)$ of P contains topological features of dimension i which, for the cases of $d = 0$ and $d = 1$, are connected components and cycles/tunnels, respectively.

Persistent homology is a computational technique used in topological data analysis that takes in an input of increasing sequences of spaces ($P : P_0 \subsetneq P_1 \subsetneq \cdots \subsetneq P_L$) referred to as a *filtration*. The idea behind persistent homology is that it extends the homology of simplicial complexes by considering the changes in homology groups over multiple scales of the distance metric, specifically connectivity-based features like connected components [34,37]. The common way this is done is via the construction of the Vietoris–Rips (VR) complex [38], which contains all the simplices of the point cloud at a given scale ϵ whose elements satisfy $d_{ij} < \epsilon$, where d_{ij} is the distance metric between two points in the point cloud ($x_i, x_j \in P$). As the construction of the VR complex only requires the distances between points, it enables us to track changes in the homology groups for different ϵ values, up to a maximum value ϵ_m, in which the connectivity remains the same. This enables us to obtain a measure of what homology groups are formed and destroyed at different ϵ values. A common way to visualize these features is via a persistence diagram. The i-dimensional persistence diagram of a VR complex contains coordinates of the form (b, d), where b refers to the value at which a topological feature of dimension i is 'birthed' in the VR complex, and d refers to the value at which it has 'died'. The intuition is that relevant topological characteristics, including connected components and voids associated with the Betti numbers for each simplex in the selected filtration, are monitored. It becomes possible to observe the duration of persistence of these topological features in the diagram as the parameter ϵ increases. Naturally, as the radius ϵ becomes sufficiently large, all pairs of points will fall within this radius, resulting in a single connected component and the absence of voids. To interpret the persistence diagram, each coordinate (b, d) denotes a topological feature being born at radius b and "dying" at radius d, where the death can be thought of as a homological feature getting filled in with a lower-dimensional simplex. From the diagram, one can measure the persistence of a feature that can be defined as $d - b$. This value describes how "long", with respect to radius, a topological feature exists before it is filled in.

A common way to measure the similarity between persistence diagrams is using the Wasserstein distance, which is a form of an optimal transport metric. The basic idea is that we can consider all possible transportation mechanisms for moving the points within one persistence diagram to the other one, a process called matching. A cost is associated with each transportation mechanism, where the distance is the infimum of these cost values [39]. Mathematically, it can be expressed as [40]:

$$W_p(d_1, d_2) = \left(\inf_\gamma \sum_{(x,y) \in \gamma} |\|x\| - \|y\||^p \right)^{\frac{1}{p}}, \tag{7}$$

where γ ranges over all bijective mappings from persistence diagram d_1 to d_2.

5.2. Persistence Diagrams

To compute and compare the persistence diagrams of both the raw higher-dimensional dynamical data and the latent representation obtained from the autoencoder, we restrict the analysis to homology groups up to the dimension of the latent space ($d = 3$). We note that, while we expect higher-dimensional topological features to be present in the raw higher-dimensional data, these are not captured in the latent representation due to the reduced dimensionality. Hence, for comparative purposes, we do not consider this analysis. Figure 8 shows the persistence diagrams for the different dynamical models considered in this study, in which the left column represents the diagrams obtained from the raw data and the right column from the latent representation obtained via the autoencoder. In the case of the traveling wave fKdV data (upper panels), we observe the similarity in the grouping of distinct homology groups. There appears to be larger number of H_1 points from the latent data, but as these lie close to the *Birth* equals *Death* line, these are likely artifacts. More importantly, however, in both the raw and latent diagrams, there appears to be a single long persistent H_1 point showing a topological consistency. (The long persistent H_0 point on all diagrams is just an artifact of the algorithm and has no topological significance.) For the case of the KS bursting dynamics model, we observe a qualitatively identical persistence diagram between the raw and latent data. The distinct homology groupings match exceedingly well and clearly show the two persistent H_1 points in both diagrams. In the bottom panel of Figure 8, we observe the persistence diagrams of the KS beating dynamics. These diagrams appear slightly more complex compared to the other models, where the consistency between the raw and latent representations appears to be less well-defined. Upon closer inspection, we see the vast majority of points for both cases lie close to the *Birth* equals *Death* line and hence arise from noise. In the case of both the raw and latent representations, we see two long-persisting H_1 points, which shows topological agreement; however, we do notice a short time persistence H_2 point in the latent persistence diagram, which we do not observe in the profile of the raw data. Due to the short persistence, this feature is likely due to noise.

We then compute the Wasserstein distance between each pair of persistence diagrams for the different dynamical models. From this, we obtain $W_{fKdV} = 113.4$, $W_{KSt} = 260.6$, and $W_{KSb} = 5.3$, where the subscripts correspond to the models being considered, namely the fKdV, KS beating traveling wave, and KS bursting dynamics. These quantitative metrics support the qualitative features we observe in the persistence diagrams seen in Figure 8.

We acknowledge here that work has been done to include topology-preserving methodologies within the autoencoder architecture using the idea of persistence homology, perhaps most prominently by [41]. However, while this work proposes a topological loss term based on the topological differences between persistence diagrams of the input and latent data, the persistent homology of the vanilla autoencoder was not investigated. Additionally, it was found in this study that the MSE of the vanilla autoencoder generally outperformed the topological autoencoder. To our knowledge, the topological properties of the vanilla autoencoder architecture have not been investigated using persistent homology, and we believe we are the first to give empirical evidence in this area.

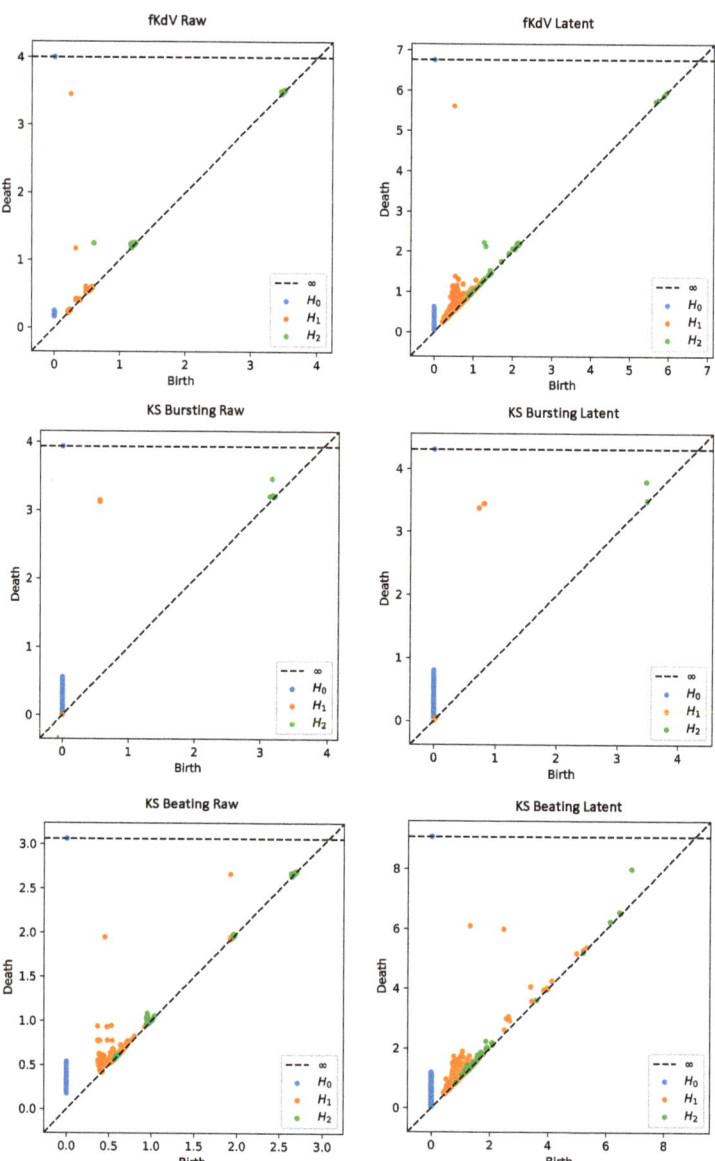

Figure 8. Persistence diagrams for the point cloud data from different dynamical models: (i) fkdv (upper panels); (ii) KS bursting dynamics (middle panels); (iii) KS beating traveling waves (lower panels). Results for the raw high-dimensional dynamical data (**left column**) and the latent representation obtained from the autoencoder (**right column**).

6. Discussion

In this study, we have developed a hybrid framework to probe the long time dynamics of dynamical systems using a combination of mathematical representations directly obtained from the numerical simulation data and the latent representation captured within the latent space of an autoencoder. The autoencoder architecture implemented in this study is purely data-driven and contains no prior information about the dynamics. In order to determine whether this framework can be generalized to arbitrary dynamical systems, we applied our methodology to both integrable and non-integrable systems that capture a rich and diverse array of solution types. Using the results from dynamical systems theory and mathematically motivated representations of the numerical simulation data, we validated that the latent representations from the autoencoder are in fact dynamically interpretable for qualitatively distinct dynamics. We show that the latent representations capture all of the qualitative dynamical characteristics present within the full order numerical simulation data though having a dimension significantly less than the full order data. We used this framework to help classify the long time dynamics of the fKdV equation using a physically motivated reformulation which, to our knowledge, is the first time this has been done. Additionally, we investigated the topological features in the latent representation of the autoencoder with respect to the raw data both qualitatively and quantitatively using persistent homology which, to our knowledge, is a novel contribution. It is important to note that this framework is generic in nature and provides clear and interpretable insights into the long time dynamics of PDE-based models without the need for vigorous mathematics. Additionally, a key part of our framework is that it does not require prior dynamical knowledge of the system being considered and hence can be used to discover the underlying dynamical behavior in a purely data-driven way. We hope to extend this framework to incorporate naturally derived geometrical information from PDE-based models, which we will present in a subsequent study.

Author Contributions: I.N. (Conceptualization: Lead; Data curation: Lead; Formal analysis: Lead; Funding acquisition: Lead; Investigation: Lead; Methodology: Lead; Project administration: Equal; Resources: Lead; Software: Lead; Supervision: Equal; Validation: Lead; Visualization: Lead; Writing—original draft: Lead; Writing—review & editing: Lead). M.E.H. (Methodology: Supporting; Supervision: Supporting; Validation: Supporting; Writing—review & editing: Supporting). All authors have read and agreed to the published version of the manuscript.

Funding: Imran Nasim acknowledges a UKRI Future Leaders Fellowship for support through the grant MR/T041862/1. The authors declare that no other funds, grants, or support were received during the preparation of this manuscript.

Data Availability Statement: The datasets generated during and/or analysed during the current study are available in the 'Numerical Data for fkdv and KS equations' repository, https://zenodo.org/records/10309413, accessed on 8 December 2023.

Conflicts of Interest: The authors declare no conflicts of interest.

Appendix A. Autoencoder Model Architecture and Parameters

The parameters used in the autoencoder architecture are listed in Table A1. The autoencoders are trained using the Adam optimizer with a learning rate of 10^{-3}. All input data are MinMax scaled, which is why we use a Sigmoid activation function in the final layer of the decoder. The MSE of the training loss for all of the models presented in this study was on the order of magnitude of 10^{-4}.

Table A1. Parameters used in neural networks for the autoencoder where d_i is the input dimension and d_z is the latent dimension. The "Dimension" column describes the dimension of each layer, and the "Activation" column describes the activation functions between layers. The "Epochs" column describes the number of epochs used for training.

Component	Dimension	Activations	Epochs
Encoder	d_i:32:64:32:d_z	Linear:ReLU:Linear:ReLU:Linear	1000
Decoder	d_z:32:64:32:d_i	Linear:ReLU:Linear:ReLU:Linear:Sigmoid	1000

Appendix B. Bifurcation Classification of the fKdV

Here, we classify the bifurcation for the fKdV equation given in Equation (1) under the steady state assumption which, to our knowledge, has not been explicitly stated.

Let us consider the standard form of the fKdV given in Equation (1). In the case of traveling waves $u(x,t) = u(\epsilon)$ with $\epsilon = x - ct$ and under the assumption of natural boundary conditions, we can turn this into a two-dimensional system that can be written as:

$$\begin{cases} u' = v \\ v' = 6u(c + F - 1) - \dfrac{9}{2}u^2 = h(u) \end{cases}. \tag{A1}$$

To find the equilibrium points, we can solve $v'(u) = 0$, which leads to $u_0 = 0$ and $u_1 = \frac{4}{3}(c + F - 1)$. To classify these equilibrium points, we can solve the linearized equation $J\mathbf{v} = \lambda \mathbf{v}$. This results in $\det(J - \lambda)$, which can be expressed as:

$$\det \begin{bmatrix} -\lambda & 1 \\ h'(u) & -\lambda \end{bmatrix}. \tag{A2}$$

Hence, the resulting characteristic equation is $\lambda^2 - h'(u) = 0$.

This results in the eigenvalues $\lambda_0 = \pm\sqrt{6(c + F - 1)}$ and $\lambda_1 = \pm\sqrt{(-6(c + F - 1))}$. The first eigenvalue λ_0 is purely imaginary if $c + F < 1$ and purely real if $c + F > 1$, which is converse to the second eigenvalue λ_1, which is purely imaginary if $c + F > 1$ and purely real if $c + F < 1$. For the case of the two-equilibrium points $u = 0$ and $u = \frac{4}{3}(c + F - 1)$, the Jacobian has a double eigenvalue, which implies a *Bogdanov–Takens* bifurcation [42].

References

1. Champion, K.; Lusch, B.; Kutz, J.N.; Brunton, S.L. Data-driven discovery of coordinates and governing equations. *Proc. Natl. Acad. Sci. USA* **2019**, *116*, 22445–22451. [CrossRef]
2. Maulik, R.; Lusch, B.; Balaprakash, P. Reduced-order modeling of advection-dominated systems with recurrent neural networks and convolutional autoencoders. *Phys. Fluids* **2021**, *33*, 037106. [CrossRef]
3. Brunton, S.L.; Proctor, J.L.; Kutz, J.N. Discovering governing equations from data by sparse identification of nonlinear dynamical systems. *Proc. Natl. Acad. Sci. USA* **2016**, *113*, 3932–3937. [CrossRef] [PubMed]
4. Lusch, B.; Kutz, J.N.; Brunton, S.L. Deep learning for universal linear embeddings of nonlinear dynamics. *Nat. Commun.* **2018**, *9*, 4950. [CrossRef]
5. Raissi, M.; Perdikaris, P.; Karniadakis, G. Physics-informed neural networks: A deep learning framework for solving forward and inverse problems involving nonlinear partial differential equations. *J. Comput. Phys.* **2019**, *378*, 686–707. [CrossRef]
6. Lee, K.; Carlberg, K.T. Model reduction of dynamical systems on nonlinear manifolds using deep convolutional autoencoders. *J. Comput. Phys.* **2020**, *404*, 108973. [CrossRef]
7. Linot, A.J.; Graham, M.D. Deep learning to discover and predict dynamics on an inertial manifold. *Phys. Rev. E* **2020**, *101*, 062209. [CrossRef] [PubMed]
8. Schonsheck, S.; Chen, J.; Lai, R. Chart auto-encoders for manifold structured data. *arXiv* **2019**, arXiv:1912.10094.
9. Floryan, D.; Graham, M.D. Data-driven discovery of intrinsic dynamics. *Nat. Mach. Intell.* **2022**, *4*, 1113–1120. [CrossRef]
10. Zeng, K.; Graham, M.D. Autoencoders for discovering manifold dimension and coordinates in data from complex dynamical systems. *arXiv* **2023**, arXiv:2305.01090.
11. Fefferman, C.; Mitter, S.; Narayanan, H. Testing the manifold hypothesis. *J. Am. Math. Soc.* **2016**, *29*, 983–1049. [CrossRef]
12. Foias, C.; Sell, G.R.; Temam, R. Inertial manifolds for nonlinear evolutionary equations. *J. Differ. Equ.* **1988**, *73*, 309–353. [CrossRef]
13. Temam, R.; Wang, X. Estimates On The Lowest Dimension Of Inertial Manifolds For The Kuramoto-Sivasbinsky Equation in The General Case. *Differ. Integral Equ.* **1994**, *7*, 1095–1108.
14. Chepyzhov, V.V.; Višik, M.I. *Attractors for Equations of Mathematical Physics*; Number 49 in Colloquium Publications; American Mathematical Society: Providence, RI, USA, 2002.
15. Zelik, S. Attractors. Then and now. *arXiv* **2022**, arXiv:2208.12101.
16. Tutueva, A.; Nepomuceno, E.G.; Moysis, L.; Volos, C.; Butusov, D. Adaptive Chaotic Maps in Cryptography Applications. In *Cybersecurity: A New Approach Using Chaotic Systems*; Abd El-Latif, A.A., Volos, C., Eds.; Springer International Publishing: Cham, Switzerland, 2022; pp. 193–205.
17. Neamah, A.A.; Shukur, A.A. A Novel Conservative Chaotic System Involved in Hyperbolic Functions and Its Application to Design an Efficient Colour Image Encryption Scheme. *Symmetry* **2023**, *15*, 1511. [CrossRef]
18. Li, R.; Lu, T.; Wang, H.; Zhou, J.; Ding, X.; Li, Y. The Ergodicity and Sensitivity of Nonautonomous Discrete Dynamical Systems. *Mathematics* **2023**, *11*, 1384. [CrossRef]
19. Ruelle, D. Small random perturbations of dynamical systems and the definition of attractors. *Commun. Math. Phys.* **1981**, *82*, 137–151. [CrossRef]

20. Katok, A.; Hasselblatt, B. *Introduction to the Modern Theory of Dynamical Systems*; Number 54; Cambridge University Press: Cambridge, MA, USA, 1995.
21. Guckenheimer, J.; Holmes, P. *Nonlinear Oscillations, Dynamical Systems, and Bifurcations of Vector Fields*; Springer: Berlin/Heidelberg, Germany, 2013; Volume 42.
22. Raugel, G. *Global Attractors in Partial Diffenrential Equations*; Département de Mathématique, Université de Paris-Sud: Orsay, France, 2001.
23. Mielke, A.; Zelik, S.V. Infinite-Dimensional Hyperbolic Sets and Spatio-Temporal Chaos in Reaction Diffusion Systems in. *J. Dyn. Differ. Equ.* **2007**, *19*, 333–389. [CrossRef]
24. Doedel, E.J.; Champneys, A.R.; Fairgrieve, T.; Kuznetsov, Y.; Oldeman, B.; Paffenroth, R.; Sandstede, B.; Wang, X.; Zhang, C. Auto-07p: Continuation and Bifurcation Software for Ordinary Differential Equations. 2007. Available online: http://indy.cs.concordia.ca/auto (accessed on 10 September 2023).
25. Dhooge, A.; Govaerts, W.; Kuznetsov, Y.A.; Meijer, H.G.E.; Sautois, B. New features of the software MatCont for bifurcation analysis of dynamical systems. *Math. Comput. Model. Dyn. Syst.* **2008**, *14*, 147–175. [CrossRef]
26. Dankowicz, H.; Schilder, F. *Recipes for Continuation*; SIAM: Philadelphia, PA, USA, 2013.
27. Binder, B.; Vanden-Broeck, J.M. Free surface flows past surfboards and sluice gates. *Eur. J. Appl. Math.* **2005**, *16*, 601–619. [CrossRef]
28. Binder, B.J. Steady Two-Dimensional Free-Surface Flow Past Disturbances in an Open Channel: Solutions of the Korteweg–De Vries Equation and Analysis of the Weakly Nonlinear Phase Space. *Fluids* **2019**, *4*, 24. [CrossRef]
29. Kuramoto, Y. Diffusion-Induced Chaos in Reaction Systems. *Prog. Theor. Phys. Suppl.* **1978**, *64*, 346–367. [CrossRef]
30. Kirby, M.; Armbruster, D. Reconstructing phase space from PDE simulations. *Z. Angew. Math. Phys.* **1992**, *43*, 999–1022. [CrossRef]
31. Rowley, C.W.; Marsden, J.E. Reconstruction equations and the Karhunen–Loève expansion for systems with symmetry. *Phys. D Nonlinear Phenom.* **2000**, *142*, 1–19. [CrossRef]
32. Lax, P.D. Almost periodic solutions of the KdV equation. *SIAM Rev.* **1976**, *18*, 351–375. [CrossRef]
33. Kevrekidis, I.G.; Nicolaenko, B.; Scovel, J.C. Back in the saddle again: A computer assisted study of the Kuramoto–Sivashinsky equation. *SIAM J. Appl. Math.* **1990**, *50*, 760–790. [CrossRef]
34. Otter, N.; Porter, M.A.; Tillmann, U.; Grindrod, P.; Harrington, H.A. A roadmap for the computation of persistent homology. *EPJ Data Sci.* **2017**, *6*, 1–38. [CrossRef]
35. Chazal, F.; Michel, B. An Introduction to Topological Data Analysis: Fundamental and Practical Aspects for Data Scientists. *Front. Artif. Intell.* **2021**, *4*. [CrossRef]
36. Rubio, J.; Sergeraert, F. Constructive algebraic topology. *Bull. Des Sci. Math.* **2002**, *126*, 389–412. [CrossRef]
37. Edelsbrunner, H.; Letscher, D.; Zomorodian, A. Topological persistence and simplification. *Discret. Comput. Geom.* **2002**, *28*, 511–533. [CrossRef]
38. Vietoris, L. Über den höheren Zusammenhang kompakter Räume und eine Klasse von zusammenhangstreuen Abbildungen. *Math. Ann.* **1927**, *97*, 454–472. [CrossRef]
39. Skraba, P.; Turner, K. Wasserstein stability for persistence diagrams. *arXiv* **2020**, arXiv:2006.16824.
40. Mileyko, Y.; Mukherjee, S.; Harer, J. Probability measures on the space of persistence diagrams. *Inverse Probl.* **2011**, *27*, 124007. [CrossRef]
41. Moor, M.; Horn, M.; Rieck, B.; Borgwardt, K. Topological autoencoders. *Proc. Mach. Learn. Res.* **2020**, *119*, 7045–7054.
42. Kuznetsov, Y.A.; Kuznetsov, I.A.; Kuznetsov, Y. *Elements of Applied Bifurcation Theory*; Springer: New York, NY, USA, 1998; Volume 112.

Disclaimer/Publisher's Note: The statements, opinions and data contained in all publications are solely those of the individual author(s) and contributor(s) and not of MDPI and/or the editor(s). MDPI and/or the editor(s) disclaim responsibility for any injury to people or property resulting from any ideas, methods, instructions or products referred to in the content.

MDPI
St. Alban-Anlage 66
4052 Basel
Switzerland
www.mdpi.com

Mathematics Editorial Office
E-mail: mathematics@mdpi.com
www.mdpi.com/journal/mathematics

Disclaimer/Publisher's Note: The statements, opinions and data contained in all publications are solely those of the individual author(s) and contributor(s) and not of MDPI and/or the editor(s). MDPI and/or the editor(s) disclaim responsibility for any injury to people or property resulting from any ideas, methods, instructions or products referred to in the content.

www.ingramcontent.com/pod-product-compliance
Lightning Source LLC
LaVergne TN
LVHW070634100526
838202LV00012B/802